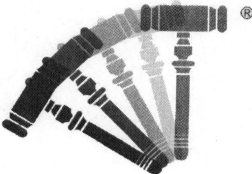

Casenote™ Legal Briefs

EVIDENCE

Keyed to

Weinstein, Mansfield, Abrams and Berger's
Evidence

ASPEN
PUBLISHERS

1185 Avenue of the Americas, New York, NY 10036
www.aspenpublishers.com

ISBN 0-7355-4129-9

4 5 6 7 8 9 0

FORMAT FOR THE CASENOTE LEGAL BRIEF

PARTY ID: Quick identification of the relationship between the parties.

NATURE OF CASE: This section identifies the form of action (e.g., breach of contract, negligence, battery), the type of proceeding (e.g., demurrer, appeal from trial court's jury instructions) or the relief sought (e.g., damages, injunction, criminal sanctions).

FACT SUMMARY: This is included to refresh the student's memory and can be used as a quick reminder of the facts.

CONCISE RULE OF LAW: Summarizes the general principle of law that the case illustrates. It may be used for instant recall of the court's holding and for classroom discussion or home review.

FACTS: This section contains all relevant facts of the case, including the contentions of the parties and the lower court holdings. It is written in a logical order to give the student a clear understanding of the case. The plaintiff and defendant are identified by their proper names throughout and are always labeled with a (P) or (D).

ISSUE: The issue is a concise question that brings out the essence of the opinion as it relates to the section of the casebook in which the case appears. Both substantive and procedural issues are included if relevant to the decision.

HOLDING AND DECISION: This section offers a clear and in-depth discussion of the rule of the case and the court's rationale. It is written in easy-to-understand language and answers the issue(s) presented by applying the law to the facts of the case. When relevant, it includes a thorough discussion of the exceptions to the case as listed by the court, any major cites to other cases on point, and the names of the judges who wrote the decisions.

CONCURRENCE / DISSENT: All concurrences and dissents are briefed whenever they are included by the casebook editor.

EDITOR'S ANALYSIS: This last paragraph gives the student a broad understanding of where the case "fits in" with other cases in the section of the book and with the entire course. It is a hornbook-style discussion indicating whether the case is a majority or minority opinion and comparing the principal case with other cases in the casebook. It may also provide analysis from restatements, uniform codes, and law review articles. The editor's analysis will prove to be invaluable to classroom discussion.

QUICKNOTES: Conveniently defines legal terms found in the case and summarizes the nature of any statutes, codes, or rules referred to in the text.

PALSGRAF v. LONG ISLAND R.R. CO.
Injured bystander (P) v. Railroad company (D)
N.Y. Ct. App., 248 N.Y. 339, 162 N.E. 99 (1928).

NATURE OF CASE: Appeal from judgment affirming verdict for plaintiff seeking damages for personal injury.

FACT SUMMARY: Helen Palsgraf (P) was injured on R.R.'s (D) train platform when R.R.'s (D) guard helped a passenger aboard a moving train, causing his package to fall on the tracks. The package contained fireworks which exploded, creating a shock that tipped a scale onto Palsgraf (P).

CONCISE RULE OF LAW: The risk reasonably to be perceived defines the duty to be obeyed.

FACTS: Helen Palsgraf (P) purchased a ticket to Rockaway Beach from R.R. (D) and was waiting on the train platform. As she waited, two men ran to catch a train that was pulling out from the platform. The first man jumped aboard, but the second man, who appeared as if he might fall, was helped aboard by the guard on the train who had kept the door open so they could jump aboard. A guard on the platform also helped by pushing him onto the train. The man was carrying a package wrapped in newspaper. In the process, the man dropped his package, which fell on the tracks. The package contained fireworks and exploded. The shock of the explosion was apparently of great enough strength to tip over some scales at the other end of the platform, which fell on Palsgraf (P) and injured her. A jury awarded her damages, and R.R. (D) appealed.

ISSUE: Does the risk reasonably to be perceived define the duty to be obeyed?

HOLDING AND DECISION: (Cardozo, C.J.) Yes. The risk reasonably to be perceived defines the duty to be obeyed. If there is no foreseeable hazard to the injured party as the result of a seemingly innocent act, the act does not become a tort because it happened to be a wrong as to another. If the wrong was not willful, the plaintiff must show that the act as to her had such great and apparent possibilities of danger as to entitle her to protection. Negligence in the abstract is not enough upon which to base liability. Negligence is a relative concept, evolving out of the common law doctrine of trespass on the case. To establish liability, the defendant must owe a legal duty of reasonable care to the injured party. A cause of action in tort will lie where harm, though unintended, could have been averted or avoided by observance of such a duty. The scope of the duty is limited by the range of danger that a reasonable person could foresee. In this case, there was nothing to suggest from the appearance of the parcel or otherwise that the parcel contained fireworks. The guard could not reasonably have had any warning of a threat to Palsgraf (P), and R.R. (D) therefore cannot be held liable. Judgment is reversed in favor of R.R. (D).

DISSENT: (Andrews, J.) The concept that there is no negligence unless R.R. (D) owes a legal duty to take care as to Palsgraf (P) herself is too narrow. Everyone owes to the world at large the duty of refraining from those acts that may unreasonably threaten the safety of others. If the guard's action was negligent as to those nearby, it was also negligent as to those outside what might be termed the "danger zone." For Palsgraf (P) to recover, R.R.'s (D) negligence must have been the proximate cause of her injury, a question of fact for the jury.

EDITOR'S ANALYSIS: The majority defined the limit of the defendant's liability in terms of the danger that a reasonable person in defendant's situation would have perceived. The dissent argued that the limitation should not be placed on liability, but rather on damages. Judge Andrews suggested that only injuries that would not have happened but for R.R.'s (D) negligence should be compensable. Both the majority and dissent recognized the policy-driven need to limit liability for negligent acts, seeking, in the words of Judge Andrews, to define a framework "that will be practical and in keeping with the general understanding of mankind." The Restatement (Second) of Torts has accepted Judge Cardozo's view.

QUICKNOTES

FORESEEABILITY – The reasonable anticipation that damage is a likely result from certain acts or omissions.

NEGLIGENCE - Failure to exercise that degree of care which a person of ordinary prudence would exercise under similar circumstances.

PROXIMATE CAUSE – Something which in natural and continuous sequence, unbroken by any new intervening cause, produces an event, and without which the injury would not have occurred.

NOTE TO STUDENTS

Aspen Publishers is proud to offer *Casenote Legal Briefs*–continuing thirty years of publishing America's best-selling legal briefs.

Casenote Legal Briefs are designed to help you save time when briefing assigned cases. Organized under convenient headings, they show you how to abstract the basic facts and holdings from the text of the actual opinions handed down by the courts. Used as part of a rigorous study regime, they can help you spend more time analyzing and critiquing points of law than on copying out bits and pieces of judicial opinions into your notebook or outline.

Casenote Legal Briefs should never be used as a substitute for assigned casebook readings. They work best when read as a follow-up to reviewing the underlying opinions themselves. Students who try to avoid reading and digesting the judicial opinions in their casebooks or on-line sources will end up shortchanging themselves in the long run. The ability to absorb, critique, and restate the dynamic and complex elements of case law decisions is crucial to your success in law school and beyond. It cannot be developed vicariously.

Casenote Legal Briefs represent but one of the many offerings in Aspen's Study Aid Timeline, which includes:

- Casenotes *Legal Briefs*
- Emanuel *Outlines*
- *Examples & Explanations* Series
- *Introduction to Law* Series
- Emanuel *Law in A Flash* Flashcards
- Emanuel *CrunchTime* Series

Each of these series is designed to provide you with easy-to-understand explanations of complex points of law. Each volume offers guidance on the principles of legal analysis and, consulted regularly, will hone your ability to spot relevant issues. We have titles that will help you prepare for class, prepare for your exams, and enhance your general comprehension of the law along the way.

To find out more about Aspen Study Aid publications, visit us on-line at www.aspenpublishers.com or e-mail us at legaledu@aspenpubl.com. We'll be happy to assist you.

Free access to Briefs and Updates on-line!

Download the cases you want in your notes or outlines using the full cut-and-paste feature accompanying our on-line briefs. On-line briefs will also contain the latest updates. Please fill out this form for full access to these useful features. No photocopies of this form will be accepted.

① **Name:** _____ **Phone:** (____) _____

   Address: _____ **Apt.:** _____

   City: _____ **State:** _____ **ZIP Code:** _____

   Law School: _____ **Year (circle one):** 1st   2nd   3rd

② **Cut out the UPC found on the lower left-hand corner of the back cover of this book. Staple the UPC inside this box. Only the original UPC from the book cover will be accepted. (No photocopies or store stickers are allowed.)**

┌─────────────────────────────┐
│   │
│   **Attach UPC**   │
│   **inside this box.**   │
│   │
└─────────────────────────────┘

③ **E-mail:** _____ **(Print LEGIBLY or you may not get access!**

④ **Title (course subject) of this book** _____

⑤ **Used with which casebook (provide author's name):** _____

⑥ **Mail the completed form to:**   Aspen Publishers, Inc.
                                        Legal Education Division
                                        Casenote On-line Access
                                        1185 Avenue of the Americas
                                        New York, NY 10036

I understand that on-line access is granted solely to the purchaser of this book for the academic year in which it was purchased. Any other usage is not authorized and will result in immediate termination of access. Sharing of codes is strictly prohibited.

_____
Signature

Upon receipt of this completed form, you will be e-mailed codes so that you may access the Briefs and Updates for this Casenote Legal Brief. On-line Briefs and Updates may not be available for all titles. For a full list of available titles please check www.aspenpublishers.com/casenotes.

HOW TO BRIEF A CASE

A. DECIDE ON A FORMAT AND STICK TO IT

Structure is essential to a good brief. It enables you to arrange systematically the related parts that are scattered throughout most cases, thus making manageable and understandable what might otherwise seem to be an endless and unfathomable sea of information. There are, of course, an unlimited number of formats that can be utilized. However, it is best to find one that suits your needs and stick to it. Consistency breeds both efficiency and the security that when called upon you will know where to look in your brief for the information you are asked to give.

Any format, as long as it presents the essential elements of a case in an organized fashion, can be used. Experience, however, has led *Casenotes* to develop and utilize the following format because of its logical flow and universal applicability.

NATURE OF CASE: This is a brief statement of the legal character and procedural status of the case (e.g., "Appeal of a burglary conviction").

There are many different alternatives open to a litigant dissatisfied with a court ruling. The key to determining which one has been used is to discover *who is asking this court for what.*

This first entry in the brief should be kept as *short as possible.* The student should use the court's terminology if the student understands it. But since jurisdictions vary as to the titles of pleadings, the best entry is the one that apprises the student of who wants what in this proceeding, not the one that sounds most like the court's language.

CONCISE RULE OF LAW: A statement of the general principle of law that the case illustrates (e.g., "An acceptance that varies any term of the offer is considered a rejection and counteroffer").

Determining the rule of law of a case is a procedure similar to determining the issue of the case. Avoid being fooled by red herrings; there may be a few rules of law mentioned in the case excerpt, but usually only one is *the* rule with which the casebook editor is concerned. The techniques used to locate the issue, described below, may also be utilized to find the rule of law. Generally, your best guide is simply the chapter heading. It is a clue to the point the casebook editor seeks to make and should be kept in mind when reading every case in the respective section.

FACTS: A synopsis of only the essential facts of the case, i.e., those bearing upon or leading up to the issue.

The facts entry should be a short statement of the events and transactions that led one party to initiate legal proceedings against another in the first place. While some cases conveniently state the salient facts at the beginning of the decision, in other instances they will have to be culled from hiding places throughout the text, even from concurring and dissenting opinions. Some of the "facts" will often be in dispute and should be so noted. Conflicting evidence may be briefly pointed up. "Hard" facts must be included. Both must be *relevant* in order to be listed in the facts entry. It is impossible to tell what is relevant until the entire case is read, as the ultimate determination of the rights and liabilities of the parties may turn on something buried deep in the opinion.

The facts entry should never be longer than one to three *short* sentences.

It is often helpful to identify the role played by a party in a given context. For example, in a construction contract case the identification of a party as the "contractor" or "builder" alleviates the need to tell that that party was the one who was supposed to have built the house.

It is always helpful, and a good general practice, to identify the "plaintiff" and the "defendant." This may seem elementary and uncomplicated, but, especially in view of the creative editing practiced by some casebook editors, it is sometimes a difficult or even impossible task. Bear in mind that the *party presently* seeking something from this court may not be the plaintiff, and that sometimes only the cross-claim of a defendant is treated in the excerpt. Confusing or misaligning the parties can ruin your analysis and understanding of the case.

ISSUE: A statement of the general legal question answered by or illustrated in the case. For clarity, the issue is best put in the form of a question capable of a "yes" or "no" answer. In reality, the issue is simply the Concise Rule of Law put in the form of a question (e.g., "May an offer be accepted by performance?").

The major problem presented in discerning what is *the* issue in the case is that an opinion usually purports to raise and answer several questions. However, except for rare cases, only one such question is really the issue in the case. Collateral issues not necessary to the resolution of the matter in controversy are handled by the court by language known as *"obiter dictum"* or merely *"dictum."* While dicta may be included later in the brief, it has no place under the issue heading.

To find the issue, the student again asks *who wants what* and then goes on to ask *why did that party succeed or fail in getting it.* Once this is determined, the "why" should be turned into a question.

The complexity of the issues in the cases will vary, but in all cases a single-sentence question should sum up the issue. *In a few cases,* there will be two, or even more rarely, three issues of equal importance to the resolution of the case. Each should be expressed in a single-sentence question.

Since many issues are resolved by a court in coming to a final disposition of a case, the casebook editor will reproduce the portion of the opinion containing the issue or issues most relevant to the area of law under scrutiny. A noted law professor gave this advice: "Close the book; look at the title on the cover." Chances are, if it is Property, the student need not concern himself with whether, for example, the federal government's treatment of the plaintiff's land really raises a federal question sufficient to support jurisdiction on this ground in federal court.

The same rule applies to chapter headings designating sub-areas within the subjects. They tip the student off as to what the text is designed to teach. The cases are arranged in a casebook to show a progression or development of the law, so that the preceding cases may also help.

It is also most important to remember to *read the notes and questions* at the end of a case to determine what the editors wanted the student to have gleaned from it.

HOLDING AND DECISION: This section should succinctly explain the rationale of the court in arriving at its decision. In capsulizing the "reasoning" of the court, it should always include an application of the general rule or rules of law to the specific facts of the case. Hidden justifications come to light in this entry; the reasons for the state of the law, the public policies, the biases and prejudices, those considerations that influence the justices' thinking and, ultimately, the outcome of the case. At the end, there should be a short indication of the disposition or procedural resolution of the case (e.g., "Decision of the trial court for Mr. Smith (P) reversed").

The foregoing format is designed to help you "digest" the reams of case material with which you will be faced in your law school career. Once mastered by practice, it will place at your fingertips the information the authors of your casebooks have sought to impart to you in case-by-case illustration and analysis.

B.   BE AS ECONOMICAL AS POSSIBLE IN BRIEFING CASES

Once armed with a format that encourages succinctness, it is as important to be economical with regard to the time spent on the actual reading of the case as it is to be economical in the writing of the brief itself. This does not mean "skimming" a case. Rather, it means reading the case with an "eye" trained to recognize into which "section" of your brief a particular passage or line fits and having a system for quickly and precisely marking the case so that the passages fitting any one particular part of the brief can be easily identified and brought together in a concise and accurate manner when the brief is actually written.

It is of no use to simply repeat everything in the opinion of the court; the student should only record enough information to trigger his or her recollection of what the court said. Nevertheless, an accurate statement of the "law of the case," i.e., the legal principle applied to the facts, is absolutely essential to class preparation and to learning the law under the case method.

To that end, it is important to develop a "shorthand" that you can use to make margin notations. These notations will tell you at a glance in which section of the brief you will be placing that particular passage or portion of the opinion.

Some students prefer to underline all the salient portions of the opinion (with a pencil or colored underliner marker), making marginal notations as they go along. Others prefer the color-coded method of underlining, utilizing different colors of markers to underline the salient portions of the case, each separate color being used to represent a different section of the brief. For example, blue underlining could be used for passages relating to the concise rule of law, yellow for those relating to the issue, and green for those relating to the holding and decision, etc. While it has its advocates, the color-coded method can be confusing and time-consuming (all that time spent on changing colored markers). Furthermore, it can interfere with the continuity and concentration many students deem essential to the reading of a case for maximum comprehension. In the end, however, it is a matter of personal preference and style. Just remember, whatever method you use, underlining must be used sparingly or its value is lost.

For those who take the marginal notation route, an efficient and easy method is to go along underlining the key portions of the case and placing in the margin alongside them the following "markers" to indicate where a particular passage or line "belongs" in the brief you will write:

N   (NATURE OF CASE)
CR   (CONCISE RULE OF LAW)
I   (ISSUE)
HC   (HOLDING AND DECISION, relates to the CONCISE RULE OF LAW behind the decision)
HR   (HOLDING AND DECISION, gives the RATIONALE or reasoning behind the decision)
HA   (HOLDING AND DECISION, APPLIES the general principle(s) of law to the facts of the case to arrive at the decision)

Remember that a particular passage may well contain information necessary to more than one part of your brief, in which case you simply note that in the margin. If you are using the color-coded underlining method instead of margin notation, simply make asterisks or checks in the margin next to the passage in question in the colors that indicate the additional sections of the brief where it might be utilized.

The economy of utilizing "shorthand" in marking cases for briefing can be maintained in the actual brief writing process itself by utilizing "law student shorthand" within the brief. There are many commonly used words and phrases for which abbreviations can be substituted in your briefs (and in your class notes also). You can develop abbreviations that are personal to you and which will save you a lot of time. A reference list of briefing abbreviations will be found elsewhere in this book.

C. USE BOTH THE BRIEFING PROCESS AND THE BRIEF AS A LEARNING TOOL

Now that you have a format and the tools for briefing cases efficiently, the most important thing is to make the time spent in briefing profitable to you and to make the most advantageous use of the briefs you create. Of course, the briefs are invaluable for classroom reference when you are called upon to explain or analyze a particular case. However, they are also useful in reviewing for exams. A quick glance at the fact summary should bring the case to mind, and a rereading of the concise rule of law should enable you to go over the underlying legal concept in your mind, how it was applied in that particular case, and how it might apply in other factual settings.

As to the value to be derived from engaging in the briefing process itself, there is an immediate benefit that arises from being forced to sift through the essential facts and reasoning from the court's opinion and to succinctly express them in your own words in your brief. The process ensures that you understand the case and the point that it illustrates, and that means you will be ready to absorb further analysis and information brought forth in class. It also ensures you will have something to say when called upon in class. The briefing process helps develop a mental agility for getting to the *gist* of a case and for identifying, expounding on, and applying the legal concepts and issues found there. Of most immediate concern, that is the mental process on which you must rely in taking law school examinations. Of more lasting concern, it is also the mental process upon which a lawyer relies in serving his clients and in making his living.

ABBREVIATIONS FOR BRIEFING

acceptance	acp	offer	O
affirmed	aff	offeree	OE
answer	ans	offeror	OR
assumption of risk	a/r	ordinance	ord
attorney	atty	pain and suffering	p/s
beyond a reasonable doubt	b/r/d	parol evidence	p/e
bona fide purchaser	BFP	plaintiff	P
breach of contract	br/k	prima facie	p/f
cause of action	c/a	probable cause	p/c
common law	c/l	proximate cause	px/c
Constitution	Con	real property	r/p
constitutional	con	reasonable doubt	r/d
contract	K	reasonable man	r/m
contributory negligence	c/n	rebuttable presumption	rb/p
cross	x	remanded	rem
cross-complaint	x/c	res ipsa loquitur	RIL
cross-examination	x/ex	respondeat superior	r/s
cruel and unusual punishment	c/u/p	Restatement	RS
defendant	D	reversed	rev
dismissed	dis	Rule Against Perpetuities	RAP
double jeopardy	d/j	search and seizure	s/s
due process	d/p	search warrant	s/w
equal protection	e/p	self-defense	s/d
equity	eq	specific performance	s/p
evidence	ev	statute of limitations	S/L
exclude	exc	statute of frauds	S/F
exclusionary rule	exc/r	statute	S
felony	f/n	summary judgment	s/j
freedom of speech	f/s	tenancy in common	t/c
good faith	g/f	tenancy at will	t/w
habeas corpus	h/c	tenant	t
hearsay	hr	third party	TP
husband	H	third party beneficiary	TPB
in loco parentis	ILP	transferred intent	TI
injunction	inj	unconscionable	uncon
inter vivos	I/v	unconstitutional	unconst
joint tenancy	j/t	undue influence	u/e
judgment	judgt	Uniform Commercial Code	UCC
jurisdiction	jur	unilateral	uni
last clear chance	LCC	vendee	VE
long-arm statute	LAS	vendor	VR
majority view	maj	versus	v
meeting of minds	MOM	void for vagueness	VFV
minority view	min	weight of the evidence	w/e
Miranda warnings	Mir/w	weight of authority	w/a
Miranda rule	Mir/r	wife	W
negligence	neg	with	w/
notice	ntc	within	w/i
nuisance	nus	without prejudice	w/o/p
obligation	ob	without	w/o
obscene	obs	wrongful death	wr/d

TABLE OF CASES

Continued on next page

TABLE OF CASES (Continued)

Continued on next pa

TABLE OF CASES (Continued)

CHAPTER 1
RELEVANCY AND RELATED PROBLEMS

QUICK REFERENCE RULES OF LAW

1. **Relevancy.** Except in rare cases of abuse, demonstrative evidence that tends to prove a material issue or clarify the circumstances of the crime is admissible despite its prejudicial tendency. (People v. Adamson)

   [For more information on highly prejudicial evidence, see Casenote Law Outline on Evidence, Chapter 2, § V, Discretionary Exclusion of Relevant Evidence.]

2. **Relevance and Prejudice.** The fact that there might be dissimilarities in the conditions under which tests were conducted and those that obtained in the case at trial does not mean that the test evidence is not relevant — although it may affect the weight of the evidence. (Robbins v. Whelan)

   [For more information on relevant evidence, see Casenote Law Outline on Evidence, Chapter 2, § III, Is the "Evidence" Relevant?.]

3. **Relevance and Prejudice.** Although it is within the sound discretion of the trial court to determine whether the inflammatory nature of offered visual evidence is outweighed by its probative value with respect to a fact in issue, it may not be admitted if all the material facts which could conceivably have been adduced had been established by other uncontradicted evidence or testimony. (State v. Poe)

   [For more information on evidence creating undue prejudice, see Casenote Law Outline on Evidence, Chapter 2, § V, Discretionary Exclusion of Relevant Evidence.]

4. **Relevance and Prejudice.** When an element of a crime is felony-convict status, a court may force the government to accept a defendant's concession to the prior conviction as proof of that element. (Old Chief v. United States)

5. **Sufficiency and Circumstantial Evidence.** Circumstantial evidence may be so overwhelming that the trier of fact is capable of inferring death, inferring that it was not by natural cause, and, given these inferences, that the evidence was sufficient to show that the defendant committed the murder. (Regina v. Onufrejczyk)

   [For more information on inferences, see Casenote Law Outline on Evidence, Chapter 2, § III, Is the "Evidence" Relevant?.]

6. **Sufficiency and Circumstantial Evidence.** In a criminal case, a defendant's failure to call any particular witness cannot create an inference as to whether or not that witness' testimony would be favorable or unfavorable. (State v. Brewer)

   [For more information on inferences, see Casenote Law Outline on Evidence, Chapter 2, § III, Is the "Evidence" Relevant?.]

7. **Probability and Statistical Evidence in Decisionmaking.** A proposition is proved by the preponderance of the evidence if it is made to appear more likely or probable in the sense that actual belief in its truth, derived from the evidence, exists in the mind or minds of the tribunal notwithstanding any doubts that may still linger there. Mathematical evidence may not be introduced without some supporting direct evidence. (Smith v. Rapid Transit, Inc.)

   [For more information on burdens of proof, see Casenote Law Outline on Evidence, Chapter 4, § I, Burdens of Proof.]

8. **Probability and Statistical Evidence in Decisionmaking.** Expert opinion as to the percentile of the population possessing a combination of three blood characteristics is not inadmissible because it is based on hearsay (e.g., reports of others) about the percentage of the population possessing each of the characteristics individually. (State v. Rolls)

   [For more information on expert opinions, see Casenote Law Outline on Evidence, Chapter 12, § III, Expert Opinions.]

9. **Preservation of Issues for Appeal.** To preserve an objection to admissibility for appeal, Federal Rule of Evidence 103(a) requires that an attorney state a specific ground for the objection unless the ground is apparent from the context. (United States v. Brewer)

PEOPLE v. ADAMSON
State (P) v. Murder suspect (D)
Cal. Sup. Ct., 27 Cal.2d 478, 165 P.2d 3 (1946); aff'd 332 U.S. 46 (1947).

NATURE OF CASE: Appeal from conviction of first-degree murder and burglary.

FACT SUMMARY: Charged with burglary and murdering the victim who was found with the top parts of her stockings torn off, Adamson (D) objected at his trial to the introduction into evidence of top parts of stockings found in his dresser on the grounds that admission of the evidence could serve no purpose except to create prejudice against him as a Negro by the implication of a fetish or sexual degeneracy.

CONCISE RULE OF LAW: Except in rare cases of abuse, demonstrative evidence that tends to prove a material issue or clarify the circumstances of the crime is admissible despite its prejudicial tendency.

FACTS: The body of an old woman was found badly beaten, with the lower parts of her stockings lying next to her. The stocking tops had been torn off. These stocking tops were eventually found in Adamson's (D) apartment dresser. Adamson (D) was charged with burglary and first-degree murder. At his trial, the tops recovered from his dresser were offered into evidence as linking him to the crime. Adamson's (D) objections that the tops could serve no other purpose than to excite and prejudice the jury against him as a sexual degenerate with a fetish, and a Negro, were overruled.

ISSUE: Is demonstrative evidence which tends to prove a material issue at trial or clarifies the circumstances of a crime excludable simply because it is also highly prejudicial to the defendant?

HOLDING AND DECISION: (Traynor, J.) No. Although the evidence is not sufficient by itself to identify Adamson (D) as the criminal, it constituted a logical link in the chain of evidence. Evidence that tends to throw light on a fact in dispute may be admitted, the jury determining its weight. The admission of the tops did not deprive Adamson (D) of due process of law. No prejudicial implication was made by the prosecutor in oral argument.

EDITOR'S ANALYSIS: This court's reasoning was reiterated in United States v. Schipani, 289 F. Supp. 43, 56 (E.D.N.Y. 1968): "Since so much of the evaluation of evidence depends upon varying hypotheses applied by triers with different backgrounds and views of life, fact-finding differences among jurors and between judge and jury are to be expected. The court's function is, in the usual sample case, only to decide whether a reasonable man might have his assessment of the probabilities of a material proposition changed by the piece of evidence sought to be admitted. If it may affect that evaluation, it is relevant and, subject to certain other rules, admissible."

[For more information on highly prejudicial evidence, see Casenote Law Outline on Evidence, Chapter 2, § V, Discretionary Exclusion of Relevant Evidence.]

QUICKNOTES
LOGICAL RELEVANCE - The relationship between offered evidence and a fact in issue that suggests such evidence makes the issue more or less public.

PROBATIVE - Tending to establish proof.

NOTES:

ROBBINS v. WHELAN
Injured passenger (P) v. Alleged negligent driver (D)
653 F.2d 47 (1st Dist. 1981); cert. denied, 454 U.S. 1123 (1982).

NATURE OF CASE: Action for damages for negligence.

FACT SUMMARY: Robbins (P) was not permitted to introduce into evidence test results in a Department of Transportation report giving the stopping distances for all cars manufactured the same year as Mercedes which Whelan (D) was allegedly driving negligently when he collided with another car.

CONCISE RULE OF LAW: The fact that there might be dissimilarities in the conditions under which tests were conducted and those that obtained in the case at trial does not mean that the test evidence is not relevant — although it may affect the weight of the evidence.

FACTS: In attempting to establish that Whelan (D) was negligent at the time his Mercedes collided with the car in which he was a passenger, Robbins (P) offered for admission into evidence a copy of a Department of Transportation report containing a table of stopping distances for all cars manufactured in that model year. It gave the maximum stopping distance for a Mercedes going 60 miles per hour, that stopping distance being less than the length of the skid marks Robbins (P) claimed the Mercedes had made just before the collision. His counsel did not specifically tell the court that the test evidence was being introduced in an effort to show the Mercedes had to be going faster than Whelan (D) claimed. The court appeared to be considering its relevance only on the issue of inadequate brakes when it sustained Whelan's (D) objection to the introduction of this evidence on the grounds that it was not relevant. After a bifurcated trial, the jury decided the issue of liability in favor of Whelan (D).

ISSUE: Is test evidence necessarily irrelevant because test conditions differ somewhat from those that obtained in the case at trial?

HOLDING AND DECISION: (Coffin, J.) No. Perfect identity between experimental and actual conditions is neither attainable nor required; dissimilarities between test and actual conditions affect the weight of evidence, not its admissibility. In this case, the test evidence was being offered as an indirect means of calculating the Mercedes' speed prior to braking. While counsel offering the evidence did not make this very clear, this court cannot say that the record is so confused that the point as to relevance was not sufficiently made. Secondly, it has not been demonstrated that there were any significant differences between the test conditions and those that existed at the time of the accident. Whelan's (D) proper course, then, would be to attack the weight to be accorded this test evidence by presenting contrary evidence about how the variance between the test and actual conditions might affect the inferences that Robbins (P) urged be drawn. That is what the trial court should have let happen — after letting the test results into evidence. There was no other evidence presented that could serve the same purpose of establishing a relationship between the skid marks Whelan (D) allegedly left and probable speed. On the close question of negligence, it is obvious that Robbins' (P) case was made considerably weaker by the error the trial court committed in not admitting the aforementioned evidence. Because it cannot be said with reasonable assurance that the jury would still have found in favor of Whelan (D) had it been given the opportunity to consider that data, there is no alternative but to remand for a new trial. Remanded.

DISSENT: (Campbell, J.) Counsel for Robbins (P) never correctly stated the purpose for which the evidence was being offered. I do not think that the indirect relationship between speed and skid marks was so obvious that counsel was excused from stating it. In general, before a party may claim error on appeal in the exclusion of evidence, he must have told the court not only what he intended to prove but for what purpose. If I saw evidence of injustice, I might be more tempted to stretch the rule, but I see no such evidence here.

EDITOR'S ANALYSIS: Counsel must be very careful in identifying the purpose for which evidence is being offered. McCormick states that if it turns out later that the evidence was not admissible for the purpose stated at trial but was indeed admissible for another purpose, counsel cannot complain of its exclusion on appeal (unless it falls within the obvious-purpose exception mentioned in Campbell's dissent).

[For more information on relevant evidence, see Casenote Law Outline on Evidence, Chapter 2, § III, Is the "Evidence" Relevant?]

QUICKNOTES
PROBATIVE - Tending to establish proof.
RELEVANCE - The admissibility of evidence based on whether it has any tendency to prove or disprove a matter at issue to the case.

NOTES:

STATE v. POE

State (P) v. Murder suspect (D)

Utah Sup. Ct., 21 Utah 2d 113, 441 P.2d 512, appl. after remand, 24 Utah 2d 355, 471 P.2d 870 (1970).

NATURE OF CASE: Appeal from conviction of first-degree murder.

FACT SUMMARY: At his trial, where he was charged with murdering a lifelong resident of a small community, Poe (D) objected to the composition of the jury and the showing of gruesome, colored slides of the victim's autopsy to the jury.

CONCISE RULE OF LAW: Although it is within the sound discretion of the trial court to determine whether the inflammatory nature of offered visual evidence is outweighed by its probative value with respect to a fact in issue, it may not be admitted if all the material facts which could conceivably have been adduced had been established by other uncontradicted evidence or testimony.

FACTS: Poe (D) was charged with murdering a lifelong resident of a small community of some 10,000 residents. Members of the jury were acquainted with the sheriff, some of the witnesses for the prosecution, the victim, the defendant, and the prosecutors. The trial court admitted into evidence black and white photographs showing the victim lying in his bed in a sleeping position, with two bullet holes in his head. It also admitted colored slides taken during the course of the autopsy. Poe's (D) counsel failed to make the proper objection at this point to the admission of the slides. The colored slides accentuated the gruesomeness of the autopsy. Poe (D) was convicted, the jury not recommending life imprisonment. On appeal, Poe (D) challenged the "community pattern of thought as expressed by potential jurors," and the introduction of the slides as being needlessly inflammatory with little probative value.

ISSUE: (1) Is the fact that potential jurors are well-acquainted with the victim and various witnesses for the prosecution sufficient to establish a denial of a fair trial? (2) Should inflammatory evidence be excluded if all of the conclusions which could have been made from the inflammatory evidence were established by other evidence?

HOLDING AND DECISION: (Callister, J.) (1) No. The trial judge had carefully and exhaustively examined the jury panel. Furthermore, the panel had been passed for cause by the defendant. There is no direct evidence that the acquaintanceships of the prospective jurors to the victim and the witnesses were prejudicial to Poe (D). (2) Yes. The colored slides had no probative value since independent testimony had established all the facts which could have been adduced from viewing them. Their only purpose was to inflame and arouse the jury. The slides could very well have tipped the scales in favor of the death penalty. Even though Poe's (D) counsel did not raise the proper objection, the court will overlook the technicality. The case is reversed and remanded for a new trial.

DISSENT: (Ellett, J.) All evidence given tends to prejudice the jury, but otherwise competent evidence which a witness could testify to should be admissible. If the defendant wished to avoid having the jury see the pictures, he could have stipulated to the cause of death. These pictures were no more gruesome than was the open heart surgery portrayed on television.

EDITOR'S ANALYSIS: A photograph is admitted usually under the theory that it is only a graphic portrayal of oral testimony to which a witness must lay the appropriate foundation. However, the vividness of colored photographs and motion pictures often leaves too strong an impression on the jury. Preliminary viewing of the film or a photograph may be done by the trial court. McCormick suggests that the difficulty posed in this regard may be diminished today by more sophisticated movie-going jurors.

[For more information on evidence creating undue prejudice, see Casenote Law Outline on Evidence, Chapter 2, § V, Discretionary Exclusion of Relevant Evidence.]

QUICKNOTES

RELEVANCE - The admissibility of evidence based on whether it has any tendency to prove or disprove a matter at issue to the case.

PROBATIVE - Tending to establish proof.

FRE 403 - Provides that a court may dismiss otherwise relevant evidence where its prejudicial effect on the proceeding outweighs any probative value it has.

NOTES:

OLD CHIEF v. UNITED STATES
Gun user (D) v. Federal government (P)
519 U.S. 172, 117 S. Ct. 644 (1997).

NATURE OF CASE: Appeal from convictions for assault with a dangerous weapon, using a firearm in a crime of violence, and possession of a firearm by a felon.

FACT SUMMARY: Old Chief (D) offered to stipulate that he had a prior conviction, but the government (P) contended that it was entitled to prove its case by evidence of its own choice, i.e., an official record of his assault conviction.

CONCISE RULE OF LAW: When an element of a crime is felony-convict status, a court may force the government to accept a defendant's concession to the prior conviction as proof of that element.

FACTS: 18 U.S.C. § 922(g)(1) prohibits possession of a firearm by anyone with a prior felony conviction, which the government can prove by introducing a record of judgment or similar evidence identifying the previous offense. Old Chief (D) was arrested after a fracas involving at least one gunshot. He was subsequently charged with assault with a dangerous weapon and using a firearm. He was also charged with a violation of § 922(g)(1) based on an earlier conviction for assault causing serious bodily injury. Fearing prejudice if the jury learned the nature of the earlier crime, he offered to concede the fact of his prior conviction. The government (P) refused to accept his concession, insisting on its right to prove its case in its own way. At trial, over Old Chief's (D) renewed objection, the government (P) introduced the order of judgment for Old Chief's (D) prior conviction, which specified the name and basis nature of the prior offense. The jury found Old Chief (D) guilty on all counts, and he appealed. The appellate court sustained the conviction, and the Supreme Court granted certiorari.

ISSUE: When an element of a crime is felony-convict status, may a court force the government to accept a defendant's concession to the prior conviction as proof of that element?

HOLDING AND DECISION: (Souter, J.) Yes. When an element of a crime is felony-convict status, a court may force the government to accept a defendant's concession to the prior conviction as proof of that element. Federal Rule of Evidence 403 authorizes a court to exclude relevant evidence whenever its probative value is substantially outweighed by the danger of unfair prejudice. In this case, the prejudicial effect of Old Chief's (D) prior assault conviction would take on added weight from his pending gun charges and assault charges. The language of § 922 shows that Congress was not concerned with the specific name or nature of the prior offense beyond what is necessary to place it within the broad category of qualifying offenses. Old Chief (D) offered to clearly stipulate that his felony did qualify. Although, in

general, the government (P) is entitled to prove its case free from any defendant's offer to stipulate the evidence away, the point at issue here is Old Chief's (D) legal status only. The government's (D) case will not lose any evidentiary depth or eventful narration merely because Old Chief (D) chooses to stipulate to a generic felony. The risk of unfair prejudice substantially outweighs the discounted probative value of the record of conviction; it was an abuse of discretion to admit the official record when an admission by Old Chief (D) was available. Reversed and remanded.

DISSENT: (O'Connor, J.) This decision precludes the government (P) from offering evidence to directly prove a necessary element of its case. Any incremental harm resulting from such an offer could be properly mitigated by appropriate jury instructions.

EDITOR'S ANALYSIS: The term "unfair prejudice" refers to the capacity of otherwise relevant evidence to lure the factfinder into declaring guilt on a ground that is not derived from the proof specific to the offense charged. Such improper grounds could include (as in the case above) the generalization of a defendant's earlier bad act into bad character, thereby causing the jury to convict for crimes other than those charged. This so-called propensity reasoning is addressed by Federal Rule of Evidence 404(b): "Evidence of other crimes, wrongs, or acts is not admissible to prove the character of a person in order to show action in conformity therewith."

QUICKNOTES
FRE 403 - Provides that a court may dismiss otherwise relevant evidence where its prejudicial effect on the proceeding outweighs any probative value it has.
RELEVANCE - The admissibility of evidence based on whether it has any tendency to prove or disprove a matter at issue to the case.
PROBATIVE - Tending to establish proof.

NOTES:

REGINA v. ONUFREJCZYK
Queen (P) v. Murder suspect (D)
Eng. Crim. App., 1 All E.R. 247 (1955).

NATURE OF CASE: Prosecution for first-degree murder.

FACT SUMMARY: Onufrejczyk (D) was charged with the murder of his partner, Sykut, even though the body could not be found and there was nothing other than circumstantial evidence that Sykut had been murdered.

CONCISE RULE OF LAW: Circumstantial evidence may be so overwhelming that the trier of fact is capable of inferring death, inferring that it was not by natural cause, and, given these inferences, that the evidence was sufficient to show that the defendant committed the murder.

FACTS: Onufrejczyk (D) and Sykut were partners in a farm. Both were registered aliens living in England. The farm was a failure and Onufrejczyk (D) had exhausted his personal assets and had attempted, unsuccessfully, to borrow money from every possible source. He had even attempted to get a fraudulent valuation of the farm in order to borrow additional money from a bank. Onufrejczyk (D) wanted to buy Sykut out. Sykut was willing to sell for £700, otherwise he wanted the farm to be put up for sale. They had quarreled before an attorney. On December 14th, Sykut disappeared. There is no record of his leaving the country and no one had seen or heard from him since then. His wife and friends in Poland did not know of his whereabouts. On December 18th, Onufrejczyk (D) wrote a letter to a Polish woman living nearby that he had given Sykut most of the £700 to buy him out and that Sykut had left town for two weeks. He tried to have a deed forged giving him the farm. When questioned about Sykut's disappearance, Onufrejczyk (D) gave a fanciful story about three men in a black car (or, in some accounts, a green car) taking Sykut away at gun point. A half hour before this was to have taken place, Onufrejczyk (D) told a sheriff that Sykut had gone to the doctor's in town (it was proved that he hadn't). Onufrejczyk (D) tried to get the local blacksmith to lie about when Sykut had picked up a horse. Minute particles of Sykut's blood were found in the farm house, though Onufrejczyk claimed these came from a cut finger. Sykut left all of his personal belongings at the farm. The jury found that Sykut was dead, that he had been murdered, and that Onufrejczyk (D) had done it.

ISSUE: Can a jury find a defendant guilty of murder where death, murder, and defendant's guilt must all be inferred from circumstantial evidence?

HOLDING AND DECISION: (Goddard, J.) Yes. Where circumstantial evidence of death by violent cause is overwhelming, a jury is permitted to infer that the alleged decedent is indeed dead and that he had been murdered. These inferences establish a corpus delicti just as certainly as if the body had been discovered. Once this inference is accepted by the jury as a fact (beyond a reasonable doubt), the evidence was such that the jury was entitled to find Onufrejczyk (D) guilty of Sykut's death. The court focused on Onufrejczyk's (D) lies, the fact that Sykut, a registered alien, could not be found in England, and that there was no record of his leaving the country. His wife and friends in Poland had not seen or heard from him. Onufrejczyk (D) had attempted to have a deed of sale registered containing a forgery of Sykut's signature. The court felt that this was inconsistent with any theory that Sykut was still alive. Onufreiczyk's (D) claim that he had paid Sykut most of the £700 for the farm were incredible based on his financial condition and the fact that no one would loan him any money. From these, and many other facts, Onufrejczyk (D) must have known that Sykut would not be coming back to refute his stories and the forged deed of sale. The court felt that if the jury believed the Sykut was dead and that it was not by natural causes, the evidence appeared overwhelming that Onufrejczyk (D) had been involved in Sykut's death. The rule that a corpus delicti must be produced is rooted in another time. To allow a murderer to go free just because he discovered a good way to dispose of a body without trace and with no witnesses to the crime would be against the best interests of justice. It is far more difficult for a person, especially a resident alien, to just disappear. The court felt that it was time to break with the past on this issue.

EDITOR'S ANALYSIS: This case allows the trier of fact to infer a corpus delicti, based on overwhelming circumstantial evidence, when a body cannot be found. Once the jury accepts the fact that someone has been murdered, then, and only then, can they decide whether the evidence warrants a finding that the defendant has committed the crime. Therefore, the only inference to be drawn from the evidence is that someone has been murdered. Guilt must be proved. Circumstantial evidence is permitted to prove a fact. The fact or facts upon which it is sought to base an inference must be proved and not left to rest in conjecture, and when proved it must appear that the inference drawn is the only one that can fairly and reasonably be drawn from the facts and that any other explanation is fairly and reasonably excluded.

[For more information on inferences, see Casenote Law Outline on Evidence, Chapter 2, § III, Is the "Evidence" Relevant?]

STATE v. BREWER
State (P) v. Alleged drunk driver (D)
Me. Sup. Jud. Ct., 505 A.2d 774 (1985).

NATURE OF CASE: Appeal of conviction of driving under the influence and with a suspended license.

FACT SUMMARY: In a DUI prosecution, the State (P) argued that Brewer's (D) failure to call a witness who allegedly could exonerate him created an implication of guilt.

CONCISE RULE OF LAW: In a criminal case, a defendant's failure to call any particular witness cannot create an inference as to whether or not that witness' testimony would be favorable or unfavorable.

FACTS: Brewer (D) was accused of driving under the influence and without a license. He had been in a vehicle, but contended that Pratt, his roommate, had been driving. No other witness could prove or disprove this. At trial, neither side called Pratt as a witness. The State (P) argued that Brewer's (D) failure to call a supposed alibi witness demonstrated guilt. Brewer (D) was convicted, and he appealed.

ISSUE: In a criminal case, can a defendant's failure to call any particular witness create an inference as to whether or not that witness' testimony would be favorable or unfavorable?

HOLDING AND DECISION: (Glassman, J.) No. In a criminal case, a defendant's failure to call any particular witness cannot create an inference as to whether or not that witness' testimony would be favorable or unfavorable. It was once held that the opposite was true. Failure to call a witness could create an inference that the witness' testimony would be unfavorable. This was based on the now-outmoded concept that a party "vouched" for his witness. Now a party can attack the credibility of his own witness. Also, in past days one party was often in a better position to produce a witness. With discovery, this is no longer true. Thus, the foundation for the old rule no longer exists. Also of significance is that a criminal defendant is under no obligation to present any evidence, so it would be improper to penalize him for exercising this prerogative. In this case the State's (P) argument tried to raise a negative presumption, and that was therefore improper. Reversed.

EDITOR'S ANALYSIS: The issue at hand illustrates one of the many problems with circumstantial evidence. Although some authorities dispute it, there is a general perception that circumstantial evidence is less reliable than direct. Most jurisdictions restrict to some extent the utility of circumstantial evidence in criminal cases.

[For more information on inferences, see Casenote Law Outline on Evidence, Chapter 2, § III, Is the "Evidence" Relevant.]

SMITH v. RAPID TRANSIT, INC.
Driver of damaged car (P) v. Bus company (D)
Mass. Sup. Jud. Ct., 317 Mass. 469, 58 N.E.2d 754 (1945).

NATURE OF CASE: Action for personal injuries as the result of negligent operation of a bus.

FACT SUMMARY: Although unable to find out which bus company owned the vehicle which forced her off the road, Smith (P) sued Rapid Transit, Inc. (D) on the theory that it was most probably owned by them.

CONCISE RULE OF LAW: A proposition is proved by the preponderance of the evidence if it is made to appear more likely or probable in the sense that actual belief in its truth, derived from the evidence, exists in the mind or minds of the tribunal notwithstanding any doubts that may still linger there. Mathematical evidence may not be introduced without some supporting direct evidence.

FACTS: Betty Smith (P) was driving her automobile at 1:00 a.m. on Main Street, Winthrop. A bus coming toward her forced her to swerve to the right to avoid being hit. Her automobile collided with a parked car. Smith (P) could not see who owned the bus. Smith (P) brought suit against Rapid Transit (D) on the theory that they were the only local bus company licensed to use Main Street as a route; they had buses running at the time of the accident which could have, based on the company's timetable, been where Smith (P) was injured at about 1:00 a.m. This made it mathematically more certain than not that Smith (P) was injured by Rapid Transit's (D) bus. The judge directed the verdict for Rapid Transit (D), and Smith (P) appealed.

ISSUE: Should a case be allowed to go to the jury where the only proof of guilt is that it is mathematically more likely than not that defendant is guilty?

HOLDING AND DECISION: (Spalding, J.) No. The ownership of the bus was a matter of conjecture. Other buslines could have been using Main Street (private, chartered, etc.). It is not enough that mathematically the chances somewhat favor the proposition to be proven. Proof by preponderance of the evidence means that the trier of fact believes in the truth of the fact asserted, based on the evidence presented, notwithstanding any lingering doubts. It is necessary to present some nonstatistical and individualized proof of identity before compelling a party to pay damages, and even before compelling him to come forward with defensive evidence, absent an adequate explanation of the failure to present such individualized proof.

EDITOR'S ANALYSIS: This case stands for the proposition that mere mathematical inference of guilt, regardless of its high probability, will be insufficient to allow the case to go to the jury without nonstatistical evidence to support it. Mere probability lacks an evidential foundation from which a valid inference can be drawn. Without adequate proof of the underlying proposition, the inference would merely be an unproven supposition. Mathematics alone cannot supply this evidential base.

[For more information on preponderance of evidence, see Casenote Law Outline on Evidence, Chapter 4, § I, Burdens of Proof.]

QUICKNOTES
DIRECTED VERDICT - A verdict ordered by the court in a jury trial.

NOTES:

STATE v. ROLLS
Plaintiff (P) v. Convicted criminal (D)
Me. Sup. Ct., 389 A.2d 824 (1978).

NATURE OF CASE: Appeal from conviction of various crimes.

FACT SUMMARY: Rolls (D) maintained that testimony estimating what percentage of the population had blood having the combination of three characteristics found in both the victim's blood and the blood still on his pants was based on hearsay as to what percentage of the population possesses each of the three characteristics taken individually.

CONCISE RULE OF LAW: Expert opinion as to the percentile of the population possessing a combination of three blood characteristics is not inadmissible because it is based on hearsay (*e.g.*, reports of others) about the percentage of the population possessing each of the characteristics individually.

FACTS: At the trial which culminated in Rolls (D) being convicted of various crimes, including burglary and rape, Special Agent Spalding of the FBI was permitted to testify concerning tests he had conducted on blood stains found on the pants that Rolls (D) was wearing when he was picked up by the police. Over the objection of Rolls (D), he testified that approximately five percent of the population would possess all three blood characteristics which the victim possessed and which were present in the bloodstain on Rolls' (D) pants. On appeal, Rolls (D) argued that this testimony was inadmissible. He claimed there was an insufficient foundation to support its admission because Agent Spalding based his opinion on hearsay (e.g., reports on FBI research and studies by Scotland Yard). That is, he reached the conclusion as to what percentage of the population would have all three blood grouping characteristics by multiplying the figures others had put out as to what percentage of the population had each individual blood characteristic.

ISSUE: Is expert opinion as to what percentage of the population has a particular combination of blood characteristics inadmissible because it is based on the reports of others as to what percentage of the population possesses each of the characteristics individually?

HOLDING AND DECISION: (Nichols, J.) No. Before the Maine Rules of Evidence were adopted, there was authority for the proposition that an expert opinion based on hearsay was as objectionable as hearsay itself. As it now stands, however, the objection registered to the testimony in this case is more properly direct to its weight rather than its admissibility. Affirmed.

EDITOR'S ANALYSIS: Blood-grouping tests have, in recent years, been extensively used in paternity cases. In combination with the Human Leukocyte Antigen blood tissue test (HLA), they can offer a 91% to 98% probability that one who tests as the possible father is in fact the actual father. This has led many courts to allow such evidence as positive proof of paternity. Historically, evidence as to blood type, which was much less conclusive, was only admissible to exclude paternity.

[For more information on expert opinions, see Casenote Law Outline on Evidence, Chapter 12, § III, Expert Opinions.]

QUICKNOTES
EXPERT WITNESS - A witness providing testimony at trial who is specially qualified regarding the particular subject matter involved.

NOTES:

UNITED STATES v. BREWER
Federal government (P) v. Cocaine dealer (D)
1 F.3d 1430 (4th Cir. 1993).

NATURE OF CASE: Appeal from conviction on eight counts of possession with intent to distribute cocaine.

FACT SUMMARY: Brewer (D) argued that the testimony of his fiancee was improper character evidence, but the government (P) argued that Brewer's (D) attorney had failed to preserve this error by not stating any basis for his objection.

CONCISE RULE OF LAW: To preserve an objection to admissibility for appeal, Federal Rule of Evidence 103(a) requires that an attorney state a specific ground for the objection unless the ground is apparent from the context.

FACT SUMMARY: At Brewer's (D) trial for possession of cocaine with intent to distribute, the government (P) called his fiancee, Scott, to testify. The government (P) requested the court to be permitted to treat Scott as a hostile witness. The court refused because the government (P) had not demonstrated adversity. When the government (P) asked her if Brewer (D) dealt drugs, Brewer's (P) counsel objected, but stated no basis for his objection. The government (P) then began to ask leading questions designed to elicit the information that Scott had previously told U.S. marshals that Brewer (D) was a drug dealer. Scott denied it. Brewer's (D) counsel again objected. The U.S. marshal then testified to rebut Scott's testimony. Brewer (D) was convicted and appealed, arguing that Scott had been called solely to provide improper character evidence and that the marshal's impeachment testimony was prejudicial.

ISSUE: To preserve an objection to admissibility for appeal, does Federal Rule of Evidence 103(a) require that an attorney state a specific ground for the objection unless that ground is apparent from the context?

HOLDING AND DECISION: (Phillips, J.) Yes. To preserve an objection to admissibility for appeal, Federal Rule of Evidence 103(a) requires that an attorney state a specific ground for the objection unless the ground is apparent from the context. In this case, the ground was not apparent. Brewer's (D) counsel focused more on the form of the government's (D) questions rather than on their content. It is unclear whether the admission of the testimony that Brewer (D) was a drug dealer was proper, since it appears to resemble forbidden character evidence. The court of appeals cannot correct a lower court error unless the error is clear under current law. There is no such error here. Furthermore, the law is unsettled as to whether a court must instruct a jury that testimony be limited to one purpose if counsel does not request such an instruction. Brewer's (D) counsel did not request the district court to instruct the jury that the marshal's

testimony was admissible only to impeach Scott and not for its substance. Therefore the court did not commit plain error by failing to make such an instruction sua sponte. Affirmed.

DISSENT: (Widener, J.) A party may not call a witness whose testimony is known to be adverse for the sole purpose of impeaching her, as the government (P) did in this case. It knew that Scott would deny that she had told the marshal that Brewer (D) was a drug dealer, which is why it asked at the outset to treat her as a hostile witness. Therefore Brewer's (D) objection was clear from the context. Furthermore, the marshal's testimony about what Scott told him was rank hearsay and should not have admitted.

EDITOR'S ANALYSIS: Rules of evidence may be bypassed in three ways. They may be implicitly waived by failure to invoke them, that is, by failing to object to the introduction of improper evidence in a timely manner. They may also be implicitly waived by "opening the door," i.e., when the objecting party mentions the evidence in its own case-in-chief. Finally, the Rules may be explicitly waived via stipulation, whereby the parties agree to concede certain facts or otherwise inadmissible evidence pertaining to such facts.

QUICKNOTES

CHARACTER EVIDENCE - Evidence of someone's moral standing in a community based on reputation.

SUA SPONTE - An action taken by the court by its own motion and without the suggestion of one of the parties.

NOTES:

2

CHAPTER 2
REAL PROOF

QUICK REFERENCE RULES OF LAW

1. **Ability of Trier to Acquire Knowledge.** Real evidence is not inadmissible simply because it calls for the jurors to make a tactile evaluation, provided that the evidence offered is not technical in nature, nor requires special knowledge or skill to assess. (McAndrews v. Leonard)

   [For more information on discretionary inclusion of evidence, see Casenote Law Outline on Evidence, Chapter 2, § V, Discretionary Exclusion of Relevant Evidence.]

2. **Ability of Trier to Acquire Knowledge.** In a paternity case, the exhibition of the child to the fact finder for the purpose of proving paternity by showing its resemblance to the alleged father is not permitted. (Almeida v. Correa)

   [For more information on discretionary exclusion of evidence, see Casenote Law Outline on Evidence, Chapter 2, § V, Discretionary Exclusion of Relevant Evidence.]

3. **Ability of Trier to Acquire Knowledge.** Where age is an element of a crime, evidence of age must be presented by the prosecution. (Watson v. State)

4. **Ability of Trier to Acquire Knowledge.** It is error for the prosecution in a criminal case to display what it knows cannot be admitted into evidence (for lack of proper foundation, etc.), and it has the burden on appeal to show "beyond a reasonable doubt that the (improper display of) inadmissible evidence did not affect the verdict." (State v. Scarlett)

   [For more information on allocation of burden of proof, see Casenote Law Outline on Evidence, Chapter 4, § I, Burdens of Proof.]

5. **Identification as a Condition of Relevancy.** Samples to be admissible as evidence must be shown to reflect the condition of the substance at the time involved in the issues. It must be shown that no substantial change has taken place in the substance to be exhibited because of lapse of time. (Anderson v. Berg)

   [For more information on preliminary questions, see Casenote Law Outline on Evidence, Chapter 5, § II, Preliminary Questions of Fact.]

6. **Demeanor.** In the event of a showing by a defendant in a criminal action of a reasonable possibility that his attitude, appearance or demeanor, as observed by a jury, had been substantially influenced or affected by circumstances over which he had no real control, grounds for a new trial exist, at least where the defendant's projected image may have prejudiced the jury in sentencing. (State v. Murphy)

7. **Views.** Proof of the fact of an unauthorized visit by jurors during a criminal trial is sufficient to warrant a new trial. Proof of how such visit may have influenced individual jurors is not needed, the visit, in and of itself, constituting inherent prejudice to the defendant. No distinction will be made between visits to a scene of a crime and other views. (People v. Crimmins)

8. **Demonstrations and Experiments.** Demonstrative evidence need not precisely replicate the situation the evidence seeks to clarify. (United States v. Wanoskia)

9. **Demonstrations and Experiments.** A test is not admissible unless the test conditions are "so nearly the

same in substantial particulars" as those involved in the episode in litigation "as to afford a fair comparison in respect to the particular issue to which the test is directed." (Hall v. General Motors Corp.)

[For more information on admissibility of evidence, see Casenote Law Outline on Evidence, Chapter 2, § III, Is the "Evidence" Relevant?]

10. **Reproductions of the Event and of Evidence of the Event.** As a general rule, photographs are admissible in evidence only when they are verified or authenticated by some other evidence. They are generally inadmissible as original or substantive evidence, and must be sponsored by a witness or witnesses whose testimony they serve to explain and illustrate. (Knihal v. State)

[For more information on authentication of photographs, see Casenote Law Outline on Evidence, Chapter 13, § I, Authentication in General.]

11. **Reproductions of the Event and of Evidence of the Event.** Where visual identification is crucial to a defense, expert testimony regarding such identification should be admitted. (United States v. Alexander)

[For more information on expert testimony, see Casenote Law Outline on Evidence, Chapter 12, § III, Expert Opinions.]

12. **Reproductions of the Event and of Evidence of the Event.** "Day in the life" films may be admitted to demonstrate the effect of injuries upon a plaintiff. (Bannister v. Town of Noble, Oklahoma)

[For more information on discretionary exclusion of evidence, see Casenote Law Outline on Evidence, Chapter 2, § V, Discretionary Exclusion of Relevant Evidence.]

13. **Reproductions of the Event and of Evidence of the Event.** The party offering tape recordings into evidence has the duty of laying the foundation that such recordings are accurate, authentic, and trustworthy. (United States v. Carbone)

[For more information on authentication, see Casenote Law Outline on Evidence, Chapter 13, § I, Authentication in General.]

14. **Reproductions of the Event and of Evidence of the Event.** Courts may rule on the issue of evidence authentication. (United States v. Sliker)

[For more information on authentication of voices, see Casenote Law Outline on Evidence, Chapter 13, § IV, Authentication of Voices.]

15. **Blackboards, Maps, Models, and the Like.** Charts demonstrating how evidence ties together are admissible. (United States v. Brennan)

[For more information on admissible evidence, see Casenote Law Outline on Evidence, Chapter 2, § I, Admissibility.]

16. **Authentication.** Printed matter in general (*e.g.*, a label) bears no mark of authorship other than as implied by its content; and, such a writing cannot go to the jury as purporting to be of more certain authorship, without extrinsic evidence of genuineness to authenticate it. (Keegan v. Green Giant Co.)

[For more information on authentication of writings, see Casenote Law Outline on Evidence, Chapter 13, § II, Authentication of Documents.]

17. **Authentication.** Before admitting evidence for consideration by a jury, the court must determine whether its proponent has offered a satisfactory foundation for which the jury could reasonably find that the evidence is authentic. (United States v. Branch)

18. **Authentication.** Computer records may properly be admitted as business records if they are made or based on information transmitted by a person with knowledge, are made in the ordinary course of business, and are trustworthy. (United States v. Moore)

19. **Authentication.** The court may condition a paperless trial upon the disclosure of all witness statements thirty days in advance of trial. (United States of America v. Labovitz)

20. **Authentication.** To be admitted into evidence, a document must be authenticated, which can be accomplished by circumstantial evidence as well as by direct testimony. (Zenith Radio Corp. v. Matsushita Electric Industrial Co., Limited)

> *[For more information on authentication of documents, see Casenote Law Outline on Evidence, Chapter 13, § II, Authentication of Documents.]*

21. **Authentication.** Where the genuineness of a party's signature is in dispute, other signatures of that party found on papers otherwise irrelevant, not connected with the case, and not admitted to be genuine, are admissible for the purpose of comparison with the signature in dispute after the genuineness of the signatures sought to be so introduced has been predetermined as a matter of law by the court. (University of Illinois v. Spalding)

> *[For more information on authentication of handwriting, see Casenote Law Outline on Evidence, Chapter 13, § II, Authentication of Documents.]*

22. **Best Evidence Rule.** In an action based on artwork copyright infringement, the Best Evidence Rule requires production of the originals or true copies thereof. (Seiler v. Lucasfilm, Ltd.)

> *[For more information on lost originals, see Casenote Law Outline on Evidence, Chapter 14, § IV, Absence of Originals Excused.]*

23. **Best Evidence Rule.** In the federal courts, the "best evidence rule" (where the content of a writing is sought to be proved, secondary evidence is inadmissible unless failure to offer the original writing as primary evidence is satisfactorily explained) is limited to cases where the contents of a writing are to be proved. (Meyers v. United States)

> *[For more information on the best evidence rule requirements, see Casenote Law Outline on Evidence, Chapter 14, § I, The Best Evidence Rule Stated.]*

24. **Best Evidence Rule.** Where copies of an order for goods is made in triplicate, as opposed to letterpress copies, any one of the copies is admissible and not subject to challenge under the Best Evidence Rule. (Federal Union Surety Co. v. Indiana Lumber & Manufacturing Co.)

> *[For more information on duplicate originals, see Casenote Law Outline on Evidence, Chapter 14, § II, Definitions.]*

25. **Best Evidence Rule.** Where the contents of a writing are to be proved, and the writing is not produced, parol evidence is not admissible to prove its contents unless its absence is satisfactorily explained. (Davenport v.

Ourisman-Mandell Chevrolet, Inc.)

[For more information on the proof of content of a writing, see Casenote Law Outline on Evidence, Chapter 14, § III, " To Prove the Content of a Writing".]

26. **Best Evidence Rule.** If all originals of a writing are lost or destroyed, Federal Rule of Evidence 1004(1) authorizes the admission of other evidence of the contents of the writing. (Amoco Production Co. v. United States)

[For more information on absence of originals, see Casenote Law Outline on Evidence, Chapter 14, § IV, Absence of Originals Excused.]

McANDREWS v. LEONARD
Injured plaintiff with head wounds (P) v. Alleged negligent driver (D)
Vt. Sup. Ct., 99 Vt. 512, 134 A. 710 (1926).

NATURE OF CASE: Action for damages to recover for personal injuries received in automobile accident.

FACT SUMMARY: Trial judge permitted McAndrews (P) to exhibit her head to the jurors in an auto accident case in order that the jurors might touch wounds she sustained.

CONCISE RULE OF LAW: Real evidence is not inadmissible simply because it calls for the jurors to make a tactile evaluation, provided that the evidence offered is not technical in nature, nor requires special knowledge or skill to assess.

FACTS: McAndrews (P) suffered head injuries in an automobile accident. An important issue at trial, in determining the extent of her injuries, was whether cracks made in her skull had been filled in with hard bone or with soft fibrous tissue. Dr. Smith, a physician called by McAndrews (P), testified that after examining McAndrews (P), he concluded the cracks were filled in with fibrous tissue. Dr. Bellerose, called by the defense, testified that the plaintiff's head was covered by callous, a substance harder than bone. In rebuttal, McAndrews' (P) counsel offered to permit the jurors to examine and touch the top of McAndrews' head in order to compare the hardness of her wound covering with the durability of the rest of her skull. Leonard (D) objected, claiming that the question is one of fact for the jury alone. After the physician called by McAndrews (P), upon questioning by the court, stated that this was a matter for a layman, the court permitted the examination. Leonard (D) appealed from this ruling.

ISSUE: Is the examination one for the jury or a matter which can be determined only by expert opinion?

HOLDING AND DECISION: (Watson, J.) The jury can examine the head of McAndrews (P). Being neither technical in nature, nor requiring special knowledge or skill, the examination was not for the purpose of ascertaining the kind of substance that had filled into the cracks. Rather, by tactile exploration, the jurors could judge for themselves the hardness of the substance. A verdict could not be based exclusively on the knowledge so acquired, yet the jurors could take the examination into consideration.

EDITOR'S ANALYSIS: It is universally thought that demonstrative evidence possesses an immediacy and reality which makes the introduction of such evidence very persuasive. The trend appears to be in favor of courts permitting greater use of all types of demonstrative evidence. However, since the judicial system is built around the reception of oral testimony, there is and will be conflict, not merely in the handling of such evidence, but in preserving such evidence in the record for possible appeal. Problems of prejudice and misleading the jury will also reoccur.

[For more information on discretionary inclusion of evidence, see Casenote Law Outline on Evidence, Chapter 2, § V, Discretionary Exclusion of Relevant Evidence.]

NOTES:

ALMEIDA v. CORREA
Alleged father (P) v. Mother (D)
Haw. Sup. Ct., 51 Haw. 594, 465 P.2d 564 (1970).

NATURE OF CASE: Appeal following finding of paternity.

FACT SUMMARY: Almeida (D) was found to be the father of Correa's (P) baby after a trial in which the baby was exhibited to the jury for the purpose of proving paternity by showing its resemblance to Almeida (D).

CONCISE RULE OF LAW: In a paternity case, the exhibition of the child to the fact finder for the purpose of proving paternity by showing its resemblance to the alleged father is not permitted.

FACTS: Almeida (D) appealed from a judgment finding him to be the father of Correa's (P) child. At trial, the child was exhibited to the jury for approximately 30 seconds so that they could assess any resemblance between the child and Almeida (D) and use that information to help resolve the paternity issue. Almeida (D) appealed maintaining that this was improper.

ISSUE: Can the child involved in a paternity case be exhibited to the fact finder for the purpose of proving paternity by showing the child's resemblance to the alleged father?

HOLDING AND DECISION: (Richardson, J.) No. A survey of the relevant scientific principles, texts, and articles has left this court unable to discern any good reason either in law or in science to warrant the exhibition of a child to a jury for the purpose of proving paternity. The face is not inherited from one parent as a unit, and neither are individual features. To properly understand and assess any specific resemblance between a child and a person alleged to be its parent, independent expert interpretation is required. So, although simple exhibition of the child to the fact finder is not to be permitted, expert testimony concerning the resemblance of a child to the alleged father is admissible to prove or disprove paternity. Reversed and remanded.

DISSENT: (Kobayashi, J.) The proper course would have been to court-test at the trial court level the scientific approach and principles that the majority insists are the absolute truth in the field of paternity. The trial court should have been given the task of adducing all necessary scientific-oriented evidence and testimony to determine what are the proper and correct facts regarding the relevancy and value of the exhibition of the child to the issue of paternity.

EDITOR'S ANALYSIS: Of those courts that do permit the child to be exhibited to the jury to show resemblance to the alleged father, one group permits such exhibition without further condition. Another group, however, imposes certain conditions. The most common one is that the child is old enough so that his features have "settled." In some jurisdictions the age at which features are considered "settled" is fixed.

[For more information on discretionary exclusion of evidence, see Casenote Law Outline on Evidence, Chapter 2, § V, Discretionary Exclusion of Relevant Evidence.]

NOTES:

WATSON v. STATE

Convicted robber (P) v. State (D)

Ind. Sup. Ct., 236 Ind. 329, 140 N.E.2d 109 (1957).

NATURE OF CASE: Appeal of conviction for armed robbery.

FACT SUMMARY: Watson (D) was convicted of armed robbery without the State (P) having presented evidence that he was over 16 years of age, which was an element of the crime.

CONCISE RULE OF LAW: Where age is an element of a crime, evidence of age must be presented by the prosecution.

FACTS: Watson (D) was charged with armed robbery. One of the elements thereof in Indiana was that the perpetrator have been at least 16 years of age at the time of the crime. During the course of the trial, Watson (D) sat in view of the jury, but no evidence of his age was introduced. Watson (D) was convicted, and he appealed.

ISSUE: Where age is an element of a crime, must evidence of age be presented by the prosecution?

HOLDING AND DECISION: (Afterburn, J.) Yes. Where age is an element of a crime, evidence of age must be presented by the prosecution. It is up to the prosecution to prove every element of its case. The purpose of trial is to confine the evidence which a jury may consider to that duly admitted. While a jury may use its collective knowledge, it simply may not come to conclusions through random observation, as any conclusion regarding age in this case must have been. Extrinsic evidence simply may not be considered by a jury. This was done here. Reversed.

EDITOR'S ANALYSIS: The court here did not say that a jury may not consider a defendant's physical appearance in deciding age. What it did say was that something must be done to bring that appearance into evidence. The failure to do so in this case required reversal of the conviction.

QUICKNOTES

EXTRINSIC EVIDENCE - Evidence that is not contained within the text of a document or contract but which is derived from the parties' statements or the circumstances under which the agreement was made.

BURDEN OF PROOF - The duty of a party to introduce evidence to support a fact that is in dispute in an action.

NOTES:

STATE v. SCARLETT
State (P) v. Convicted criminal (D)
N.H. Sup. Ct., 118 N.H. 904, 395 A.2d 1244 (1978).

NATURE OF CASE: Appeal from conviction for aggravated felonious sexual assault.

FACT SUMMARY: No mistrial was called even though the State (P), in attempting to prove its criminal charge against Scarlett (D), had displayed a blood-stained bedspread to the jury without thereafter providing the testimony necessary to establish the proper foundation for its admissibility.

CONCISE RULE OF LAW: It is error for the prosecution in a criminal case to display what it knows cannot be admitted into evidence (for lack of proper foundation, etc.), and it has the burden on appeal to show "beyond a reasonable doubt that the (improper display of) inadmissible evidence did not affect the verdict."

FACTS: While in the process of eliciting testimony from a police officer during Scarlett's (D) trial on charges of sexually assaulting a six-year-old girl, the State (P) displayed to the jury what appeared to be a blood-stained bedspread. It had the bedspread marked for identification and began an attempt to admit it into evidence. The State (P) did not have present and did not even have scheduled to testify the chemist who had conducted tests on the stains and whose testimony would be necessary to establish that they were blood stains and thus provide the proper foundation for admitting the bedspread into evidence. When no such proper foundation was forthcoming, defense counsel requested a mistrial, but the court considered a strict admonition to the jury to disregard the bedspread as evidence to be sufficient. Scarlett (D) appealed after his conviction.

ISSUE: Is it the burden of the prosecution on appeal to prove beyond a reasonable doubt that its improper display of evidence it knew was inadmissible did not affect the verdict?

HOLDING AND DECISION: (Bois, J.) Yes. Public prosecutors, who are held to a high standard of conduct, overreach and err when they display to the fact finder what they know to be inadmissible as evidence (because a proper foundation cannot then be provided, etc.). The State (P), which committed error in displaying the bedspread knowing that it could not have been admitted into evidence, now has the burden of establishing that the error was harmless beyond a reasonable doubt, i.e., that the improper display of the inadmissible evidence did not affect the verdict. It has not done so. Remanded for a new trial.

EDITOR'S ANALYSIS: The victory of Scarlett (D) was short-lived. At his new trial, the prosecution successfully introduced the bedspread into evidence, having made certain that the chemist who had analyzed the stains thereon to be blood was present at the new trial to testify and provide the necessary foundation for its introduction into evidence.

[For more information on allocation of burden of proof, see Casenote Law Outline on Evidence, Chapter 4, § I, Burdens of Proof.]

QUICKNOTES

BURDEN OF PROOF - The duty of a party to introduce evidence to support a fact that is in dispute in an action.

FOUNDATION - The validity of proffered evidence that must be established prior to as admission at trial, usually by demonstrating its authenticity or that it is what it purports to be.

NOTES:

ANDERSON v. BERG
Slip and fall victim (P) v. Building owner (D)
Kan. Sup. Ct., 202 Kan. 659, 451 P.2d 248 (1969).

NATURE OF CASE: Action to recover damages for alleged negligent injury.

FACT SUMMARY: In a negligence trial where Anderson (P) allegedly slipped upon a heavy accumulation of wax in Berg's (D) building, the trial court reopened the case after the jury had started deliberations in order to comply with a request from the jury to offer and admit into evidence a bottle of wax.

CONCISE RULE OF LAW: Samples to be admissible as evidence must be shown to reflect the condition of the substance at the time involved in the issues. It must be shown that no substantial change has taken place in the substance to be exhibited because of lapse of time.

FACTS: Anderson (P) alleged she slipped and fell in Berg's (D) building because the floors had been overwaxed by Berg's (D) employees. During the course of the trial, a small bottle containing a sample of the wax was identified by Anderson (P) but not admitted into evidence. It did not appear that either party made any use of it or desired it in evidence. The bottle of wax was obtained a month or two after the accident had occurred. The sample remained in the bottle for four and one-half years. There is no indication how many times the bottle cork was removed or how well the cork was fitted. The specific nature of the wax had not been established. After the jury retired for deliberations, it returned and requested to have the bottle of wax, stating they wanted to see how thin the sample was. The judge complied with this request over Anderson's (P) objection to reopening the case.

ISSUE: Is it reversible error for a trial judge to admit into evidence an exhibit, at any stage of the trial, without requiring preliminary proof that the exhibit has not changed substantially since the time in controversy?

HOLDING AND DECISION: (Hatcher, J.) Yes. While an appellate court would not ordinarily interfere with a trial court's discretion to reopen a case for introduction of evidence, the exhibit must still be shown to have been admissible in the first place. Here, no foundation had been laid for admitting the sample of wax. It had not been proved that no substantial change in the sample had occurred which would render it misleading if introduced as evidence. Although the fact that a sample may have undergone some change would not, without more, exclude it, here there was no evidence, whatsoever, offered as to the condition of the sample. The only foundation laid for its admission was its source and chain of possession. These are not sufficient by themselves: the thinness or thickness of the wax would mean nothing to a jury unless it was the same now as at the time of the accident.

EDITOR'S ANALYSIS: McCormick believes that most courts are predisposed to look disfavorably on jury experiments with tangible evidence. The basic objection is that such experiments are shielded from critical, adversary scrutiny. As this case holds, jury experimentation is improper, so long as the party adverse to the introduction of the evidence could mount an attack on the reliability of the tangible evidence, or on the nature and conduct of the experiments. On the other hand, jury experiments substantially similar to in-court experiments are generally permitted.

[For more information on preliminary questions, see Casenote Law Outline on Evidence, Chapter 5, § II, Preliminary Questions of Fact.]

QUICKNOTES

FOUNDATION - The validity of proffered evidence that must be established prior to as admission at trial, usually by demonstrating its authenticity or that it is what it purports to be.

NOTES:

STATE v. MURPHY
State (P) v. Tranquilized suspect (D)
Wash. Sup. Ct., 56 Wash. 2d 761, 355 P.2d 323 (1960).

NATURE OF CASE: Appeal from conviction of murder.

FACT SUMMARY: Murphy (D), having been given a tranquilizer while in custody by a fellow prisoner, testified in his own behalf and admitted guilt, but appealed on the ground that the tranquilizer caused him to project a cool, lackadaisical attitude, thereby prompting the jury to impose the death penalty.

CONCISE RULE OF LAW: In the event of a showing by a defendant in a criminal action of a reasonable possibility that his attitude, appearance or demeanor, as observed by a jury, had been substantially influenced or affected by circumstances over which he had no real control, grounds for a new trial exist, at least where the defendant's projected image may have prejudiced the jury in sentencing.

FACTS: Murphy (D) was charged with murder in the first degree. His court-appointed counsel stated that his demeanor prior to trial was "extremely nervous and taut." While being conducted to the courthouse, Murphy (D) was given a tranquilizer by a prisoner who was also a trustee. Murphy (D) had never taken a tranquilizer before and was unaware of its effects. Taking the stand in his own defense, Murphy (D), in the undisputed opinion of his counsel, appeared casual, cool, and somewhat lackadaisical, and freely admitted commission of the acts with which he was charged. The jury found him guilty and imposed the death penalty. Murphy (D) appealed, claiming not that the tranquilizer affected the content of his testimony, but rather that his drug-induced image caused the jury to impose the death penalty. At his trial, the judge denied his motion for a new trial believing that while the drug relaxed Murphy (D), it did not affect the jury in their verdict.

ISSUE: Should a new trial be automatically granted to a defendant who presents a reasonable showing that his demeanor was affected by circumstances beyond his control and thus, perhaps, prejudicing the jury in their verdict?

HOLDING AND DECISION: (Finley, J.) Yes. In the event of a showing by a defendant in a criminal action of a reasonable possibility that his attitude, appearance or demeanor, as observed by a jury, had been substantially influenced or affected by circumstances over which he had no real control, grounds for a new trial exist, at least where the defendant's projected image may have prejudiced the jury in sentencing. Neither the trial judge nor the appellate court can know to what extent, if any, Murphy's (D) attitude and appearance as a witness influenced the jury. Although the jury is not bound to follow any set criteria in reaching a verdict, common sense suggests that the jury quite possibly did consider Murphy's (D) attitude. It has already been held that a defendant has a right to appear with his physical faculties unfettered. This right is particularly important in capital cases. The tranquilizer may have so affected Murphy (D) that he was not aware of its effect on his actions. Especially since the drug was administered by a prison trustee, strong grounds exist for the granting of a new trial.

EDITOR'S ANALYSIS: When a defendant does not take the stand to testify in his own behalf, the trier of fact is permitted to take into consideration the defendant's demeanor while sitting in the courtroom. Courts view demeanor as something which the jury cannot be sensibly instructed to exclude from their considerations. The real problems arise in cases where it can be determined that the defendant's demeanor clearly prejudiced the jury. An appellate court will not reverse a verdict if the evidence in the record was sufficient by itself to sustain the verdict. However, when the issue on appeal is that the jury was so prejudiced by the defendant's demeanor as to impose a harsher sentence on him than would otherwise have been given, courts are more inclined to order a new trial. Less proof that the defendant's demeanor had actually prejudiced the jury is required.

NOTES:

PEOPLE v. CRIMMINS

State (P) v. Convicted murderer (D)

N.Y. Ct. App., 26 N.Y.2d 319, 258 N.E.2d 708 (1970).

NATURE OF CASE: Appeal from conviction of murder.

FACT SUMMARY: In the midst of a criminal trial, three jurors, on their own authority, visited the neighborhood which was the subject of a key prosecution witness' testimony.

CONCISE RULE OF LAW: Proof of the fact of an unauthorized visit by jurors during a criminal trial is sufficient to warrant a new trial. Proof of how such visit may have influenced individual jurors is not needed, the visit, in and of itself, constituting inherent prejudice to the defendant. No distinction will be made between visits to a scene of a crime and other views.

FACTS: Crimmins (D) was charged with killing her daughter. At her trial, the prosecution presented a witness who testified she saw defendant Crimmins, accompanied by a man, and a little boy, carrying a bundle. When the man threw the bundle into an automobile, the witness, who was watching from her third-floor window across the street heard Crimmins (D) say, "My God, don't do that to her." Shortly after this key witness' testimony, three jurors visited the area which was the subject of the testimony. The witness had testified she saw the defendant Crimmins at 2:00 a.m.; the jurors went at 2:00 a.m. and again at 5:30 p.m. At a hearing ordered by the appellate court, it was revealed that during the jury's deliberations, the lighting was discussed and one of the jurors commented that the area was well lit. The jurors had never been admonished not to visit any place which had been the subject of testimony. A request by defense counsel for the court to arrange a controlled visit had been earlier denied by the court as unnecessary. Crimmins (D) was convicted.

ISSUE: Is an unauthorized visit by jurors in a criminal proceeding to a scene which was the subject of testimony, but not the scene where the crime was allegedly committed, sufficient to warrant a new trial without proof of actual prejudice to the defendant?

HOLDING AND DECISION: (Burke, J.) Yes. Although one of the dangers sought to be avoided is that jurors will reenact the scene of the crime, there are others. Here, the witness' ability to see and hear the events to which she testified depended very much on the lighting in the area and the distances involved; her credibility is also essential to the prosecutor's case. Unless there is court supervision, there is no assurance the jurors on their own will attempt to duplicate all the circumstances of the original scene.

EDITOR'S ANALYSIS: On whether a "view" constitutes independent evidence, courts are divided with some holding that its purpose is to enable the jury to better understand the evidence, and not to supply evidence. Others hold that it is independent evidence and maintain that it is nonsense to distinguish between exhibits brought into the courtroom and a view. Like demeanor, a view cannot be adequately incorporated into a record for appellate review.

NOTES:

UNITED STATES v. WANOSKIA
Federal government (P) v. Murder suspect (D)
800 F.2d 235 (10th Cir. 1986).

NATURE OF CASE: Appeal of second-degree murder conviction.

FACT SUMMARY: Wanoskia (D) was convicted of murder following the prosecution's use of demonstrative evidence which did not exactly duplicate the situation surrounding the alleged crime.

CONCISE RULE OF LAW: Demonstrative evidence need not precisely replicate the situation the evidence seeks to clarify.

FACTS: Wanoskia (D) was accused of having shot his wife to death. He contended that she shot herself. At trial, the Government (P) presented a demonstration wherein it attempted to prove that the decedent could not have shot herself, as expert testimony indicated that the front of the gun was 18 inches from her at the time the gun was fired. The demonstration showed that a woman of similar size holding a gun to herself in no position could get the muzzle 18 inches away and point the gun at herself. Wanoskia (D) was convicted. He appealed, contending that the woman in the demonstration was of similar but not exact size to the decedent.

ISSUE: Must demonstrative evidence precisely replicate the situation the evidence seeks to clarify?

HOLDING AND DECISION: (Logan, J.) No. Demonstrative evidence need not precisely replicate the situation the evidence seeks to clarify. Fairness demands that the evidence approximate the conditions at issue but exact duplication is not required. Where the details of the two situations vary, the differences go to the weight of the evidence, not its admissibility. Here, the two situations were basically the same. The differences, therefore, did not affect the admissibility of the evidence, and it was properly admitted. Affirmed.

EDITOR'S ANALYSIS: Demonstrative evidence has to be carefully handled by trial courts. This is the practical result of the old adage about a picture being worth a thousand words. The prejudicial potential of demonstrative evidence is great, and Fed. R. Evid. 403-type objections are common.

QUICKNOTES

FRE 403 - Provides that a court may dismiss otherwise relevant evidence where its prejudicial effect on the proceeding outweighs any probative value it has.

EXPERT TESTIMONY - Testimonial evidence about a complex area of subject matter relevant to trial, presented by a person competent to inform the trier of fact due to specialized knowledge or training.

DEMONSTRATIVE EVIDENCE – Evidence that consists of tangible objects and not testimony.

NOTES:

HALL v. GENERAL MOTORS CORP.
Driver (P) v. Automobile manufacturer (D)
647 F.2d 175 (D.C. Cir. 1980).

NATURE OF CASE: Appeal from an award of damages for personal injuries.

FACT SUMMARY: On the grounds that the test conditions were not sufficiently comparable to those that existed when Mrs. Hall's (P) car left the road and collided with a tree, the trial court judge hearing her personal injury suit did not admit some of the tests conducted by General Motors (D).

CONCISE RULE OF LAW: A test is not admissible unless the test conditions are "so nearly the same in substantial particulars" as those involved in the episode in litigation "as to afford a fair comparison in respect to the particular issue to which the test is directed."

FACTS: Mrs. Hall (P) was rendered a quadriplegic when the five-month-old General Motors (D) car she was driving surged off the highway and rammed into a tree. She contended that this had resulted from a defect in the drive shaft. General Motors (D) maintained that it was caused by her momentary inattention to the road, followed by panic, which led her to apply the accelerator instead of the brake. General Motors (D) appealed a judgment awarding Mrs. Hall (P) $5 million in damages and her husband $1.5 million. Among the errors it claimed the trial court committed was a refusal by the court to let into evidence tests General Motors (D) had conducted with a drive shaft that was taped (not bolted, as it was in Mrs. Hall's (D) car) to a car that was pushed (not driven) to a speed of 50 miles per hour.

ISSUE: To be admissible, must a test have been conducted under conditions so substantially similar as those involved in the episode in litigation so as to afford a fair comparison in respect to the particular issue to which the test is directed?

HOLDING AND DECISION: (Ginsburg, J.) Yes. In order for a test to be admissible, it must have been conducted under conditions that are "so nearly the same in substantial particulars (as those involved in the episode in litigation) as to afford a fair comparison in respect to the particular issue to which the test is directed." In making this determination, the trial judge has great leeway, and her ruling will not be upset unless it is clearly erroneous. There was no abuse of discretion in this case, the trial judge having acted to keep from the jury experiments conducted under conditions not sufficiently similar to the circumstances surrounding the accident. Affirmed.

EDITOR'S ANALYSIS: A number of courts have used their discretion to disallow experiments when the opposing party is not given an opportunity to be present or have representatives present during the test. The underlying presumption is that tests should be subject to adversary scrutiny. Immunity from adversary scrutiny is cited by McCormick as one reason why experiments conducted by the jury during deliberations are generally improper.

[For more information on admissibility of evidence, see Casenote Law Outline on Evidence, Chapter 2, § III, Is the "Evidence" Relevant?]

QUICKNOTES
BURDEN OF PROOF - The duty of a party to introduce evidence to support a fact that is in dispute in an action.

NOTES:

KNIHAL v. STATE

Murder suspect (D) v. State (P)

Neb. Sup. Ct., 150 Neb. 771, 36 N.W.2d 109, 9 A.L.R.2d 891 (1949).

NATURE OF CASE: Appeal from conviction of murder in the second degree.

FACT SUMMARY: Trial court permitted introduction of photographs, allegedly taken at the scene of a murder, with the only testimony accompanying the pictures being that of the photographer who only stated that they were taken an hour after the shooting, they were true reflections, and that one of the pictures included Knihal (D).

CONCISE RULE OF LAW: As a general rule, photographs are admissible in evidence only when they are verified or authenticated by some other evidence. They are generally inadmissible as original or substantive evidence, and must be sponsored by a witness or witnesses whose testimony they serve to explain and illustrate.

FACTS: Knihal (D), owner of a tavern, was accused of shooting one of his patrons. At Knihal's (D) trial, and over his objections, two photographs were admitted into evidence. One showed a man with his back turned to the camera standing in a tavern, with what appeared to be the legs of another man on the floor. The other showed a man, with black blotches on various parts of his head, lying outstretched on his back. The photographer who took these pictures testified only to the effect that they were taken an hour after the shooting, were accurate reflections of what he saw at the time, and that one of the pictures included Knihal (D). There was no other testimony presented, either by the photographer or any other witness for the prosecution on what the pictures were supposed to prove, or what was described in them, or who were the people represented in them. Knihal (D) did not object to the admission of a third photograph taken by the same photographer.

ISSUE: May photographs be admitted into evidence independent of some testimony describing or authenticating the events portrayed in the photographs?

HOLDING AND DECISION: (Simmons, J.) No. (Because no timely objection was made as to the third photograph, its admission may not be appealed.) A map, picture or diagram, for evidentiary purposes, must have the force of testimony behind it. When offered to prove a thing or event as therein represented, it must be part of someone's testimony. In other words, someone must swear, under oath, what the picture goes to prove. Otherwise, the picture is merely paper which is open to anyone's interpretation. The witness must have competent knowledge of the facts portrayed in the pictures, and be able to describe them so as to give the pictures some meaning.

EDITOR'S ANALYSIS: The witness who lays the foundation for a photograph does not have to be the photographer. All he need know about is that the facts represented can be verified, and that the photograph correctly depicts these facts.

[For more information on authentication of photographs, see Casenote Law Outline on Evidence, Chapter 13, § I, Authentication in General.]

QUICKNOTES

FOUNDATION - The validity of proffered evidence that must be established prior to as admission at trial, usually by demonstrating its authenticity or that it is what it purports to be.

AUTHENTICATION (OF DOCUMENTARY EVIDENCE) - The validity of documentary evidence that must be established prior to its admission into evidence, usually by showing that a document is that it purports to be.

NOTES:

UNITED STATES v. ALEXANDER
Federal government (P) v. Convicted robber (D)
816 F.2d 164 (5th Cir. 1987).

NATURE OF CASE: Appeal of conviction for robbery.

FACT SUMMARY: Alexander (D) was convicted of bank robbery on the basis of photographic evidence after the exclusion of testimony of two proffered experts in fields related to visual identification.

CONCISE RULE OF LAW: Where visual identification is crucial to a defense, expert testimony regarding such identification should be admitted.

FACTS: Alexander (D) was charged with bank robbery. The only basis for the charge was identification with photos taken from security cameras. A police search uncovered no further evidence. At trial, Alexander (D) attempted to introduce testimony from a doctor who specialized in head shapes and from a photographic expert. The trial court excluded the testimony. Alexander (D) was convicted and appealed.

ISSUE: Where visual identification is crucial to a defense, should expert testimony regarding such identification be admitted?

HOLDING AND DECISION: (Williams J.) Yes. Where visual identification is crucial to a defense, expert testimony regarding such identification should be admitted. Federal Rule of Evidence 702 provides that in areas technical or scientific, expert testimony which will help the trier of fact with any given issue is appropriate. The vital issue in this case was related to visual identification. Alexander (D) wished to introduce the testimony of qualified experts to assist the jury in reaching its conclusion. Photographic identification is not a simple matter, as many factors may militate for or against identification. It seems clear that this was an appropriate situation for expert testimony, and it was therefore error to exclude it. Reversed.

EDITOR'S ANALYSIS: Litigation has become increasingly complex. As a result the use of experts has proliferated. There are now experts qualified to testify on almost any issue imaginable. It appears unlikely that this trend will reverse.

[For more information on expert testimony, see Casenote Law Outline on Evidence, Chapter 12, § III, Expert Opinions.]

BANNISTER v. TOWN OF NOBLE, OKLAHOMA
Injured Plaintiff (P) v. Town (D)
812 F.2d 1265 (10th Cir. 1987).

NATURE OF CASE: Appeal of award of damages for personal injury.

FACT SUMMARY: Bannister (P), suing the town of Noble (D), introduced a film showing his daily routine (a "day in the life" film) after his being injured.

CONCISE RULE OF LAW: "Day in the life" films may be admitted to demonstrate the effect of injuries upon a plaintiff.

FACTS: Bannister (P) sued the municipality of Noble, Oklahoma (D), for personal injuries. [The casebook excerpt did not note the facts giving rise to the accident or the nature of the injuries.] Bannister (P) introduced a "day in the life" film, showing how the injuries had affected his daily routine. The jury awarded damages, and Noble (D) appealed, contending that the film, which was also used during closing argument, was improperly admitted.

ISSUE: May "day in the life" films be admitted to demonstrate the effect of injuries upon a plaintiff?

HOLDING AND DECISION: (Tacha, J.) Yes. "Day in the life" films may be admitted to demonstrate the effect of injuries upon a plaintiff. These films can provide the jury with a useful guide in deciding how much should be awarded in the way of general damages. There definitely is a danger of prejudice. A film of this nature must realistically depict a plaintiff's lifestyle, and any film exaggerating the plaintiff's problems should be excluded. Whether or not such a film is proper is soundly a matter for the trial court to decide, and its judgment will not be disturbed unless plainly wrong. Here, the trial court did exercise its discretion, and this court sees no reason to reverse the trial court's decision. Affirmed.

EDITOR'S ANALYSIS: As any film buff can attest, almost anything is possible in film. The use of film as evidence is fraught with the potential for prejudice, and a trial court should examine the film carefully before admitting it. The usual practice is for the court to hold an in camera viewing of the film.

[For more information on discretionary exclusion of evidence, see Casenote Law Outline on Evidence, Chapter 2, § V, Discretionary Exclusion of Relevant Evidence.]

UNITED STATES v. CARBONE
Federal government (P) v. Narcotics suspect (D)
798 F.2d 21 (1st Cir. 1986).

NATURE OF CASE: Appeal from drug-related conviction.

FACT SUMMARY: At his trial, Carbone (D) challenged the use of transcripts as a jury aid and the admission of tape recordings on the grounds that the recordings were unauthenticated, inaudible, and enhanced.

CONCISE RULE OF LAW: The party offering tape recordings into evidence has the duty of laying the foundation that such recordings are accurate, authentic, and trustworthy.

FACTS: Prior to Carbone's (D) trial for drug-related offenses, the government (P) furnished Carbone (D) with copies of the tape recordings it planned to offer in evidence, along with transcripts of the recordings. The recordings were of drug transactions, conducted in Spanish between Carbone (D) and government (P) informants. At trial, the agent in charge of the investigations described how the conversations had been recorded. An expert witness also testified about the enhancement process used to make one of the tapes clear and understandable. At trial, Carbone (D) objected to the admissibility of the recordings, claiming they were inaudible and poorly authenticated. He also objected to the use of the transcripts of the tapes as a jury aid. The trial judge admitted the recordings and permitted the use of the transcripts. Carbone (D) appealed.

ISSUE: Does the party offering tape recordings into evidence have the duty of laying the foundation that such recordings are accurate, authentic, and trustworthy?

HOLDING AND DECISION: (Bownes, J.) Yes. The party offering tape recordings into evidence has the duty of laying the foundation that such recordings are accurate, authentic, and trustworthy. Once this is done, the party challenging the recordings bears the burden of showing they are inaccurate. In this case, the government (P) properly authenticated the recordings and ascertained beforehand that all the jurors spoke Spanish. None of the tapes were so inaudible or unintelligible as to make them more misleading than helpful. As to the issue of tape enhancement, the credibility of the expert witnesses was properly left to the jury. As to the transcripts, permitting the jury to listen to the tapes while following along with the transcripts was in accord with the law. Carbone (D) had ample time to make more accurate transcripts, if necessary. He did not do so. Nor did he raise specific accuracy objections at trial. Affirmed.

EDITOR'S ANALYSIS: The Carbone court emphasized that the preferred way of handling challenges to the accuracy and audibility of tape recordings is a pretrial motion in limine. For tactical reasons, the opponent usually prefers to prevent the proponent from even mentioning the evidence during trial. Otherwise, the jury may hear about nonadmissible evidence and conclude that the opponent has something to hide. Advanced rulings based on motions in limine also influence trial strategies.

[For more information on authentication, see Casenote Law Outline on Evidence, Chapter 13, § I, Authentication in General.]

QUICKNOTES

EXPERT TESTIMONY - Testimonial evidence about a complex area of subject matter relevant to trial, presented by a person competent to inform the trier of fact due to specialized knowledge or training.

BURDEN OF PROOF - The duty of a party to introduce evidence to support a fact that is in dispute in an action.

AUTHENTICATION (OF DOCUMENTARY EVIDENCE) - The validity of documentary evidence that must be established prior to its admission into evidence, usually by showing that a document is that it purports to be.

FOUNDATION - The validity of proffered evidence that must be established prior to as admission at trial, usually by demonstrating its authenticity or that it is what it purports to be.

NOTES:

UNITED STATES v. SLIKER
Federal government (P) v. Conspirator for bank fraud (D)
751 F.2d 477 (2d Cir. 1984); cert. denied 470 U.S. 1058 (1985).

NATURE OF CASE: Appeal of conviction for bank fraud.

FACT SUMMARY: Prior to admitting a tape recording of a conversation between Carbone (D) and Sliker (D), the court made a preliminary ruling that the voice was in fact that of Carbone (D).

CONCISE RULE OF LAW: Courts may rule on the issue of evidence authentication.

FACTS: Carbone (D), Sliker (D), and Saluzzi (D) were indicted on 20 counts of bank fraud. At trial, the Government (P) wished to introduce an incriminating tape with an alleged conversation between Carbone (D) and Sliker (D). Carbone (D) contended that the voice on the tape was not his. The court ruled to the contrary, and allowed the jury to hear the tape. The Government (P) introduced no evidence that the voice was Carbone's (D). Carbone (D) was convicted, and he appealed.

ISSUE: May courts rule on the issue of evidence authentication?

HOLDING AND DECISION: (Friendly, J.) Yes. Courts may rule on the issue of evidence authentication. Factual issues are properly the province of the jury. However, it is the function of the court to decide preliminary factual questions relating to evidence admissibility. Whether a piece of evidence is in fact what it purports to be is one such preliminary factual question, and a court properly exercises its duties when it makes a determination on this issue. A jury cannot make decisions of this nature, as its role is to rule on weight of evidence, not admissibility. The court in this instance properly fulfilled its role. Affirmed.

EDITOR'S ANALYSIS: Like films or video, tapes can present special problems in evidence law. The issue of authentication is obviously bound to arise. Also, portions of a tape played out of context can be misleading. As is often the solution in this area, an in camera review is often necessary for an admissibility ruling.

[For more information on authentication of voices, see Casenote Law Outline on Evidence, Chapter 13, § IV, Authentication of Voices.]

UNITED STATES v. BRENNAN
Federal government (P) v. Bribed judge (D)
629 F. Supp. 283 (E.D.N.Y. 1986); aff'd, 798 F.2d 581 (2d Cir. 1986).

NATURE OF CASE: Sentence hearing following a bribery conviction.

FACT SUMMARY: Brennan (D), a judge, was convicted of bribery partly through the admission of charts tying various pieces of evidence together.

CONCISE RULE OF LAW: Charts demonstrating how evidence ties together are admissible.

FACTS: The FBI, suspecting Judge William Brennan (D) of accepting bribes, operated a "sting" in which incriminating evidence was gathered. At closing argument, the Government (P) used a chart demonstrating how the various bits of evidence tied together. Brennan (D) was convicted and appealed.

ISSUE: Are charts demonstrating how evidence ties together admissible?

HOLDING AND DECISION: (Weinstein, J.) Yes. Charts demonstrating how evidence ties together are admissible. [The casebook excerpt gave no reasoning behind the holding.]

EDITOR'S ANALYSIS: It is no secret that litigation is growing increasingly complex, a reflection of society at large. Often the various pieces of evidence in a case will be many and have occurred over a great period of time. Visual compilations such as those used in this case can be crucial in these instances.

[For more information on admissible evidence, see Casenote Law Outline on Evidence, Chapter 2, § I, Admissibility.]

KEEGAN v. GREEN GIANT CO.

Injured pea swallower (P) v. Canned food distributor (D)

Me. Sup. Jud. Ct., 150 Me. 283, 110 A.2d 599 (1954).

NATURE OF CASE: Action for products liability damages.

FACT SUMMARY: Keegan (P) was injured after swallowing a piece of steel concealed in a can of peas bearing Green Giant's (D) label.

CONCISE RULE OF LAW: Printed matter in general (e.g., a label) bears no mark of authorship other than as implied by its content; and, such a writing cannot go to the jury as purporting to be of more certain authorship, without extrinsic evidence of genuineness to authenticate it.

FACTS: Keegan's (P) wife swallowed a piece of steel which had been concealed in a can of peas purchased by his mother-in-law. The can bore the label "Green Giant Brand Great Big Tender Sweet Peas. Distributed by Green Giant Company, La Sueur, Minn. C66 Co. Reg. U.S. Pat. Off. Packed in U.S.A. Replacement or refund of money . . . Guaranteed by Good Housekeeping . . . If not as advertised therein." In addition, the can was imprinted with the letters "ACFC5, 3L4." Keegan (P) sued for damages. At trial, he attempted to offer the can and label into evidence as self-evident proof that Green Giant (D) had produced it. The offer was denied and excepted to. From directed verdict for Green Giant (D), Keegan (P) appealed.

ISSUE: Is a commercial label prima facie evidence of its authorship?

HOLDING AND DECISION: (Tapley, J.) No. Printed matter in general (e.g., a label) bears no mark of authorship other than as implied by content; and, such a writing cannot go to the jury as purporting to be of more certain authorship, without extrinsic evidence of genuineness to authenticate it. There is no judicial justification for considering contents alone as sufficient proof of authorship, however. Here, extrinsic evidence linking the label and/or the code letters on the can to Green Giant (D) might well have been discovered and introduced. In such circumstances, the contents of the label and can printing could have been introduced. No such evidence was offered, however, so authentication was defective. Judgment below must be affirmed.

DISSENT: (Williamson, J.) Justice Williamson would permit introduction of the can to allow further inquiry into whether the code numbers and label were authentic. Effectively, he would shift the burden of proof (of non-authenticity) to Green Giant (D).

EDITOR'S ANALYSIS: This case points up the general rule that writings carry with them no presumption of authenticity. Extrinsic evidence of authorship must always be produced before a writing may be admitted as authentic (*i.e.*, as being prepared by the person purported to be the author). Authentication may be accomplished by direct evidence (*e.g.*, testimony of attesting witnesses, handwriting analysis), or by circumstantial evidence (e.g., by custody or reference to other communications, etc.).

[For more information on authentication of writings, see Casenote Law Outline on Evidence, Chapter 13, § II, Authentication of Documents.]

QUICKNOTES

BURDEN OF PROOF - The duty of a party to introduce evidence to support a fact that is in dispute in an action.

AUTHENTICATION (OF DOCUMENTARY EVIDENCE) - The validity of documentary evidence that must be established prior to its admission into evidence, usually by showing that a document is that it purports to be.

EXTRINSIC EVIDENCE - Evidence that is not contained within the text of a document or contract but which is derived from the parties' statements or the circumstances under which the agreement was made.

DIRECTED VERDICT - A verdict ordered by the court in a jury trial.

NOTES:

UNITED STATES v. BRANCH
Federal government (P) v. Drug dealer (D)
970 F.2d 1368 (4th Cir. 1992).

NATURE OF CASE: Appeals from convictions for conspiracy, distribution of heroin and cocaine, and for attempting to evade income taxes.

FACT SUMMARY: Branch (D) contended that the district court conducted an in camera hearing in lieu of requiring the government (P) to present sufficient evidence at trial to support a finding that tape recordings it had made of his telephone conversations were authentic.

CONCISE RULE OF LAW: Before admitting evidence for consideration by a jury, the court must determine whether its proponent has offered a satisfactory foundation for which the jury could reasonably find that the evidence is authentic.

FACTS: Branch (D) and his co-conspirators were suspected of dealing heroin and cocaine. The government (P) began an investigation in these activities and subsequently obtained authorization to place wiretaps on certain telephone lines. Before Branch's (D) trial, the government (P) requested an in camera hearing to present testimony to establish the authenticity of the tape recording made as a result of the wiretaps. During the hearing, the government (P) presented testimony of twenty-six government agents who monitored the recording of the conversations. The court overruled Branch's (D) objections that this procedure prevented the jury from properly evaluating the tapes' accuracy and genuineness. At trial, the FBI supervisor testified about the tape recordings but the monitors did not. Branch (D) was convicted and appealed, arguing that the government (P) had failed to present sufficient evidence to allow the jury to find that the tapes were authentic.

ISSUE: Before admitting evidence for consideration by a jury, must the court determine whether its proponent has offered a satisfactory foundation for which the jury could reasonably find that the evidence is authentic?

HOLDING AND DECISION: (Wilkins, J.) Yes. Before admitting evidence for consideration by a jury, the court must determine whether its proponent has offered a satisfactory foundation for which the jury could reasonably find that the evidence is authentic. Of course, although the district court must make this preliminary determination, the ultimate resolution of authenticity is a question for the jury. It is particularly appropriate in situations like Branch's (D), where an in camera hearing insures that the jury will not tainted by hearing prejudicial evidence and the court may rule on hearsay objections to co-conspirators' statements out of the hearing of the jury. In this case, not only was the in camera procedure proper, but the government (P) then went on to present sufficient evidence at trial that the tapes were accurately recorded conversations involving Branch (D) and his co-conspirators. Affirmed.

EDITOR'S ANALYSIS: United States v. McKeever, 169 F. Supp. 426 (S.D.N.Y. 1958) set forth the criteria to be evaluated when ruling on authentication issues regarding tape recordings. According to McKeever, the proponent of the recordings should prove that the recording device was capable of taping the conversation, that the operator of the device was competent to operate it, and that the recording is authentic and correct. The proponent should also identify the speakers and show that changes, additions, or deletions have not been made, and that the conversation was made voluntarily and in good faith.

QUICKNOTES

AUTHENTICATION (OF DOCUMENTARY EVIDENCE) - The validity of documentary evidence that must be established prior to its admission into evidence, usually by showing that a document is that it purports to be.

FOUNDATION - The validity of proffered evidence that must be established prior to as admission at trial, usually by demonstrating its authenticity or that it is what it purports to be.

IN CAMERA - In private chambers.

NOTES:

UNITED STATES v. MOORE
Federal government (P) v. Fraudulent bank employee (D)
923 F.2d 910 (1st Cir. 1991).

NATURE OF CASE: Appeal from conviction for conspiring fraudulently to obtain money from a bank.

FACT SUMMARY: Moore (D) argued that the government (P) did not lay an adequate foundation to admit computer-generated loan histories under the business records exception to the hearsay rule.

CONCISE RULE OF LAW: Computer records may properly be admitted as business records if they are made or based on information transmitted by a person with knowledge, are made in the ordinary course of business, and are trustworthy.

FACTS: Moore (D), a bank teller, and two other bank employees hatched a scheme whereby one employee would write up a phony loan application and someone else pretending to be the borrower would present the $5,000 check for the approved loan to Moore (D) to cash. When it was discovered that the borrowers did not exist, the government (P) brought charges against all three co-conspirators. The two other employees agreed to testify against Moore (D). Other than that testimony, the government's (P) evidence against Moore (D) consisted of fourteen computer-generated loan histories, one for each of the bad loans. At trial, the head of the bank's consumer loan department testified for the government (P) that the loan histories were made in the regular course of the bank's business and that they were compiled by a service bureau connected by phone to the bank's receiving officers. The histories, although hearsay, were admitted into evidence under the business records exception to the hearsay rule. Moore (D) was convicted as charged. She appealed, contending that the government (P) had failed to lay an adequate foundation for the admission of the computer records.

ISSUE: May computer records properly be admitted as business records if they are made or based on information transmitted by a person with knowledge, are made in the ordinary course of business, and are trustworthy?

HOLDING AND DECISION: (Breyer, C.J.) Yes. Computer records may properly be admitted as business records if they are made or based on information transmitted by a person with knowledge, are made in the ordinary course of business, and are trustworthy. In this case, the government (P) did lay an adequate foundation for the records. Its witness, the head of consumer loans, was "qualified" to testify that the information was kept in the "regular course of business," that the records were made on the basis of information transmitted by a "person with knowledge" — the service bureau, and that it was the "regular practice" of the bank and bureau to keep such records. The ordinary business circumstances described by the government's (P) witness suggest trustworthiness. Affirmed.

EDITOR'S ANALYSIS: Note that the qualified witness who is laying the foundation for business records need not be the person who actually prepared the record. However, the records must be kept pursuant to some routine procedure designed to assure their accuracy. The business records exception is laid out in Federal Rule of Evidence 803(6).

QUICKNOTES

HEARSAY - An out-of-court statement made by a person other than the witness testifying at trial that is offered in order to prove the truth of the matter asserted.

BUSINESS RECORD - A record made as a part of routine procedure. Admissible as an exception to the hearsay rule.

NOTES:

ZENITH RADIO CORP. v. MATSUSHITA ELECTRIC INDUSTRIAL CO., LIMITED

American electronics company (P) v. Japanese electronics company (D)

505 F. Supp. 1190 (E.D. Pa. 1980); rev'd on related grounds, 723 F.2d 238 (3d Cir. 1983); rev'd on other grounds, 475 U.S. 574 (1986).

NATURE OF CASE: Pretrial evidentiary hearings in business litigation.

FACT SUMMARY: The court in which complex business litigation between Zenith (P) and Mitsushita (D) and others was pending decided that it was necessary to hold pretrial evidentiary hearings to rule on the admissibility of the key documents Zenith (P) wanted to introduce into evidence to prove its case.

CONCISE RULE OF LAW: To be admitted into evidence, a document must be authenticated, which can be accomplished by circumstantial evidence as well as by direct testimony.

FACTS: The complex business litigation involving Zenith (P) and Matsushita (D) included charges of conspiratorial activity by several Japanese companies. The key documents Zenith (P) wanted to introduce at trial to prove its case included the diaries (in Japanese) of several employees of the Japanese companies allegedly involved in the conspiratorial activities complained of. They also included "protocols" of a number of other officials of Japanese companies, i.e., statements given during interviews submitted to in the course of the Six Company Case proceedings in Japan. Finally, there were the records of formal testimony given at hearings before the Japanese FTC. The protocols and testimony contained significant evidence of conspiratorial activity by Matsushita (D) and the other defendants, according to Zenith's (P) submission, and would serve to authenticate the diaries and qualify them as business records within the meaning of the Federal Rules of Evidence. Zenith (P) had chosen not to take depositions of the alleged authors of the diaries, who were in Japan, as a means of authenticating them. Thus, when the court held pretrial evidentiary hearings to rule on the admissibility of these key documents, one of the questions it faced was whether Zenith's (P) failure to take such depositions for the purpose of laying foundations for the admissibility of the documents (which is the customary route taken) was fatal to their attempt to have the documents admitted into evidence or whether they could be authenticated in some other manner.

ISSUE: Must a document be authenticated by circumstantial evidence or otherwise to be admissible?

HOLDING AND DECISION: (Becker, J.) Yes. A document must be authenticated before it can be admitted into evidence. Federal Rule of Evidence 910(a) provides: "The requirement of authentication or identification as a condition precedent to admissibility is satisfied by evidence sufficient to support a finding that the matter in question is what its proponent claims." The notion of authentication is a narrow one and is akin to the notion of genuineness. The first step in the course of authentication is for the court to determine whether or not a prima facie showing has been made that the document is what its proponent claims. In making this determination the court may not, as some have argued, consider inadmissible evidence. Its duty is to determine whether admissible evidence exists which is sufficient to support a jury finding of authenticity. If so, the document should be admitted. At that point, the burden of going forward with respect to authentication shifts to the opponent to rebut the prima facie showing by presenting evidence to the trier of fact which would raise questions as to the genuineness of the document. In all of this, it must be remembered that the required prima facie showing of authentication need not consist of a preponderance of the evidence; all that is required is substantial evidence from which the trier of fact might conclude that a document is authentic. Furthermore, testimony is not essential to establish authenticity. As McCormick states, "authentication by circumstantial evidence is uniformly recognized as permissible." The very fact that the defendants produced certain documents in answer to interrogatories may provide circumstantial evidence of authenticity. As McCormick notes, a prima facie showing of authenticity is made by the emergence of a document from public custody. Expansion of that rule to private custody cases is not warranted because the circumstances of private custody are too varied, but "proof of private custody, together with other circumstances, is frequently strong circumstantial evidence of authenticity." The characteristics of the document itself are also a basis for establishing authentication. They include its appearance (e.g., a postmark, a return address, a letterhead, a signature, typing or form which corresponds to usual practice); its contents or substance (subject matter in the document referring to knowledge which only one individual would have had is sufficient to authenticate the document); etc. Testimony in other proceedings may also establish authenticity. Where such testimony does not deal directly with any particular document offered, it may still be helpful in proving authenticity circumstantially. Answers to interrogatories may be considered as "testimony" where they directly identify a document's source or author, corroborate the contents of particular documents, indicate the presence of a purported author at a meeting or a meeting's limited attendance, or otherwise establish the document's authenticity. However, since interrogatories may not

Continued on next page.

be admissible against all defendants unless the plaintiffs' conspiracy theory is accepted, this presents a difficult situation. Where authentication depends on the admissibility of an interrogatory, which itself depends on the plaintiffs' establishment of a conspiracy, the documents may be admitted "subject to" such a showing. Another method of authentication allows the trier of fact to compare a document to another authenticated document in order to establish its authenticity. This often occurs where documents are members of a "group" of documents, sharing similar characteristics. The authentication of one document in the group may serve as the basis for authenticating the others in the group on the basis of comparison, initially by the court, and ultimately by the trier of fact. Another element that may be considered in determining authenticity is the age of the document. Federal Rule of Evidence 901 (b)(8)(C) sets 20 years as the age requirement for "Ancient Documents." None of the documents in this case are now that old, but some may reach that age by the time of trial. However, the 20-year age period for a document is dated from the time it is offered. Where, as in the case, all of the documents fall short of the 20-year limit, some additional indicia of authenticity are needed. These are the principles which will be used to determine the admissibility of the documents in this case.

EDITOR'S ANALYSIS: Certain documents are "self-authenticating," i.e., no extrinsic evidence of authenticity is needed. Among them are properly certified copies of public documents. At common law, it was necessary to have a witness who had made the copy or had compared it with the original and who would swear that the copy to be introduced into evidence was a true and correct copy of the original.

[For more information on authentication of documents, see Casenote Law Outline on Evidence, Chapter 13, § II, Authentication of Documents.]

QUICKNOTES

AUTHENTICATION (OF DOCUMENTARY EVIDENCE) - The validity of documentary evidence that must be established prior to its admission into evidence, usually by showing that a document is that it purports to be.

ANCIENT DOCUMENTS – A document that is admissible into evidence without authentification if, on its face, it shows evidence of being twenty years old or more and it in the proper location.

FOUNDATION - The validity of proffered evidence that must be established prior to as admission at trial, usually by demonstrating its authenticity or that it is what it purports to be.

NOTES:

UNITED STATES OF AMERICA v. LABOVITZ
Federal government (P) v. Criminal suspect (D)
1996 WL 417113 (D. Mass. 1996).

NATURE OF CASE: Motion to conduct a paperless trial.

FACT SUMMARY: The government (P) requested permission to image and index all of its documentary exhibits on a computer for use at trial.

CONCISE RULE OF LAW: The court may condition a paperless trial upon the disclosure of all witness statements thirty days in advance of trial.

FACTS: Prior to its trial of Labovitz (D), the government (P) made a motion to be allowed to conduct a paperless trial. Under the paperless approach, the government (P) would create computer images of documentary exhibits and then transfer the images to CD-ROMS for use at trial. Under the Jencks Act, the court lacks the power in ordinary circumstance to require the government (P) to produce witness statements before the witness has completed his direct examination at trial. In its response to the government's (P) motion, Labovitz (D) asked for disclosure of the so-called Jencks material ninety days prior to trial. The court issued a memorandum and order regarding the motion.

ISSUE: May the court condition a paperless trial upon the disclosure of all witness statements thirty days in advance of trial?

HOLDING AND DECISION: (Ponsor, J.) Yes. The court may condition a paperless trial upon the disclosure of all witness statements thirty days in advance of trial. A paperless trial presents special problems, which requires the court to be alert to possible unfairness to Labovitz (D). He must be given sufficient time to prepare his case through the special techniques used in such a trial. Literal enforcement of the Jencks Act would place him at an unfair disadvantage. He needs an opportunity to review witness statements before trial, select the documents he will need for cross-examination, and prepare them for use at trial. Therefore, the use of the paperless procedure proposed by the government (P) will be conditioned upon the disclosure by the government (P) of Jencks materials thirty days in advance of trial. This strikes a fair balance between the government's (P) right to retain witness statements and Labovitz's (D) legitimate need for time to adequately prepare using the innovative procedure that will be employed in this trial. So ordered.

EDITOR'S ANALYSIS: Judge Ponsor also required the government (P) to arrange for setting up monitors for himself, the clerk, the witness box, the defense table, the prosecution table, the jury, and the technician monitoring the projection of the images. The government (P) had to pay for the installation. It was also required to provide Labovitz (D) with an index correlating all the government (P) exhibit numbers with the image document numbers.

UNIVERSITY OF ILLINOIS v. SPALDING
Debt collector (P) v. Surety (D)
N.H. Sup. Ct., 71 N.H. 163, 51 A. 731, 62 L.R.A. 817 (1901).

NATURE OF CASE: Action for debt on a bond.

FACT SUMMARY: Trial court permitted Spalding (D) to introduce into evidence, for purposes of comparing signatures, papers containing his handwriting which were not part of the action.

CONCISE RULE OF LAW: Where the genuineness of a party's signature is in dispute, other signatures of that party found on papers otherwise irrelevant, not connected with the case, and not admitted to be genuine, are admissible for the purpose of comparison with the signature in dispute after the genuineness of the signatures sought to be so introduced has been predetermined as a matter of law by the court.

FACTS: The University of Illinois (P), trying to collect against a penniless debtor, sued the surety, Spalding (D), for the amount owed. A major issue in the trial was whether Spalding's (D) signature appeared on the bond. Spalding (D) denied that the signature was in his handwriting, and was permitted to introduce into evidence, for the purpose of comparison, his signatures on some stock certificates which were not otherwise a part of the case. Before the stock certificates were admitted, Spalding (D) and the treasurer of the corporation which issued the certificates swore that the signatures were genuine. The University (P) objected on the ground that it did not recognize the signatures as genuine and, furthermore, they were not found on papers which were connected with the case.

ISSUE: Is it error to admit into evidence, for purposes of having a standard with which to determine the genuineness of disputed handwritings, samples of handwriting neither admitted by the opposing party to be genuine nor found on papers connected with the case?

HOLDING AND DECISION: (Remick, J.) No. At common law, the only recognized method to test the genuineness of a disputed signature was to have a witness who had seen the real signature testify from memory. The fact that the witness may have had little familiarity with the party's real handwriting was of no real consequence. The reasons for this approach were threefold: (1) the inability of jurors to make intelligent comparisons; (2) the danger of unfairness and fraud in the selection of samples; (3) the introduction of collateral issues raised by writings not themselves in evidence would only confuse and distract the jury. However, the common law approach no longer carries much weight. Jurors today are more intelligent and discerning. Besides, before any writing can be admitted for purposes of comparison, its genuineness must be preliminarily determined by the trial court,

although it does not have to be supported by direct evidence. The fear that nonrepresentative or false samples will be chosen is too slight to exclude otherwise competent evidence, particularly since both parties have the right to produce samples which are open to examination and cross-examination. Finally, comparison is not really possible without using some genuine standard. Accurate comparison should not be defeated simply because a sample is found on papers not otherwise in evidence.

EDITOR'S ANALYSIS: The genuineness of a standard for comparison may be admitted by both parties. However, if not, it may still be used if it is either a part of the pleadings or has been introduced into evidence for some other purpose. If the sample writing was made after an action was commenced or subsequent to the immediate dispute, it is admissible so long as the writing was made in the ordinary course of business and not for the self-serving purpose of being made specially for use at trial. This latter rule is based on the theory that a writing, or signature, naturally made, is the best proof of a person's customary handwriting.

[For more information on authentication of handwriting, see Casenote Law Outline on Evidence, Chapter 13, § II, Authentication of Documents.]

QUICKNOTES
AUTHENTICATION (OF DOCUMENTARY EVIDENCE) - The validity of documentary evidence that must be established prior to its admission into evidence, usually by showing that a document is that it purports to be.

SURETY - A party who guarantees payment of the debt of another party to a creditor.

NOTES:

SEILER v. LUCASFILM, INC.
Designer (P) v. Movie company (D)
797 F.2d 1504 (9th Cir. 1986).

NATURE OF CASE: Appeal of dismissal of action for damages for copyright infringement.

FACT SUMMARY: Seiler (P), claiming that Lucasfilm (D) violated copyrights on certain drawings he had made, could not produce the original drawings or copies thereof.

CONCISE RULE OF LAW: In an action based on artwork copyright infringement, the Best Evidence Rule requires production of the originals or true copies thereof.

FACTS: Seiler (P) contended the "Imperial Walkers" featured in the film The Empire Strikes Back were improperly based on creatures he had designed in the late 1970's called "barthian striders." Seiler (P) did not obtain his copyright until 1981. The film had been released in 1980. Prior to trial, Seiler (P) informed the court that he no longer had the original designs or copies thereof, but planned to use reconstructions. Following an evidentiary hearing, the court held that the Best Evidence Rule mandated that originals or copies thereof be introduced, as Seiler (P) had not lost the originals in good faith. The court dismissed, and Seiler (P) appealed.

ISSUE: In an action based on artwork copyright infringement, does the Best Evidence Rule require production of the originals or true copies thereof?

HOLDING AND DECISION: (Farris, J.) Yes. In an action based on artwork copyright infringement, the Best Evidence Rule requires production of the originals or true copies thereof. The common law rule, which requires introduction of the original or a true copy of a writing, is grounded on a recognition of the fact that where the contents of a writing are at issue, the best place to look for the decision on this issue is the writing itself. Use of the original avoids the hazards of inaccurate memory or duplication. While some authority exists for the proposition that only narrative writings will be covered by the Rule, the logic behind the Rule is equally applicable to drawings, and originals or copies should be presented. Fed. R. Evid. 1008 permits a court to grant relief if it finds that the failure to produce originals was in good faith; however, the court found that not to be so, and this was within its discretion. Affirmed.

EDITOR'S ANALYSIS: As a final effort, Seiler (P) had argued that 17 U.S.C. § 410(c), part of the Copyright Law, superseded the Rule. This section creates a presumption that work deposited with the Copyright Office is admissible. The court held that only the certificate issued by the Office was presumptively admissible, not the copies themselves.

[For more information on lost originals, see Casenote Law Outline on Evidence, Chapter 14, § IV, Absence of Originals Excused.]

QUICKNOTES
BEST EVIDENCE RULE – An evidentiary rule requiring that an original document be introduced if possible; secondary evidence is only admissible after proof that the original was lost or destroyed through no fault of the proponent.

NOTES:

MEYERS v. UNITED STATES
Perjurer (D) v. Federal government (P)
84 U.S. App. D.C. 101, 171 F.2d 800 (D.C. Cir. 1948), cert. denied 336 U.S. 912 (1949).

NATURE OF CASE: Appeal from conviction of perjury and subornation.

FACT SUMMARY: Trial court permitted the chief counsel to a senate committee to testify on the testimony given by Lamarre (D) before that body, and later in the trial permitted the government to introduce into evidence a stenographic transcript of Lamarre's (D) testimony.

CONCISE RULE OF LAW: In the federal courts, the "best evidence rule" ("where the content of a writing is sought to be proved, secondary evidence is inadmissible unless failure to offer the original writing as primary evidence is satisfactorily explained") is limited to cases where the contents of a writing are to be proved.

FACTS: Lamarre (D) was indicted for perjuring his testimony before a U.S. Senate subcommittee, and for suborning the perjuries of Meyers (D). The words and expressions charged to Lamarre (D) in the indictment did not appear in the transcript, but were, the Government (P) argued, to be inferred from his answers to the many questions put to him. Rogers, chief counsel to the committee, had heard all of Lamarre's (D) testimony before the Senate body. Rogers was permitted to testify early in the trial as to what Lamarre (D) had sworn to the subcommittee. Towards the close of the trial, the Government (P) introduced into evidence a stenographic transcript of Lamarre's (D) testimony at the hearing. Lamarre (D) objected to this staggered introduction of the oral testimony as a "bizarre procedure."

ISSUE: Is the best evidence rule limited to cases where the contents of a writing are to be proved?

HOLDING AND DECISION: (Miller, J.) Yes. The best evidence rule is limited to cases where the contents of a writing are to be proved. The prosecution, by having Rogers testify, did not attempt to prove the contents of a writing; the issue was what Lamarre had said, not what the transcript contained. Hence, the "best evidence rule" was inapplicable here. Rogers' testimony was equally competent and was admissible, whether it was given before or after the transcript was received in evidence. Statements alleged to be perjured may be proved by any person who heard them, as well as by a reporter who recorded them in shorthand. Since both methods of proving the perjury were permissible, the prosecution could present its proof in any order it chose. Lamarre's (D) and Meyers' (D) counsel had full opportunity to study the transcript and to cross-examine Rogers in the light of that study. There was no indication that Meyers' (D) position before the jury would have been more favorable had the transcript been offered on an earlier day of the trial. Affirmed.

DISSENT: (Prettyman, J.) The prosecutor could not have first put into evidence the transcript of Lamarre's (D) testimony and thereafter have produced Rogers to give the jury from the witness box his own summation, since this would have been met with a ruling that "the transcript speaks for itself." Summation and interpretation are aspects of argument, and not evidence. The impression given by a succinct summation by a live witness on the stand cannot be corrected or offset by the later reading of a long, cold record. Stenographic recording has become highly developed and should be considered the best evidence of testimony when presented.

EDITOR'S ANALYSIS: In substantiating the former testimony of a party or defendant, four methods are generally approved: (1) a first-hand observer may testify from his memory without use of any aids. The observer need not give a word-by-word account, but may give the purport of the former testimony; (2) a first-hand observer may refresh his present memory by use of some note prepared by a court officer; (3) under the hearsay exception based on official writings, official court reports or notes may be admitted; (4) a witness may rely on his own written notes made at the time of the former testimony. These notes come in under the past recollection recorded rule.

[For more information on the best evidence rule requirements, see Casenote Law Outline on Evidence, Chapter 14, § I, The Best Evidence Rule Stated.]

QUICKNOTES

BEST EVIDENCE RULE – An evidentiary rule requiring that an original document be introduced if possible; secondary evidence is only admissible after proof that the original was lost or destroyed through no fault of the proponent.

BUSINESS RECORD - A record made as a part of routine procedure. Admissible as an exception to the hearsay rule.

NOTES:

FEDERAL UNION SURETY CO. v. INDIANA LUMBER & MANUFACTURING CO.

Contractor (D) v. Lumber company (P)

Ind. Sup. Ct., 176 Ind. 328, 95 N.E. 1104 (1911).

NATURE OF CASE: Action on contract for value of goods received.

FACT SUMMARY: Trial court permitted lumber company (P) to introduce into evidence a triplicate copy of an order for lumber, rather than the original written memorandum taken by its sales agent, or the copy of the delivery slip handed to Suzio (D).

CONCISE RULE OF LAW: Where copies of an order for goods is made in triplicate, as opposed to letterpress copies, any one of the copies is admissible and not subject to challenge under the Best Evidence Rule.

FACTS: Suzio (D), a contractor, placed an order for lumber with the Indiana Lumber & Manufacturing Co. (P). The two had done business before. The procedure for ordering and delivery was as follows: An agent for the company would take the order over the phone, write it down as a memorandum, hand it to a yard clerk who, in turn, gave it to a loader. The loader placed the goods on a wagon and returned the memo to the clerk. Before delivery, the clerk made three "original copies" on an automatic register: each copy was on a printed form with blanks for amount of charge, quantity, destination, description of goods, etc., and the machine filled in the appropriate information, numbering each copy. One copy was delivered with the goods to Suzio (D); the original memorandum and the two copies were retained by the company (P). In an action by the lumber company (P) against Suzio's surety (D), the trial court permitted the company (P) to introduce into evidence one of its slip copies.

ISSUE: Was it error for the trial court to admit the slip copy when the original memorandum of the order was the best evidence?

HOLDING AND DECISION: (Morris, J.) No. The memorandum, like a shop-book entry, would have been inadmissible. The register slip was admissible because it was delivered to Suzio (D) and was introduced to prove the kind and quantity of lumber delivered. There was no need to account for the slip delivered to Suzio (D) before the slip copy held by the lumber company (P) could be introduced. Since all three copies were made at the same time, and were identical in all respects, no purpose would be served by requiring production of the slip delivered to Suzio (D).

EDITOR'S ANALYSIS: Although, as this case demonstrates, courts have experienced little difficulty in dealing with copies which are "duplicate originals," the problems increase where the "original" writings are not perfectly identical in all respects. To get around the Best Evidence Rule, most courts have come to recognize certain means of copying so reliable as to dispense with the need for producing the original. Carbon copies are generally admissible despite the danger of corrections made on a ribbon copy. While photostats made for litigation purposes are not admissible (too easy to doctor), the usual practice is for the parties involved, in the interests of expediency, to stipulate to accuracy after inspection of these copies has been conducted.

---

*[For more information on duplicate originals, see **Casenote Law Outline on Evidence, Chapter 14, § II, Definitions.**]*

QUICKNOTES

BEST EVIDENCE RULE – An evidentiary rule requiring that an original document be introduced if possible; secondary evidence is only admissible after proof that the original was lost or destroyed through no fault of the proponent.

SURETY - A party who guarantees payment of the debt of another party to a creditor.

NOTES:

DAVENPORT v. OURISMAN-MANDELL CHEVROLET, INC.
Car buyer (P) v. Car dealership (D)
195 A.2d 743 (D.C. Cir. 1963).

NATURE OF CASE: Action for misrepresentation in the sale of an automobile.

FACT SUMMARY: In order to prove that the automobile in question was not new, Davenport (P) testified that service stickers on the car indicated that it had over 7,000 miles.

CONCISE RULE OF LAW: Where the contents of a writing are to be proved, and the writing is not produced, parol evidence is not admissible to prove its contents unless its absence is satisfactorily explained.

FACTS: Davenport (P) purchased a car from Ourisman-Mandell (D). Davenport (P) claimed that he believed the car was new, and that he later discovered it was a demonstrator. In order to prove that there were over seven thousand miles on the car, Davenport (P) testified that the service stickers on the car so indicated. The stickers were not introduced into evidence, but Davenport (P) memorized them, and wrote down the contents prior to testifying. The car was outside the courthouse.

ISSUE: Can the contents of a writing be proven without introducing the writing itself into evidence?

HOLDING AND DECISION: (Quinn, J.) No. Where the contents of a writing are to be proved, and the writing is not produced, parol evidence is not admissible to prove its contents unless its absence is satisfactorily explained. In this case, there was no reason given as to why the service stickers themselves were not offered into evidence. It was not shown, for example, that they could not be severed from the car, or that they could not be reproduced. Absent such a showing of unavailability, the best evidence rule requires that the original writing, i.e., the service sticker, be produced. It is not sufficient that the car containing the stickers was outside the court room.

EDITOR'S ANALYSIS: Modernly, the "best evidence rule" has been limited to requiring the production of the original writing when the proof of its contents are at issue. Therefore, many scholars have changed the name of the rule to the "original document rule" as it does not apply outside the realm of documentary evidence. The original reason for the rule was broadly to prevent a fraud on the courts. Scholars attacked this rationale on the ground that it is at times in conflict with the way in which the rule operates. The modern position, then, is to require the original writing to be offered if its contents are at issue because the exact wording and appearance of a document may be critical in determining the rights of the parties. This is especially true in such documents as deeds, wills, and formal contracts.

[For more information on the proof of content of a writing, see Casenote Law Outline on Evidence, Chapter 14, § III, " To Prove the Content of a Writing".]

QUICKNOTES

BEST EVIDENCE RULE – An evidentiary rule requiring that an original document be introduced if possible; secondary evidence is only admissible after proof that the original was lost or destroyed through no fault of the proponent.

NOTES:

AMOCO PRODUCTION CO. v. UNITED STATES
Company (P) v. Government (D)
619 F.2d 1383 (10th Cir. 1980).

NATURE OF CASE: Action to quiet title to mineral rights.

FACT SUMMARY: Amoco (P) and the Government (D) disagreed as to whether the Federal Farm Mortgage Corporation had reserved a one-half mineral interest in certain land it had sold, the original deed having been destroyed and the recorded version in Summit County containing no such reservation.

CONCISE RULE OF LAW: If all originals of a writing are lost or destroyed, Federal Rule of Evidence 1004(1) authorizes the admission of other evidence of the contents of the writing.

FACTS: In Amoco's (P) action to quiet title to certain mineral rights, the central question was whether, as the Government (D) claimed, the Federal Farm Mortgage Corporation had reserved a one-half mineral interest in a piece of property it had sold in 1942. The Government (D) contended that such an interest had been reserved in the 1942 deed conveying the land to the Newtons. However, the original deed and all copies other than the recorded version kept in the Summit County Recorder's Office were no longer in existence, and the recorded version contained no such reservation. After a summary judgment was granted in favor of Amoco (P), the Government (D) appealed and cited as error the trial court's exclusion of all the evidence it proffered bearing on the contents of the 1942 deed. Such exclusion was based on the notion that the recorded version of the deed fell within Federal Rule of Evidence 1005, which authorizes the admission of certified copies of public records, and that it precluded admission of any other evidence of the contents of the deed.

ISSUE: Can other evidence of the contents of a writing be admitted if all the originals are lost or destroyed?

HOLDING AND DECISION: (McKay, J.) Yes. If all originals of a writing are lost or destroyed, Federal Rule of Evidence 1004(1) authorizes the admission of other evidence of the contents of the writing. This is the rule that should have been applied by the court below in dealing with the 1942 deed. The rule covering public documents is simply inapplicable. While certified copies of public documents are admissible, this term encompasses only documents "authorized to be recorded or filed and actually recorded or filed." In this case, it would be the actual record maintained by the public office to which the public document rule would apply, not the original deed from which that record is made. Where, as in the case, the original deed is returned to the parties after it is recorded, it is not a public record — and it is the contents of the deed (not the record made from it) that was at issue. Reversed and remanded.

EDITOR'S ANALYSIS: The Federal Rules of Evidence take the position of the American rule, which holds that the next best evidence of a lost paper is a copy thereof and that if such a copy is available then oral evidence as to the contents of the lost paper is inadmissible. A recorded version of a deed, however, is not necessarily a copy.

[For more information on absence of originals, see Casenote Law Outline on Evidence, Chapter 14, § IV, Absence of Originals Excused.]

NOTES:

CHAPTER 3
TESTIMONIAL PROOF

QUICK REFERENCE RULES OF LAW

1. **Disqualifications under the Common Law.** A criminal defendant may not be prevented as a matter of law from introducing testimony influenced by hypnosis. (Rock v. Arkansas)

   [For more information on precedential relevance of evidence, see Casenote Law Outline on Evidence, Chapter 2, § VI, Precedential Relevance.]

2. **The Dead Man Rule.** A "dead man's" statute, which precludes testimony by a party when the other party to the transaction is dead, does not apply to disinterested third parties, or to testimony which could not have been contradicted by the deceased party's own knowledge. (Zeigler v. Moore)

   [For more information on defunct declarant, see Casenote Law Outline on Evidence, Chapter 10, § XI, "Unavailability" of Declarant Exception.]

3. **Truthfulness.** It is reversible error for a district court to prevent a party from testifying solely on the basis of the party's religiously based objections to the form of the oath. (United States v. Ward)

4. **Ability to Observe, Remember, and Relate.** Where an opportunity for observation is shown, even though slight, a witness is considered competent to testify as to the observation. (Gladden v. State)

   [For more information on personal knowledge of witness, see Casenote Law Outline on Evidence, Chapter 11, § IV, Personal Knowledge.]

5. **Ability to Observe, Remember, and Relate.** If a witness lacks personal knowledge of a matter, that witness is deemed incompetent to testify with respect to that matter. (State v. Ranieri)

6. **Ability to Observe, Remember, and Relate.** Although Missouri statute sets up a rebuttable presumption that a child under 10 years of age is incompetent to testify as a witness, there is no fixed age at which a child may be a competent witness, and it is up to the court to make the competency determination in each case. (State v. Singh)

   [For more information on witness competency, see Casenote Law Outline on Evidence, Chapter 11, § II, Witness Competence.]

7. **Ability to Observe, Remember, and Relate.** Once it is shown that a witness has the capacity to observe, recollect, and communicate, he is competent to testify, and any deficiency is considered only so far as it affects the weight of the testimony. (Schneiderman v. Interstate Transit Lines)

   [For more information on witness competency, see Casenote Law Outline on Evidence, Chapter 11, § II, Witness Competence.]

8. **Ability to Observe, Remember, and Relate.** A witness is incompetent to testify if his ability to communicate is so limited as to violate the opposing party's right of cross-examination. (People v. White)

   [For more information on witness competency, see Casenote Law Outline on Evidence, Chapter 11, § II, Witness Competence.]

9. Ability to Observe, Remember, and Relate. While a mentally retarded person can be called to testify at the hearing held to decide if he should be civilly committed to the state Department of Health, he may refuse to testify regarding any criminal conduct in which he might have engaged or about any other matter which would tend to implicate him in criminal activity. (Cramer v. Tyars)

> *[For more information on witness competency, see Casenote Law Outline on Evidence, Chapter 11, § II, Witness Competence.]*

10. Preparation of Witnesses. It is appropriate and proper for an attorney to prepare his witness before trial by refreshing her memory before she takes the stand, reviewing her testimony before trial, etc. as long as the witness' essential testimony is neither altered nor colored by emphasis or suggestion. (People v. McGuirk)

> *[For more information on the scope of examination, see Casenote Law Outline on Evidence, Chapter 11, § V, Order and Scope of Examination.]*

11. Preparation of Witnesses. Placing statements in a draft affidavit that have not been previously discussed with a witness does not automatically constitute bad-faith conduct. (Resolution Trust Corp. v. Bright)

12. Form of Examination — Questioning. Where the trial judge does not maintain control of leading questions or ignores them, and they continue throughout the trial, thereby producing a warped version of the issues to the jury, the judgment based on such a trial must be set aside. (Straub v. Reading Co.)

> *[For more information on leading questions, see Casenote Law Outline on Evidence, Chapter 11, § VI, The Form of Questions.]*

13. Refreshing Recollection. There is a distinction between present recollection revived and past recollection recorded in that in the first instance the witness' memory is revived and she presently recollects the facts and testifies to them, while, in the latter case, the witness has no present recollection of the matter contained in the writing. In the case of present recollection revived, the primary evidence is not the writing but the oral testimony of the witness, while in the case of past recollection recorded, the writing is a substitute for the witness' memory and as such is an independent probative force which is required to meet certain standards. (United States v. Riccardi)

> *[For more information on past recollection recorded, see Casenote Law Outline on Evidence, Chapter 10, § VI, Past Recollection Recorded.]*

14. Lay Opinions. Generally, a lay witness may testify only to facts and not to opinions or conclusions, but witnesses may be permitted to use shorthand descriptions, which are, in reality, opinions, in presenting to the court their impressions of the general physical condition of a person. (State v. Garver)

> *[For more information on opinions of a lay witness, see Casenote Law Outline on Evidence, Chapter 12, § II, Lay Witness Opinions.]*

15. Cross-Examination. While liberal discretion is vested in the trial court as to order of proof, departure from the regular order should not be allowed where it will work injustice to either party. Cross-examination must be limited to the subject matter of the direct examination. (Finch v. Weiner)

> *[For more information on the scope of cross-examination, see Casenote Law Outline on Evidence, Chapter 11, § V, Order and Scope of Examination.]*

16. Cross-Examination. Cross-examinations may be on any matter germane to the direct examination, qualifying or destroying it, or tending to elucidate, modify, explain, contradict, or rebut testimony. (People v. Sallis)

[For more information on scope of cross-examination, see Casenote Law Outline on Evidence, Chapter 11, § V, Order and Scope of Examination.]

17. **Cross-Examination.** Federal Rule of Evidence 611(b) provides that cross-examination should be limited to the subject matter of the direct examination and matters affecting the credibility of the witness. (United States v. Segal)

[For more information on the scope of cross-examination, see Casenote Law Outline on Evidence, Chapter 11, § V, Order and Scope of Examination.]

18. **Redirect and Recross Examination.** Unless new matter is elicited for the first time on redirect examination, a defendant has no right to recross-examination. (Commonwealth v. O'Brien)

[For more information on scope of recross-examination, see Casenote Law Outline on Evidence, Chapter 11, § V, Order and Scope of Examination.]

19. **Accrediting.** Witness cooperation agreements may be admitted in their entirety only after the credibility of the witness has been attacked. (United States v. Cosentino)

[For more information on bolstering credibility, see Casenote Law Outline on Evidence, Chapter 11, § VII, Impeachment of Witnesses.]

20. **Own Witness.** A prior inconsistent statement may not be introduced to impeach one's own witness, thus circumventing the hearsay exclusion, where the original testimony was not damaging and the impeachment testimony is both prejudicial and lacking probative value as impeachment evidence. (United States v. Ince)

[For more information on prior inconsistent statements, see Casenote Law Outline on Evidence, Chapter 9, § VII, Exemption: Prior Statements of Witnesses.]

21. **Bias, Interest, and Corruption.** A district court is accorded a wide discretion in determining the admissibility of evidence under the Federal Rules. (United States v. Abel)

[For more information on admissibility of evidence, see Casenote Law Outline on Evidence, Chapter 2, § I, Admissibility.]

22. **Prior Convictions.** So long as probative value outweighs its prejudicial effect, a certified copy of a prior conviction may be introduced against a defendant when the defendant has attempted to minimize the severity of the crime on direct examination. (United States v. Valencia)

[For more information on prior convictions for impeachment, see Casenote Law Outline on Evidence, Chapter 6, § V, Character to Impeach.]

23. **Prior Convictions.** The willful failure to file a tax return does not constitute a crime of dishonesty and false statement, and evidence of the conviction may not be used to impeach a witness. (Cree v. Hatcher)

[For more information on prior convictions to impeachment character, see Casenote Law Outline on Evidence, Chapter 6, § V, Character to Impeach.]

24. **Prior Bad Acts.** A defendant, like any other witness, may be interrogated upon cross-examination in regard to any criminal or immoral act that has a bearing on his credibility, and it does not matter that the acts inquired about are similar to the crime for which the defendant is being tried, that there are a number of acts, or that the defendant denies committing the acts. (People v. Sorge)

[For more information on testimony regarding other crimes, see Casenote Law Outline on Evidence, Chapter 6, § IV, The "Other Crimes" Loophole.]

25. **Reputation and Opinion of Character.** When a defendant in a criminal case takes the witness stand, he subjects himself to cross-examination the same as any other witness, and the state has a right to impeach him as a witness to the extent of proving by witnesses that his general reputation for truth and veracity in the community where he resides is bad. (State v. Ternan)

> *[For more information on character evidence, see Casenote Law Outline on Evidence, Chapter 6, § V, Character to Impeach.]*

26. **Reputation and Opinion of Character.** The credibility of a witness may not be attacked by evidence in the form of opinion or reputation for untruthfulness where no foundation for such an opinion is first offered. (United States v. Dotson)

> *[For more information on reputation and opinion of character, see Casenote Law Outline on Evidence, Chapter 6, § I, Definitions and Distinctions.]*

27. **Reputation and Opinion of Character.** It is not proper to cross-examine a witness as to whether he had not given the same testimony during previous trials at which he was convicted. (Newton v. State)

> *[For more information on prior statements of witnesses, see Casenote Law Outline on Evidence, Chapter 9, § VII, Exemption: Prior Statements of Witnesses.]*

28. **Prior Inconsistent Statements.** A witness may properly be impeached by introduction of extrinsic evidence of a prior statement inconsistent with his present testimony where he denies having made the prior inconsistent statement. (Denver City Tramway Co. v. Lomovt)

> *[For more information on prior inconsistent statements, see Casenote Law Outline on Evidence, Chapter 9, § III, The Out-of-Court ("O.C.C.") Statement.]*

29. **Rehabilitation.** Where an attack is made on the veracity of a witness, it is proper to permit testimony that the witness has a good reputation for truth and veracity. (Rodriguez v. State)

> *[For more information on evidence of good character, see Casenote Law Outline on Evidence, Chapter 6, § III, Character to Prove Conduct.]*

ROCK v. ARKANSAS
Hypnotized wife (D) v. State (P)
483 U.S. 44 (1987).

NATURE OF CASE: Appeal of conviction for voluntary manslaughter.

FACT SUMMARY: Rock (D) was not permitted to testify as to matters in which her recollection had been refreshed by hypnosis.

CONCISE RULE OF LAW: A criminal defendant may not be prevented as a matter of law from introducing testimony influenced by hypnosis.

FACTS: Rock (D) was involved in an altercation with her husband which ended in his death by shooting. Rock (D) claimed to have only a vague memory of what occurred. While in a hypnotic trance, she purportedly recalled that her finger was not on the trigger when the gun discharged. Expert examination revealed that the gun did have a propensity to fire at improper times. In response to a motion in limine, the trial court excluded all testimony possibly aided by the hypnosis as unreliable. Rock (D) was convicted. On appeal, the state supreme court laid down a rule that no hypnosis-induced testimony would be admissible in any case, civil or criminal. The U.S. Supreme Court granted review.

ISSUE: May a criminal defendant be prevented as a matter of law from introducing testimony influenced by hypnosis?

HOLDING AND DECISION: (Blackmun, J.) No. A criminal defendant may not be prevented from introducing testimony influenced by hypnosis. One of the most basic rules in our system of criminal justice is that a defendant has an absolute right to testify in his own behalf. This right is implied from provisions of the Fifth, Sixth, and Fourteenth Amendments. A necessary component of this right is the ability of the defendant to "tell his story" in his own words. States have at various times created competency rules based on the notion that the right of the witness to give his testimony is subordinate to the state's interest in guaranteeing reliable evidence. This is not so. A state certainly has an interest in preventing perjury, but where it cannot show that a per se incompetency rule is absolutely necessary, such a rule cannot be condoned. Here, hypnosis as a memory-enhancing device is still largely an unexplored area; it simply cannot be said that testimony gained therefrom is inherently unreliable. While a state can devise rules to enhance its probative value, such as requiring proper credentials by those employing it, the state cannot, on a per se basis, exclude all hypnotically induced testimony. Reversed.

DISSENT: (Rehnquist, J.) An individual's right to present evidence has always been subject to reasonable restrictions.

There is much in hypnosis literature to suggest that testimony gained therefrom is inherently unreliable, and it should be within the power of a state to exclude it.

EDITOR'S ANALYSIS: The Arkansas Supreme Court borrowed much of its reasoning from People v. Shirley, 31 Cal. 3d 18 (1982). This, one of the first major cases to deal with hypnotically induced testimony, also laid down a broad exclusionary rule. Unlike in the present case, however, the court there excepted criminal defendants from the ambit of the decision.

[For more information on precedential relevance of evidence, see Casenote Law Outline on Evidence, Chapter 2, § VI, Precedential Relevance.]

QUICKNOTES

MOTION IN LIMINE - Motion by one party brought prior to trial to exclude the potential introduction of highly prejudicial evidence.

PRIVILEGE AGAINST SELF-INCRIMINATION - A privilege guaranteed by the Fifth Amendment to the federal Constitution in a criminal proceeding for communications made by an accused and protecting an accused or witness from having to give testimony that may incriminate himself.

NOTES:

ZEIGLER v. MOORE
Injured plaintiff (P) v. Administrator of the estate (D)
Nev. Sup. Ct., 75 Nev. 91, 335 P.2d 425 (1959).

NATURE OF CASE: Action for damages on a theory of negligent operation of an automobile.

FACT SUMMARY: Because the defendant driver, Christ (D), had died after the auto collision and before trial, the trial court refused to permit the Sheriff to testify as to oral statements made by Christ (D) to him, and Zeigler (P) from testifying as to her own actions, the road conditions, and her medical expenses.

CONCISE RULE OF LAW: A "dead man's" statute, which precludes testimony by a party when the other party to the transaction is dead, does not apply to disinterested third parties, or to testimony which could not have been contradicted by the deceased party's own knowledge.

FACTS: Zeigler (P) sued Christ (D) for damages allegedly suffered in an automobile collision with Christ's (D) vehicle. The accident was unwitnessed. Before the trial could be commenced, Christ (D) died so the administrator of his estate, Moore (D), was substituted in his place. According to Nevada law, no person may testify when the other party to the transaction is dead if the testimony would seek to prove facts which transpired before the death of the other party. Relying on this statute, the trial judge refused to permit the Sheriff to testify as to a conversation he had with Christ (P) after the accident when Christ had come to his office to fill out an accident report. Zeigler (P) was also precluded from testifying that she had not driven in a reckless manner, the extent of her medical costs, and the road conditions at the time of the accident.

ISSUES: (1) Is the Sheriff's testimony within the scope of the "Dead Man's" statute? (2) May a party in a tort action testify as to matters which could not have been contradicted by an opposing deceased party because these matters were not within the dead party's knowledge?

HOLDING AND DECISION: (Badt, J.) (1) No. Under Nevada law, the "Dead Man's" statute has been held not to apply to the testimony of disinterested third parties. (2) Yes. The reasons for excluding testimony under a "Dead Man's" statute is to prevent the living from obtaining unfair advantage by giving an uncontradicted and unexplained account of what transpired beyond possibility of contradiction by the decedent. The statute is to place the living and the dead on terms of perfect equality. Where these reasons do not appear, the testimony of an interested party will not be excluded. Mrs. Zeigler (P) may testify to any matter related to the accident which could not possibly be contradicted by Christ (D) had he lived: this determination is for the trial court to make. It has been claimed that the survival of tort actions against the estate of a decedent is undermined by "Dead Man" statutes, particularly where the transaction is unwitnessed by third parties. However, it is for the legislature, and not the courts, to weigh the chance of injustice in individual cases against the protection of estates from fraudulent demands.

EDITOR'S ANALYSIS: Some states have sought an intermediate ground with respect to permitting testimony when the opposing party is dead by adopting the following approaches: (1) Interested party testimony is admissible only when accompanied by other disinterested evidence. (2) Interested parties may testify, but if they do so, hearsay statements of the deceased are admissible (California follows this rule). (3) "Dead Man" prohibitions are preserved, but the trial judge has discretionary power to permit interested survivors to testify when exclusion would result in injustice.

[For more information on defunct declarant, see Casenote Law Outline on Evidence, Chapter 10, § XI, "Unavailability" of Declarant Exception.]

QUICKNOTES
DEAD MAN'S STATUTE – Evidence of a deceased's promises or statements may not be introduced by a claimant against the deceased's estate.

NOTES:

UNITED STATES v. WARD
Federal government (P) v. Tax evader (D)
989 F.2d 1015 (9th Cir. 1992).

NATURE OF CASE: Appeal from convictions for attempt to evade income tax and failure to file income taxes.

FACT SUMMARY: Ward (D) argued that the district court did not allow him to swear to an oath of his own creation, thereby precluding him from testifying in his own defense and violating his First Amendment right to free exercise of religion.

CONCISE RULE OF LAW: It is reversible error for a district court to prevent a party from testifying solely on the basis of the party's religiously based objections to the form of the oath.

FACTS: Prior to his trial for income tax evasion, Ward (D) filed a motion to challenge the oath, proposing an alternative oath that replaced the word "truth" with the phrase "fully integrated Honesty." The oath would then read, "Do you affirm to speak with fully integrated Honesty, only with fully integrated Honesty and nothing but fully integrated Honesty?" The district court denied the motion. At trial, Ward (D) offered to take both the standard oath and his oath. The district court refused to allow it. Ward (D) did not testify and presented no witnesses. The jury convicted Ward (D) on all counts. He appealed, contending that the court's insistence on his taking the "truth" oath abridged his First and Fifth Amendment rights.

ISSUE: Is it reversible error for a district court to prevent a party from testifying solely on the basis of the party's religiously based objections to the form of the oath?

HOLDING AND DECISION: (Fletcher, J.) Yes. It is reversible error for a district court to prevent a party from testifying solely on the basis of the party's religiously based objections to the form of the oath. There is no constitutionally or statutorily required form of oath. Federal Rule of Evidence 603 requires only that a witness declare that he will testify truthfully, by oath or affirmation administered in a form calculated to awaken his conscience and impress his mind with the duty to do so. In this case, Ward (D) offered to take both oaths; he did not attempt to create some cleverly worded oath that would give him a safe harbor for perjury. Therefore the district court abused its discretion in refusing his request and preventing his testimony. Reversed and remanded.

DISSENT: (Poole, J.) Ward's (D) proposed alternative oath does not contain an acknowledgment of the duty to speak truthfully and does not ensure that he is aware of the cost of dishonesty. Accommodating his concerns will result in numerous wasteful and time-consuming attacks on the standard oath.

EDITOR'S ANALYSIS: A witness will be found competent to testify after swearing to an oath including the term "so help you God" even if, on cross-examination, he states that he does not believe in God. See Flores v. State, 443 P.2d 73 (Alaska 1968). Furthermore, the opposing party may not inquire into the reasons why a Muslim elected to affirm rather than to swear on the Koran. See United States v. Kalaydjian, 784 F.2d 53 (2d Cir. 1975). Federal Rule of Evidence 610 prohibits inquiry into the religious beliefs of witnesses.

NOTES:

GLADDEN v. STATE

Drunk driving suspect (D) v. State (P)

Ala. Ct. App., 36 Ala. App. 197, 54 So.2d 607 (1951); cert. denied, 256 Ala. 368, 54 So.2d 610.

NATURE OF CASE: Appeal from a conviction of drunk driving.

FACT SUMMARY: A deputy sheriff testified that after observing Gladden (D) driving, he concluded that he was drunk.

CONCISE RULE OF LAW: Where an opportunity for observation is shown, even though slight, a witness is considered competent to testify as to the observation.

FACTS: Deputy Hurley observed Gladden (D) driving in an erratic manner. He stopped Gladden (D) and placed him under arrest. At trial, the deputy testified that Gladden (D) was drunk when arrested. On cross-examination, the deputy stated that he saw Gladden (D) prior to concluding that he was intoxicated while driving.

ISSUE: Was the deputy qualified by observation or knowledge to testify as to Gladden's (D) condition when he was driving?

HOLDING AND DECISION: (Harwood, J.) Yes. Where an opportunity for observation is shown, even if slight, a witness is considered competent to testify. In this jurisdiction, nonexpert opinion evidence is permissible without the necessity of first detailing the factual basis of the opinion on matters that are not of a complex nature. Intoxication is just such a matter. There is no way to measure the exact capacity for observation except by presenting the evidence to a jury. Therefore, the witness is competent to testify as to what he observes as long as there is a opportunity for observation shown.

EDITOR'S ANALYSIS: This case is based on the general rule related to all testimony. That rule is the requirement that a witness testifying to objective facts must have and means of knowing them from observation. In this case, the deputy was really stating that it was his opinion that Gladden (D) was drunk. However, as is generally the case, such general matters may be testified to by a nonexpert. Therefore, while really stating opinion, the court treated the statement as factual, and allowed the testimony to stand. As long as there was a slight opportunity for the witness to observe Gladden (D), and to base his testimony on such observation, the testimony was valid.

[For more information on personal knowledge of witness, see Casenote Law Outline on Evidence, Chapter 11, § IV, Personal Knowledge.]

QUICKNOTES

COMPETENCY TO TESTIFY - Those qualifications necessary for a witness to give testimony at a trial consistent with the requirements of law.

NOTES:

STATE v. RANIERI
State (P) v. Assulter (D)
R.I. Sup. Ct., 586 A.2d 1094 (1991).

NATURE OF CASE: Appeal from conviction for burglary and assault.

FACT SUMMARY: Elsie was suddenly able, on the eve of Ranieri's (D) trial, to remember that Ranieri (D) was the man who assaulted her, although she never actually saw her attacker.

CONCISE RULE OF LAW: If a witness lacks personal knowledge of a matter, that witness is deemed incompetent to testify with respect to that matter.

FACTS: Elsie was brutally assaulted by someone who broke into her apartment at night. She was grabbed from behind moments after she awoke at 4 a.m. She never saw her assailant come up behind her and was unable to identify him for eighteen months after the attack. During that eighteen months, Ranieri (D) was arrested and charged with the assault on Elsie and with burglary. A local newspaper published his photograph several times. On the eve of Ranieri's (D) trial, Elsie suddenly came forward and identified him as her attacker, saying she knew all along that he was her assailant and that she had been afraid to come forward before. Ranieri (D) was convicted. He appealed, challenging Elsie's in and out-of-court identifications on the basis that Elsie was not a competent witness.

ISSUE: If a witness lacks personal knowledge of a matter, is that witness deemed incompetent to testify with respect to that matter?

HOLDING AND DECISION: (Judge not listed) Yes. If a witness lacks personal knowledge of a matter, that witness is deemed incompetent to testify with respect to that matter. Under Federal Rule of Evidence 602, a witness may not testify to a matter unless evidence is introduced to support a finding that the witness has personal knowledge of the matter. In making that determination, the trial judge must determine whether a witness had a sufficient opportunity to perceive the subject matter about which she is testifying. In this case, Elsie is not competent under Rule 602. At trial, Elsie claimed that she "knew" Ranieri (D) had been spying on her and had previously broken into her apartment, although she never saw him or anyone else actually enter her house. She had absolutely no factual basis for any of her allegations against Ranieri (D). Since sufficient evidence was not introduced that Elsie had personal knowledge of her assailant's identity, her identifications should have been suppressed. Reversed and remanded.

EDITOR'S ANALYSIS: Rule 602 is derived from the common law system of proof, which insists on the most reliable source of information. The same policy is reflected in Rule 801, the hearsay rule, and in Rule 701, the opinion rule. Rule 701 states that if a witness is not testifying as an expert, his testimony in the form of opinions or inferences must be rationally based on his own perceptions and helpful to a clear understanding of his testimony or the determination of a fact in issue.

QUICKNOTES
COMPETENCY TO TESTIFY - Those qualifications necessary for a witness to give testimony at a trial consistent with the requirements of law.

OPNION TESTIMONY – Evidence as to a witness' opinion rather than facts and which are not admissible at trial.

NOTES:

STATE v. SINGH
State (P) v. Convicted Murderer (D)
Mo. Ct. App., 586 S.W.2d 410 (1979).

NATURE OF CASE: Appeal from a manslaughter conviction.

FACT SUMMARY: Singh (D) objected to the fact that his six-year-old daughter was permitted to testify at his trial as to what happened the night his wife was shot.

CONCISE RULE OF LAW: Although Missouri statute sets up a rebuttable presumption that a child under 10 years of age is incompetent to testify as a witness, there is no fixed age at which a child may be a competent witness, and it is up to the court to make the competency determination in each case.

FACTS: Following his conviction for manslaughter of his wife, Singh (D) appealed on the grounds that the trial judge erred by actively participating in the voir dire examination to determine if Singh's (D) daughter (aged six years eight months at the time of trial and five years nine and one-half months at the time of the mother's death) should be permitted to testify. Singh (D) also claimed that the trial court erred in determining that his daughter was a competent witness and letting her testify as to what happened the night his wife was shot.

ISSUE: In each case, is it ultimately up to the court to determine if a child, regardless of his age, is competent to testify as a witness?

HOLDING AND DECISION: (Maus, J.) Yes. In this state, there is a statute which sets up a rebuttable presumption that a child under 10 years of age is incompetent to act as a witness. Thus, while there is no fixed age at which a child may be a competent witness, the burden was upon the state to establish the child's competency in this case. It is, of course, up to the court to determine the competency of a child offered as a witness. The established procedure is for this determination to be made upon a voir dire examination held outside the presence of the jury — an examination in which the court may participate actively within the bounds of fairness and impartiality. This is precisely what occurred in this case. After the examination, the court found the child competent under the applicable standards, which require that the witness have (1) present understanding of or intelligence to understand, on instruction, an obligation to speak the truth; (2) mental capacity at the time of the occurrence in question truly to observe and to register such occurrence; (3) memory sufficient to retain an independent recollection of the observations made; and (4) capacity truly to translate into words the memory of such observation. Since the proper procedures and standards were used, the trial court acted properly. Affirmed.

EDITOR'S ANALYSIS: Both England and Canada have a unique way of dealing with the problems in this area. They allow certain children to give unsworn testimony, but only if it is corroborated.

SCHNEIDERMAN v. INTERSTATE TRANSIT LINES
Injured driver (P) v. Bus company (D)
Ill. Sup. Ct., 394 Ill. 569, 69 N.E.2d 293 (1946).

NATURE OF CASE: Action for damages for personal injuries resulting from a traffic accident.

FACT SUMMARY: The injuries to Schneiderman (P) were such that at times he could not speak coherently, and he could answer only very simple questions. Nevertheless, he was allowed to testify at the trial.

CONCISE RULE OF LAW: Once it is shown that a witness has the capacity to observe, recollect, and communicate, he is competent to testify, and any deficiency is considered only so far as it affects the weight of the testimony.

FACTS: Schneiderman's (P) car was struck by a bus owned by the Interstate Transit Lines (D). The injuries suffered by Schneiderman (P) were such that at times he could not speak coherently, and he could only answer very simple questions. The court did allow him to testify and at times he was confused. He did answer some questions but, upon repeated questioning, he was contradictory and he easily became tired.

ISSUE: Once it is shown that a witness has the capacity to observe, recollect, and communicate, is he competent to testify, and is any deficiency considered only so far as it affects the weight of the testimony?

HOLDING AND DECISION: (Murphy, J.) Yes. Once it is shown that a witness has the capacity to observe, recollect, and communicate he is competent to testify. Any mental deficiency affecting that testimony will be considered only as to the weight the trier of fact gives to it. It was clear that Schneiderman (P) did possess the ability to communicate, at least in a limited manner. The credibility of that communication is a question for the jury to decide. Credibility is a question of degree, and the court will not attempt to measure it as long as there is some ability on the part of the witness to observe, recollect, and communicate. It was for the jury to determine what, if any, of the testimony was not accurate because of the witness's condition.

EDITOR'S ANALYSIS: As was indicated in the last case, capacity is measured in very loose terms. While that case dealt with the lack of ability to recollect, this one deals with the ability to communicate. The trend of the law is away from any test for capacity, and merely to let the trier of fact weigh any evidence and give it weight according to apparent credibility. However, the courts are reluctant to put the question of capacity solely in the hands of the jury. The reason for this is the court's distrust in the ability of the jury to discriminate between competent and incompetent testimony, and the probability of emotional rather than factual verdicts.

PEOPLE v. WHITE
State (P) v. Convinted thief (D)
Ill. Sup. Ct., 40 Ill. 2d 137, 238 N.E.2d 389 (1968).

NATURE OF CASE: Criminal prosecution for misdemeanor theft of property.

FACT SUMMARY: The only eyewitness to the crime was unable to testify orally due to illness, but indicated that White (D) was the thief by responding to questions with gestures, indicating a "yes" or "no" answer.

CONCISE RULE OF LAW: A witness is incompetent to testify if his ability to communicate is so limited as to violate the opposing party's right of cross-examination.

FACTS: White (D) was convicted of forcibly taking a ring from the finger of a patient at a nursing home where she was employed. The victim was incompetent to testify, but her roommate, Kallick, was an eyewitness to the crime. However, Kallick was unable to speak, but had learned to communicate by answering questions with gestures. She would raise her right knee to indicate a "yes" answer, and remain still to indicate "no." By so gesturing she indicated to the head nurse that White (D) had taken the ring. The head nurse then instigated the criminal prosecution. At trial, Kallick was allowed to testify using the knee gestures in response to the questions. Her testimony indicated that White (D) had taken the ring.

ISSUE: Is a witness competent to testify if his ability to communicate is so limited as to violate the opposing party's right of cross-examination?

HOLDING AND DECISION: (House, J.) Yes. A witness whose capacity to communicate is so limited as to prevent a complete cross-examination, is incompetent, for to allow only the direct examination would deny the opposition a fair trial. In this case, White (D) could not cross-examine Kallick on several key areas, such as the identification that she made to the head nurse, or details surrounding the crime. Perhaps the most important area that cross-examination usually provides, but could not in this case, was the possibility of bias or outside influence on the testimony. White (D) being denied this fundamental right to cross-examine and confront her accuser was, thereby, denied a fair trial when the court allowed Kallick's direct examination.

EDITOR'S ANALYSIS: Traditionally the courts have looked to mental capacity in questions of lack of competence to testify. However, physical disabilities can also render a witness incompetent. Most jurisdictions have a twofold requirement for capacity; that is, an understanding of the duty to tell the truth and the capacity to communicate. The former deals generally with the lack of mental capacity and the latter, as in this case, deals with a physical disability which limits the witness's ability to either express himself or to be understood. Here, the witness could not express herself sufficiently to allow a full examination of the knowledge of the crime, therefore it was error to allow her testimony. It should be noted that the federal rules of evidence are more liberal in this area and allow the admission of the evidence, but the failure to communicate or understand the duty to tell the truth are weighed by the truth of fact. In other words, competency is a question of credibility rather than admissibility and, therefore, a federal court would probably have allowed this testimony and the jury would be allowed to weigh its trustworthiness.

[For more information on witness competency, see Casenote Law Outline on Evidence, Chapter 11, § II, Witness Competence.]

QUICKNOTES

COMPETENCY TO TESTIFY - Those qualifications necessary for a witness to give testimony at a trial consistent with the requirements of law.

CONFRONTATION CLAUSE - A provision in the Sixth Amendment to the United States Constitution that an accused in a criminal action has the right to confront the witnesses against him, including the right to attend the trial and to cross-examine witnesses called on behalf of the prosecution.

CREDIBILITY - Believability; plausibility; whether or not a witness' testimony is believable.

NOTES:

CRAMER v. TYARS

Party attempting to commit (P) v. Mentally retarded person (D)

Cal. Sup. Ct., 23 Cal.3d 131, 588 P.2d 793 (1979).

NATURE OF CASE: Civil commitment proceedings.

FACT SUMMARY: Tyars (D) was a mentally retarded person who questioned the ability of the court to force him to testify at the hearing regarding his commitment to the state Department of Health.

CONCISE RULE OF LAW: While a mentally retarded person can be called to testify at the hearing held to decide if he should be civilly committed to the state Department of Health, he may refuse to testify regarding any criminal conduct in which he might have engaged or about any other matter which would tend to implicate him in criminal activity.

FACTS: Tyars (D) raised the issue on appeal of the propriety of calling him, over objections, as a witness in his own civil commitment hearing. He was found to be subject to civil commitment under a statutory provision providing for the commitment of those mentally retarded persons who constitute a danger to themselves or others. The trial court had expressly found that Tyars (D), while incapable of understanding the witness oath, did understand the obligation to tell the truth.

ISSUE: Can a mentally retarded person be forced to testify at his civil commitment hearing?

HOLDING AND DECISION: (Richardson, J.) Yes. One who is the subject of a hearing designed to determine if he is a mentally retarded person who should be civilly committed to the state Department of Health can be forced to testify at the hearing. However, as with any witness in a civil or criminal proceeding, he has the right to decline to answer questions which may tend to incriminate him in criminal activity. This privilege against self-incrimination does not, however, give any witness in any proceeding the right to refuse to reveal to the trier of fact his physical or mental characteristics where they are relevant to the issue under consideration. Thus, Tyars (D) was subject to call a witness and could be required to respond to noncriminatory questioning which may have revealed his mental condition to the jury, whose duty it was to determine whether he was mentally retarded. While the trial court did not follow this guideline, it is clear that any erroneous questioning of Tyars (D) was harmless beyond all reasonable doubt. This is clear from the weight and nature of the uncontradicted and overwhelming evidence from two medical experts as to his severe and irreversible mental retardation. Affirmed.

EDITOR'S ANALYSIS: Giving the jury in this type of case the chance to observe the person who is the subject of the commitment proceeding and to hear him speak and respond so as to give some indication of his mental and intellectual function has been likened to the situation in a criminal trial where the defendant can be compelled to give a handwriting sample, don certain clothing, etc.

[For more information on witness competency, see Casenote Law Outline on Evidence, Chapter 11, § II, Witness Competence.]

QUICKNOTES

COMPETENCY TO TESTIFY - Those qualifications necessary for a witness to give testimony at a trial consistent with the requirements of law.

PRIVILEGE AGAINST SELF-INCRIMINATION - A privilege guaranteed by the Fifth Amendment to the federal Constitution in a criminal proceeding for communications made by an accused and protecting an accused or witness from having to give testimony that may incriminate himself.

NOTES:

PEOPLE v. McGUIRK
State (P) v. Convicted rapist (D)
Ill. App. Ct., 106 Ill. App. 2d 266, 245 N.E.2d 917 (1969), cert. denied 396 U.S. 972 (1969).

NATURE OF CASE: Appeal from a conviction for rape and indecent liberties.

FACT SUMMARY: On appeal from a conviction for rape and taking indecent liberties with a nine-year-old girl, McGuirk (D) contended that the prosecutor had acted improperly in preparing the girl for her testimony at the trial.

CONCISE RULE OF LAW: It is appropriate and proper for an attorney to prepare his witness before trial by refreshing her memory before she takes the stand, reviewing her testimony before trial, etc. as long as the witness' essential testimony is neither altered nor colored by emphasis or suggestion.

FACTS: McGuirk (D) was convicted of having raped and taken indecent liberties with a nine-year-old girl who lived in the building where he was employed as a janitor. The child testified at the trial. On cross-examination she said that the prosecutor had read something to her (it turned out to be a transcript of her grand jury testimony) and told her to say the same thing that was on the paper. She also answered affirmatively to questions regarding whether it was not true she would do what the "nice man" (the prosecutor) told her because he was a good man, and whether he had told her that McGuirk (D) would be the only black man sitting at the table. She also testified, however, that she had informed the prosecutor that McGuirk (D) had raped her, and that the prosecutor never used McGuirk's (D) name until she mentioned it to him.

ISSUE: Is it proper for an attorney to prepare his witness in ways that do not alter or color by emphasis or suggestion their essential testimony?

HOLDING AND DECISION: (Dempsey, J.) Yes. There is nothing improper in an attorney's refreshing the memories of his witnesses before they take the stand or in reviewing their testimony before trial. It often makes for better direct examination, facilitates the trial, and lessens the possibility of irrelevant and perhaps prejudicial interpolations. In fact, there is nothing wrong with going over the story of the prosecutrix in a sex case, easing her embarrassment, or even suggesting sexual terms she can use in telling her story as long as the witness' essential testimony is neither altered nor colored by emphasis or suggestion. In this case, the defendant was almost caught in the act and conviction did not rest solely on the prosecutrix' testimony. There is no reason to suspect that the prosecutor colored her testimony by his preparation before trial. Affirmed in part.

EDITOR'S ANALYSIS: One trial judge sought to prevent improper coaching by prohibiting a criminal defendant from speaking with his attorney during the overnight recess called after his direct testimony and before his cross-examination. The Supreme Court held this violated his right to counsel and suggested any improper coaching could be revealed by proper cross-examination. Geders v. United States, 425 U.S. 80 (1976).

[For more information on the scope of examination, see Casenote Law Outline on Evidence, Chapter 11, § V, Order and Scope of Examination.]

NOTES:

RESOLUTION TRUST CORP. v. BRIGHT
Investigating Entity (P) v. Bank (D)
6 F.3d 336 (5th Cir. 1993).

NATURE OF CASE: Appeal of sanctions and attorney fees assessed in shareholder suit.

FACT SUMMARY: After conducting aggressive presuit interviews with a witness in which they tried to elicit certain statements, Resolution Trust Corp. (P) attorneys were sanctioned for tampering with a witness.

CONCISE RULE OF LAW: Placing statements in a draft affidavit that have not been previously discussed with a witness does not automatically constitute bad-faith conduct.

FACTS: Resolution Trust Corp. (RTC) (P) began to investigate potential fraud, among other wrongs, perpetrated by two officers (D) of Bright Banc Savings Ass'n. As part of RTC's (P) prefiling investigation, Erhart, formerly employed by Bright Banc, was interviewed by RTC (P) attorneys. After several days of vigorous interviews, RTC's (P) attorneys presented Erhart with an affidavit summarizing what she had told them. They warned her to read the affidavit carefully, as it contained material they had not discussed in their interviews. Erhart refused to sign the affidavit, and a protracted session of editing and discussion followed. During that discussion the RTC (P) attorneys tried unsuccessfully to get Erhart to agree with their version of events at Bright Banc. Finally, Erhart signed a draft acceptable to her. After the suit was filed, Bright (D) and Reeder (D), the officers of Bright Banc, moved for sanctions against the attorneys for RTC (P) based upon their aggressive questioning and the initial affidavit presented to Erhart. The district judge sanctioned the RTC (P) attorneys, disbarring them from practicing before him, assessing $110,000 in attorney fees, and removing their law firm from further appearances in the underlying case. The RTC (P) attorneys appealed.

ISSUE: Does placing statements in a draft affidavit that have not been previously discussed with a witness automatically constitute bad-faith conduct?

HOLDING AND DECISION: (Kazen, J.) No. Placing statements in a draft affidavit that have not been previously discussed with a witness does not automatically constitute bad-faith conduct. So long as interviewing attorneys disclose the contents of an affidavit clearly, it is not sanctionable conduct for the attorneys to present the affiant with an affidavit that contains material that was not discussed in presuit interviews. Since disbarment is a quasi-criminal proceeding, all rules used to impose the sanction must be strictly construed in favor of the person charged. In this case, the sanctioning court failed to make specific findings as to how any Disciplinary Rules were violated. No finding of false

statements was ever made. The RTC (P) attorneys clearly warned Erhart to read the affidavit in detail, and she did so, since a lengthly discussion ensued about alterations and corrections to the affidavit. The district court abused its discretion by issuing sanctions against the RTC (P) attorneys. Reversed.

EDITOR'S ANALYSIS: Attorneys are advocates for their clients. So long as a witness is never asked to swear to false statements, it is well within valid conduct for an attorney to present the case in the light most favorable to the client. However, a witness should never be misled in an interview, since such conduct is sanctionable.

NOTES:

STRAUB v. READING CO.

Injured employee (P) v. Employer (D)

220 F.2d 177 (3d Cir. 1955).

NATURE OF CASE: Action to recover damages for negligence.

FACT SUMMARY: At trial Straub's (P) attorney asked leading questions during his direct examination of Straub (P) and of Straub's (P) witness.

CONCISE RULE OF LAW: Where the trial judge does not maintain control of leading questions or ignores them, and they continue throughout the trial, thereby producing a warped version of the issues to the jury, the judgment based on such a trial must be set aside.

FACTS: Straub (P) brought this action against his employer, Reading Co. (D) under the Federal Employers' Liability Act to recover for back injuries. Straub's (P) claim was proved, to an unconscionably large extent, by leading questions. Reading's (D) counsel asked the court to caution Straub's (P) counsel not to ask such questions. The court responded by asking Straub's (P) attorney to refrain from asking leading questions, but such questioning continued. Reading (D) contended that it was deprived of a fair trial by the deliberate conduct of Straub's (P) attorney throughout the trial.

ISSUE: Where leading questions have been asked throughout a trial and, hence, a warped version of the issues has been produced, may a new trial be ordered?

HOLDING AND DECISION: (McLaughlin, J.) Yes. Generally, the problem of leading questions is within the control of the trial court. However, this rule only applies in ordinary lawsuits. Where the control is lost or at least palpably ignored and such conduct continues throughout the trial, thereby producing a warped version of the issues to the jury, the judgment based on such a trial must be set aside. This is because the jury did not have the opportunity to pass upon the whole case. In this case, Straub's (P) attorney used leading questions in the direct examination of Straub's (P) witnesses in the presentation of Straub's (P) claim. Such conduct was grossly improper and was properly objected to by Reading (D). The judgment for Straub (P) must be reversed and a new trial ordered.

EDITOR'S ANALYSIS: The entire matter of the allowability of leading questions is discretionary. The judge's action will not be reviewed unless it is charged that such action as to leading questions amounted to, or contributed to, the denial of a fair trial, as was the case in Straub. A leading question is one which improperly suggests to the witness the answer desired. In determining this, it is necessary to consider, in addition to verbal form, the nature of the topic, the temper and bias of the witness, and the tone and inflection of the examiner's voice together with his emphasis upon the words and phrases and their arrangement.

[For more information on leading questions, see Casenote Law Outline on Evidence, Chapter 11, § VI, The Form of Questions.]

QUICKNOTES

LEADING QUESTIONS – A question that suggests the answer to the witness.

NOTES:

UNITED STATES v. RICCARDI
Federal government (P) v. Convicted felon (D)
174 F.2d 883 (3d Cir. 1949), cert. denied, 337 U.S. 941 (1949).

NATURE OF CASE: Appeal from conviction of felonious transportation of stolen property in interstate commerce.

FACT SUMMARY: At trial, the owner of the chattels involved testified with respect to the chattels by using copies of notes she had made at the time the chattels were moved from her house. A second witness used the some notes to testify as to the chattel's value.

CONCISE RULE OF LAW: There is a distinction between present recollection revived and past recollection recorded in that in the first instance the witness' memory is revived and she presently recollects the facts and testifies to them, while, in the latter case, the witness has no present recollection of the matter contained in the writing. In the case of present recollection revived, the primary evidence is not the writing but the oral testimony of the witness, while in the case of past recollection recorded, the writing is a substitute for the witness' memory and as such is an independent probative force which is required to meet certain standards.

FACTS: Riccardi (D) was convicted of felonious transportation of stolen property in interstate commerce. The property involved included numerous household items and was stolen from Farid. Riccardi (D) did not deny receiving some of Farid's chattels, but he denied both the quantity and quality alleged. Farid testified that as the chattels were being moved from her house, she made notes which she later copied on her typewriter. Only one of the original notes was produced. With the aid of the typed lists, Farid testified that her recollection was refreshed, and that she presently recognized and could identify each item on the list. The lists were not offered into evidence. An expert, Berlow, testified that he had visited Farid's home many times in his capacity as an antique dealer and that he was very familiar with the furnishings therein. He was shown the lists and with their aid testified that he could recall most of the items and could give an opinion as to their value. He was permitted to do so. Riccardi (D) contended that the lists should not have been used because they were not made by Farid and Berlow at or shortly after the time of the transaction while the facts were fresh in memory.

ISSUE: Can witnesses who are testifying to an essential transaction refresh their memory with writings which were not made at or shortly after the time of the transaction?

HOLDING AND DECISION: (Kalodner, J.) Yes. There is an important distinction between present recollection revived and past recollection recorded. In the first instance, the witness' memory is revived, and he presently recollects the facts and testifies to them. In the latter case, the witness has no present recollection of the matter contained in the writing and must ask the court to accept a writing for the truth of its contents because he is willing to swear that the contents are true. In cases of present recollection revived, the primary evidence is not the writing but the oral testimony of the witness. A song, a scent, a photograph, an allusion, even a past statement known to be false may revive a memory. The only evidence recognized where the memory is revived is the witness' testimony. In cases of past recollection recorded, the witness does not have a present recollection, and the writing is offered as a substitute. As such, it assumes a distinct significance as an independent probative force which is required to meet certain standards to determine that the writing may be safely received as a substitute for the witness' memory. It is up to the trial judge to determine whether the witness testifies upon a record or from his own recollection. In the instant case, the trial judge determined that Farid and Berlow testified from present recollection. Looking to the facts, this court cannot say it was plainly not so. Farid testified that she was present when the chattels were moved, and Berlow testified that he was familiar with them and could testify as to their value. The judge recognized that the chattels involved were so numerous that no one would be expected to recite them all from memory. The trial judge did not abuse his discretion, either in determining that Berlow and Farid testified from present recollection or in permitting their use of the lists. The judgment is affirmed.

EDITOR'S ANALYSIS: The safeguards which have been developed for admitting writings in a case of past recollection recorded require that the writing must have been written by the witness or examined and found correct by such witness, and that they must have been prepared so promptly after the events recorded that the events must have been fresh in the mind of the witness when the record was made. Some cases hold that writings used in cases of present recollection revived must also meet these requirements. However, most courts, when faced with the clear distinction between the two types of cases, will follow the classical rule that any memorandum or any other object may be used as a stimulus to present memory without restriction as to authorship, guarantee of correctness, or time of making. The adverse party is entitled to inspect the writing, in such cases, and to have it available for reference in cross-examining the witness. The adverse party may also submit such writings to the jury for their inspection.

[For more information on past recollection recorded, see Casenote Law Outline on Evidence, Chapter 10, § VI, Past Recollection Recorded.]

QUICKNOTES

PAST RECOLLECTION RECORDED – An exception to the hearsay rule for statements contained in a document as to which the witness no longer has recollection.

STATE v. GARVER

State (P) v. Insane convicted murderer

Or. Sup. Ct., 190 Or. 291, 225 P.2d 771 (1950).

NATURE OF CASE: Appeal from conviction of first-degree murder.

FACT SUMMARY: At trial, Mitchell, Garver's (D) mother, testified on the issue of Garver's (D) insanity and related history. The court struck the phrases used by her: "such a terrible shape" and "physically ill."

CONCISE RULE OF LAW: Generally, a lay witness may testify only to facts and not to opinions or conclusions, but witnesses may be permitted to use shorthand descriptions, which are, in reality, opinions, in presenting to the court their impressions of the general physical condition of a person.

FACTS: At his trial for murder, Garver (D) pleaded the defense of insanity. His mother, Mitchell, testified on the issue of his insanity and related history of Garver (D) from infancy to the day of the alleged crime, including his illnesses, both mental and physical, his moral delinquencies, his crimes, and "whatever else might throw light on his mental condition." The court struck the following phrases used by her: "such a terrible shape" and "physically ill."

ISSUE: May witnesses be permitted to use shorthand descriptions, which are, in reality, opinions, in presenting to the court their impressions of the general physical condition of a person?

HOLDING AND DECISION: (Lusk, J.) Yes. The general rule is that a lay witness may testify only to facts and not to opinions or conclusions. However, too strict an adherence to the "opinion" rule is undesirable. Lay witnesses are frequently allowed to use shorthand descriptions, which are, in reality, opinions, to give their impression of the general physical condition of a person. This seems to this court to be a common sense view. It leaves the witness free to testify in ordinary language, unbewildered by admonition from the judge to testify to facts. The jury understands what the witness means, and the right of cross-examination safeguards the opposing party. In this case, Mitchell was a fairly intelligent witness, but she became confused and frustrated by the objections and rulings. She used the expressions which were stricken while she was trying to explain Garver's (D) physical and mental condition. The lower court's ruling striking the expressions may not have been reversible error, but the court should have let the stricken testimony stand. The case is reversed and remanded on other grounds.

EDITOR'S ANALYSIS: Much has been written on the artificiality of the opinion/fact distinction. McCormick states, "This classic formula, based as it is on the assumption that 'fact' and 'opinion' stand in contrast and, hence, are readily distinguishable, has proven the clumsiest of all tools furnished the judge for the regulation of witnesses. It is clumsy because its basic assumption is an illusion." Exceptions to the rule were, at first, limited to cases of strict necessity, and that remains the rule followed by many courts. However, the actual practice in the trial courts is more liberal and allows the admission of opinions on the grounds of expediency or convenience. The short-hand description rule seems to incorporate this latter rule.

[For more information on opinions of a lay witness, see Casenote Law Outline on Evidence, Chapter 12, § II, Lay Witness Opinions.]

QUICKNOTES

LAY WITNESS – A witness that is not an expert with respect to the testimony he is giving.

NOTES:

FINCH v. WEINER

Passenger of car (P) v. Owner of truck (D)

Conn. Sup. Ct. Err., 109 Conn. 616, 145 A. 31 (1929).

NATURE OF CASE: Action to recover damages for personal injuries.

FACT SUMMARY: At the trial arising out of an accident between a car in which Finch (P) was riding and Weiner's (D) truck, Finch (P) called the driver of the truck (at the beginning of presentation of evidence) and asked only whether he was employed by Weiner (D) and that he identify an accident report. Weiner's (D) counsel, then, cross-examined the driver, eliciting from him his version of the accident.

CONCISE RULE OF LAW: While liberal discretion is vested in the trial court as to order of proof, departure from the regular order should not be allowed where it will work injustice to either party. Cross-examination must be limited to the subject matter of the direct examination.

FACTS: There was a collision between a car, in which Finch (P) was riding, and a truck owned by Weiner (D). At the beginning of the presentation of evidence by Finch (P), the driver of the truck, Skinner, was called as a witness. He was asked whether he was employed by Weiner (D) and to identify an accident report. Then Weiner's (D) counsel, over Finch's (P) objection, cross-examined Skinner and elicited from him his version of the accident and the events preceding and following it, none of which had been touched in the direct examination.

ISSUE: Can a party cross-examine a witness, called by the opposing party at the beginning of the latter's presentation of evidence, as to matters which had not been covered in direct examination?

HOLDING AND DECISION: (Hinman, J.) No. First of all it is true that liberal discretion is vested in the trial judge as to the order of proof. However, the purpose of allowing discretionary variances from the regular order of proof is to facilitate the forwarding of the trial, i.e., to avoid the necessity of detaining a witness. The discretion must be exercised with regard to the substantial rights involved, and departure from the regular order should not be allowed where it will work injustice on one of the parties. In this case, the effect of the order allowed was to permit Weiner (D) to place before the jury at the outset of the trial a version of the accident which was favorable to him, proceeding from a witness called by Finch (P). Secondly, the admission of this evidence involved a conspicuous transgression of the established rule that cross-examination shall be limited to the subject matter of the direct examination. Particularly where a witness is called for examination as to some particular or formal point only, the adversary is not entitled to examine the witness generally or to draw out facts having no connection with the direct testimony and tending to establish a substantive claim or defense. Such was the case here, and the admission of Weiner's (D) cross-examination of Skinner was so prejudicial to Finch (P) that it was not within the limits of permissible exercise of the trial court's decision. A new trial is ordered.

EDITOR'S ANALYSIS: Finch v. Weiner illustrates an approach to the scope of cross-examination involving substantial restrictions. This approach is sometimes referred to as the American rule and is followed by a majority of jurisdictions, including the federal courts. As stated in the case, this approach restricts cross-examination more or less tightly to matters stated in direct examination. A minority of jurisdictions follow the English or wide-open rule which allows a cross-examiner to interrogate as to the whole case. A second minority permits the scope of cross-examination to cover matters tending to modify or explain away the effect, immediate or inferential, of the direct examination.

[For more information on the scope of cross-examination, see Casenote Law Outline on Evidence, Chapter 11, § V, Order and Scope of Examination.]

QUICKNOTES

CROSS EXAMINATION - The interrogation of a witness by an adverse party either to further inquire as to the subject matter of the direct examination or to call into question the witness' credibility.

NOTES:

PEOPLE v. SALLIS

State (P) v. Sexual assault suspect (D)

Colo. Ct. of App., 857 P.2d 572 (1993).

NATURE OF CASE: Appeal of evidenciary ruling after an acquittal on sexual assault charges.

FACT SUMMARY: In a sexual assault prosecution, the court strictly limited the people's (P) cross-examination of Sallis (D) to only seven questions.

CONCISE RULE OF LAW: Cross-examinations may be on any matter germane to the direct examination, qualifying or destroying it, or tending to elucidate, modify, explain, contradict, or rebut testimony.

FACTS: Sallis (D) was charged with sexually assaulting a friend's child. At trial, Sallis (D) answered only two questions on direct examination. He was asked whether he sexually assaulted the child and whether he threatened the child. Sallis (D) answered both questions with a denial. On cross-examination outside the jury's presence, the people (P) sought to ask Sallis (D) about his relationship with the child, details of a motorcycle ride, and a dinner with the child and mother a week after the assault. The trial court sustained objections to all of the questions as being beyond the scope of direct examination. Arguing that this ruling rendered any cross-examination completely ineffective, the people (P) declined to cross-examine Sallis (D). Sallis (D) was acquitted. The people (P) appealed.

ISSUE: May cross-examinations be on any matter germane to the subject matter of the direct examination?

HOLDING AND DECISION: (Pierce, J.) Yes. Cross-examinations may be on any matter germane to the direct examination, qualifying or destroying it, or tending to elucidate, modify, explain, contradict, or rebut testimony. When a defendant makes a general denial of the offense charged, he cannot hide from questions reasonably related to the ultimate act. In this case, the history of Sallis's (P) relationship with the child was reasonably related to the denial of the assault. The trial court too severely limited the people's (P) ability to develop facts surrounding the incident. Reversed and remanded for a new trial.

EDITOR'S ANALYSIS: When a defendant takes the stand, two issues arise. First, a limited cross-examination rule as a procedural matter applies to the defendant just as it does to all witnesses. And second, a constitutional question arises as to whether a defendant has entirely waived the privilege against self-incrimination when answering any question. It is generally accepted that a waiver of the privilege does not destroy the procedural rules surrounding the scope of cross-examination.

[For more information on scope of cross-examination, see Casenote Law Outline on Evidence, Chapter 11, § V, Order and Scope of Examination.]

QUICKNOTES

CROSS EXAMINATION - The interrogation of a witness by an adverse party either to further inquire as to the subject matter of the direct examination or to call into question the witness' credibility.

DIRECT EXAMINATION - The initial interrogation of a witness, conducted by the party who called the witness.

NOTES:

UNITED STATES v. SEGAL
Federal government (P) v. Bribery suspect (D)
534 F.2d 578 (3d Cir. 1976).

NATURE OF CASE: Appeal from convictions for conspiracy and bribery of a public official.

FACT SUMMARY: It was Segal's (D) contention that the cross-examination his attorney had attempted to conduct of the prosecution's witnesses was improperly restricted.

CONCISE RULE OF LAW: Federal Rule of Evidence 611(b) provides that cross-examination should be limited to the subject matter of the direct examination and matters affecting the credibility of the witness.

FACTS: At the trial that resulted in Segal's (D) being convicted of conspiracy and bribery of a public official (IRS Agent Sigmond), the prosecution introduced into evidence excerpts from recordings that had been made of conversations between the parties. They had been obtained by having Agent Sigmond wear a body recorder when he visited Segal's (D) office and by having him simply record the telephone conversations he had with Segal (D), a CPA, and Hurst (D), one of Segal's (D) clients. On cross-examination, Segal's (D) counsel sought to replay some of the tape excerpts played on direct examination, but the court insisted that he rely on the transcripts (which had been supplied to the jurors for their use when the excerpts were played on direct). Defense counsel was also prevented from playing parts of the recordings that were not heard on direct, the court insisting that such was not proper during cross-examination because it went beyond the scope of the direct examination that had been conducted.

ISSUE: Do the Federal Rules of Evidence limit cross-examination to the subject matter of the direct examination and matters affecting the credibility of the witness?

HOLDING AND DECISION: (Weis, J.) Yes. It is often said that cross-examination should not exceed the scope of direct, and under the Federal Rules of Evidence the scope is to be measured by the subject matter of the direct examination rather than by specific exhibits which are introduced at that time. Federal Rule of Evidence 611 (b) provides that cross-examination should be limited to the subject matter of the direct examination and matters affecting the credibility of the witness. It is clear that the court below unduly limited cross-examination. The fact that some of the tape evidence the defense sought to explore on cross-examination could have been introduced by them when they put on their case does not preclude its use on cross-examination if the prosecution made the subject matter part of its direct testimony. Reversed and remanded for a new trial.

EDITOR'S ANALYSIS: Fed. R. Evid. 611(b) is more restrictive than the rule proposed by the Advisory Committee and promulgated by the Supreme Court, only to be rejected by Congress. That rule would have permitted cross-examination as to any issue in the case, with the caveat that the judge could — in the interests of justice — limit it to matters testified to on direct.

[For more information on the scope of cross-examination, see Casenote Law Outline on Evidence, Chapter 11, § V, Order and Scope of Examination.]

QUICKNOTES
CROSS EXAMINATION - The interrogation of a witness by an adverse party either to further inquire as to the subject matter of the direct examination or to call into question the witness' credibility.

DIRECT EXAMINATION - The initial interrogation of a witness, conducted by the party who called the witness.

NOTES:

COMMONWEALTH v. O'BRIEN
State (P) v. Murder suspect (D)
Mass. Sup. Jud. Ct., 419 Mass. 470, 645 N.E.2d 1170 (1995).

NATURE OF CASE: Appeal of evidentiary ruling after a conviction for murder.

FACT SUMMARY: In his trial for the murder of an infant, O'Brien (D) was denied the opportunity to question a witness for the Commonwealth (P) during recross-examination about a potentially impeaching second statement not inquired into during cross-examination.

CONCISE RULE OF LAW: Unless new matter is elicited for the first time on redirect examination, a defendant has no right to recross-examination.

FACTS: Shanahan's child died as a result of a head injury caused by O'Brien (D). Shanahan's sister testified that O'Brien (D) threw the child on the floor in the evening after the child vomited on his shoulder. The defense theory of the case was that O'Brien (D) dropped the child by accident earlier in the day. Crucial to resolving the divergent theories was Shanahan's testimony as to when she observed certain symptoms in her child during the afternoon. On cross-examination, Shanahan was challenged with a statment made to the police that she had noticed "cold" symptoms in her child during the afternoon. O'Brien's (D) attorney theorized that the "cold" symptoms were actually signs of head injury, bolstering O'Brien's (D) story. On redirect examination, the Commonwealth (P) elicited that Shanahan had been questioned the day after her child's funeral, suggesting that her statement at that time was unreliable, and that her in-court testimony was accurate. On recross-examination, O'Brien's (D) attorney sought to challenge Shanahan with an entirely separate statement made in preparation for trial, a statement that had not been brought out at any point on direct, cross, or redirect examination. The judge sustained objections to that testimony as beyond the scope of redirect. O'Brien (D) was convicted. He appealed.

ISSUE: Does a defendant have an automatic right to recross-examination?

HOLDING AND DECISION: (Liacos, C.J.) No. Unless new matter is elicited for the first time on redirect examination, a defendant has no right to recross-examination. The Constitution guarantees defendants the right to challenge witnesses under the Confrontation Clause of the Sixth Amendment via cross-examination. However, no such right exists with respect to recross-examination. But if new information is elicited on redirect examination, the new information can be challenged during recross-examination. In this case, the Commonwealth (P) used redirect examination to explain why the impeaching police statement made by Shanahan was unreliable. The use of redirect examination to explain an apparent inconsistency does not constitute the introduction of new material such that a fresh right to cross-examine arises. O'Brien's (D) attorney made a tactical error when he did not use the second statement to impeach during his initial cross-examination. Affirmed.

DISSENT: (O'Connor, J.) O'Brien (D) had no reason to introduce the second statement, which was similar to the statement given to the police after the funeral, until after the Commonwealth (P) elicited testimony that downplayed the significance of the initial police statement. O'Brien (D) could not predict that such an explanation would follow cross-examination. His attorney should have been permitted to challenge the new and unexpected explanation as to why the statements given to the police by the child's mother were unreliable.

EDITOR'S ANALYSIS: The Constitution does not clearly specify a right to recross-examination. However, a total bar on recross-examination has been determined to violate the Confrontation Clause, unless the court gives notice of such a policy. The right to confront witnesses implies that confrontation cannot be circumvented by eliciting new testimony during redirect examination.

[For more information on scope of recross-examination, see Casenote Law Outline on Evidence, Chapter 11, § V, Order and Scope of Examination.]

QUICKNOTES
CROSS EXAMINATION - The interrogation of a witness by an adverse party either to further inquire as to the subject matter of the direct examination or to call into question the witness' credibility.

NOTES:

UNITED STATES v. COSENTINO
Federal government (P) v. Extortionist (D)

844 F.2d 30 (2nd. Cir. 1988), cert. denied, 488 U.S. 923 (1988).

NATURE OF CASE: Appeal of evidentiary rulings after a conviction for extortion and bribery by mail.

FACT SUMMARY: Vendors who had dealt with Cosentino (D) were given plea bargains in exchange for testimony, a fact mentioned by the prosecutor during opening statements and direct testimony.

CONCISE RULE OF LAW: Witness cooperation agreements may be admitted in their entirety only after the credibility of the witness has been attacked.

FACTS: Cosentino (D), the Project Supervisor of the New York Housing Authority, was charged with extortion and use of the mails to bribe. Vendors who had dealt with Cosentino (D) were given plea bargains in exchange for their testimony. The prosecutor (P) mentioned the plea bargains in his opening statement. Furthermore, the entire contents of the witness cooperation agreements signed by the vendors were entered into evidence during direct examination. These agreements included promises to testify truthfully as well as the penalties for failure to do so. Cosentino (D) was convicted. He appealed the evidentiary rulings admitting the plea bargain cooperation agreements.

ISSUE: May a witness cooperation agreement be introduced into evidence by the prosecution at any time?

HOLDING AND DECISION: (Meskill, J.) No. Witness cooperation agreements may be admitted in their entirety only after the credibility of the witness has been attacked. If, for example, the credibility of a witness is questioned during a defendant's opening statement, a witness cooperation agreement, including any promises to testify truthfully, may be introduced during direct examination to bolster credibility. This is in line with the general rule that, absent an attack, no evidence may be admitted to support a witness's credibility. A witness cooperation agreement has value to both the defense and the prosecution. The defense will often use the agreement to show that the testimony offered is in exchange for something of great value, such as immunity from prosecution. The credibility of the witness is thus diminished. But the prosecution can negate this bias by showing that the agreement insists that any testimony given be truthful. Such bolstering, however, cannot be used by the prosecution unless the credibility of the witness has first been questioned. On the other hand, the mere fact that an agreement has been made may be brought out by the prosecution even in the absence of an attack, in order to avoid the appearance that the prosecution is hiding something. In this case, Cosentino's (D) counsel raised matters of credibility in his opening statement; therefore the prosecution (P) could counter with the entire body of the agreement on direct examination. Moreover, the prosecutor (P) properly restricted his opening statement to the existence of the agreements and the witness's criminal backgrounds. Affirmed.

EDITOR'S ANALYSIS: Other circuits have allowed the full contents of witness cooperation agreements to be introduced into evidence on direct examination with no prior attack on credibility. The argument adopted in those cases is that revealing the truth-telling portion of the agreement promises nothing that the law does not already require. Thus, the jury can be made aware by the defense that the agreement offers no special indicia of reliability.

[For more information on bolstering credibility, see Casenote Law Outline on Evidence, Chapter 11, § VII, Impeachment of Witnesses.]

QUICKNOTES

BIAS - Predisposition; preconception; refers to the tendency of the judge to favor or disfavor a particular party.

CREDIBILITY - Believability; plausibility; whether or not a witness' testimony is believable.

NOTES:

UNITED STATES v. INCE
Federal government (P) v. Firearms user (D)
21 F.3d 576 (4th Cir. 1994).

NATURE OF CASE: Appeal of evidentiary ruling after a conviction for assault.

FACT SUMMARY: The government (P) introduced hearsay evidence to impeach a witness who it knew would refuse to testify about a conversation with Ince (D).

CONCISE RULE OF LAW: A prior inconsistent statement may not be introduced to impeach one's own witness, thus circumventing the hearsay exclusion, where the original testimony was not damaging and the impeachment testimony is both prejudicial and lacking probative value as impeachment evidence.

FACTS: After a gun was fired at a concert on a military base, Ince (D) and his companions were stopped as they attempted to leave the base. Ince's (D) friend Neumann gave an unsworn statement to MP Stevens. She told Stevens that Ince (D) admitted to firing the gun, but he no longer had the weapon. Ince (D) was charged with assault with a dangerous weapon. Ince (D) was tried twice, with the first jury deadlocking. At both trials, the government (P) called Neumann to testify. She said she could not recall the details of her conversation with Ince (D). The government (P) attempted to refresh her recollection with the statement taken by Stevens. She still said she could not recall the conversation clearly. The prosecutor then called Stevens, over Ince's (D) objection, to testify as to what Neumann told him. The government (P) was permitted to proceed when it was argued that the hearsay evidence was intended to impeach the credibility of Neumann, since she had claimed that she could not recall the conversation. Ince (D) was convicted after the second trial. Ince (D) appealed.

ISSUE: May a prior inconsistent statement be introduced to impeach one's own witness, thus circumventing the hearsay exclusion, if the impeachment testimony is prejudicial and of little probative value?

HOLDING AND DECISION: (Murnaghan, J.) No. A prior inconsistent statement may not be introduced to impeach one's own witness, thus circumventing the hearsay exclusion, where the original testimony was not damaging and the impeachment testimony is both prejudicial and lacking probative value as impeachment evidence. Impeachment by prior inconsistent statement was not intended as a vehicle to circumvent the hearsay rule. Where the witness has not damaged the case, an attack on credibility by impeachment is not necessary. Here, Neumann merely refused to give testimony that the government (P) hoped she would give. There was no reason to attack her credibility. By allowing Stevens to testify as to Ince's (D)

supposed confession to Neumann, the jury was able to hear extremely prejudicial information. Reversed and remanded.

EDITOR'S ANALYSIS: One original justification for the rule that prohibited impeaching one's own witness was that a witness being attacked by both parties might just as well lie to end the confrontation. However, such concerns proved unpersuasive, and the rule has been abolished. Impeachment is now available to either party. But the tool may not be used where it is a ruse to introduce otherwise inadmissable evidence.

[For more information on prior inconsistent statements, see Casenote Law Outline on Evidence, Chapter 9, § VII, Exemption: Prior Statements of Witnesses.]

QUICKNOTES

PRIOR INCONSISTENT STATEMENT – A statement made before a witness' testimony that contradicts such testimony and which may be admitted in order to impeach the witness; the prior statements may not be admitted, however, to prove the truth of the matter asserted.

PROBATIVE - Tending to establish proof.

NOTES:

UNITED STATES v. ABEL

Federal government (P) v. Convicted bank robber (D)

469 U.S. 45 (1984).

NATURE OF CASE: Appeal from reversal of conviction for bank robbery.

FACT SUMMARY: In the Government's (P) prosecution of Abel (D) for bank robbery, the Government (P) contended that rebuttal testimony of one of Abel's (D) co-defendants was more probative than prejudicial and, therefore, was properly admitted into evidence.

CONCISE RULE OF LAW: A district court is accorded a wide discretion in determining the admissibility of evidence under the Federal Rules.

FACTS: Abel (D) and two cohorts were indicted for robbing a savings and loan. The cohorts pleaded guilty, but Abel (D) went to trial. One of the cohorts, Ehle, agreed to testify against Abel (D) and identify him as a participant in the robbery. Abel (D) sought to counter Ehle's testimony with that of Mills, a friend of both Abel (D) and Ehle, who had spent time with them in prison. The prosecutor tried to discredit Mills' testimony by calling Ehle back to the stand to rebut Mills' testimony, but defense counsel objected, stating that Ehle's rebuttal testimony was too prejudicial to be allowed into evidence. The Government (P) contended that Ehle's testimony was more probative than prejudicial and should be admitted. The district court upheld the Government's (P) position and allowed Ehle to testify. Abel (D) appealed, and the court of appeals reversed, holding that the district court improperly admitted testimony which was more prejudicial than probative. The Government (P) appealed.

ISSUE: Is a district court accorded a wide discretion in determining the admissibility of evidence under the Federal Rules?

HOLDING AND DECISION: (Rehnquist, J.) Yes. A district court is accorded a wide discretion in determining the admissibility of evidence under the Federal Rules. Assessing the probative value of evidence and weighing any factors counseling against admissibility is a matter first for a district court's sound judgment under Federal Rules of Evidence 401 and 403 and ultimately, if the evidence is admitted, for the trier of fact. Before admitting Ehle's testimony, this district court gave heed to the extensive arguments of counsel, both in chambers and at the bench, in an attempt to avoid undue prejudice to Abel. These precautions may not have prevented all prejudice to Abel (D) from Ehle's testimony, but they did ensure that the admission of highly probative evidence did not unduly prejudice Abel (D). There was no abuse of discretion under Rule 403 in admitting Ehle's testimony. Reversed.

EDITOR'S ANALYSIS: Relevant evidence is that which in some degree advances the inquiry. It is material and probative and, as such, it is admissible. However, evidence may be excluded under Federal Rule of Evidence 403 if its probative value is substantially outweighed by the danger of unfair prejudice.

[For more information onFederal Rule 404 , see Casenote Law Outline on Evidence, Chapter 2, § V, Discretionary Exclusion of Relevant Evidence.]

QUICKNOTES

FRE 403 - Provides that a court may dismiss otherwise relevant evidence where its prejudicial effect on the proceeding outweighs any probative value it has.

PROBATIVE - Tending to establish proof.

NOTES:

UNITED STATES v. VALENCIA
Federal government (P) v. Cocaine dealer (D)
61 F.3d 616 (8th Cir. 1995).

NATURE OF CASE: Appeal of conviction for the possession and distribution of cocaine.

FACT SUMMARY: Valencia (D) was confronted on cross-examination by the prosecutor (P) with a copy of a prior conviction after Valencia (D) had attempted to minimize the significance and severity of the prior crime.

CONCISE RULE OF LAW: So long as probative value outweighs its prejudicial effect, a certified copy of a prior conviction may be introduced against a defendant when the defendant has attempted to minimize the severity of the crime on direct examination.

FACTS: Valencia (D) was charged with the possession and distribution of cocaine. Valencia (D) testified in his own defense. On direct examination Valencia (D) admitted to a prior conviction for possession, but he attempted to explain away the severity and significance of the conviction. On cross-examination, the prosecutor introduced a certified copy of the prior conviction for impeachment purposes. The court had previously disallowed the previous conviction under a Fed. R. Evid. 404(b) other crimes ruling, but allowed it this time for impeachment purposes pursuant to Fed. R. Evid. 609. Valencia (D) was subsequently convicted on all counts. Valencia (D) appealed.

ISSUE: May a certified copy of a prior conviction be introduced against the defendant after he has attempted to minimize the severity of the crime on direct examination?

HOLDING AND DECISION: (Bogue, J.) Yes. So long as its probative value outweighs its prejudicial effect, a certified copy of a prior conviction may be introduced against a defendant when the defendant has attempted to minimize the severity of the crime on direct examination. A ruling under Fed. R. Evid. 404(b) does not govern a decision or foreclosure analysis in a later-presented Fed. R. Evid. 609 question. The respective rules operate in two completely different situations; 404(b) evidence goes to guilt, while 609 evidence goes to credibility. Here, the government (P) properly cross-examined Valencia (D) after he attempted to minimize his past behavior on direct examination. Valencia (D) opened the door to impeachment in this matter. Affirmed.

EDITOR'S ANALYSIS: Much criticism has been offered against the use of prior offenses to challenge credibility. One legitimate criticism arises when the prior offense is unrelated to the current situation. While the prior conviction will likely prejudice the jury against the individual, it might well be impossible to articulate a sound reason why the prior conviction offers any insight into current credibility.

[For more information on prior convictions for impeachment, see Casenote Law Outline on Evidence, Chapter 6, § V, Character to Impeach.]

QUICKNOTES

FRE 403 - Provides that a court may dismiss otherwise relevant evidence where its prejudicial effect on the proceeding outweighs any probative value it has.

PROBATIVE - Tending to establish proof.

NOTES:

CREE v. HATCHER
Injured patient (P) v. Doctor (D)
969 F.2d 34 (3rd Cir. 1992), cert. dismissed, 506 U.S. 1017 (1992).

NATURE OF CASE: Appeal of a defense verdict in a medical malpractice suit.

FACT SUMMARY: Cree's (P) expert pathologist was impeached by evidence of a prior conviction of failure to file an income tax return.

CONCISE RULE OF LAW: The willful failure to file a tax return does not constitute a crime of dishonesty and false statement, and evidence of the conviction may not be used to impeach a witness.

FACTS: Cree (P) was diagnosed with a Class II irregularity in her Pap test. Dr. Hatcher (D) told her to return in six months, but failed to tell Cree (P) that such an irregularity could progress to cancer. Cree (P) moved before returning for another exam, and she subsequently was diagnosed with cancer of the cervix. She sued Hatcher (D) for medical malpractice. At the trial, Hatcher (D) impeached Cree's (P) expert pathologist with evidence of a prior conviction of willful failure to file a federal income tax return. The jury found for Hatcher (D); Cree (P) appealed.

ISSUE: Does willful failure to file a tax return constitute a crime involving "dishonesty and false statement" such that evidence of the conviction may be used to impeach a witness?

HOLDING AND DECISION: (Pollack, J.) No. The willful failure to file a tax return does not constitute a crime of dishonesty and false statement, and evidence of the conviction may not be used to impeach a witness. Prior convictions may be used to impeach where the underlying offense indicates a propensity for falsehood. Such offenses include perjury, false statement, criminal fraud, embezzlement, and false pretense. Willful failure to file a tax return, however, is not such a crime. One convicted of it need not have intended to defraud the government. Here, the pathologist's failure to file a tax return is not significantly linked to his ability to testify truthfully on medical matters. Since he was a key witness, the impeachment prejudiced Cree (P). Reversed and remanded for a new trial.

EDITOR'S ANALYSIS: Commentators worry that the automatic admissibility of convictions involving dishonesty and false statements could cause tremendous prejudice in certain cases. Since Congress had an opportunity to address those concerns in a 1990 amendment by adding a balancing requirement to Rule 609, but did not do so, the implication is that the court is not allowed to balance prejudice against probative value when admitting evidence of prior convictions for impeachment purposes. Though not entirely consoling, it is unlikely that this problem arises with any great regularity.

_____

[For more information on prior convictions to impeachment character, see Casenote Law Outline on Evidence, Chapter 6, § V, Character to Impeach.]

NOTES:

PEOPLE v. SORGE
State (P) v. Abortionist (D)
N.Y. Ct. App., 301 N.Y. 198, 93 N.E.2d 637 (1950).

NATURE OF CASE: Appeal from conviction for abortion.

FACT SUMMARY: At trial the prosecutor interrogated Sorge (D) about abortions she had performed on other women, and when she answered in the negative, pressed her further.

CONCISE RULE OF LAW: A defendant, like any other witness, may be interrogated upon cross-examination in regard to any criminal or immoral act that has a bearing on his credibility, and it does not matter that the acts inquired about are similar to the crime for which the defendant is being tried, that there are a number of acts, or that the defendant denies committing the acts.

FACTS: At trial, the prosecutor interrogated Sorge (D) about abortions she had allegedly performed upon four other women. After she answered his questions in the negative, he pressed her further as to whether she had not signed a statement admitting that she had aborted one of the women, as to whether that particular operation had not been the basis for her plea of guilty to the crime of practicing medicine without a license, and as to whether she had not been present while a fifth abortion was committed. The outcome of the case depended largely upon whether the jury believed Sorge (D) or the victim.

ISSUE: Can a defendant be interrogated upon cross-examination in regard to a criminal or immoral act which is similar to the crime for which the defendant is being tried or which was committed a number of times or which the defendant denies committing?

HOLDING AND DECISION: (Fuld, J.) Yes. A defendant, like any other witness, may be interrogated upon cross-examination in regard to a criminal or immoral act that has a bearing on her credibility as a witness. It does not matter that the offenses or acts inquired about are similar to the crime for which the defendant is being tried. Nor are they rendered improper merely because of their number as long as they have a basis in fact and are asked in good faith. Nor is it improper to continue cross-examination about a specific crime after a defendant has denied it. As long as the questioning is done in good faith, it is proper. While a witness' testimony regarding collateral matters may not be refuted by the calling of other witnesses or by the production of extrinsic evidence, there is no prohibition against examining the witness, himself, further on the chance that he may change his testimony. In this case, none of the questions was improper as a matter of law. Nor is it possible to say that prejudice resulted from the cumulative effect of the prosecutor's questions nor that permitting the vigorous cross-examination constituted an abuse of discretion. The evidence against Sorge (D) was clear and, since the outcome of the case depended almost entirely upon whether the jury believed Sorge (D) or the victim, there was good reason to give both sides a relatively free hand on cross-examination in order to give the jury full opportunity to weigh and evaluate the credibility of each witness.

EDITOR'S ANALYSIS: The majority of courts limit cross-examination concerning acts of misconduct as an attack upon character to acts which have some relation to the credibility of the witness. Some courts, such as the one here, permit an attack upon character by fairly wide-open cross-examination upon acts of misconduct which show bad character and have only an attenuated relation to credibility. A substantial number of courts prohibit altogether cross-examination as to acts of misconduct for impeachment. McCormick feels that this latter view is the fairest because of dangers of prejudice, especially where the witness is a party, distraction and confusion, abuse, and the difficulties or appeal of ascertaining whether particular acts relate to credibility

---

[For more information on testimony regarding other crimes, see Casenote Law Outline on Evidence, Chapter 6, § IV, The "Other Crimes' Loophole.]

QUICKNOTES

ABUSE OF DISCRETION - A determination by an appellate court that a lowe court's decision was based on an error of law.

CREDIBILITY - Believability; plausibility; whether or not a witness' testimony i believable.

CROSS EXAMINATION - The interrogation of a witness by an adverse part either to further inquire as to the subject matter of the direct examination or to ca into question the witness' credibility.

EXTRINSIC EVIDENCE - Evidence that is not contained within the text of document or contract but which is derived from the parties' statements or th circumstances under which the agreement was made.

IMPEACHMENT - The discrediting of a witness by offering evidence to show tha the witness lacks credibility.

NOTES:

STATE v. TERNAN
State (P) v. Assaulter (D)
Wash. Sup. Ct., 32 Wash. 2d 584, 203 P.2d 342 (1949).

NATURE OF CASE: Appeal from conviction of assault.

FACT SUMMARY: In rebuttal to Ternan's (D) testimony at his trial, the State (P) called witnesses who testified that Ternan's (D) reputation for truth and veracity was bad.

CONCISE RULE OF LAW: When a defendant in a criminal case takes the witness stand, he subjects himself to cross-examination the same as any other witness, and the state has a right to impeach him as a witness to the extent of proving by witnesses that his general reputation for truth and veracity in the community where he resides is bad.

FACTS: Ternan (D) testified at his trial. In rebuttal, the State (P) called witnesses who testified that Ternan's (D) general reputation for truth and veracity in a certain community was bad. The court instructed the jury that "evidence relative to the reputation of the defendants for truth and veracity was admitted solely for the purpose of affecting their credibility as a witness, and is to be considered by you for that purpose only, and in connection with all the other evidence in the case, in deciding how much weight or credence you will give their testimony."

ISSUE: When a defendant in a criminal case takes the witness stand, does the state have a right to impeach him as a witness to the extent of proving by witnesses that his general reputation for truth and veracity in the community where he resides is bad?

HOLDING AND DECISION: (Grady, J.) Yes. The controlling statute provided that an accused person may offer himself as a witness on his own behalf and shall be allowed to testify as other witnesses, but when he does so testify he shall be subject to all the rules of law relating to cross-examination of other witnesses. This statute has been construed to mean that such persons may be impeached with reference to their general reputation for truth and veracity in the community where they reside. An important distinction exists between the character of a person and a person's reputation. The character of a defendant in a criminal case is not open to inquiry unless he himself puts it in issue. But once a defendant has taken the witness stand, the State can impeach him to the extent of proving that his general reputation for truth and veracity in the community where he resides is bad. Hence, in this case, once Ternan (D) testified, it was proper for the State to call witnesses who testified that Ternan's (D) reputation for truth and veracity was bad. The judgment is affirmed.

EDITOR'S ANALYSIS: The majority of courts follow the rule expressed in this case and limit the inquiry of a witness' reputation to reputation for truth and veracity. A few allow inquiry as to reputation for general character or moral character, and fewer still permit proof of reputation for specific traits other than veracity.

UNITED STATES v. DOTSON
Government (P) v. Paroled felon (D)
799 F.2d 189 (5th Cir. 1986).

NATURE OF CASE: Appeal of conviction on three counts of receiving firearms.

FACT SUMMARY: Dotson (D), a paroled felon, argued that he obtained firearms in violation of parole only to protect himself; the prosecution (P) maligned Dotson's (D) witnesses as lacking truthful character.

CONCISE RULE OF LAW: The credibility of a witness may not be attacked by evidence in the form of opinion or reputation for untruthfulness where no foundation for such an opinion is first offered.

FACTS: Dotson (D) was paroled after felony convictions for drug possession. As a parole condition, Dotson (D) was not to knowingly receive a firearm. However, after threats and assaults on his person, including a hail of bullets being fired into his home, Dotson (D) sought out handguns for his protection. At trial, Dotson (D) offered several witnesses who supported and bolstered his defense of necessity. Several government (P) agents were called as witnesses, each testifying that they had formed a negative opinion regarding Dotson (D) and his witnesses. Dotson (D) was convicted, and he then appealed.

ISSUE: May the credibility of a witness be attacked by evidence in the form of opinion or reputation for untruthfulness where no foundation for such an opinion is first offered?

HOLDING AND DECISION: (Clark, J.) No. The credibility of a witness may not be attacked by evidence in the form of opinion or reputation for untruthfulness where no foundation for such an opinion is first offered. Federal Rule of Evidence 608(a) allows witness credibility to be attacked by opinion and reputation evidence of untruthfulness. However, the right to introduce such evidence is not unchecked. A foundation for such an opinion must be given, or else the prosecution could parade a series of witnesses across the stand, each saying that the defendant and other witnesses are essentially unbelievable. Here, that was exactly what was attempted. The prosecution (P) witnesses offered no underlying facts to support their opinions. Dotson (D) was substantially prejudiced by this testimony. Reversed.

EDITOR'S ANALYSIS: Recent trends, including this case, suggest that reputation or opinion of character evidence must be supported by more than a showing of relevance. A foundation for the opinion or reputation must be solid enough to allow the trier of fact to weigh the testimony beyond its nature as a mere assertion. For example, the time span over which such reputation evidence is developed must be long enough to reflect on character. Reputation in a community must be from a large enough segment to establish a general sentiment, not just a few personal opinions.

NEWTON v. STATE

Criminal conspirator (D) v. State (P)

Md. Ct. App., 147 Md. 71, 127 A. 123 (1924).

NATURE OF CASE: Appeal from conviction for criminal conspiracy to defraud by misrepresenting the financial condition of a business concern.

FACT SUMMARY: The State (P) cross-examined a defense witness as to whether or not he had given the same testimony at his own trial and whether or not he had been convicted.

CONCISE RULE OF LAW: It is not proper to cross-examine a witness as to whether he had not given the same testimony during previous trials at which he was convicted.

FACTS: Newton (D) was jointly indicted with Dickey and Gillespie but was tried separately. Newton (D) called Dickey as a defense witness. The State (P) cross-examined Dickey as to whether he had not given the same testimony at his own trial and at Gillespie's trial. When Dickey responded affirmatively, the prosecutor said, "And you were convicted, were you not?" The prosecutor further asked Dickey whether he was not convicted in his trial in the same court as Newton's (D) trial was being held.

ISSUE: Is it proper to cross-examine a witness as to whether he had not given the same testimony during previous trials at which he was convicted?

HOLDING AND DECISION: (Offutt, J.) No. If an examiner seeks to impeach the credibility of a witness by showing that he had been convicted of a crime, the examiner should ask the question directly. Or if an examiner intends to show that in another case the witness swore to statements contrary to his testimony in the present case, the witness should be asked whether he made such conflicting statements. The method of cross-examining Dickey used in this case was improper. In addition to intimidating Dickey, the only apparent purpose was to point out to the jury that in Dickey's own case, when he was tried for the same crime, he had made the same statements as he was making at Newton's (D) trial and that the three judges before whom he was tried discredited his statements and convicted him. The obvious purpose was to induce the jury to believe that since Dickey's testimony had already been discredited by judges in the same court, they should likewise discredit it. The judgment of conviction is reversed and a new trial is ordered.

EDITOR'S ANALYSIS: The approach tried in Newton is often rejected. In German v. German, 3 A.2d 849 (1938), involving alimony, a reference to a report in a previous related action that one party had given untrue testimony was held improper. In Shewbart v. State, 33 Ala.App. 195 (1947), it was held proper to prevent cross-examination of peace officers who apparently testified against defendant as to whether they had testified against defendant before the grand jury, the grand jury thereafter refusing to indict. State v. Williams, 487 P. 2d 100 (1971) held that it was not error to prevent cross-examination of an informer as to whether, in other cases in which he had testified, there had been acquittals.

[For more information on prior statements of witnesses, see Casenote Law Outline on Evidence, Chapter 9, § VII, Exemption: Prior Statements of Witnesses.]

QUICKNOTES

CREDIBILITY - Believability; plausibility; whether or not a witness' testimony is believable.

CROSS EXAMINATION - The interrogation of a witness by an adverse party either to further inquire as to the subject matter of the direct examination or to call into question the witness' credibility.

IMPEACHMENT - The discrediting of a witness by offering evidence to show that the witness lacks credibility.

NOTES:

DENVER CITY TRAMWAY CO. v. LOMOVT
City transit company (P) v. Injured pedestrian (D)
Colo. Sup. Ct., 53 Colo. 292, 126 P. 276 (1912).

NATURE OF CASE: Personal injury negligence suit.

FACT SUMMARY: Lomovt (P) sued Denver City Tramway (D) for personal injuries sustained when a street car ran over her. Murray testified for Denver (D) that the motorman acted prudently and Lomovt introduced the testimony of two witnesses to the accident that Murray had stated that the motorman ought to be lynched.

CONCISE RULE OF LAW: A witness may properly be impeached by introduction of extrinsic evidence of a prior statement inconsistent with his present testimony where he denies having made the prior inconsistent statement.

FACTS: Lomovt (P) was injured when she was run over by a street car operated by Denver City Tramway Co. (D). She brought suit alleging negligent operation by the motorman. Denver City (D) produced Murray, a witness, who testified, in essence, that the motorman was not negligent. Lomovt's (P) attorney confronted Murray with a statement he allegedly made at the time of the accident when he said the motorman ought to be lynched. When Murray denied the statement, Lomovt (P) introduced the testimony of two other witnesses that Murray had made the statement in question. Denver City (D) appealed judgment against them, claiming the two witnesses' testimonies should not have been admitted.

ISSUE: May a witness be impeached by the introduction of extrinsic evidence of a prior inconsistent statement where the witness denies at trial that he made the prior statement?

HOLDING AND DECISION: (Hill, J.) Yes. Murray was given ample opportunity to explain the prior statement when he was cross-examined. His denial properly laid a foundation to introduce contradicting evidence. Since Murray testified that the motorman was not negligent, the prior statement, if made, was at least an inference on his part that the motorman had committed a wrong and was, therefore, inconsistent. The test of materiality is whether the prior statement, if true, would tend to prove the adverse party's case. Since that is true in this case, the two witnesses' testimonies were properly admitted.

EDITOR'S ANALYSIS: If the witness completely admits the prior inconsistent statement, then he must be given an opportunity to explain, if he can. Once the admission is made, no further evidence can be introduced as to the prior statement. This is not true where the admission is equivocal. It has been held that present testimony of a witness that he does not remember anything about the occurrence is not inconsistent with a prior statement made in reference to the occurrence and the prior statement is not admissible.

RODRIGUEZ v. STATE
Aggravated assault suspect (P) v. State (D)
Tx. Ct. Civ. App., 165 Tex. Cr. 179, 305 S.W.2d 250 (1957).

NATURE OF CASE: Aggravated assault conviction appeal.

FACT SUMMARY: Rodriguez (D), who was convicted of aggravated assault for attempting to molest a seven-year-old girl, argued that the State (P) should not have been permitted to show the reputation for truth and veracity of its witness against him.

CONCISE RULE OF LAW: Where an attack is made on the veracity of a witness, it is proper to permit testimony that the witness has a good reputation for truth and veracity.

FACTS: Rodriguez (D) was convicted of aggravated assault. Cathalina Gavia testified that she had come into a room and found Rodriguez (D) attempting to remove the pants off her seven-year-old foster daughter. Rodriguez (D) denied the charge of assault and testified that on the day before the incident he had seen Cathalina in a car on a country road with a man lying on her legs; that when he came to see Cathalina's father, Rodriguez (D) spoke to her about what he had seen, she denied it angrily, and shortly thereafter charged Rodriguez (D) with assaulting the child. Cathalina was then recalled and denied the incidents testified to by Rodriguez (D). After the testimony was given by Rodriguez (D) and Gavia, the State (P) was permitted over objection to prove that Cathalina's reputation for truth and veracity in the community was good. On appeal, Rodriguez (D) argued that the admission of this testimony was error.

ISSUE: Is it proper to permit testimony that a witness has a good reputation for truth and veracity when an attack is made on the veracity of that witness?

HOLDING AND DECISION: (Woodley, J.) Yes. The general rule is that where there is no evidence to impeach the testimony of a witness except contradictory evidence, it is not permissible to bolster the testimony of the witness by proof of his good reputation for truth and veracity. However, where an attack is made upon the veracity of the witness, such as by evidence that the witness has conspired with another to falsely accuse the defendant, or where it is attempted to be shown that the witness is testifying under corrupt motives, or is fabricating testimony, it is proper to permit testimony that the witness has a good reputation for truth and veracity. Here, the introduction of the reputation evidence was under proper circumstances. Affirmed.

EDITOR'S ANALYSIS: In general, a witness will be given an opportunity to explain or deny those facts which are alleged to give rise to bias or interest. In addition, evidence of a witness' good reputation for veracity and truthfulness is usually admissible to rehabilitate that witness when he has been impeached by the showing of a prior criminal conviction.

CHAPTER 4
HEARSAY

QUICK REFERENCE RULES OF LAW

1. **Definition and Rationale.** The hearsay rule makes extrajudicial assertions inadmissible unless the assertor is brought to testify in court where he may be probed and cross-examined as to the grounds of his assertion and his qualifications to make it. (Leake v. Hagert)

   [For more information on hearsay evidence, see Casenote Law Outline on Evidence, Chapter 9, Hearsay: Definitions and Exemptions, § IV, Hearsay Defined.]

2. **Definition and Rationale.** Testimony by a witness in court as to statements made out of court by a physician are inadmissible as hearsay. (Central of Georgia Railway Co. v. Reeves)

   [For more information on admissibility of out-of-court statements, see Casenote Law Outline on Evidence, Chapter 9, § IV, Hearsay Defined.]

3. **Definition and Rationale.** Multiple hearsay is admissible provided that each level of hearsay satisfies an exception to the hearsay rule. (Hickey v. Settlemier)

   [For more information on legally operative conduct and hearsay within hearsay, see Casenote Law Outline on Evidence, Chapter 9, § IV, Hearsay Defined; § VI, "Multiple Hearsay."]

4. **Definition and Rationale.** Statements offered, not to prove the truth of the matter asserted therein, but as circumstantial evidence of the declarant's state of mind, are admissible nonhearsay when relevant. (Banks v. State)

   [For more information on admissible hearsay and other exclusionary rules, see Casenote Law Outline on Evidence, Chapter 10, § XVI, Admissible Hearsay and Other Exclusionary Rules.]

5. **Definition and Rationale.** Hearsay admissible under an exception to hearsay exclusion must also be both relevant and not so unfairly prejudicial as to outweigh its probative value. (United States v. Reyes)

   [For more information on admissible hearsay and other exclusionary rules, see Casenote Law Outline on Evidence, Chapter 10, § XVI, Admissible Hearsay and Other Exclusionary Rules.]

6. **Definition and Rationale.** Written or oral evidence of the opinion of an out-of-court declarant which is not made subject to an oath or cross-examination is inadmissible as hearsay. (Wright v. Doe D. Tatham)

   [For more information on hearsay evidence, see Casenote Law Outline on Evidence, Chapter 9, § IV, Hearsay Defined.]

7. **Definition and Rationale.** Out-of-court statements made by an unidentified individual can be admitted as nonhearsay if they provide circumstantial evidence of the defendant's knowledge and intent to commit the charged crime, and do not directly assert the issue of the case as fact. (Headley v. Tilghman)

   [For more information on co-conspirator admissions, see Casenote Law Outline on Evidence, Chapter 9, § VIII, Exemption: Statements by Parties.]

8. **Definition and Rationale.** Testimony as to conduct of an out-of-court declarant, which is not asserted

testimonially, is made subject to cross-examination, and is based upon personal knowledge, is not hearsay. (Kinder v. Commonwealth)

> *[For more information on nonassertive conduct as hearsay, see Casenote Law Outline on Evidence, Chapter 9, § II, "Statement" Defined.]*

9. **Definition and Rationale.** If an extrajudicial declaration comports with the definition of hearsay and does not fall within any specific exception, it may still be admitted if there are circumstantial guarantees of trustworthiness, as specified by Federal Rule of Evidence 803(24). (United States v. Muscato)

> *[For more information on "wildcard" hearsay exceptions, see Casenote Law Outline on Evidence, Chapter 10, § X, The "Wildcard" Exceptions.]*

10. **Prior Statements of Witnesses.** A party may use a prior inconsistent statement as substantive evidence if the declarant is available for cross-examination. (Rowe v. Farmers Insurance Company, Inc.)

> *[For more information on use of prior inconsistent statements, see Casenote Law Outline on Evidence, Chapter 9, § VII, Exemption: Prior Statements of Witnesses.]*

11. **Prior Statements of Witnesses.** Testimony of a witness at a preliminary hearing, subject to full cross-examination at that time, can be introduced as substantive evidence against defendant, and does not violate defendant's right of confrontation. (California v. Green)

> *[For more information on the Rights of Confrontation Rule, see Casenote Law Outline on Evidence, Chapter 9, § X, Hearsay and the Right of Confrontation.]*

12. **Prior Statements of Witnesses.** Fed. R. Evid. 801(d)(1)(B) permits prior consistent statements to be used for substantive purposes after the statements are admitted to rebut the existence of an improper influence or motive. (Tome v. United States)

13. **Prior Statements of Witnesses.** A witness in a criminal trial may testify about an earlier identification even if he can no longer testify as to the basis for that identification. (United States v. Owens)

> *[For more information on the Confrontation Clause, see Casenote Law Outline on Evidence, Chapter 9, § X, Hearsay and the Right of Confrontation.]*

14. **Admissions.** A gesture such as shaking your head that has a universal meaning is an admission as much as specific words with the same meaning, and it is a question for the jury to determine the meaning of the gesture. (Bill v. Farm Bureau Life Insurance Co.)

> *[For more information on nonverbal conduct, see Casenote Law Outline on Evidence, Chapter 9, § II, "Statement" Defined.]*

15. **Admissions.** Argument from a prior trial may be used as evidence if it involves an assertion of fact inconsistent with factual assertions in the subsequent trial. (United States v. McKeon)

16. **Admissions.** Federal Rule of Evidence 801(d)(2)(D) makes statements made by agents within the scope of their employment admissible, and there is no implied requirement that the declarant have personal knowledge of the facts underlying his statement. (Mahlandt v. Wild Canid Survival & Research Center, Inc.)

> *[For more information on vicarious admissions, see Casenote Law Outline on Evidence, Chapter 9, § VIII, Exemption: Statements by Parties.]*

17. Admissions. The Confrontation Clause does not require a court to embark on an independent inquiry into the reliability of statements that satisfy the requirements of Federal Rule of Evidence 801(d)(2)(E). (Bourjaily v. United States)

[For more information on the Confrontation Clause, see Casenote Law Outline on Evidence, Chapter 9, § X, Hearsay and the Right of Confrontation.]

18. Declarations against Interest. A decedent's out-of-court declarations in disparagement of his title are admissible as a declaration against interest even where the testimony is offered by one who would benefit from admission. (Cole v. Cole)

[For more information on declarations against interest, see Casenote Law Outline on Evidence, Chapter 10, § XIV, Declarations Against Interest.]

19. Declarations against Interest. A declaration against interest made by a person now unavailable to testify will be admissible only insofar as it contains statements of fact and not statements of opinion as to legal fault. (Carpenter v. Davis)

[For more information on declarations against interest, see Casenote Law Outline on Evidence, Chapter 10, § XIV, Declarations Against Interest.]

20. Declarations against Interest. Statements against a penal interest are sufficient to invoke the exception to the hearsay rule, and the declarant is unavailable if he refuses to testify based on constitutional privilege. (People v. Brown)

[For more information on declarations contrary to penal interest, see Casenote Law Outline on Evidence, Chapter 10, § XIV, Declarations Against Interest.]

21. Declarations against Interest. Fed. R. Evid. 804(b)(3) does not allow admission of non-self-exculpatory statements, even if they are made within a broader narrative that is generally self-inculpatory. (Williamson v. United States)

[For more information on declarations against interest, see Casenote Law Outline on Evidence, Chapter 10, § XIV, Declarations against Interest.]

22. Spontaneous, Contemporaneous, and Excited Utterances. Various courts throughout the United States have embraced the precepts underlying an exception to the hearsay rule for declarations of present sense impressions. (Commonwealth v. Coleman)

[For more information on present sense impressions, see Casenote Law Outline on Evidence, Chapter 10, § II, Present Sense Impressions.]

23. Physical or Mental Condition of Declarant. Expressions of present physical state are admissible to prove such physical state. (Fidelity Service Insurance Co. v. Jones)

[For more information on expressions of present physical state, see Casenote Law Outline on Evidence, Chapter 10, § IV, Present State-of-Mind Exception.]

24. Physical or Mental Condition of Declarant. The test for admissibility of medical professional hearsay under Rule 803(4) is whether the subject matter of the statements is reasonably pertinent to diagnosis or treatment. (United States v. Tome)

[For more information on statements for medical diagnosis, see Casenote Law Outline on Evidence, Chapter 10, § V, Statements for Medical Diagnosis.]

25. Physical or Mental Condition of Declarant. A statement of a defendant's then-existing state of mind is not rendered inadmissible by the hearsay rule. (United States v. DiMaria)

[For more information on the state of mind exception, see Casenote Law Outline on Evidence, Chapter 10, § IV, Present State-of-Mind Exception.]

26. Physical or Mental Condition of Declarant. Declarations of state of mind which tend to evince a plan or intent to perform an act may be introduced into evidence as proof that the act has, in fact, been committed. (Mutual Life Insurance Co. v. Hillmon)

[For more information on the present state of mind exception, see Casenote Law Outline on Evidence, Chapter 10, § IV, Present State-of-Mind Exception.]

27. Physical or Mental Condition of Declarant. Hearsay evidence of statements in which the declarant has stated his intention to do something with another person are admissible under the state of mind exception to the hearsay rule to show that he intended to do it, from which the trier of fact may draw the inference that he carried out his intention and did it. (United States v. Pheaster)

[For more information on the present state of mind exception, see Casenote Law Outline on Evidence, Chapter 10, § IV, Present State-of-Mind Exception.]

28. Physical or Mental Condition of Declarant. Declarations of present memory, looking backward to a prior occurrence, are inadmissible to prove, or tend to prove, the existence of the occurrence. (Shepard v. United States)

[For more information on present state of mind exception, see Casenote Law Outline on Evidence, Chapter 10, § IV, Present State-of-Mind Exception.]

29. Physical or Mental Condition of Declarant. Out-of-court statements which tend to prove a plan, design, or intention of the declarant are admissible to prove that the plan, design, or intention was carried out. (United States v. Annunzziato)

[For more information on the present state of mind exception, see Casenote Law Outline on Evidence, Chapter 10, § IV, Present State-of-Mind Exception.]

30. Business Entries and Public Records. A document containing hearsay is admissible under the business records exception of Rule 803(6) if it is prepared in the regular course of business, even if the particular document is not routine. (United States v. Jacoby)

[For more information on business records exception, see Casenote Law Outline on Evidence, Chapter 10, § VII, The Business Records Exception.]

31. Business Entries and Public Records. A business record, to be in the regular course of business, must be made in relation to the inherent nature of the business and in the methods systematically employed for the conduct of the business as a business. (Palmer v. Hoffman)

[For more information on the admissibility of business record, see Casenote Law Outline on Evidence, Chapter 10, § VII, The Business Records Exception.]

32. Business Entries and Public Records. Even if a statute allows business records to be admitted without firsthand knowledge of the recorder if done in the regular course of business, this does not include entries that include hearsay statements of third parties not engaged in the business related to the record. (Johnson v. Lutz)

[For more information on requirements for the business records exception, see Casenote Law Outline on Evidence, Chapter 10, § VII, The Business Records Exception.]

33. Business Entries and Public Records. Statements in public records and reports in the form of opinions or conclusions are admissible unless the sources of information or other circumstances indicate lack of trustworthiness. (Beech Aircraft Corp. v. Rainey)

[For more information on official records, see Casenote Law Outline on Evidence, Chapter 10, § VIII, The Official Records Exception.]

34. Business Entries and Public Records. Medical records may be admissible under the business records exception to the hearsay rule but not to show the diagnosis or medical opinion placed therein by a doctor who is unavailable for cross-examination. (Commonwealth v. DiGiacomo)

[For more information on requirements for the business records exception, see Casenote Law Outline on Evidence, Chapter 10, § VII, The Business Records Exception.]

35. Business Entries and Public Records. Entries in hospital records are considered admissible as records made in the regular course of business of the hospital only if they are germane to medical history, diagnosis, or treatment (*i.e.*, medically relevant). (Wadena v. Bush)

[For more information on the business record exception, see Casenote Law Outline on Evidence, Chapter 10, § VII, The Business Records Exception.]

36. Former Testimony. Prior testimony is admissible when the issues are the same and the party against whom the testimony is offered had a fair and adequate opportunity to cross-examine at the former trial. (Gaines v. Thomas)

[For more information on prior statements of witnesses, see Casenote Law Outline on Evidence, Chapter 9, § VII, Exemption: Prior Statements of Witnesses.]

37. Former Testimony. The prior testimony of an unavailable witness is admissible under Federal Rule of Evidence 804(b)(1) if the party against whom it is offered or a "predecessor in interest" had the "opportunity and similar motive to develop the testimony by direct, cross or redirect examination." (Lloyd v. American Export Lines, Inc.)

[For more information on the former testimony exception, see Casenote Law Outline on Evidence, Chapter 10, § XII, The Former Testimony Exception.]

38. Former Testimony. In a criminal trial, the statement of one who is not present for cross-examination is admissible (under an exception to the hearsay rule) only if it is shown that he is unavailable and if the statement bears adequate "indicia of reliability." (Ohio v. Roberts)

[For more information on statements bearing "indices of reliability," see Casenote Law Outline on Evidence, Chapter 9, § X, Hearsay and the Right of Confrontation.]

39. Former Testimony. Similarity of motive for Rule 804(b)(1) is shown where the party resisting the offered testimony at a pending proceeding had, at a prior proceeding, an interest of substantially similar intensity to prove (or disprove) the same side of a substantially similar issue. (United States v. DiNapoli)

[For more information on former testimony, see Casenote Law Outline on Evidence, Chapter 10, § XII, The Former Testimony Exception.]

40. Dying Declarations. All that is required to admit a dying declaration is that the declarant is dying and is aware of that fact. The weight given to the declaration is a question for the jury. (Wilson v. State)

[For more information on dying declarations, see Casenote Law Outline on Evidence, Chapter 10, § XIII, Dying Declarations.]

41. Ancient Documents. Ancient documents, if authenticated, are presumed reliable by their nature, and no further evidence of reliability is required for admission of the document into evidence. (Bowers v. Fibreboard Corporation)

[For more information on ancient documents, see Casenote Law Outline on Evidence, Chapter 10, § IX, Miscellaneous Hearsay Exceptions.]

42. Learned Treatises. Since the purpose of the creation of a document pertains directly to its reliability as a learned treatise, it is not proper, under Rule 803(18), to admit a document into evidence as a learned treatise while redacting the purpose of its creation. (Graham v. Wyeth Laboratories)

[For more information on learned treatises, see Casenote Law Outline on Evidence, Chapter 10, § IX, Miscellaneous Hearsay Exceptions.]

43. Nonclass Exceptions. To be admissible under the residual hearsay exception provided for in the Federal Rules of Evidence, evidence offered must fulfill five requirements relating to its trustworthiness, its materiality, its probative importance, whether its admission will best serve the interests of justice, and whether the opponent received adequate notice of its use. (Robinson v. Shapiro)

[For more information on the residual exceptions, see Casenote Law Outline on Evidence, Chapter 10, § X, The "Wildcard" Exceptions.]

44. Nonclass Exceptions. The admission of statements of a child-victim in a molestation prosecution under the residual hearsay exception may violate the Confrontation Clause. (Idaho v. Wright)

[For more information on the medical diagnosis exception in child abuse cases, see Casenote Law Outline on Evidence, Chapter 10, § V, Statements for Medical Diagnosis.]

45. Contitutional Restraints. The Sixth Amendment Confrontation Clause does not prohibit the admission of testimony under the "spontaneous declaration" and "medical examination" exceptions to the hearsay rule. (White v. Illinois)

[For more information on excited utterances, see Casenote Law Outline on Evidence, Chapter 10, § III, Excited Utterances.]

LEAKE v. HAGERT
Driver of tractor (P) v. Driver of car (D)
N.D. Sup. Ct., 175 N.W.2d 675 (1970).

NATURE OF CASE: Action to recover damages for personal injury.

FACT SUMMARY: Leake (P) alleged that the collision between his tractor and Hagert's (D) car was caused by Hagert's (D) negligence. An insurance adjustor was allowed to testify that Leake's (P) son had told him that the tractor's rear light had not been working for some time.

CONCISE RULE OF LAW: The hearsay rule makes extrajudicial assertions inadmissible unless the assertor is brought to testify in court where he may be probed and cross-examined as to the grounds of his assertion and his qualifications to make it.

FACTS: Leake (P) alleged that Hagert (D) negligently drove her car into Leake's (P) tractor. Hagert (D) admitted that the collision occurred, but denied that it was caused by her negligence. She alleged that it was caused by the lack of proper lights on Leake's (P) tractor. An insurance adjustor testified that Leake's (P) son told him that the tractor's rear light had been out for some time. The son was not available to testify at the trial. The jury returned a verdict dismissing Leake's (P) complaint. Leake (P) contended on appeal that it was reversible error for the trial court to allow the adjustor to testify as to Leake's (P) son's statement over Leake's (P) objection. Leake (P) contended that whether the light was out or not is a question of fact.

ISSUE: Are extrajudicial assertions admissible where the assertor is not brought to testify in court?

HOLDING AND DECISION: (Paulson, J.) No. The hearsay rule prohibits use of a person's assertion, as equivalent to testimony of the fact asserted, unless the assertor is brought to testify in court, where she may be probed and cross-examined as to the grounds of her assertion and her qualifications to make it. In this case the adjustor's testimony concerning the statement of Leake's (P) son was hearsay. The son did not testify in this action. He was not a party. His statement was not made under oath and was not subject to cross-examination. Nor was he available as a witness at the time of trial. Hence, it was error for the trial court to admit the adjustor's testimony concerning the son's statement. However, such error was not prejudicial, and the judgment is affirmed.

EDITOR'S ANALYSIS: The Anglo-American tradition has evolved three conditions under which witnesses ordinarily will be required to testify: oath, personal presence at trial, and cross-examination. The rule against hearsay is designed to insure compliance with these conditions, and when one of them is absent, the hearsay objection becomes pertinent. The out-of-court declarant speaks without the solemnity of the oath administered on witnesses in a court. As to the second factor, there is no opportunity to observe the out-of-court declarant's demeanor. Also, personal presence eliminates the danger of a witness' reporting statements inaccurately. It is generally agreed, however, that the third factor is the main justification for the exclusion of hearsay, that is the lack of opportunity for the adverse party to cross-examine the out-of-court declarant.

[For more information on hearsay evidence, see Casenote Law Outline on Evidence, Chapter 9, Hearsay: Definitions and Exemptions, § IV, Hearsay Defined.]

QUICKNOTES

CROSS EXAMINATION - The interrogation of a witness by an adverse party either to further inquire as to the subject matter of the direct examination or to call into question the witness' credibility.

DECLARANT - Any human speaker who is the source of offered testimony, often hearsay spoken outside of court.

EXTRA JUDICIAL - Outside of court: taking place outside of formal proceedings.

HEARSAY - An out-of-court statement made by a person other than the witness testifying at trial that is offered in order to prove the truth of the matter asserted.

NEGLIGENCE - Conduct falling below the standard of care that a reasonable person would demonstrate under similar conditions.

OUT-OF-COURT STATEMENT - A statement made outside of the proceeding and generally considered hearsay since opposing counsel's opportunity to cross-examine the declarant regarding the statement has been denied.

NOTES:

CENTRAL OF GEORGIA RAILWAY CO. v. REEVES
Railroad company (D) v. Injured plaintiff (P)
Ala. Sup. Ct., 257 So. 2d 839 (1972).

NATURE OF CASE: Action under the Federal Employers' Liability Act to recover damages for personal injuries.

FACT SUMMARY: Reeves (P) sought damages for injuries arising out of the derailment of Central's (D) train. He testified, over Central's (D) objection, as to what an examining physician told him about his condition.

CONCISE RULE OF LAW: Testimony by a witness in court as to statements made out of court by a physician are inadmissible as hearsay.

FACTS: Reeves (P) sought damages for injuries arising out of the derailment of one of Central's (D) trains. At trial, Reeves (P) testified, over Central's (D) objection, as to what an examining physician had told him about his condition. He testified that the doctor told him that he had a weakness in his arm, a stiffness in his neck, nerve trouble in his back, and that he was not physically able to do his work any more. Central (D) argued on appeal that the admission of such testimony violated the hearsay rule and constituted reversible error.

ISSUE: Is testimony by a witness in court as to statements made out of court by a physician inadmissible?

HOLDING AND DECISION: (Bloodworth, J.) Yes. A witness' testimony as to statements made out of court by a physician is inadmissible as hearsay. In this case, Reeves' (P) attorney argued that the testimony concerning the doctor's statements was offered to show Reeves' (P) mental anguish and his present mental state, rather than his physical condition. Hence, he argued, the question was whether the doctor made the statements, not whether they were true. The court found little support for this argument. It concluded that to allow a patient to testify as to statements made to him out of court by a doctor in order to show that he, the patient, was caused mental anguish as a result of the statements would open wide the door to hearsay evidence, without the opportunity afforded to cross-examine the declarant. The judgment is reversed.

EDITOR'S ANALYSIS: In a similar situation, the court in Brown v. Coca-Cola, 344 P. 2d 207 (1959), reached an opposite result. It held that a plaintiff's testimony as to statements made to him out of court by a physician were not hearsay since the statements were not offered to prove their truth or falsity, but merely to establish the plaintiff's state of mind which resulted from the physician's statements. In Kingdon v. Subrant, 158 N.W. 2d 863 (N.D. 1968), the court stated, "The theory of the hearsay rule is that when a human utterance is offered as evidence of the truth asserted in it, the credit of the assertor becomes the basis of the

inference and, therefore, the assertion can be received only when made upon the stand and subject to the test of cross-examination. However, where it becomes relevant to show that a certain statement or declaration was made, regardless of its truth or falsity, such proof is not hearsay and should be admitted. It is evidence of what is sometimes called a verbal or operative fact."

[For more information on admissibility of out-of-court statements, see Casenote Law Outline on Evidence, Chapter 9, § IV, Hearsay Defined.]

QUICKNOTES
HEARSAY - An out-of-court statement made by a person other than the witness testifying at trial that is offered in order to prove the truth of the matter asserted.

OUT-OF-COURT STATEMENT - A statement made outside of the proceeding and generally considered hearsay since opposing counsel's opportunity to cross-examine the declarant regarding the statement has been denied.

STATE OF MIND – A person's intent in performing a particular act.

NOTES:

HICKEY v. SETTLEMIER
Accused animal shooter (P) v. Defamer (D)
Or. Sup. Ct., 318 Or. 196, 864 P.21d 372 (1993).

NATURE OF CASE: Appeal of a suit for defamation.

FACT SUMMARY: Settlemier (D) made two videotaped statements about Hickey (P) that were potentially defamatory, and had a third such statement attributed to her by the reporter that taped the other statements.

CONCISE RULE OF LAW: Multiple hearsay is admissible provided that each level of hearsay satisfies an exception to the hearsay rule.

FACTS: The television news magazine "20/20" aired a program in which Settlemier (D) accused her neighbor, Hickey (P), of shooting animals not suitable for resale and housing other animals in poor conditions on his property. The reporter for the segment also related that Settlemier (D) was certain that Hickey (P) was dealing in stolen pets. Settlemier (D) denied ever saying that. Hickey (P) filed a suit for defamation on the basis of the three statements and attempted to use the videotape of the program as evidence that the statements had been made. An appeal followed.

ISSUE: Is multiple hearsay admissible if each level of hearsay satisfies an exception to the hearsay rule?

HOLDING AND DECISION: (Peterson, J.) Yes. Multiple hearsay is admissible provided that each level of hearsay satisfies an exception to the hearsay rule. Unless an exception to the hearsay rule exists for both the reporter's statement in this case and the comment that the reporter claims to have heard, a videotape of the reporter relating an off-camera statement is inadmissible to establish publication. Out-of-court statements are generally inadmissible as hearsay unless a hearsay exception exists. If the out-of-court statement relates another statement, then an avenue for admission must be found for both the out-of-court statement and the comment it purports to relate. One nonhearsay category exists for statements that have legal significance. If the out-of-court statement is offered as evidence that the statement took place, rather than as proof of the fact asserted in the statement, the statement is admissible as a verbal act. Thus the statements made directly by Settlemier (D) on the videotape are not hearsay. The comment allegedly made by Settlemier (D) to the reporter about stolen pets also had legal significance; the act of making a defamatory statement is the issue, not the truth of the statement. Thus the statement attributed to Settlemier (D) is nonhearsay. However, the videotape of the reporter's statement is offered to prove its truth, that Settlemier (D) said exactly what was reported. Thus, while Settlemier's (D) statement could have been admitted had it been taped, the reporter's taped recounting of the statement is inadmissible hearsay.

EDITOR'S ANALYSIS: Words with legal significance carve out a substantial exception to the hearsay rule. Defamatory statements are one of the clearest examples, but others are harder to identify. For example, testimony relating an out-of-court statement to a plaintiff, warning of a slippery puddle, appears to be hearsay, offered to prove the contents of the warning. But the warning also has legal significance, tending to prove that due care was exercised by warning of a known hazard. An attorney must be prepared to argue whether a statement is offered to prove its contents or merely to prove that the statement was uttered at all.

[For more information on legally operative conduct and hearsay within hearsay, see Casenote Law Outline on Evidence, Chapter 9, § IV, Hearsay Defined; § VI, "Multiple Hearsay."]

QUICKNOTES
DEFAMATION - An intentional false publication, communicated publicly in either oral or written form, subjecting a person to scorn, hatred or ridicule, or injuring him or her in relation to his or her occupation or business.

NOTES:

BANKS v. STATE

Murder suspect (D) v. State (P)

Md. Ct. App., 92 Md. App. 422, 608 A.2d 1249 (1992).

NATURE OF CASE: Appeal of a conviction for murder.

FACT SUMMARY: Banks (D) was convicted of murder after out-of-court statements about her violent nature, allegedly made by the decedent, were admitted as verbal acts.

CONCISE RULE OF LAW: Statements offered, not to prove the truth of the matter asserted therein, but as circumstantial evidence of the declarant's state of mind, are admissible nonhearsay when relevant.

FACTS: Banks (D) was accused of fatally stabbing her boyfriend, McDonald. At trial, Banks (D) testified that McDonald was abusive, and that she was defending herself when she stabbed him. Several witnesses corroborated Banks' (D) testimony of past abuse. However, the State (P) offered testimony from McDonald's relatives that McDonald had expressed fear of Banks (D). Police officers testified that on several domestic dispute calls, McDonald had told them that he had been assaulted by Banks (D). Banks (D) was convicted. She appealed.

ISSUE: Are statements offered as circumstantial evidence of the declarant's state of mind admissible nonhearsay when relevant?

HOLDING AND DECISION: (Motz, J.) Yes. Statements offered, not to prove the truth of the matter asserted therein, but rather to show circumstantial evidence of the declarant's state of mind, are admissible nonhearsay when relevant. Once a determination has been made that the testimony is not excludable as hearsay, its relevance and risk of prejudice must still be evaluated. Here, McDonald's statements of fear to his relatives fall within a nonhearsay category as evidence of his state of mind. However, the state of mind of McDonald is not relevant to determining whether Banks (D) committed the crime, or whether Banks (D) was a battered woman. Due to the highly prejudicial nature of the testimony, the conviction is reversed.

EDITOR'S ANALYSIS: There are cases where a victim's state of mind would be relevant in a murder trial. If the defendant's defense included the argument that the victim committed suicide, then statements of the victim's emotional condition would be admissible and relevant. Put another way, just because testimony falls within an exception to hearsay exclusion does not mean that the admissibility of the evidence has been decided. It must still be relevant and not unduly prejudicial.

[For more information on admissible hearsay and other exclusionary rules, see Casenote Law Outline on Evidence, Chapter 10, § XVI, Admissible Hearsay and Other Exclusionary Rules.]

QUICKNOTES

DECLARANT - Any human speaker who is the source of offered testimony, often hearsay spoken outside of court.

RELEVANT EVIDENCE - Evidence having any tendency to prove or disprove a disputed fact.

NOTES:

UNITED STATES v. REYES
Federal government (P) v. Smuggling co-conspiritor (D)
18 F.3d 65 (2d Cir. 1994).

NATURE OF CASE: Appeal of a conviction for conspiracy to import cocaine.

FACT SUMMARY: A government agent was allowed to testify that during interviews with captured drug smugglers, Stein (D) was indentified by the smugglers as a co-conspirator.

CONCISE RULE OF LAW: Hearsay admissible under an exception to hearsay exclusion must also be both relevant and not so unfairly prejudicial as to outweigh its probative value.

FACTS: Customs agents identified a ship on which cocaine was being smuggled into the country. After capturing two individuals whose van contained scuba gear capable of removing the drugs from the ship, other co-conspirators were identified, including Stein (D). At trial, an agent testified that during her questioning of the first two smugglers, they identified Stein (D) as a co-conspirator. While the statements of the two were never directly quoted, Stein's (D) counsel raised a hearsay objection. The government (P) contended that it was offering the agent's statements as background, to show the agent's state of mind and not for the truth of the matter asserted. The testimony was admitted. Other testimonial evidence of the same character was introduced and admitted over objections. Stein (D) was convicted; he appealed on the basis of the evidentiary rulings.

ISSUE: Must hearsay admissible under an exception to hearsay exclusion also be both relevant and not so unfairly prejudicial as to outweigh its probative value?

HOLDING AND DECISION: (Leval, J.) Yes. Hearsay admissible under an exception to hearsay exclusion must also be both relevant and not so unfairly prejudicial as to outweigh its probative value. Testimonial evidence that appears to be hearsay can, at times, be admitted to show the investigator's state of mind at the time. But such evidence must be relevant. And once found relevant, the risk of unfair prejudice must not be so great as to outweigh any probative value of the evidence. Here, virtually every variable argues against receipt of the evidence. First, the agent's state of mind during the investigation was not particularly relevant. Second, Stein (D) had offered no evidence opening the door to rebuttal. The agent's reasons for investigating Stein (D) had not been questioned. Third, the prejudicial nature of the evidence goes right to the core issue in the case; the issue was whether Stein (D) was a co-conspirator. Even without a direct quote, the agent allowed the testimony of complicity to be heard by the jury. Finally, Stein (D) was not accorded the opportunity to cross-examine the other smugglers.

The admission of such prejudicial testimony going to the core issue of the case was error. Reversed.

EDITOR'S ANALYSIS: Other criminal cases have allowed similar testimony and have been upheld on appeal. See, e.g., United States v. Walker, 636 F.2d 194 (8th Cir. 1980). But in those cases, the testimony focused on a confidential informant providing information that caused further investigation by the officer. Such testimony did not directly indicate that the defendant had been identified as the perpetrator of a crime. Rather, the testimony only explained the next actions of the officer.

[For more information on admissible hearsay and other exclusionary rules, see Casenote Law Outline on Evidence, Chapter 10, § XVI, Admissible Hearsay and Other Exclusionary Rules.]

QUICKNOTES

RELEVANT EVIDENCE - Evidence having any tendency to prove or disprove a disputed fact.

TRUTH OF THE MATTER – A term of art used in evidence that renders out of court statements inadmissible to prove the truth of those statements.

STATE OF MIND – A person's intent in performing a particular act.

NOTES:

WRIGHT v. DOE D. TATHAM
Contests that will is valid (D) v. Contests will as not valid (P)
H.L., 5 Clark & Fennelly 670 (1838).

NATURE OF CASE: Action to contest a will on the ground of the testator's incompetency to make a will.

FACT SUMMARY: At trial letters written to the testator, one of which concerned business, were introduced to demonstrate the testator's competency to make a will.

CONCISE RULE OF LAW: Written or oral evidence of the opinion of an out-of-court declarant which is not made subject to an oath or cross-examination is inadmissible as hearsay.

FACTS: Tatham (P) contested Marsden's, the testator, will on the grounds of Marsden's mental incompetency. At the trial, certain letters written to Marsden between 1784 and 1799, one of which concerned business matters, were rejected as inadmissible. Wright (D) wanted to introduce the letters to show that the writers of the letters treated Marsden as a sane man. Marsden executed his will in 1822 and a codicil in 1822.

ISSUE: Are letters expressing the opinion of out-of-court declarants not subject to oath or cross-examination inadmissible as hearsay?

HOLDING AND DECISION: (Coleridge, J.) Yes. The general rule is that evidence must be given under oath, and this case does not fall within any of the established exceptions to that rule. The letters express the writers' opinions which were formed from facts which were not before the jury. The issue of competency is a question of fact to be decided by the jury on the basis of the evidence of the facts before it not on the basis of opinions formed by facts which are not known to the jury. Further, there is no opportunity for Tatham (P), the opposing party, to test by cross-examination the foundation upon which the opinions in the letter rest. Without the writers of the letters being present to testify as to what factors shaped their opinions of Marsden's competency, the letters are inadmissible. Further, the issue in this case is not what Marsden's mental capacity was reputed to be, but what it actually was. The letters are inadmissible as to this issue. Finally, the letters are not made admissible by the reason that the writers do not merely express their opinions in the letters but prove their belief of it by acting upon it to the extent of sending the letters. The opinion of a person is inadmissible. The act which proves that the person believed the truth of the opinion, and which is irrelevant to the issue, except for that purpose, cannot render the act admissible.

EDITOR'S ANALYSIS: This landmark case held non-assertive conduct to be excludable as hearsay. In subsequent cases, the hearsay issue has often gone unrecognized, especially where the conduct in question was nonverbal. When the issue has been raised the rulings have been divided. The current trend seems to oppose exclusion.

[For more information on hearsay evidence, see Casenote Law Outline on Evidence, Chapter 9, § IV, Hearsay Defined.]

QUICKNOTES
DECLARANT - Any human speaker who is the source of offered testimony, often hearsay spoken outside of court.

HEARSAY - An out-of-court statement made by a person other than the witness testifying at trial that is offered in order to prove the truth of the matter asserted.

CROSS EXAMINATION - The interrogation of a witness by an adverse party either to further inquire as to the subject matter of the direct examination or to call into question the witness' credibility.

NOTES:

HEADLEY v. TILGHMAN
Suspected drug trafficker (D) v. State (P)
53 F.3d 472 (2d Cir. 1995).

NATURE OF CASE: Appeal of a granted petition for a writ of habeas corpus after state appellate court affirmed a conviction for possession of narcotics and conspiracy to sell narcotics.

FACT SUMMARY: Out-of-court statements made by an unidentified individual were admitted when an officer described returning a beeper page made to Headley (D), a suspected drug trafficker who had just been arrested.

CONCISE RULE OF LAW: Out-of-court statements made by an unidentified individual can be admitted as nonhearsay if they provide circumstantial evidence of the defendant's knowledge and intent to commit the charged crime, and do not directly assert the issue of the case as fact.

FACTS: Headley (D) was arrested after a search of a friend's apartment where he was staying. Drug paraphernalia and cash were found. During processing at the police station, Headley's (D) beeper received a call. Officer Manzi returned the call, and a man said, "Are you up? Can I come by? Are you ready?" When Manzi spoke, the man hung up. Headley (D) was charged with possession of narcotics and conspiracy to sell narcotics. At trial, Manzi's testimony of his exchange on the phone was admitted as the statements of a co-conspirator made in furtherance of conspiracy, over defense objections. Headley (D) was convicted and appealed, but the conviction was affirmed. Headley (D) then sought a writ of habeas corpus from the federal district court, and his petition was granted. The petition was appealed.

ISSUE: Can out-of-court statements made by an unidentified indvidual be admitted as nonhearsay if they provide circumstantial evidence of the defendant's knowledge and intent to commit the charged crime, and do not directly assert the issue of the case as fact?

HOLDING AND DECISION: (McLaughlin, J.) Yes. Out-of-court statments made by an unidentified individual can be admitted as nonhearsay if they provide circumstantial evidence of the defendant's knowledge and intent to commit the charged crime, and do not directly assert the issue of the case as fact. Just because a statement is used as circumstantial evidence of a conspiracy does not mean that the statement must be analyzed under the co-conspirator statement exception to the hearsay rule. In this case, the statements were used as circumstantial evidence that Headley (D) was known as a drug dealer. The statement did not state as fact that he was a dealer; rather, the statement showed another individual's belief that Headley (D) was a dealer. The officer's interpretations of the statement could readily have been discounted by the jury as an incorrect analysis of the caller's

meaning. It is not necessary to even reach the co-conspirator exception to the hearsay rule, as the testimony was not hearsay. Reversed and remanded with instructions to deny the petition.

EDITOR'S ANALYSIS: There is much debate among commentators as to how implied assertations should be classified. Some commentators argue for a case-by-case approach, reviewing each statement for the risk of prejudice. Other commentators suggest that so long as the statement is not a direct assertion, the implied information falls outside the hearsay rule. Finally, some have suggested that the context of the situation should control; calls seeking drugs, for example, would be viewed primarily as actions rather than as assertions.

[For more information on co-conspirator admissions, see Casenote Law Outline on Evidence, Chapter 9, § VIII, Exemption: Statements by Parties.]

QUICKNOTES
CIRCUMSTANTIAL EVIDENCE - Evidence that, though not directly observed, supports the inference of principal facts.

NOTES:

KINDER v. COMMONWEALTH
Convicted thief (D) v. State (P)
Ky. Ct. App., 306 S.W. 2d 265 (1957).

NATURE OF CASE: Appeal from conviction for grand larceny.

FACT SUMMARY: At trial, police officers were allowed to testify, over Kinder's (D) objection, that they were led to the location of stolen property by a five-year-old child who did not testify.

CONCISE RULE OF LAW: Testimony as to conduct of an out-of-court declarant, which is not asserted testimonially, is made subject to cross-examination, and is based upon personal knowledge, is not hearsay.

FACTS: At Kinder's (D) grand larceny trial, a coal company vice-president testified to the loss of certain property. He testified that he recognized part of the property in a truck which was being operated by Kinder's (D) father. The truck was later stopped by police officers, but the property was not in it. The property was later found by the officers underneath a shack near to where the property had first been recognized. Over Kinder's (D) objection, the officers testified that a five-year-old child (Kinder's (D) nephew) had directed them to the location of the property. The officers were not permitted to say what the child had said. At the time of the trial, the child was in another state.

ISSUE: Is testimony as to conduct of an out-of-court declarant, which is not asserted testimonially, is made subject to cross-examination, and is based upon personal knowledge, hearsay?

HOLDING AND DECISION: (Montgumery, J.) No. Hearsay is evidence which derives its value not solely from the credit to be given to the witness upon the stand, but, in part, from the veracity and competency of some other person. In this case, the statements objected to by Kinder (D) were made subject to cross-examination and were based upon personal knowledge. The officers were testifying to what they had seen and heard. Further, no merit is found in Kinder's (D) objection to the testimony because of the child's age since the child did not testify, and also because the child's age would not necessarily have rendered his testimony incompetent. The competency of an infant-witness is determined by the witness' intelligence. The judgment of conviction is affirmed.

EDITOR'S ANALYSIS: This case presents the question of whether the hearsay rule will exclude evidence of conduct, as well as statements. Under the traditional common law definition of hearsay "statement" included nonassertive conduct. Non assertive conduct as hearsay utilizes hearsay inferences in that the conduct is offered as a basis for the inferences first, of the actor's belief and, second, that the facts were in accord with the belief. The non assertive conduct in this case was the Kinder child's directing the police officers to the stolen property. Kentucky does not recognize such non-assertive conduct as hearsay.

[For more information on nonassertive conduct as hearsay, see Casenote Law Outline on Evidence, Chapter 9, § II, "Statement" Defined.]

NOTES:

UNITED STATES v. MUSCATO
Federal government (P) v. Illegal gunmaker (D)
534 F. Supp. 969 (E.D.N.Y. 1982).

NATURE OF CASE: Motion for a new trial after a conviction for producing illegal firearms.

FACT SUMMARY: Muscato (D) lent Gollender a pistol while he used Gollender's pen gun as a prototype for mass production; later, Gollender's out-of-court identification of the pistol was introduced as evidence.

CONCISE RULE OF LAW: If an extrajudicial declaration comports with the definition of hearsay and does not fall within any specific exception, it may still be admitted if there are circumstantial guarantees of trustworthiness, as specified by Federal Rule of Evidence 803(24).

FACTS: Gollender possessed a gun shaped like a pen. Muscato (D) was shown the pen gun by others so he could determine if it could be replicated. Muscato (D) agreed to make copies, so he lent Gollender a pistol while the pen gun was serving as a model. Gollender placed a label on the gun to describe the operation of the safety; he returned the pistol when his pen gun was no longer needed. Later, Muscato (D) and others were arrested. Gollender described the pistol he had been loaned during a debriefing by government officials. Gollender was shown the gun that had been seized in the arrest, and he identified it based upon the remnants of his label. At trial, an agent testified as to Gollender's out-of-court description of the gun prior to being shown the seized pistol; Muscato's (D) attorney objected to the testimony as hearsay. Muscato (D) was convicted; he filed a motion for a new trial.

ISSUE: If an extrajudicial declaration comports with the definition of hearsay and does not fall within any specific exception, may it still be admitted if there are circumstantial guarantees of trustworthiness?

HOLDING AND DECISION: (Weinstein, C.J.) Yes. If an extrajudicial declaration comports with the definition of hearsay and does not fall within any specific exception, it may still be admitted if there are circumstantial guarantees of trustworthiness, as specified by Federal Rule of Evidence 803(24). The Federal Rules of Evidence specify twenty-three specific classes of exceptions to hearsay exclusion. The twenty-fourth category, the catch-all exception, covers situations not listed but having similar circumstantial guarantees of trustworthiness. In this case, Gollender's testimony had specific indicators of reliability. First, he described the pistol before it was shown to him. Second, Gollender identified the pistol again in court. Finally, he was available for examination in court. Gollender's out-of-court statement, offered essentially to prove that the pistol shown in court was given to him by Muscato (D), has sufficient hallmarks of reliability to allow admission of the statement under Rule 803(24). Motion for a new trial denied.

EDITOR'S ANALYSIS: The specific exceptions to the hearsay rule listed in the Federal Rules of Evidence were not intended as exhaustive. Rather, they indicate the majority of all situations where an exception would properly apply. However, the "catch-all" category of 803(24) allows for hearsay to be admitted at any time where it has the same level of reliability as the specific categories.

[For more information on "wildcard" hearsay exceptions, see Casenote Law Outline on Evidence, Chapter 10, § X, The "Wildcard" Exceptions.]

QUICKNOTES
EXTRA JUDICIAL DECLARATION - Outside of court: declaration taking place outside of formal proceedings.

NOTES:

ROWE v. FARMER'S INSURANCE CO. INC.
Owner of destroyed vehicle (P) v. Insurer (D)
Mo. Sup. Ct., en banc, 699 S.W.2d 423 (1985).

NATURE OF CASE: Appeal of award of damages in action to collect on an insurance policy.

FACT SUMMARY: Farmer's Insurance (D) was not permitted to introduce a prior inconsistent statement of its own witness for impeachment or as substantive evidence.

CONCISE RULE OF LAW: A party may use a prior inconsistent statement as substantive evidence if the declarant is available for cross-examination.

FACTS: Rowe's (P) vehicle was destroyed by fire. His insurer, Farmer's (D), believed that Rowe (P) had burned it intentionally and had refused to indemnify. Rowe (P) brought an action to collect the proceeds. At trial, Carroll, an acquaintance of Rowe (P), was expected by Farmer's (D) to testify that Rowe (P) had told him that he intended to burn the car. This was based on an earlier statement. However, he denied ever saying this. The trial court did not allow Farmer's (D) to introduce the inconsistent statement. The jury returned a verdict in favor or Rowe (P), and Farmer's (D) appealed.

ISSUE: May a party use a prior inconsistent statement as substantive evidence if the declarant is available for cross-examination?

HOLDING AND DECISION: (Welliver, J.) Yes. A party may use a prior inconsistent statement as substantive evidence if the declarant is available for cross-examination. The fact is that a prior statement made by a witness is often more reliable and believable than a statement made at trial. As time passes, memories fade. Further, witnesses will tend to fill in gaps in memory with material that may not be true. In short, the search for the truth will be aided if prior inconsistent statements are allowed to be used as substantive evidence. However, fairness demands that the party opposing the statement be allowed to cross-examine. As the statement itself cannot be cross-examined, the party intending to introduce the statement must produce the declarant at trial. Here, Farmer's (D) was not permitted to introduce an important prior statement, and the witness was available. It was error to exclude the statement. Reversed.

CONCURRENCE: (Blackmar, J.) One can easily disagree with the dissent's assertion that there may be no adequate cross-examination of an out-of-court statement. There is ample room for exploration if the declarant is available.

CONCURRENCE: (Donnelly, J.) The rule adopted here would be unconstitutional if applied against criminal defendants.

DISSENT: (Billings, J.) Prior out-of-court statements are often made in an offhand manner, with the declarant not realizing its future import. Also, they can often be taken out of context. Most importantly, the majority's assertions notwithstanding, it is not possible to adequately cross-examine an out-of-court statement, even if the declarant is in court.

EDITOR'S ANALYSIS: The rule here is still in the minority of American jurisdictions. However, the trend appears to be toward adopting it. The arguments against the rule are basically those contained in the dissent, particularly the cross-examination argument.

[For more information on use of prior inconsistent statements, see Casenote Law Outline on Evidence, Chapter 9, § VII, Exemption: Prior Statements of Witnesses.]

QUICKNOTES
IMPEACHMENT - The discrediting of a witness by offering evidence to show that the witness lacks credibility.

DECLARANT - Any human speaker who is the source of offered testimony, often hearsay spoken outside of court.

CROSS EXAMINATION - The interrogation of a witness by an adverse party either to further inquire as to the subject matter of the direct examination or to call into question the witness' credibility.

SUBSTANTIVE EVIDENCE – Evidence that is admitted to prove a disputed fact.

PRIOR INCONSISTENT STATEMENT – A statement made before a witness' testimony that contradicts such testimony and which may be admitted in order to impeach the witness; the prior statements may not be admitted, however, to prove the truth of the matter asserted.

NOTES:

CALIFORNIA v. GREEN
State (P) v. Seller of marijuana
399 U.S. 149 (1970).

NATURE OF CASE: Criminal action for furnishing marijuana to a minor.

FACT SUMMARY: Porter, arrested for selling marijuana to an undercover police officer, identified Green (D) as his supplier.

CONCISE RULE OF LAW: Testimony of a witness at a preliminary hearing, subject to full cross-examination at that time, can be introduced as substantive evidence against defendant, and does not violate defendant's right of confrontation.

FACTS: While in custody, Porter, a minor charged with selling marijuana, said that Green (D) had personally delivered the "grass" to him. One week later, at Green's (D) preliminary hearing, Porter testified that Green (D) had merely indicated where Porter was to pick up the "grass." Two months later, at Green's (D) trial, Porter claimed he could not remember how he had obtained the "grass," claiming that he had been on LSD at the time. Green (D) claimed that he was denied his right of confrontation because Porter's lack of memory made it impossible adequately to cross-examine him.

ISSUE: Is it a denial of a defendant's right of confrontation to introduce testimony of a witness at a previous hearing, when the witness, though present in court, cannot be adequately cross-examined because he doesn't remember?

HOLDING AND DECISION: (White, J.) No. If there was opportunity for full cross-examination at the previous hearing, testimony of a witness at that preliminary hearing can be introduced as substantive evidence against the defendant without violating the Sixth Amendment right of confrontation. This case rejects the reasoning in the California case, People v. Johnson, 68 Cal.2d 646, 441 P.2d 111 (1968), which had a similar fact situation. The court in that case had reversed a conviction because of the introduction of prior statements of a witness which were not subject to cross-examination when originally made. The court here holds that the confrontation clause is not violated when the declarant/witness is subject to cross-examination at the time the statements are being introduced into evidence. The main danger in belated cross-examination substituted for timely cross-examination is that false testimony is apt to "harden." Here, however, the witness repudiates his earlier testimony. The court finds no confrontation problem when declarant is actually in court and subject to being asked to defend or explain the inconsistency between his prior and present statements. Even if declarant Porter had been unavailable at the trial, the court would have admitted the earlier testimony since it had been given in circumstances affording an opportunity for full cross-

examination. Since, if Porter had died, his testimony would have been admissible, the fact that he is alive and in court does not change its admissibility. The question of the admissibility of Porter's statements while in custody, on the other hand, was remanded to the state court: the record on this point was inadequate on the question of reliability. Also, there may be a harmless error question, more appropriate for the state court to decide.

CONCURRENCE: (Harlan, J.) "Confrontation" only requires production of an available witness, not his cross-examination. Incorporating a "cross-examination" right into the Fourteenth Amendment would result in a constitutionalization of hearsay rules, and would limit the flexibility of the States in this "evolving area of the law." The case should be remanded to determine the reliability of Porter's statements while in custody, and the sufficiency of evidence to sustain a conviction "beyond a reasonable doubt."

DISSENT: (Brennan, J.) When a witness cannot (or will not) testify about events reflected in preliminary hearing testimony, defendant cannot effectively challenge those prior assertions.

EDITOR'S ANALYSIS: This case affirms the constitutionality of California Evidence Code, § 1235 (Inconsistent Statement Exception to the Hearsay Rule), effective 1967. The California case of People v. Johnson had excluded prior statements unless the declarant had been subject to cross-examination when the statements were originally made. The California Supreme Court in Green had attempted to extend this ban even to cases in which cross-examination had been effected, if the witness/declarant could not effectively be cross-examined at the time the statements were being introduced. The United States Supreme Court rejects both bans, thus finding Ev. Code, § 1235, constitutional with respect to the confrontation clause. It should be noted that a result of this case is that the use of prior inconsistent statements is not limited to impeaching a witness, but that such statements also can be used as substantive evidence.

[For more information on the Rights of Confrontation Rule, see Casenote Law Outline on Evidence, Chapter 9, § X, Hearsay and the Right of Confrontation.]

QUICKNOTES

CROSS EXAMINATION - The interrogation of a witness by an adverse party either to further inquire as to the subject matter of the direct examination or to call into question the witness' credibility.

DECLARANT - Any human speaker who is the source of offered testimony, often hearsay spoken outside of court.

SUBSTANTIVE EVIDENCE – Evidence that is admitted to prove a disputed fact.

UNITED STATES v. McKEON
Federal government (P) v. Firearms regulations violator (D)
738 F.2d 26 (2d Cir. 1984).

NATURE OF CASE: Appeal of conviction for violation of federal firearms regulations.

FACT SUMMARY: McKeon (D) was convicted of a firearms violation after the Government (P) was allowed to introduce a portion of the opening statement of a prior trial which had ended in a mistrial.

CONCISE RULE OF LAW: Argument from a prior trial may be used as evidence if it involves an assertion of fact inconsistent with factual assertions in the subsequent trial.

FACTS: McKeon (D) was accused of violating federal firearms regulations. His first two trials ended in mistrials. In the second trial, McKeon's (D) attorney asserted in his opening statement that McKeon's (D) wife had not made certain photocopies. In the third trial, aware of an imminent change in the Government's (P) strategy, the attorney changed this factual assertion. The trial court allowed the Government (P) to introduce the factual assertions of the prior opening statement to show the change between the two opening statements. McKeon (D) appealed.

ISSUE: May argument from a prior trial be used as evidence if it involves an assertion of fact inconsistent with factual assertions in the subsequent trial?

HOLDING AND DECISION: (Winter, J.) Yes. Argument from a prior trial may be used as evidence if it involves an assertion of fact inconsistent with factual assertions in the subsequent trial. While little authority on this point exists, this court sees little material difference between the situation at hand and a party's right to introduce changes in pleadings to point out inconsistencies. However, when dealing with argument there are issues of special concern. The use of prior argument can consume substantial time in pursuit of marginal matters. Second, inferences drawn may be inaccurate or unfair. Third, free use of prior argument could deter robust advocacy. Fourth, explanation of a seeming inconsistency could seriously affect other aspects of the defense. Finally, admissibility of argument could lead to attorney disqualification. Therefore, free use of prior argument cannot be condoned. Only when the argument makes factual assertions regarding material issues should the evidence be admitted. Here, the opening statements made contrasting factual assertions, and therefore the prior opening statement was admitted properly, to show the change in the defense's position. Affirmed.

EDITOR'S ANALYSIS: The issue here comes under the rubric of authorized admissions. Specifically, the question arose as to the extent to which a defendant is bound by his attorney's prior statements. The court made as a dividing line factual assertions as opposed to legal argument or factual speculation.

COLE v. COLE
Wife of decedent (P) v. Children of decedent (D)
Ga. Ct. App., 205 Ga. App. 332, 422 S.E.2d 230 (1992).

NATURE OF CASE: Review of appeal of a probate court ruling awarding one-half a marital home to decedent's wife.

FACT SUMMARY: Over objections, Mrs. Cole (P), the decedent's second wife, testified that the decedent had told her that he would contribute to the purchase of their home once he was no longer obligated to pay child support, but not before.

CONCISE RULE OF LAW: A decedent's out-of-court declarations in disparagement of his title are admissible as a declaration against interest even where the testimony is offered by one who would benefit from admission.

FACTS: Mr. Cole died intestate. His second wife, Mrs. Cole (P), and the children (D) of his first marriage survived him. The probate court awarded only one-half interest in the home to Mrs. Cole (P). Mrs. Cole (P) appealed the ruling to the superior court. Mrs. Cole (P) testified that once she and the decedent were married, she sold her home and bought a new one with no help from the decedent. Over a hearsay objection, she testified that the decedent told her that he could not contribute to purchase of the property until his child support obligations from his first marriage ended. The jury awarded the entire home to Mrs. Cole (P). The children (D) appealed.

ISSUE: Are a decedent's out-of-court declarations in disparagement of his title admissible when offered by one who would benefit from admission?

HOLDING AND DECISION: (Carley, J.) Yes. A decedent's out-of-court declarations in disparagement of his title are admissible as a declaration against interest even where the testimony is offered by one who would benefit from admission. Declarations made by a person since deceased against his interest and not made with a view to pending litigation shall be admissible in evidence in any case. Here, Mr. Cole stated that he possessed no share of the property, a statement generally seen as against his pecuniary interests. That Mrs. Cole (P) would benefit from introduction of the evidence is irrelevant. The jury is free to evaluate her credibility and did so here. Affirmed.

EDITOR'S ANALYSIS: Note that it is the interests of the out-of-court declarant that must be evaluated. The credibility of the witness may be questioned by identifying the potential benefit to the witness. The presumption of reliability attached to statements against interest remains; credibility of the witness is another issue entirely.

[For more information on declarations against interest, see Casenote Law Outline on Evidence, Chapter 10, § XIV, Declarations Against Interest.]

TOME v. UNITED STATES

513 U.S. 150, 115 S. Ct. 696 (1995).

NATURE OF CASE: Appeal from conviction of felony sexual abuse of a child.

FACT SUMMARY: Tome (D), convicted of felony sexual abuse of a child, appealed, contending that the trial court abused its discretion by admitting out-of-court consistent statements made by his daughter to six prosecution witnesses who testified as to the nature of Tome's (D) sexual assaults on his daughter.

CONCISE RULE OF LAW: Fed. R. Evid. 801(d)(1)(B) permits prior consistent statements to be used for substantive purposes after the statements are admitted to rebut the existence of an improper influence or motive.

FACTS: Tome (D) was charged by the United States (P) with felony sexual abuse of his daughter, A.T., who was four years old at the time of the alleged crime. Tome (D) and the child's mother were divorced in 1988, and the mother was finally awarded custody in 1990. Thereafter, the mother contacted authorities with allegations that Tome (D) had committed sexual abuse against A.T. Tome (D) argued that A.T.'s allegations were concocted so that the child would not be returned to Tome (D) for visitation purposes. At trial, A.T. testified first for the United States (P). Thereafter, cross-examination took place over two trial days. On the first day, A.T. answered all questions placed to her. Under cross-examination, however, A.T. was questioned regarding her conversations with the prosecutor but was reluctant to discuss them. The United States (P) then produced six witnesses who testified about seven statements made by A.T. describing Tome's (D) sexual assaults upon her. A.T.'s out-of-court statements, recounted by these witnesses, were offered by the United States (P) under Fed. R. Evid. 801(d)(1)(B). The trial court admitted all of the statements over Tome's (D) objections, accepting the United State's (P) argument that they rebutted the implicit charges that A.T.'s testimony was motivated by a desire to live with her mother. Tome (D) was convicted and sentenced to twelve years' imprisonment. On appeal, the Tenth Circuit Court of Appeals affirmed, and Tome (D) again appealed, contending that the district court judge had abused his discretion in admitting A.T.'s out-of-court statements.

ISSUE: Does Fed. R. Evid. 801(d)(1)(B) permit prior consistent statements to be used for substantive purposes after the statements are admitted to rebut the existence of an improper motive?

HOLDING AND DECISION: (Kennedy, J.) Yes. Fed. R. Evid. 801(d)(1)(B) permits prior consistent statements to be used for substantive purposes after the statements are admitted to rebut the existence of an improper motive. The prevailing common law rule, before adoption of the Federal Rules of Evidence, was that a prior consistent statement introduced to rebut a charge of recent fabrication or improper influence or motive was admissible if the statement had been made before the alleged fabrication, influence, or motive came into being but inadmissible if made afterward. Rule 801 defines prior consistent statements as nonhearsay only if they are offered to rebut a charge of recent fabrication or improper influence or motive. Prior consistent statements may not be admitted to counter all forms of impeachment or to bolster the witness merely because she has been discredited. Here, the question is whether A.T.'s out-of-court statements rebutted the alleged link between her desire to be with her mother and her testimony, not whether they suggested that A.T.'s testimony was true. The Rule speaks of a party's rebutting an alleged motive, not bolstering the veracity of the story told. However, the requirement is that consistent statements must have been made before the alleged influence or motive to fabricate arose. The language of the Rule suggests that it was intended to carry over the common law premotive rule. If the Rule were to permit introduction of prior statements as substantive evidence to rebut every implicit charge that a witness' in-court testimony results from recent fabrication, improper influence, or motive, the whole emphasis of the trial could shift to the out-of-court statements rather than the in-court ones. In response to a rather weak charge that A.T.'s testimony was a fabrication so that she could stay with her mother, the United States (P) was allowed to present a parade of witnesses who did no more than recount A.T.'s detailed out-of-court statements to them. Although those statements might have been probative on the question of whether the alleged conduct had occurred, they shed minimal light on whether A.T. had the charged motive to fabricate. Reversed and remanded.

CONCURRENCE: (Scalia, J.) There was no need for the majority to discuss the Advisory Committee's Notes pertinent to Rule 801(d)(1)(B). The promulgated Rule says what it says, regardless of the intent of its drafters. While the Notes are persuasive scholarly commentaries concerning the meaning of the Rules, they bear no special authoritativeness as the work of the draftsmen. It is the words of the Rules that have been authoritatively adopted by this Court and by Congress.

Continued on next page.

DISSENT: (Breyer, J.) The basic issue here concerns not hearsay, but relevance. The majority believes that a hearsay-related rule, Fed. R. Evid. 801(d)(1)(B), codifies this absolute timing requirement. It does not. Rule 801(d)(1)(B) has nothing to do with relevance. Rather, that Rule carves out a subset of prior consistent statements that were formerly admissible only to rehabilitate a witness. It thus says that members of such a subset are "not hearsay." That is, if such a statement is admissible for a particular rehabilitative purpose, its proponent may use it substantively, for a hearsay purpose, as well. The Federal Rules do authorize a district court to allow (where probative in respect to rehabilitation) the use of postmotive prior consistent statements to rebut a charge of recent fabrication, improper influence, or motive.

EDITOR'S ANALYSIS: Justice Breyer, in his dissent, commented that prior consistent statements may rehabilitate a witness whose credibility has been questioned. Justice Breyer also cited Judge Friendly's opinion in United States v. Rubin, 609 F.2d 51 (2d Cir. 1979). In that case, Judge Friendly argued that Rule 801(d)(1)(B)'s timing requirement applied exclusively to those prior consistent statements offered for their truth after a challenge of recent fabrication or improper influence or motive. When used just to rehabilitate after other varieties of challenge and credibility, the statement is admissible under Rule 801(c) for a limited purpose of questioning credibility rather than for the truth of the statement. Friendly argued that Rule 801(d)(1)(B)'s timing restrictions were inapplicable. In these circumstances, no improper influence or motive is alleged, and the prior statement does not need to precede.

NOTES:

UNITED STATES v. OWENS

Federal government (P) v. Convicted murderer (D)

484 U.S. 554 (1988).

NATURE OF CASE: Appeal of conviction for attempted murder.

FACT SUMMARY: Owens (D) was convicted of attempted murder after victim Foster, while unable to identify Owens (D) in court, testified that he had earlier identified him.

CONCISE RULE OF LAW: A witness in a criminal trial may testify about an earlier identification even if he can no longer testify as to the basis for that identification.

FACTS: Foster, a prison guard, was severely beaten. While in the hospital, he identified Owens (D) as the attacker. He later lost independent recollection of the attack and could not explain the basis for his hospital identification. Over defense objection, Foster was allowed to testify regarding his hospital identification. Owens (D) was convicted and appealed. The Ninth Circuit reversed, holding that the Confrontation Clause barred such testimony. The Supreme Court granted review.

ISSUE: May a witness in a criminal trial testify about an earlier identification even if he can no longer testify as to the basis for that identification?

HOLDING AND DECISION: (Scalia, J.) Yes. A witness in a criminal trial may testify about an earlier identification even if he can no longer testify as to the basis for that identification. The Confrontation Clause of the Sixth Amendment has been read to require only the opportunity for effective cross-examination, not whatever sort of cross-examination the defense might wish. When a witness cannot recall the basis for an earlier identification, the opposing party already has a potent cross-examination tool, as a forgetful witness has inherent credibility problems. It has long been held that an expert may give an opinion even if he has forgotten the basis therefor, and this situation is no different. Here, Owens (D) had the opportunity to attack Foster on the basis of his forgetfulness, and that was all the Confrontation Clause required. Reversed.

DISSENT: (Brennan, J.) Had Foster died and the individual to whom he made his identification attempted to testify as to the identification, he surely would have been precluded therefrom. Foster, having forgotten how he identified Owens (D), was no more susceptible to effective cross-examination than the investigator to whom he made the identification. In both instances, effective cross-examination was denied.

EDITOR'S ANALYSIS: Owens (D) also contended that Foster's testimony violated the Federal Rules of Evidence. Specifically, Owens (D) contended that Fed. R. Evid. 801(d)(1)(C)'s exclusion from hearsay of a prior identification required that the declarant be subject to cross-examination. Foster, stated Owens (D), was not so subject due to his memory loss. The court disagreed for the same reasons noted in the discussion on the Confrontation Clause.

[For more information on the Confrontation Clause, see Casenote Law Outline on Evidence, Chapter 9, § X, Hearsay and the Right of Confrontation.]

QUICKNOTES

CONFRONTATION CLAUSE - A provision in the Sixth Amendment to the United States Constitution that an accused in a criminal action has the right to confront the witnesses against him, including the right to attend the trial and to cross-examine witnesses called on behalf of the prosecution.

DECLARANT - Any human speaker who is the source of offered testimony, often hearsay spoken outside of court.

NOTES:

BILL v. FARM BUREAU LIFE INS. CO.

Father of deceased insured (P) v. Insurer (D)

Iowa Sup. Ct., 254 Iowa 1215, 119 N.W.2d 768 (1963).

NATURE OF CASE: Action to compel the payment of death benefits on a life insurance policy.

FACT SUMMARY: The court refused to allow testimony of a doctor that after the deceased had died, his father, Mr. Bill (P), shook his head indicating a negative answer to the question, "Is there any doubt that your son committed suicide?"

CONCISE RULE OF LAW: A gesture such as shaking your head that has a universal meaning is an admission as much as specific words with the same meaning, and it is a question for the jury to determine the meaning of the gesture.

FACTS: Bill (P), the father of the deceased, had taken out a life insurance policy on the life of his son with the Farm Bureau Life Ins. Co. (D). The policy provided that no benefits would be paid if the cause of death was suicide. Bill's (P) son's body was found with a noose around his neck, and Farm Bureau (D) refused to pay the death benefits under the policy because they contended that the son committed suicide. On this issue of suicide, the court refused to admit testimony of the medical examiner that he had a conversation with Bill (P), and when he asked him if there was any doubt that his son had committed suicide he shook his head in a negative manner.

ISSUE: Is the shaking of a head in response to a question so indefinite a response as to give rise to conjecture, and thereby not be admissible as an admission?

HOLDING AND DECISION: (Thompson, J.) No. A gesture such as the shaking of a head, that is subject to a universal meaning, is admissible as an admission if it fits the other requirements, and it is a question of fact for the jury to determine if any unusual meaning was meant by the gesture. If Bill (P) admitted that his son had killed himself, it would be admissible as an admission, and the fact that he indicated that this was his belief by shaking his head in response to a question rather than affirmatively stating does not change the admissibility. Shaking the head is universally recognized as meaning "no," and while it may be also used to indicate confusion or bewilderment, it is up to the jury to determine the meaning of the gesture, and it was, therefore, error to refuse to admit the testimony and thereby prevent the jury from learning of the gesture.

EDITOR'S ANALYSIS: Admissions are words or acts of a party opponent, or of his predecessor or representative, offered as evidence against him. As specific words were not spoken, the type of admission that is present in this case is an adoptive admission, or conduct that indicates that the party agrees that a statement of the someone else is truthful. In this case, by shaking his head, Bill (P) indicated that he believed his son committed suicide. When a party affirmatively acts to indicate his assent to the truth of a statement, such as here, it is an express admission and, therefore, is an exception to the hearsay rule.

[For more information on nonverbal conduct, see Casenote Law Outline on Evidence, Chapter 9, § II, "Statement" Defined.]

NOTES:

MAHLANDT v. WILD CANID SURVIVAL & RESEARCH CENTER, INC.

Boy bitten by wolf (P) v. Animal research center (D)

588 F.2d 626 (8th Cir. 1978).

NATURE OF CASE: Appeal from denial of damages for negligence.

FACT SUMMARY: The trial court hearing Daniel Mahlandt's (P) civil action against the Center (D) refused to let into evidence certain conclusionary statements against interest made by an employee of the Center (D).

CONCISE RULE OF LAW: Federal Rule of Evidence 801(d)(2)(D) makes statements made by agents within the scope of their employment admissible, and there is no implied requirement that the declarant have personal knowledge of the facts underlying his statement.

FACTS: Nobody actually saw what happened, but young Daniel Mahlandt (P), who was just under four years old at the time, wound up in the enclosure where Mr. Poos (D), the Director of the Center (D), kept Sophie, a wolf belonging to the Center (D) but which he took around to schools and institutions where he showed films and gave programs regarding the nature of wolves. Sophie had been raised at the children's zoo and had there acted in a good-natured and stable manner while in contact with thousands of children. Sophie apparently bit Mahlandt (P), causing him serious injuries. There was some evidence indicating that the child might have crawled under the fence and thereby received his injuries. An offer was made to disprove this theory by introducing evidence that Poos (D) had left a note on the door of the Center's (D) president saying the wolf had bitten a child and that he had made a similar statement later that day when he met the president and was asked what happened. There was also an offer to introduce minutes of a meeting of the Center's (D) board that reflected a great deal of discussion about the legal aspects of the incident of Sophie biting the child. None of this was let into evidence, the judge reasoning that in each case those making the statements had no personal knowledge of the facts and the statements were thus hearsay. A judgment for the Center (D) followed.

ISSUE: Is it necessary to show that the agent had personal knowledge of the facts underlining his statement for a statement made by an agent within the scope of his employment to be admissible under Federal Rule of Evidence 801 (d)(2)(D)?

HOLDING AND DECISION: (Van Sickle, J.) No. Federal Rule of Evidence 801(d)(2)(D) makes admissible statements made by agents within the scope of their employment. Rule 403 provides for the exclusion of relevant evidence if its probative value is substantially outweighed by the danger of unfair prejudice, etc. Rule 805 recites, in effect, that a statement containing hearsay within hearsay is admissible if each part of the statement falls within an exception to the hearsay rule. While each provides

additional bases for excluding otherwise acceptable evidence, neither rule mandates the introduction into Rule 801 (d)(2)(D) of an implied requirement that the declarant have personal knowledge of the facts underlying his statement. Thus, the two statements made by Poos (D) (one in the note he wrote and one he made verbally) were admissible against the Center (D). As to the minutes of the Center's (D) board meeting, there was no servant or agency relationship which justified admitting the evidence of these minutes as against Poos (D) (who was a nonattending, nonparticipating employee). The only remaining question is whether the trial court's rulings excluding these three items of evidence are at all justified under Rule 403. It is true that none of the statements involved were based on the personal knowledge of the declarant. However, it was recognized by the Advisory Committee on Proposed Rules that this does not necessarily mean they must be rejected as too unreliable to be admitted into evidence. In its discussion of 801 (d)(2) exceptions to the hearsay rule, the Committee said: "The freedom which admissions have enjoyed from technical demands of searching for an assurance of trustworthiness in some against-interest circumstances, and form the restrictive influences of the opinion rule and the rule requiring first-hand knowledge, when taken with the apparently prevalent satisfaction with the results, calls for generous treatment of this avenue to admissibility." 28 U.S.C.A., Volume of Federal Rules of Evidence, Rule 801, p. 527, at p. 530. So here, remembering that relevant evidence is usually prejudicial to the cause of the side against which it is presented and that the prejudice which concerns us is unreasonable prejudice — and applying the spirit of Rule 801 (d)(2) — Rule 403 does not warrant the exclusion of the evidence of Poos' (D) statements as against himself or the Center (D). But the limited admissibility of the corporate minutes, coupled with the repetitive nature of the evidence and the low probative value of the minute record, all justify supporting the judgment of the trial court, under Rule 403, not to admit them into evidence. Reversed and remanded for a new trial.

EDITOR'S ANALYSIS: One of the questions courts have struggled with in this area is whether or not in order to qualify as an admission the statement must have been made by the agent to an outsider (i.e., one other than his principal or another agent). This often comes up when the opposing party in a suit against the principal wants to introduce into evidence a report written or given orally by an agent to the principal or another agent. Just as many courts have refused to let such evidence in as have let it in against the principal as an admission. The Federal Rules of Evidence have been interpreted as recognizing what Wigmore observed: that "communication to an outsider has not generally been thought to be an essential characteristic of an admission." Wigmore on Evidence, § 1557.

BOURJAILY v. UNITED STATES

Narcotics distribution conspiritor (D) v. Federal government (P)

483 U.S. 171 (1987).

NATURE OF CASE: Appeal from conviction for conspiracy to distribute cocaine and possession of cocaine with intent to distribute.

FACT SUMMARY: In the Government's (P) case against Bourjaily (D) for conspiracy to distribute cocaine and possession of cocaine with intent to distribute, Bourjaily (D) contended that the admission of a coconspirator's statement implicating Bourjaily (D) in the crimes violated Bourjaily's (D) constitutional right to confront the witnesses against him because he could not cross-examine the coconspirator, Lonardo.

CONCISE RULE OF LAW: The Confrontation Clause does not require a court to embark on an independent inquiry into the reliability of statements that satisfy the requirements of Federal Rule of Evidence 801(d)(2)(E).

FACTS: Bourjaily (D) was charged with conspiring to distribute cocaine and with possession of cocaine with intent to distribute. Over Bourjaily's (D) objection at trial, the Government (P) introduced the telephone statement of Lonardo, one of Bourjaily's (D) coconspirators, which implicated Bourjaily (D) in the crimes. The court decided that the Government (P) had established, by a preponderance of the evidence, that a conspiracy involving Lonardo and Bourjaily (D) existed and Lonardo's statements over the phone had been made in the course of and in furtherance of the conspiracy. Thus, the statements satisfied Federal Rule of Evidence 801(d)(2)(E) and were not hearsay. Bourjaily (D) was convicted on both counts and appealed. The court of appeals affirmed, rejecting Bourjaily's (D) contention that because he could not cross-examine Lonardo, the admission of Lonardo's statement violated Bourjaily's (D) constitutional right to confront the witnesses against him. Bourjaily (D) appealed.

ISSUE: Does the Confrontation Clause require a court to embark on an independent inquiry into the reliability of statements that satisfy the requirements of Federal Rule of Evidence 801(d)(2)(E)?

HOLDING AND DECISION: (Rehnquist, C.J.) No. The Confrontation Clause does not require a court to embark on an independent inquiry into the reliability of statements that satisfy the requirements of Federal Rule of Evidence 801(d)(2)(E). A court, in making a preliminary factual determination under 801(d)(2)(E), may examine the hearsay statements sought to be admitted. The judge should receive the evidence and give it such weight as his judgment counsels. Here, the trial court properly considered Lonardo's statement in finding that the Government (P) had established by a preponderance of the evidence that Lonardo was involved in a conspiracy with Bourjaily (D). There is

no reason to believe that the trial court's fact-finding of this point was clearly erroneous, and thus, Lonardo's out-of-court statement was properly admitted against Bourjaily (D). Also, the court of appeals was correct in holding that the requirements for admission of evidence under Rule 801(d)(2)(E) are identical to the requirements of the Confrontation Clause, and since the statement was admissible under the Rule, there was no constitutional problem. Affirmed.

CONCURRENCE: (Stevens, J.) An otherwise inadmissible hearsay statement cannot provide the sole evidentiary support for its own admissibility — it cannot lift itself into admissibility entirely by tugging on its own bootstraps. It may, however, use its own bootstraps, together with other support to overcome the objection.

DISSENT: (Blackmun, J.) The Court's reasoning is wrong in three respects. First, the Federal Rules of Evidence changed the well-settled law that preliminary questions of fact, relating to admissibility of a nontestifying coconspirator's statement, must be established by evidence independent of that statement itself. Second, the Court's conclusion that allowing the coconspirator's statement to be considered in the resolution of these factual questions will remedy problems of the statement's unreliability is erroneous. Third, because the Court alters the traditional hearsay exemption, the Court cannot rely on firmly rooted hearsay exception rationale to avoid a determination whether any "indicia of reliability" support the coconspirator's statement, as the Confrontation Clause surely demands.

EDITOR'S ANALYSIS: Under Federal Rule of Evidence 801(d)(2)(E), the existence of a conspiracy in fact is sufficient to support admissibility of evidence. A conspiracy count in the indictment is not required nor does the declarant need be indicted. The evidence is similarly admissible in civil cases, where the conspiracy rule applies to tortfeasors acting in concert.

[For more information on the Confrontation Clause, see Casenote Law Outline on Evidence, Chapter 9, § X, Hearsay and the Right of Confrontation.]

QUICKNOTES

CONSPIRACY - Concerted action by two or more persons to accomplish some unlawful purpose.

CONFRONTATION CLAUSE - A provision in the Sixth Amendment to the United States Constitution that an accused in a criminal action has the right to confront the witnesses against him, including the right to attend the trial and to cross-examine witnesses called on behalf of the prosecution.

HEARSAY - An out-of-court statement made by a person other than the witness testifying at trial that is offered in order to prove the truth of the matter asserted.

CARPENTER v. DAVIS

Wrongful death plaintiff (P) v. Truck driver/owner (D)

Mo. Sup. Ct., 435 S.W.2d 382 (1968).

NATURE OF CASE: Suit for wrongful death.

FACT SUMMARY: Carpenter's (P) wife was killed in an auto collision, and he brought suit for wrongful death. At trial the driver of the other car was allowed to testify as to a statement made by Carpenter's (P) wife at the scene that the truck driver was not at fault.

CONCISE RULE OF LAW: A declaration against interest made by a person now unavailable to testify will be admissible only insofar as it contains statements of fact and not statements of opinion as to legal fault.

FACTS: Carpenter's (P) wife was killed when the car in which she was riding was struck broadside by a truck at an intersection. Carpenter (P) brought a wrongful death suit against the driver and owner of the truck. At trial, the driver was allowed to testify, over objection, that at the scene of the accident he said to Mrs. Carpenter, "I'm sorry, lady, you pulled right out in front of me" and that she replied, "Yes, I know, it's not your fault." The statement was admitted as a declaration against interest, and Carpenter (P) appealed a judgment in favor of the driver and owner, contending the statement was inadmissible.

ISSUE: Where a statement is sought to be introduced as a declaration against interest of an unavailable witness, will the statement be admissible where it contains opinions of legal fault rather than statements of fact?

HOLDING AND DECISION: (Donnelly, J.) No. This statement is not an admission since Mrs. Carpenter is not a party and her husband's cause of action being a separate cause created by the state does not place him in privity with her. The statement should not have been admitted in its entirety since it contained both a statement of fact and an opinion of fault. Her statement, "Yes, I know," was a factual response to the driver's description of what had occurred. However, "It's not your fault" was an opinion and cannot be used on retrial. If it were an admission, the entire statement would be admissible. The judgment for the driver and owner is reversed.

DISSENT: (Finch, J.) The majority opinion allows the husband a greater possibility of recovery than his wife would have had were she to have survived and brought an action on her own. Since the statement would be an admission as to her, it would be admissible in its entirety. I would hold that where a statement would be admissible as an admission, it is also admissible as a declaration against interest against a party bringing a wrongful death suit for the death of the declaring person.

DISSENT: (Seiler, J.) The entire statement does contain the circumstantial probability of trustworthiness to qualify it as an exception to the hearsay rule. The entire statement could be considered as an opinion, as all statements may be either fact or opinion based on the circumstances. The fact that some of this statement may be opinion should affect the weight given to the statement, not its admissibility.

DISSENT: (Storckman, J.) The majority would exclude opinion in a declaration against interest since the testifying witness may intentionally or unintentionally alter the meaning by a slight change in wording. However, the punctuation in this statement was supplied by the court reporter. If the comma is removed from, "Yes, I know, it's not your fault," then the entire statement is either fact or opinion, depending on interpretation. Beyond that, this statement, if it is to be a declaration against interest, must be based on the peculiar knowledge of the declarant and must be known by the declarant to be against his interest. This statement fails on both counts, since Mrs. Carpenter was not in the best position to judge the occurrence and there is no indication that she was aware of any adverse connotations of her statement. She might very well have just been trying to be solicitous at the time.

EDITOR'S ANALYSIS: The unavailability requirement may be satisfied by the death of the witness, mental or physical incapacity, absence from the jurisdiction, or exemption from testifying by reason of privilege. The declaration must be adverse to some pecuniary or proprietary interest of the declarant. Traditionally, statements that subject a person to criminal liability or make him an object of hatred, ridicule, or social disgrace have not been held to be against interest since no property or pecuniary interest is involved. Modernly, however, the trend is to include such statements in this exception to the hearsay rule.

[For more information on declarations against interest, see Casenote Law Outline on Evidence, Chapter 10, § XIV, Declarations Against Interest.]

QUICKNOTES

HEARSAY - An out-of-court statement made by a person other than the witness testifying at trial that is offered in order to prove the truth of the matter asserted.

NOTES:

PEOPLE v. BROWN
State (P) v. Convicted murderer (D)
N.Y. Ct. App., 26 N.Y.2d 88, 257 N.E.2d 16 (1970).

NATURE OF CASE: Appeal from a murder conviction.

FACT SUMMARY: To prove that the person Brown (D) shot had a gun, the defense attempted to introduce a statement made by Seals that he had picked up the deceased's gun and used it in a robbery shortly after the shooting.

CONCISE RULE OF LAW: Statements against a penal interest are sufficient to invoke the exception to the hearsay rule, and the declarant is unavailable if he refuses to testify based on constitutional privilege.

FACTS: Brown (D) was convicted of murder. His defense at trial was self-defense based on the contention that the deceased had a gun. No gun was found at the scene. Seals had told Brown's (D) attorney that he had picked the gun up shortly after the shooting and used it in a robbery. The attorney was not allowed to testify at the trial because the statement was hearsay, and Seals refused to testify, asserting his privilege against self-incrimination.

ISSUES: (1) Are declarations against interest satisfied if the statement is against a penal interest? (2) Is the declarant unavailable if he refuses to testify based on a constitutional privilege?

HOLDING AND DECISION: (Bergan, J.) (1) Yes. A declaration against a penal interest is sufficiently trustworthy to satisfy that exception to the hearsay rule. Even if the rule required the statement to be against pecuniary interests, being convicted of a crime would hurt the declarant's economic situation and therefore be against his pecuniary interest. (2) To use this exception to the hearsay rule, it is also necessary that the declarant be unavailable to testify. A witness who refuses to testify based on his constitutional privilege against self-incrimination is no less unavailable than if he were dead or insane. Therefore, it was error to exclude Seals' statement in this case.

EDITOR'S ANALYSIS: Although there has been substantial argument for doing away with the unavailability requirement of declarations against interest, it is still uniformly a requirement. Traditionally, death was the only acceptable reason for the required unavailability. Insanity became the next proper reason, and the courts are expanding the permissible reasons, as this case indicates. The decision in this case, that successful claim of privilege renders a declarant unavailable, represents the outer limits of the decision today, and, in fact, other courts have ruled that such a declarant is not unavailable. The trend, however, is to do away with the requirement altogether, although no case to date has so held.

[For more information on declarations contrary to penal interest, see Casenote Law Outline on Evidence, Chapter 10, § XIV, Declarations Against Interest.]

NOTES:

FIDELITY SERVICE INSURANCE CO. v. JONES
Insurer (D) v. Insured (P)
Ala. Sup. Ct., 280 Ala. 195, 191 So.2d 20 (1966).

NATURE OF CASE: Appeal from award of damages on an insurance policy.

FACT SUMMARY: Fidelity (D) contended testimony of relatives concerning complaints by the deceased insured were hearsay and inadmissible to disprove a preexisting physical condition which may have contributed to the death.

CONCISE RULE OF LAW: Expressions of present physical state are admissible to prove such physical state.

FACTS: Jones was insured by Fidelity (D) under a policy which paid benefits if his death by drowning was not due to any disease or infirmity. Jones died when he drowned in the bathtub under circumstances wherein inferences could be made that the death was either purely accidental or contributed to by Jones' alleged infirmity. Fidelity (D) refused to pay the policy benefits, contending that Jones blacked out and drowned. His beneficiaries (P) sued, contending the drowning was purely accidental. The beneficiaries (P) presented testimony that Jones had never complained of blackouts or of not feeling well. Judgment for the beneficiaries (P) was appealed on the basis such testimony was inadmissible hearsay.

ISSUE: Are expressions of present physical state admissible to prove such physical state?

HOLDING AND DECISION: (Coleman, J.) Yes. Expressions of present physical state are admissible to prove that physical state. Such statements are original evidence of the declarant's physical state. Because Fidelity (D) was able to introduce evidence of the supposed blackouts, Jones' physical state was placed in issue, allowing for his statements concerning his physical state to be admitted. Affirmed.

EDITOR'S ANALYSIS: The type of statements described in this case are given more weight if made to a physician in the course of an examination. The circumstances are such as to add to their reliability. Such statements are particularly important in cases where the victim cannot testify at trial.

[For more information on expressions of present physical state, see Casenote Law Outline on Evidence, Chapter 10, § IV, Present State-of-Mind Exception.]

QUICKNOTES

HEARSAY - An out-of-court statement made by a person other than the witness testifying at trial that is offered in order to prove the truth of the matter asserted.

STATE OF MIND – A person's intent in performing a particular act.

UNITED STATES v. DI MARIA
Federal government (P) v. Possessor of stolen cigarettes (D)
727 F.2d 265 (2d Cir. 1984).

NATURE OF CASE: Appeal from a conviction for possession of stolen cigarettes.

FACT SUMMARY: Di Maria (D) contended that his statement to federal agents at the time of his arrest was evidentiary of his mental state and was thus admissible.

CONCISE RULE OF LAW: A statement of a defendant's then-existing state of mind is not rendered inadmissible by the hearsay rule.

FACTS: Di Maria (D) was arrested by the FBI and convicted of possession of stolen cigarettes, possession of contraband cigarettes, and conspiracy. At trial he attempted unsuccessfully to admit into evidence his statement, made at the scene of the arrest, that he "only came here to get some cigarettes real cheap." Di Maria (D) contended that the statement tended to show his mental state was not to obtain stolen cigarettes but rather to obtain bootleg cigarettes. The Government (P) contended that the statement was unbelievable and excludable. Di Maria (D) appealed.

ISSUE: Is a statement of a defendant's then-existing state of mind admissible?

HOLDING AND DECISION: (Friendly, J.) Yes. A statement of a defendant's then-existing state of mind is not rendered inadmissible by the hearsay rule. Statements of present state of mind are a recognized exception to the hearsay rule. While such statements may be self-serving and untrue, this goes to the weight of the evidence rather than to its admissibility. As a result, such was admissible, and it was error to exclude the statement. Reversed and remanded.

DISSENT: (Manfield, J.) Admission of the statement would violate the spirit of the hearsay rule.

EDITOR'S ANALYSIS: State of mind, despite its nebulous nature and difficulty in proof, is a necessary element in many civil causes of action and criminal offenses. Hearsay statements are often the only tangible evidence of the declarant's state of mind. Thus, despite their inherent unreliability, they are admissible subject to intense cross-examination.

[For more information on the state of mind exception, see Casenote Law Outline on Evidence, Chapter 10, § IV, Present State-of-Mind Exception.]

GAINES v. THOMAS
Injured bystander (P) v. Defendent (D)
S.C. Sup. Ct., 241 S.C. 412, 128 S.E.2d 692 (1962).

NATURE OF CASE: Action for damages for personal injuries from automobile accident.

FACT SUMMARY: In a prior action brought by Thomas (D), a now-deceased witness testified about the accident. That testimony was admitted at this trial.

CONCISE RULE OF LAW: Prior testimony is admissible when the issues are the same and the party against whom the testimony is offered had a fair and adequate opportunity to cross-examine at the former trial.

FACTS: Martin, who is represented by Thomas (D), was involved in a traffic accident with a truck driven by Byers. The accident also injured Gaines (P), who was working at the side of the road. Thomas (D) brought a prior action against the trucking company. At that trial, Byers testified, but before this action was brought by Gaines (P) against Thomas (D), Byers died.

ISSUE: May the former testimony of a witness, on the same issues, from an earlier trial where he was subject to cross-examination be admissible in a later trial?

HOLDING AND DECISION: (Brailsford, J.) Yes. Prior testimony is admissible when the issues are the same and the party against whom the testimony is offered had a fair and adequate opportunity to cross-examine the witness at the prior trial. The old rule on prior testimony required that there be the exact same parties. This rule placed an unnecessary restriction on the use of former testimony, however. There is no reason to believe that the cross-examination of Martin's representative in the first case would have been different than it would have been in this case had Byers not died. This rule is formulated to insure fairness to the opposing party. This fairness is established by the former opportunity to cross-examine, and the exact same parties are not required.

EDITOR'S ANALYSIS: The old view on prior testimony, which this court disregards, was based on a mutuality type of argument. It was said that because the party attempting to offer the prior testimony was not a party to the previous action, the testimony at that action could not be offered against him. Therefore, it was reasoned that it was unfair for him to be able to use it. This reciprocity doctrine was finally determined to have little bearing on the question of what is fair in respect to the actual situation where former testimony is offered against a party who did have adequate opportunity to cross-examine. Therefore, it was abandoned.

[For more information on prior statements of witnesses, see Casenote Law Outline on Evidence, Chapter 9, § VII, Exemption: Prior Statements of Witnesses.]

WILLIAMSON v. UNITED STATES
Convicted cocaine dealer (D) v. Federal government (P)
512 U.S. 594, 114 S. Ct. 2431 129 L.Ed.2d 476 (1994).

NATURE OF CASE: Appeal from conviction of possession of cocaine with intent to distribute, conspiracy to possess cocaine with intent to distribute, and traveling interstate to promote the distribution of cocaine.

FACT SUMMARY: Williamson (D) contended that the district court erred in allowing the testimony of a DEA agent in court who related arguably self-inculpatory statements made out of court to him by Harris, one of Williamson's (D) employees, regarding the possession and transport of the cocaine.

CONCISE RULE OF LAW: Fed. R. Evid. 804(b)(3) does not allow admission of non-self-exculpatory statements, even if they are made within a broader narrative that is generally self-inculpatory.

FACTS: Harris, an employee of Williamson (D), was stopped by the police while he was driving. The police, after searching the car, found 19 kilograms of cocaine in the car and arrested Harris. After his arrest, Harris was interviewed by telephone by a DEA agent, Walton. Harris told Walton that he had gotten the cocaine from a Cuban, that the cocaine belonged to Williamson (D), and that Harris was delivering it to a particular dumpster for pickup. Shortly thereafter, Walton interviewed Harris personally; Harris then told Walton that he was transporting the cocaine to Atlanta for Williamson (D), that Williamson (D) was traveling ahead of him in another car at the time of the arrest, and that Williamson (D) had apparently seen the police searching Harris' car and had fled. Harris told Walton that he had initially lied about the source of the cocaine because he was afraid of Williamson (D). Harris implicated himself in his statements to Walton but did not want his story to be recorded and refused to sign a written transcript of the statement. Walton later testified that Harris was not promised any reward for cooperating. Williamson (D) was eventually charged and convicted of various drug-related offenses. When Harris was called to testify at Williamson's (D) trial, he refused to do so. The district court then ruled that, under Fed. R. Evid. 804(b)(3), Agent Walton could relate what Harris told him because Harris' statements were against his own interests. Williamson (D) was convicted, and the court of appeals affirmed. On appeal, Williamson (D) argued that both lower courts erred by allowing Walton to testify regarding Harris' out-of-court statements.

ISSUE: Does Fed. R. Evid. 804(b)(3) allow admission of non-self-inculpatory statements, even if they are made within a broader narrative that is generally self-inculpatory?

HOLDING AND DECISION: (O'Connor, J.) No. Fed. R. Evid. 804(b)(3) does not allow admission on non-self-inculpatory

statements, even if they are made within a broader narrative that is generally self-inculpatory. The district court may not just assume, for purposes of Rule 804(b)(3), that a statement is self-inculpatory because it is part of a fuller confession, and this is especially true when the statement implicates someone else. The question under the Rule is always whether the statement was sufficiently against the declarant's penal interest that a reasonable person would not have made the statement unless believing it to be true. This question can only be answered in light of all the surrounding circumstances. In this case, some of Harris' confession would clearly have been admissible under the Rule. For instance, when he said he knew there was cocaine in the car, he forfeited his only defense to the charge of cocaine possession — lack of knowledge. But other parts of his confession, especially those in which he implicated Williamson (D), did little to subject Harris to criminal liability. A reasonable person in Harris' position might think that implicating someone else would decrease his own exposure to criminal liability at sentencing. Nothing in the record shows that the district court or court of appeals inquired whether each of the statements in Harris' confession was truly self-inculpatory. Remanded to the court of appeals to conduct this inquiry.

CONCURRENCE: (Scalia, J.) A declarant's statement is not magically transformed from a statement against penal interest into one that is inadmissible merely because the declarant names another person or implicates a possible codefendant. The relevant inquiry, however — and one that is not furthered by clouding the waters with manufactured categories such as "collateral neutral" and "collateral self-serving" — must always be whether the particular remark at issue (and not the extended narrative) meets the standard set forth in the Rule.

CONCURRENCE: (Ginsburg, J.) Fed. R. Evid. 804(b)(3) excepts from the general hearsay rule only those declarations or remarks within a narrative that are individually self-inculpatory. However, Harris' statements, as recounted by Walton, do not fit, even in part, within the exception described in the Rule for Harris' arguably inculpatory statements are too closely intertwined with his self-serving declarations to be ranked as trustworthy. To the extent that some of these statements tended to incriminate Harris, they provided only marginal or cumulative evidence of his guilt. They project the image of a person's acting not against his penal interest but striving mightily to shift principal responsibility to someone else. Therefore, Harris' hearsay statements should not be admissible under Rule 804(b)(3).

CONCURRENCE: (Kennedy, J.) Rule 804(b)(3) establishes a hearsay exception for statements against penal, proprietary,

Continued on next page.

pecuniary, and legal interest. The text of the Rule does not tell us whether collateral statements are admissible. The Court resolves this issue by adopting the extreme position that no collateral statements are admissible under the Rule. The Court reaches that conclusion by relying on the "principle behind the Rule" that reasonable people do not make statements against their interest unless they are telling the truth, and reasons that this policy "expressed in the statutory text" simply does not extend to collateral statements. To the contrary, three sources indicate that the Rule allows the admission of some collateral statements: first, the Advisory Committee Note to the Rule establishes that some collateral statements are admissible; second, at common law, collateral statements were admissible, and we can presume that Congress intended the principle and terms used in the Federal Rules of Evidence to be applied as they were at common law; third, absent a textual direction to the contrary, we should assume that Congress intended the penal interest exception for inculpatory statements to have some meaningful effect. The exclusion of collateral statements would cause the exclusion of almost all inculpatory statements.

EDITOR'S ANALYSIS: As indicated by the Court in Williamson, Rule 804(b)(3) requires that self-inculpatory statements should be examined in terms of the reasonable person and that the declarant believe the statement to be against interest. In order to analyze whether the declarant truly believes his statement was against interest, the identity of the person to whom the statement was made should be considered. Although the situation wherein a declarant makes his statement to the authorities is the prime example of a statement against interest, if such a statement was made to a trusted friend (who was expected to keep the information secret), it has not necessarily been held that this eliminates the disserving nature of the statement.

[For more information on declarations against interest, see Casenote Law Outline on Evidence, Chapter 10, § XIV, Declarations against Interest.]

NOTES:

COMMONWEALTH v. COLEMAN
State (P) v. Murderer (D)
Pa. Sup. Ct., 458 Pa. 112, 326 A.2d 387 (1974).

NATURE OF CASE: Appeal from convictions for second-degree murder and other offenses.

FACT SUMMARY: Coleman (D) was convicted of the second-degree murder of his girlfriend after a trial in which the girlfriend's mother was permitted to testify as to statements her daughter had made to her in a telephone conversation just minutes before she was stabbed to death.

CONCISE RULE OF LAW: Various courts throughout the United States have embraced the precepts underlying an exception to the hearsay rule for declarations of present sense impressions.

FACTS: Coleman's (D) live-in girlfriend called her mother at 6:15 one morning and said that Coleman (D) had just awakened her with several facial punches, that he would not let her leave the apartment, and that he was going to hang up the phone and then kill her. At 6:25 the connection broke; the mother called the police as her daughter had implored her to do. Meanwhile, Coleman (D), covered with blood and cut about the face and hands, hailed a patrol car on a nearby street. By 6:35 they found his girlfriend in the apartment — dead from 102 stab wounds. Insisting that he acted in self-defense after attacked with a letter opener, Coleman (D) objected to introduction of the telephone conversation under the res gestae exception to the hearsay rule. It was nonetheless admitted, and he was convicted of second-degree murder and other related offenses.

ISSUE: Have courts recognized an exception to the hearsay rule for declaration of present sense impressions?

HOLDING AND DECISION: (Jones, J.) Yes. As McCormick indicates, within the scope of res gestae there exist four distinct exceptions to the hearsay rule: (1) declarations of present bodily condition; (2) declarations of present mental state and emotion; (3) excited utterances; and (4) declarations of present sense impression. Various courts throughout this country have embraced the precepts underlying an exception to the hearsay rule for declarations of present sense impressions, under which the mother's testimony in this case is properly admissible. Her daughter's statements fall within that exception rather than the exception long recognized for excited utterances. Affirmed.

CONCURRENCE: (Pomeroy, J.) I agree that the statements are admissible, but I believe they come with the "excited utterance" exception to the hearsay rule. This is, therefore, not the proper case to use as a vehicle for the adoption of the "present sense impression" exception.

EDITOR'S ANALYSIS: U.S. v. Medico, 557 F.2d 309 (2d Cir. 1977), suggests that present sense impressions or excited utterances of an unidentified declarant may be admissible. There, an employee of the bank that was robbed heard an unidentified bystander relay the getaway car's license number through the bank door, another unidentified bystander having first seen the car and yelled out its license number.

[For more information on present sense impressions, see Casenote Law Outline on Evidence, Chapter 10, § II, Present Sense Impressions.]

QUICKNOTES

HEARSAY - An out-of-court statement made by a person other than the witness testifying at trial that is offered in order to prove the truth of the matter asserted.

SECOND-DEGREE MURDER - The unlawful killing of another person, without premeditation, and characterized by either an intent to kill or by a reckless disregard for human life.

EXCITED UTTERANCE – An exception to the hearsay rule for statements made or caused by the happening of a startling occurrence and that is related to that occurrence.

PRESENT SENSE IMPRESSION - Statements made as an event is being observed describing the event.

NOTES:

UNITED STATES v. TOME
Federal government (P) v. Sexual abuse suspect (D)
61 F.3d 1446 (10th Cir. 1995).

NATURE OF CASE: Review on remand of reversal of conviction for sexual abuse.

FACT SUMMARY: Testimony from pediatricians was admitted at Tome's (D) trial; the testimony, admitted under Rule 803(4), consisted of out-of-court statements by the victim identifying her father, Tome (D), as her assailant.

CONCISE RULE OF LAW: The test for admissibility of medical professional hearsay under Rule 803(4) is whether the subject matter of the statements is reasonably pertinent to diagnosis or treatment.

FACTS: Tome (D) was convicted for sexually abusing his daughter. At trial, several pediatricians testified that the daughter had identified Tome (D) as the abuser. The hearsay testimony of the doctors was admitted. Dr. Kuper interviewed the daughter to identify what injuries had occurred. The daughter described the abuse to her. Dr. Reich interviewed the daughter before examining her; Dr. Reich stated that the interview was to put the child at ease to facilitate the exam. The daughter told Dr. Reich of the abuse. Dr. Spiegel examined the daughter to verify that sexual abuse had occurred. The daughter told Dr. Spiegel of the abuse. Ecklebarger, a caseworker, interviewed the daughter. Ecklebarger related the detailed account given by the daughter at trial. Tome (D) appealed his conviction on the basis of evidentiary admission errors. The conviction was affirmed, but the Supreme Court reversed and remanded for further consideration.

ISSUE: Is the test for admissibility of medical professional hearsay under Rule 803(4) whether the subject matter of the statements is reasonably pertinent to diagnosis or treatement?

HOLDING AND DECISION: (Tacha, J.) Yes. The test for admissibility of medical professional hearsay under Rule 803(4) is whether the subject matter of the statements is reasonably pertinent to diagnosis or treatment. The rationale for permitting the admission of hearsay statments made to doctors is that the patient has a strong interest in telling the truth to the doctor; however, the admissibility is limited to statements needed for diagnosis and treatment. Here, the three pediatricians each needed an accurate account of the sexual abuse suffered by the daughter in order to diagnose and treat her. But Ecklebarger did not diagnose the daughter. Nor did Ecklebarger treat the daughter in any way. Given the strength and detail of Ecklebarger's testimony, the error cannot be said to be harmless. Conviction reversed.

CONCURRENCE AND DISSENT: (Holloway, J.) There is no reason to believe that a young child understands the need of doctors to receive accurate information to make a diagnosis. Thus, the presumption of truth in the statements is not reasonable in this case. None of the statements should have been admitted.

EDITOR'S ANALYSIS: The assumption that patients are aware that doctors require truthful information to treat them underlies rule 803(4). This explains why the prior distinction between treating and diagnosing physicians was removed. If patients are aware that doctors need accurate information to safely treat them, then the presumption is that all doctors will be given the same truthful information.

[For more information on statements for medical diagnosis, see Casenote Law Outline on Evidence, Chapter 10, § V, Statements for Medical Diagnosis.]

NOTES:

MUTUAL LIFE INSURANCE CO. v. HILLMON
Insurance company (D) v. Estate of decedent (P)
145 U.S. 285 (1892).

NATURE OF CASE: Action to recover on a life insurance policy.

FACTUAL SUMMARY: Where the issue at trial was whether a body found at a creek was Hillmon, so as to establish his death and thus enable his widow (P) to collect under a life insurance policy, Mutual Life Insurance Co. (D) sought to introduce letters sent by Walters to his fiancee and sister which stated Walters' intention to accompany Hillmon.

CONCISE RULE OF LAW: Declarations of state of mind which tend to evince a plan or intent to perform an act may be introduced into evidence as proof that the act has, in fact, been committed.

FACTS: Hillmon had a life insurance policy, issued by Mutual Life Insurance Co. (D), naming his widow (P) as beneficiary. When Hillmon disappeared, his widow (P) brought an action to collect under the policy. The widow (P) introduced evidence that Hillmon had left Wichita on or about March 5, 1879 and that on March 18, he was accidentally killed at a creek. The insurance company (D) introduced evidence which suggested that the body found at the creek was one Walters, not Hillmon. To substantiate this claim, the insurance company (P) sought to introduce letters written by Walters to his fiancee and sister in which Walters, just before March 5, expressed his intention of leaving Wichita with Hillmon. Apparently, Walters was also missing, and the body found at the creek was unidentifiable. The trial judge refused to admit the letters into evidence.

ISSUE: Are out-of-court statements which tend to prove the intention of the declarant at a particular moment in time admissible?

HOLDING AND DECISION: (Gray, J.) Yes. When the intention to be proved is important only as qualifying an act, its connection with that act must be shown in order to warrant the admission of declarations of the intention. But whenever the intention is, of itself, a distinct and material fact in a chain of circumstances, it may be proved by contemporaneous oral or written declarations of the party. Especially where the declarant is, or believed, dead, there can hardly be any other way of proving his intention. Even when alive, his memory is probably less trustworthy than letters written by him at the very time and under circumstances precluding a suspicion of misrepresentation. The letters in question were competent, not as narratives of facts or as proof that Hillman had actually left Wichita, but that he had the intention of doing so, which made it more probable that he, in fact, did leave.

EDITOR'S ANALYSIS: Questionable sincerity and remoteness in time, of course, act as limitations on the admissibility of a declarant's past intentions in order to prove the commission of some act by the declarant. Some commentators have suggested two further limitations to the rule given in this case: (1) such evidence should only be admitted when the declarant himself is unable to testify; (2) declarations used to establish subsequent conduct should not be admitted when the plan expressed by the intention required the cooperation of another person. The reason for this latter limitation is that the chances of carrying out the plan are reduced where another person is involved.

[For more information on the present state of mind exception, see Casenote Law Outline on Evidence, Chapter 10, § IV, Present State-of-Mind Exception.]

QUICKNOTES

STATE OF MIND - A declarant's mental state; testimony regarding state is ordinarily not considered hearsay because it is indicative of motivation and therefore has circumstantial guarantees of trustworthiness.

RELEVANCE - The admissibility of evidence based on whether it has any tendency to prove or disprove a matter at issue to the case.

NOTES:

UNITED STATES v. PHEASTER

Federal government (P) v. Kidnapping conspirator (D)

544 F.2d 353 (9th Cir. 1976); cert. denied, 429 U.S. 1099 (1977).

NATURE OF CASE: Appeal from various criminal convictions, including conspiracy.

FACT SUMMARY: Inciso (D) claimed that it was error for the trial court to have admitted into evidence statements made by the party that he and others, including Pheaster (D), had allegedly conspired to kidnap to the effect that he was going to meet Inciso (D) in the parking lot and would be back.

CONCISE RULE OF LAW: Hearsay evidence of statements in which the declarant has stated his intention to do something with another person are admissible under the state of mind exception to the hearsay rule to show that he intended to do it, from which the trier of fact may draw the inference that he carried out his intention and did it.

FACTS: Inciso (D), Pheaster (D), and others were allegedly part of a plot to kidnap and hold for ransom Larry Adell, the 16-year-old son of a Palm Springs multimillionaire. Larry disappeared forever after leaving his friends at a table at a local restaurant known as Sambo's North, telling them he was going to meet Angelo and he'd be right back. Earlier that day, he had told his girlfriend that he was going to meet Angelo at Sambo's North at 9:30 that night to pick up a pound of marijuana Angelo had promised him for free. She had been with Larry another time when he met a man named Angelo. At trial she identified Inciso (D) as that man. Inciso (D) objected to the introduction of this testimony concerning the statements Larry made to others. The Government (P) insisted it was admissible under the Hillmon doctrine to show Larry's state of mind and thus prove by inference that he parted in accordance with his intention to meet Angelo and did meet him.

ISSUE: Does the Hillmon doctrine permit hearsay evidence of statements by a declarant that he intended to do something with another person to be admitted to show that the declarant had the intention to do it, thus permitting the trier of fact to infer that he carried out his intention and did it?

HOLDING AND DECISION: (Renfrew, J.) Yes. The Hillmon doctrine is a particular species of the "state of mind" exception to the general rule that hearsay evidence is inadmissible. Under the Hillmon doctrine, which takes its name from a famous Supreme Court decision, the state of mind of the declarant is used inferentially to prove other matters which are in issue. It does not require that the state of mind of the declarant be an actual issue in the case. Stated simply, the doctrine provides that when the performance of a particular act by an individual is an issue in a case, his intention (state of mind) to perform that act may be shown. From that intention, the trier of fact may draw the inference that the person carried out his intention and performed the act. Within this conceptual framework, hearsay evidence of statements by the person which tend to show his intention is deemed admissible under the state of mind exception. Inciso's (D) objection concerns application of this doctrine to situations in which the declarant has stated his intention to do something with another person, and the issue is whether he did so. When hearsay evidence concerns the declarant's statement of his intention to do something with another person, the Hillmon doctrine requires that the trier of fact infer from the state of mind of the declarant the probability of a particular act not only by the declarant but also by the other person. Several objections can be raised against a doctrine that would allow such an inference to be made. First, it is an unreliable inference. More importantly, however, such an inference is inconsistent with the state of mind exception. Part of the statement that is admitted has nothing to do with the declarant's state of mind. If Larry's friends had testified that he said, "Angelo is going to be in the parking lot of Sambo's North tonight with a pound of grass," no state of mind exception of any other exception to the hearsay rule would be available. Yet, this is in effect at least half of what the testimony did attribute to Larry. Despite the theoretical awkwardness associated with the application of the Hillmon doctrine to facts such as those in this case, the authority in favor of such an application is impressive and must be followed. Therefore, although this court recognizes the force of the objection to the application of the Hillmon doctrine in the instant case, it cannot conclude that the district court erred in permitting the testimony concerning Larry Adell's statements.

EDITOR'S ANALYSIS: Although the new Federal Rules of Evidence were not in force when this case came to trial, both the Advisory Committee on the Proposed Rules and the House Committee on the Judiciary specifically addressed the Hillmon doctrine in making statements concerning Rule 803(3), which codifies the state of mind exception to the hearsay rule but does not provide a direct statement of the Hillmon doctrine. The language they used indicates that both bodies perceived the then-prevailing common law view to be that the Hillmon doctrine could be applied in cases where the hearsay statement of intent by a declarant was admitted to prove he did something with another person. However, the Notes of the House Committee stated its intention that the Rule be construed to limit the Hillmon doctrine "so as to render statements of intent by a declarant admissible only to prove his future conduct, not the future conduct of another person." This is contrary to the view which the Advisory Committee obviously had of the effect of Rule 803(3) on the Hillmon doctrine. It states, "(t)he rule of Mutual Life Ins. Co. v. Hillmon, 145 U.S. 285 (1892), ... allowing evidence of intention as tending to prove the doing of the act intended is, of course, left undisturbed." Note to Paragraph (3), 28 U.S.C.A. at 585.

[For more information on the present state of mind exception, see Casenote Law Outline on Evidence, Chapter 10, § IV, Present State-of-Mind Exception.]

SHEPARD v. UNITED STATES
Physician (D) v. Federal government (P)
290 U.S. 96 (1933).

NATURE OF CASE: Appeal from conviction for murder.

FACT SUMMARY: Trial court had permitted the introduction of testimony that Mrs. Shepard, the victim, had stated shortly before her death, "Dr. Shepard (D) has poisoned me."

CONCISE RULE OF LAW: Declarations of present memory, looking backward to a prior occurrence, are inadmissible to prove, or tend to prove, the existence of the occurrence.

FACTS: Dr. Shepard (D) was charged with the poison-killing of his wife, who was also his patient. At his trial, the court permitted the prosecution to introduce testimony of a nurse who attended Mrs. Shepard shortly before her death. The nurse testified that Mrs. Shepard asked her to fetch a bottle of whisky from the Doctor's (D) room. The nurse said the wife had drunk from this bottle before collapsing, requested a test, insisted that the smell and taste were strange, and added, "Dr. Shepard (D) has poisoned me." On appeal following Dr. Shepard's (D) conviction, the U.S. Supreme Court ruled that the evidence could not be justified under the rule which makes dying declarations admissible.

ISSUE: Though incompetent as dying declarations, are the mere statements made to the nurse admissible, either as (1) an indication of a state of mind inconsistent with the presence of suicidal intent or (2) as evidence of present memory to prove that Mrs. Shepard had observed the matter remembered?

HOLDING AND DECISION: (Cardozo, J.) (1) No. Since the testimony had been offered and received as proof of a dying declaration, the government may not now argue on appeal that the declarations were offered to show a persistency of a will to live. Because of the stated purpose of the testimony, Dr. Shepard (D) was put off his guard. It would now be unfair for the government to shift its ground. The purpose for which normally hearsay evidence is sought to be admitted must be made clear at the time it is introduced. (2) No. The government did not use the declarations by Mrs. Shepard to prove her present thoughts and feelings or even her thoughts and feelings in times past. Rather, they were offered as proof of an act committed by someone else, as evidence that she was dying of poison by her husband. The jury is incapable of distinguishing in its mind between these declarations as mere indications of a state of mind and as pointing the finger of guilt at Dr. Shepard (D). The ruling in Mutual Life Ins. Co. v. Hillmon, 145 U.S. 285 (1892), represents the high-water line beyond which courts may not go; in that case, the testimony looked forward to prove an occurrence. Here, it looks backward to a past act and, more importantly, to an act by someone not the speaker.

EDITOR'S ANALYSIS: The rule enunciated here has been heavily criticized but has, nonetheless, survived in the case law. One exception has been in probate cases where the testator's declarations made after the disputed occurrence are admitted to prove that he has made or revoked a will. The reason for this is that the testator is unavailable. Extending this rationale, the Model Code of Evidence would admit all hearsay declarations, including statements of memory, when the declarant is unavailable to testify.

[For more information on present state of mind exception, see Casenote Law Outline on Evidence, Chapter 10, § IV, Present State-of-Mind Exception.]

QUICKNOTES
STATE OF MIND – A person's intent in performing a particular act.

PRESENT SENSE IMPRESSION - Statements made as an event is being observed describing the event.

DYING DECLARATION - A statement spoken upon belief of impending death, usually not considered hearsay due to its circumstantial guarantees of trustworthiness.

NOTES:

UNITED STATES v. ANNUNZIATO
Federal government (P) v. Union agent (D)
293 F.2d 373 (2d Cir. 1961); cert. denied 368 U.S. 919 (1961).

NATURE OF CASE: Appeal from conviction of violation of a statute making it unlawful for a representative of employees in an industry affecting interstate commerce to accept money from the employer of such employee.

FACT SUMMARY: Annunziato (D) was the business agent for a union, members of which were working for the Terry Co. building a turnpike. Terker testified that his deceased father and late president of Terry Co. told him that he had received a call from Annunziato (D) requesting some money for the turnpike project and that he intended to give it to him.

CONCISE RULE OF LAW: Out-of-court statements which tend to prove a plan, design, or intention of the declarant are admissible to prove that the plan, design, or intention was carried out.

FACTS: The Terry Co. was building a turnpike using out-of-state materials. Annunziato (D) was the business agent for the union, whose members were being employed by Terry to work on the project. At trial, Terker testified that his deceased father and late president of Terry Co. had told him that he had received a call from Annunziato (D) requesting some money for the turnpike project. Terker further testified that his father went on to say that he intended to deliver the money to Annunziato (D).

ISSUE: Are out-of-court statements which tend to prove a plan, design, or intention of the declarant admissible?

HOLDING AND DECISION: (Friendly, J.) Yes. The existence of a design or plan to a specific act is relevant to show that the act was probably done as planned, and that plan or design may be evidence under an exception to the hearsay rule by the person's own statements as to its existence. This exception also applies where the declarant accompanied the statement of a future plan with an explanation of the reason, in the recent past, that prompted the plan. It is true that the statement of the past event would not be admitted if it stood alone, but where the event is recent, is within the personal knowledge of the declarant, and is so integrally included in the declaration of the design as to make it unlikely that the design would be true and the reason false, the reason will be admissible. Since all of these elements were present in this case, not only is Terker's testimony that his father intended to send Annunziato (D) the money admissible but also his reference to the phone call from Annunziato (D) which produced the plan to produce the money.

EDITOR'S ANALYSIS: As indicated by this case, out-of-court statements which tend to prove a design, plan, or intention of the declarant are admissible to prove that the design, plan, or

intention was carried out. Admissibility is subject to the usual limitations as to remoteness in time and apparent sincerity common to all declarations of mental state. This case also indicates an increased judicial willingness to admit evidence of memory or belief to prove the fact remembered or believed when this is closely related to declarations tending to prove intent or plan.

[For more information on the present state of mind exception, see Casenote Law Outline on Evidence, Chapter 10, § IV, Present State-of-Mind Exception.]

QUICKNOTES

HEARSAY - An out-of-court statement made by a person other than the witness testifying at trial that is offered in order to prove the truth of the matter asserted.

OUT-OF-COURT STATEMENT - A statement made outside of the proceeding and generally considered hearsay since opposing counsel's opportunity to cross-examine the declarant regarding the statement has been denied.

DECLARANT - Any human speaker who is the source of offered testimony, often hearsay spoken outside of court.

AGENT - An individual who has the authority to act on behalf of another.

NOTES:

UNITED STATES v. JACOBY
Federal government (P) v. Officer of bank (D)
955 F.2d 1527 (11th Cir. 1992), cert. denied, 507 U.S. 920 (1993).

NATURE OF CASE: Appeal of a conviction for several financial violations.

FACT SUMMARY: A memo, prepared by Scheer and describing the mechanics of financial violations charged to officers (D) of Sunrise Savings and Loan, was admitted under the residual hearsay exception Fed. R. Evid. 804(b)(5); Scheer was unavailable after using his Fifth Amendment privilege.

CONCISE RULE OF LAW: A document containing hearsay is admissible under the business records exception of Rule 803(6) if it is prepared in the regular course of business, even if the particular document is not routine.

FACTS: Officers of Sunrise Savings and Loan circumvented financial laws by lending funds to individuals in excess of Federal Savings and Loan Insurance Corp. (FSLIC) maximum levels. Jacoby (D) and other officers were indicted and prosecuted for their actions. At their trial, a memorandum, prepared by Scheer, was introduced into evidence. The memorandum contained hearsay statements identifying some of the mechanics of the fraudulent practices. It was Scheer's practice to write such explanatory memos to the file where the circumstances were sufficiently unusual to merit clarification. Jacoby (D) objected to the admission, but the document was admitted under the residual hearsay exception Rule 804(b)(5) for declarants like Scheer who are unavailable as a witness. The court did not rule on an alternative ground for admission, the business records exception. Jacoby (D) was convicted, and he appealed contending that the document lacked guarantees of trustworthiness.

ISSUE: Is a document containing hearsay admissible under the business records exception of Rule 803(6) even if the document was not of a type routinely prepared in the course of business?

HOLDING AND DECISION: (Friedman, J.) Yes. A document containing hearsay is admissible under the business records exception of Rule 803(6) if it is prepared in the regular course of business, even if the particular document is not routine. The hallmark of Rule 803(6) is not the routineness with which a document is prepared; it is, rather, that the document be one that is drafted during the regular course of business. In this case, it was the practice of Scheer to draft memos to the file in unusual cases that needed explanation. While the memo was not routine, it was done in the regular course of business. Thus, the memo was admissible under Rule 803(6) as a business record exception to hearsay exclusion. Affirmed.

EDITOR'S ANALYSIS: Business records that are regularly generated are presumed to have a greater level of reliability because of the consistent nature of the record-keeping. So long as a document is prepared as a result of a specific type of occurrence, it does not matter that the occurrence is rare. Furthermore, it does not matter that other businesses in the industry do not follow such a documentary practice; if the business in question regularly prepares a document, it will suffice for purposes of Rule 803(6).

[For more information on business records exception, see Casenote Law Outline on Evidence, Chapter 10, § VII, The Business Records Exception.]

QUICKNOTES
BUSINESS RECORD - A record made as a part of routine procedure. Admissible as an exception to the hearsay rule.

NOTES:

PALMER v. HOFFMAN
Railroad trustee (D) v. Injured claimant (P)
318 U.S. 109 (1943).

NATURE OF CASE: Action for personal injuries arising out of a railroad accident.

FACT SUMMARY: The engineer of a train involved in an accident, who died before trial, made a statement to the railroad company regarding the accident. This statement was not allowed in evidence.

CONCISE RULE OF LAW: A business record is considered to be "in the regular course of business" if made systematically or as a matter of routine to reflect events or transactions of the business.

FACTS: Hoffman (P) was injured in an accident with a railroad train and brought suit against Palmer (D), a trustee of the railroad. Shortly after the accident, the engineer of the train made a statement to the superintendent of the railroad and to a representative of the public utilities commission. It was the custom of the railroad to record such statements whenever there was an accident. The engineer died before the trial, and Palmer (D) attempted to introduce the statement into evidence. A statute allowed business records to be admitted if made in the course of regular business, but the court would not allow it into evidence.

ISSUE: Was the accident report made in the regular course of business?

HOLDING AND DECISION: (Douglas, J.) No. To be considered made in the regular course of business, a record must be made in relation to the inherent nature of the business and in the methods systematically employed for the conduct of the business as a business. The keeping of accident reports, while customary, is not essential to the efficient operation of a railroad. If the mere custom of making a record of nonessential activity could bring that record within the meaning of "regular course" of business, then any company could bring any type of record into court. The primary purpose of the record in this case was not for the efficient management of a railroad, but it was for litigation. Therefore, the record was not within the regular course of business and thereby was properly excluded.

EDITOR'S ANALYSIS: This case is the leading case on what is the regular course of business. Many scholars have criticized the decision as being contrary to the statute, and therefore many lower courts have dealt with the case in varying ways. The accepted analysis of this case today is that it does not create a blanket rule of exclusion for "self-serving" accident reports or other such records kept by businesses. Instead, it gives trial courts the discretion to exclude evidence which falls under the business records exception to the hearsay rule. The motive and the opportunity to falsify are the primary factors in using this case to exclude records.

[For more information on the admissibility of business records, see Casenote Law Outline on Evidence, Chapter 10, § VII, The Business Records Exception.]

QUICKNOTES

BUSINESS RECORD - A record made as a part of routine procedure. Admissible as an exception to the hearsay rule.

NOTES:

JOHNSON v. LUTZ
Estate of decedent (P) v. Driver (D)
N.Y. Ct. App., 253 N.Y. 124, 170 N.E. 517 (1930).

NATURE OF CASE: Wrongful death action based on a traffic accident.

FACT SUMMARY: Lutz (D) attempted to get an accident report filed by a policeman into evidence. The report contained statements of witnesses to the traffic accident.

CONCISE RULE OF LAW: Even if a statute allows business records to be admitted without firsthand knowledge of the recorder if done in the regular course of business, this does not include entries that include hearsay statements of third parties not engaged in the business related to the record.

FACTS: Johnson (P) was killed in a traffic accident with Lutz (D). In order to prove that he was not at fault, Lutz (D) attempted to have an accident report admitted into evidence. The report was made by a police officer on duty and included statements of witnesses to the accident. A statute in effect provided that records kept in the normal course of business are admissible without the firsthand knowledge of the recorder. However, the court did not allow the report into evidence.

ISSUE: Does the statute extend to allow records that include statements of persons not engaged in the business into evidence?

HOLDING AND DECISION: (Hubbs, J.) No. Even if a statute allows records made in the course of business to be admitted without firsthand knowledge, this does not extend to records that include statements of third parties that are not engaged in the business related to the record. The purpose of the statute was to allow proof of business transactions without the necessity of calling all the parties involved in situations involving normal business conditions. The essence of this statute was to provide credence to records made by persons in the exercise of the business duty. The intent of the legislature was not to extend this rule to statements made by persons outside the business for which the report was made, such as witnesses to an accident. Therefore, the report was properly excluded.

EDITOR'S ANALYSIS: The statute in question in this case was passed to remedy situations such as the one that existed in the previous case. Had this statute been in effect in that case, as it would have been in most jurisdictions today, the shopbook would have been admissible to prove the account receivable. However, as this case indicates, to apply this type of statute to a record, not only must the recorder be under a business duty to record the information, but the persons giving him the information must be under a similar duty. In other words, it's not enough that the policeman was under a business duty to make the report in this case, but the witnesses must have also been under a business duty in reporting to the police. Obviously, they were not under such a duty, and, therefore, the report was not admissible. This rule has been severely criticized but still stands as the majority rule.

[For more information on the business records exception to the hearsay rule, see Casenote Law Outline on Evidence, Chapter 10, § VII, The Business Records Exception.]

QUICKNOTES
BUSINESS RECORD - A record made as a part of routine procedure. Admissible as an exception to the hearsay rule.

NOTES:

BEECH AIRCRAFT CORP. v. RAINEY
Aircraft manufacturer (D) v. Navy pilot (P)
488 U.S. 153 (1988).

NATURE OF CASE: Appeal from reversal of a judgment for the defendant in a product liability action.

FACT SUMMARY: In this product liability suit filed against Beech (D) for the deaths of two Navy pilots that occurred when a Beech (D) aircraft crashed during training maneuvers, the trial judge allowed some conclusions and opinions in an investigative report to be admitted but excluded others.

CONCISE RULE OF LAW: Statements in public records and reports in the form of opinions or conclusions are admissible unless the sources of information or other circumstances indicate lack of trustworthiness.

FACTS: When the crash of a Navy training aircraft resulted in the death of both pilots on board, Rainey (P) and the other surviving spouse (P) brought a product liability suit against Beech (D), manufacturer of the plane. Rainey (P) alleged that the crash had been caused by a loss of engine power due to some defect in the aircraft's fuel control system, while Beech (D) advanced the theory of pilot error. The trial judge determined that an investigative report prepared by a Navy lieutenant was sufficiently trustworthy to be admissible, not only as to its factual findings, but also as to some of its conclusions. However, the trial judge did not allow Rainey (P), who was a Navy flight instructor, to testify as to his opinion of the probable primary cause of the crash. The jury returned a verdict for Beech (D). The court of appeals, having concluded that Fed. R. Evid. 803(8)(C) does not except conclusions and opinions contained in investigatory reports from the hearsay rule, reversed and remanded for a new trial. On rehearing en banc, a divided court of appeals reinstated the panel judgment. Beech (D) appealed.

ISSUE: Are statements in public records and reports in the form of opinions or conclusions admissible?

HOLDING AND DECISION: (Brennan, J.) Yes. Statements in public records and reports in the form of opinions or conclusions are admissible evidence unless the sources of information or other circumstances indicate lack of trustworthiness. Neither the language of Rule 803 nor the intent of its framers calls for a distinction between fact and opinion. As long as a conclusion is based on a factual investigation and satisfies the Rule's trustworthiness requirement, it should be admissible along with other portions of a report. However, the district court erred in refusing to permit Rainey (P) on cross-examination to present a more complete picture of his theory of the primary cause of the crash, about which he had testified on direct. Reversed in part, affirmed in part, and remanded.

EDITOR'S ANALYSIS: Federal Rule of Evidence 803 provides that certain types of hearsay statements are not made excludable by the hearsay rule, whether or not the declarant is available to testify. Controversy over what public records and reports are made not excludable by Rule 803(8)(C) has divided the federal courts from the beginning. While the Fifth and Eleventh Circuits follow a narrow interpretation, holding that the term "factual findings" do not encompass opinions or conclusions, other courts of appeal have generally adopted a broader interpretation.

[For more information on official records, see Casenote Law Outline on Evidence, Chapter 10, § VIII, The Official Records Exception.]

QUICKNOTES
PUBLIC RECORD – Records kept by a governmental agency pursuant to law.

NOTES:

COMMONWEALTH v. DiGIACOMO

State (P) v. Putative defender of friend (D)

Pa. Sup. Ct., 463 Pa. 449, 345 A.2d 605 (1975).

NATURE OF CASE: Prosecution for murder.

FACT SUMMARY: At his trail, DiGiacomo (D) sought to introduce medical records (under the business records exception) to show the admitting diagnosis of a doctor unavailable to testify at trial.

CONCISE RULE OF LAW: Medical records may be admissible under the business records exception to the hearsay rule but not to show the diagnosis or medical opinion placed therein by a doctor who is unavailable for cross-examination.

FACTS: DiGiacomo (D) claimed that he had shot and killed the party beating his friend Hruska in order to protect Hruska's life. Hruska's hospital records were admitted into evidence under the business records exception but only to prove the fact of hospitalization and length of stay. DiGiacomo (D) was not permitted to use them to show the admitting diagnosis, written by a doctor who was not available to testify at the trial.

ISSUE: Are hospital records admissible as business records for the purpose of showing the diagnosis or medical opinion written therein by a doctor who is not available to testify at trial?

HOLDING AND DECISION: (Nix, J.) No. Under the business records exception, hospital records are admissible to show the fact of hospitalization, treatment prescribed, and symptoms given, but they are not admissible to show the diagnosis or medical opinion rendered therein by a doctor who is not available for crossexamination. Such is in the nature of expert opinion testimony, which requires that the expert be available for cross-examination.

CONCURRENCE: (Roberts, J.) There should not be a blanket prohibition on the admission of all hospital records to show the diagnoses contained therein. Such diagnoses are unusually reliable, especially when a particular diagnosis is one upon which "competent physicians would not differ." Their reliability stems from their being used to prescribe treatment, etc. However, even if such evidence had been admitted, it would not have changed the judgment in this case.

CONCURRENCE: (Pomeroy, J.) The trial judge committed an error, albeit a harmless one, when he held that hospital records are per se inadmissible for diagnostic purposes. They are admissible for such purposes (as business records) at the discretion of the trial judge (i.e., if, in his opinion, the sources of information, method, and time of preparation were such as to justify their admission).

EDITOR'S ANALYSIS: Federal Rule of Evidence 803(6) has dropped the distinction federal courts once made (and some state courts still make) between routine and speculative diagnoses. It permits either to be admitted but gives the trial court the power to exclude a particular record where indications of trustworthiness are lacking. A number of state courts have held diagnoses admissible, at least in some situations.

[For more information on requirements for the business records exception, see Casenote Law Outline on Evidence, Chapter 10, § VII, The Business Records Exception.]

QUICKNOTES

BUSINESS RECORD - A record made as a part of routine procedure. Admissible as an exception to the hearsay rule.

CROSS EXAMINATION - The interrogation of a witness by an adverse party either to further inquire as to the subject matter of the direct examination or to call into question the witness' credibility.

HEARSAY - An out-of-court statement made by a person other than the witness testifying at trial that is offered in order to prove the truth of the matter asserted.

NOTES:

WADENA v. BUSH
Injured plaintiff (P) v. Negligent driver (D)
Minn. Sup. Ct., 305 Minn. 134, 232 N.W.2d 753 (1975).

NATURE OF CASE: Action for damages resulting from an automobile accident.

FACT SUMMARY: Bush (D) was allowed to introduce into evidence the emergency room records that were prepared when she and others involved in an automobile accident were taken to the hospital, but the court deleted therefrom certain references to the alleged intoxication of Wadena (P) and his friends.

CONCISE RULE OF LAW: Entries in hospital records are considered admissible as records made in the regular course of business of the hospital only if they are germane to medical history, diagnosis, or treatment (*i.e.*, medically relevant).

FACTS: Wadena (P) was riding with his friends in his car when it was involved in a collision with the car owned and driven by Mrs. Bush (D). All of the persons involved in the accident admitted drinking intoxicating liquor during the evening prior to the collision. Mrs. Bush (D) was permitted to introduce into evidence the emergency room records from the hospital to which those involved in the accident were taken for treatment. However, upon a motion from Wadena (P), notations therein making reference to the alleged intoxication of Wadena (P) and his companions were deleted. A physician called by Mrs. Bush (D) for cross-examination offered testimony indicating that intoxication would be relevant to rendering proper treatment, but some of the questions and answers suggested this was so only if the patient was in shock or unconscious. The notations in the hospital records were not conclusive as to whether the parties were in shock or unconscious either at the scene of the accident or when admitted.

ISSUE: Are entries in hospital records admissible only if they are medically relevant?

HOLDING AND DECISION: (Knutson, J.) Yes. To be admissible as records made within the regular course of business, entries in hospital records must have been germane to medical history, diagnosis, or treatment (i.e., medically relevant). The medical relevance of intoxication is a question of fact for the trial court and should be disturbed on appeal only if clearly erroneous. In this case, the evidence created a fact issue as to whether or not the intoxication notations were medically relevant. The trial court did not abuse its discretion in deciding they were not. At any rate, such notations would never be admissible in the absence of a showing of the identity of the person who made them and his source of information. This foundation was not provided at trial. Affirmed.

EDITOR'S ANALYSIS: Reports in the hospital record of statements made by the patient may still be admissible (even if not medically relevant) if they can qualify as admissions of a party opponent, dying declarations, declarations against interest, or excited utterances. The excited utterance exception to the hearsay rule has often been used to admit such otherwise inadmissible portions of records.

[For more information on the business record exception, see Casenote Law Outline on Evidence, Chapter 10, § VII, The Business Records Exception.]

QUICKNOTES
BUSINESS RECORD - A record made as a part of routine procedure. Admissible as an exception to the hearsay rule.

RELEVANCE - The admissibility of evidence based on whether it has any tendency to prove or disprove a matter at issue to the case.

NOTES:

LLOYD v. AMERICAN EXPORT LINES, INC.

Combative crew member (P) v. Shipping company (D)

580 F.2d 1179 (3d Cir. 1978); cert. denied, 439 U.S. 969 (1978).

NATURE OF CASE: Counterclaim for damages for negligence and unseaworthiness.

FACT SUMMARY: In defending against a counterclaim brought by Alvarez (D), Export (D) sought to introduce into evidence testimony that Lloyd (P) (who was unavailable) had given at a Coast Guard hearing regarding the fight between himself and Alvarez (D) aboard one of Export's (D) ships.

CONCISE RULE OF LAW: The prior testimony of an unavailable witness is admissible under Federal Rule of Evidence 804(b)(1) if the party against whom it is offered or a "predecessor in interest" had the "opportunity and similar motive to develop the testimony by direct, cross or redirect examination."

FACTS: There was a fight between two crew members, Lloyd (P) and Alvarez (D), aboard one of Export's (D) ships. Lloyd (P) sued Export (D), alleging negligence and unseaworthiness. Export (D) joined Alvarez (D) as a third-party defendant, and he then counterclaimed against Export (D), alleging negligence and unseaworthiness (based on Export's [D] supposed failure to use reasonable precautions to safeguard him from one it knew to have dangerous propensities, i.e., Lloyd [P]). Lloyd's (P) case was dismissed when he repeatedly failed to show up for pretrial depositions and when his case was called for trial. Alvarez (D) proceeded with his counterclaim, testifying to his version of the fight that had occurred between himself and Lloyd (P). The trial court did not permit Export (D) to introduce into evidence Lloyd's (P) prior testimony at a Coast Guard hearing that had been held to determine whether his merchant mariner's document should have been suspended or revoked on the basis of charges of misconduct brought against him for the fight with Alvarez (D). That testimony contained Lloyd's (P) quite different account of the fight that had occurred. At the hearing, both Lloyd (P) and Alvarez (D) were represented by counsel and testified under oath. On appeal, Export (D) argued that the trial court had erred in ruling that this prior testimony was not admissible under Federal Rule of Evidence 804(b)(1), which renders admissible the prior testimony of an unavailable witness if the party against whom it is offered or a "predecessor in interest" had the "opportunity and similar motive to develop the testimony by direct, cross or redirect examination."

ISSUE: If a witness is unavailable, does Federal Rule of Evidence 804(b)(1) make his prior testimony admissible if the party against whom it is offered or a "predecessor in interest" had the "opportunity and similar motive to develop the testimony by direct, cross or redirect examination"?

HOLDING AND DECISION: (Aldisert, J.) Yes. Under Federal Rule of Evidence 804(b)(1), the prior testimony of a witness who is "unavailable" is admissible if the party against whom it is offered or a "predecessor in interest" had the "opportunity and similar motive to develop the testimony by direct, cross or redirect examination." In this case, it is clear that the proponent of Lloyd's (P) statement was unable to procure his attendance by process or other reasonable means and that he must thus be considered to have been "unavailable." As to whether Export (D) can be considered a "predecessor in interest" of Lloyd (P), that is a more difficult question. Congress did not define that phrase, leaving it up to the courts to interpret it. As originally submitted by the Supreme Court, Rule 804(b)(1) would have allowed prior testimony of an unavailable witness to be received in evidence if the party against who it was offered, or a person with "motive and interest similar," had an opportunity to examine the witness. The change in wording that occurred thereafter to that which is now set forth in Rule 804(b)(1) did not signal a return to the common law approach to former testimony — which required privity or a common property interest between the parties. With that in mind, this court is satisfied that there was a sufficient community of interest shared by the Coast Guard in its hearing and Alvarez (D) in the subsequent civil trial to satisfy Rule 804(b)(1). The Coast Guard investigating officer attempted to establish at the Coast Guard hearing what Alvarez (D) attempted to establish at the later trial: Lloyd's (P) intoxication, his role as the aggressor, and his prior hostility toward Alvarez (D). While the result sought in the two proceedings differed, the basic interest advanced by both was that of determining culpability and, if appropriate, exacting a penalty for the same condemned behavior thought to have occurred. Under the circumstances, this court is satisfied that there existed sufficient "opportunity and similar motive (for the Coast Guard investigating officer) to develop (Lloyd's) testimony" at the former hearing to justify its admission against Alvarez (D) at the later trial. It is this court's belief that Congress intended that when a party in a former suit had a like motive to cross-examine regarding the same matters as the present party would have and had an adequate opportunity to do so, the testimony thus procured in that former suit is admissible against the present party because the previous party was, in the final analysis, a predecessor in interest to the present party.

CONCURRENCE: (Stern, J.) While I agree with the result, I cannot agree with the analysis. I would hold that the prior testimony is admissible under the catchall exception to the hearsay rule, 804(b)(5), and not under 804(b)(1). Under the majority's approach, it is sufficient that the Coast Guard

Continued on next page.

investigator and Alvarez (D) shared a community of interest, which the majority seems to think means nothing more than similarity of interest or similarity of motive. But similar motive is a separate prerequisite to admissibility under 804(b)(1), and thus the majority's analysis which reads "predecessor in interest" to mean nothing more than a person with "similar motive" eliminates the predecessor in interest requirement entirely. It seems clear that the phrase "predecessor in interest" is a term of art having a narrow, substantive law sense that historically requires it to be defined in terms of a privity relationship. No such relationship existed in this case. While the interests of Alvarez (D) and the Coast Guard may overlap, they do not coincide. The Coast Guard investigating officer was under no duty to advance every arguable issue against Lloyd (P) in vindication of Alvarez's (D) interests. He simply did not represent Alvarez (D).

EDITOR'S ANALYSIS: Just precisely when a witness is "unavailable" so that his prior testimony may be admissible is a problem that has plagued the courts. While some have held that a witness' loss of memory of the relevant matters does not render him "unavailable," the general consensus is that it does; so too does his refusal to testify.

———————————

[For more information on the former testimony exception, see Casenote Law Outline on Evidence, Chapter 10, § XII, The Former Testimony Exception.]

QUICKNOTES

NEGLIGENCE - Conduct falling below the standard of care that a reasonable person would demonstrate under similar conditions.

FORMER TESTIMONY – Testimony given in a prior proceeding that may be offered in a later proceeding under certain circumstances.

UNAVAILIABILITY – An exception to the hearsay rule for out-of-court statements made by a witness who is unavailable due to death, insanity or because the witness is beyond the jurisdiction of the court.

NOTES:

OHIO v. ROBERTS
State (P) v. Forgery convict (D)
448 U.S. 56 (1980).

NATURE OF CASE: Appeal from a conviction for forgery.

FACT SUMMARY: Roberts (D) claimed that his constitutional right to confront the witnesses against him had been violated when the prosecution was allowed to introduce into evidence, under the prior testimony exception to the hearsay rule, testimony a witness had given at a preliminary hearing.

CONCISE RULE OF LAW: In a criminal trial, the statement of one who is not present for cross-examination is admissible (under an exception to the hearsay rule) only if it is shown that he is unavailable and if the statement bears adequate "indicia of reliability."

FACTS: Roberts (D) was being tried for forgery of a check and possession of stolen credit cards. Although he claimed the victim's daughter had given him the items and said he could use them, the daughter had testified at the preliminary hearing, at which time she denied giving him the items without telling him she had no permission to use them. This testimony was admitted at his trial, over his objection, under the prior testimony exception to the hearsay rule. It was Roberts' (D) claim that this violated his constitutional right to confront the witnesses against him.

ISSUE: If a witness is not available for a criminal trial, can a statement he made be admitted as long as it bears adequate "indicia of reliability"?

HOLDING AND DECISION: (Blackmun, J.) Yes. When a hearsay declarant is not present for cross-examination at a criminal trial, the Confrontation Clause of the Constitution normally requires a showing that he is unavailable. Even then, his extrajudicial statement is admissible only if it bears adequate "indicia of reliability." This requirement has been applied principally by concluding that certain hearsay exceptions rest upon such solid foundations that admission of virtually any evidence within them comports with the "substance of the constitutional protection" the Confrontation Clause is designed to provide criminal defendants. Reliability can be inferred without more in a case where the evidence falls within a firmly rooted hearsay exception. In other cases, the evidence must be excluded at least absent a showing of particularized guarantees of trustworthiness.

EDITOR'S ANALYSIS: A criminal defendant's right to a fair trial was found to have been violated when he was not permitted to put into evidence the fact that another man, one McDonald, had told his close friends that he had committed the murder in question. The trial court had not permitted the defendant to call those to whom the confessions had been made to testify to this "hearsay," nor had it let him get such confessions in by impeaching McDonald after calling him as a witness (because of Mississippi's "voucher" rule). Chambers v. Mississippi, 410 U.S. 284 (1973).

[For more information on statements bearing "indices of reliability," see Casenote Law Outline on Evidence, Chapter 9, § X, Hearsay and the Right of Confrontation.]

QUICKNOTES

HEARSAY - An out-of-court statement made by a person other than the witness testifying at trial that is offered in order to prove the truth of the matter asserted.

CROSS EXAMINATION - The interrogation of a witness by an adverse party either to further inquire as to the subject matter of the direct examination or to call into question the witness' credibility.

CONFRONTATION CLAUSE - A provision in the Sixth Amendment to the United States Constitution that an accused in a criminal action has the right to confront the witnesses against him, including the right to attend the trial and to cross-examine witnesses called on behalf of the prosecution.

NOTES:

UNITED STATES v. DINAPOLI
Federal government (P) v. Racketeer (D)
8 F.3d 909 (2d Cir. 1993).

NATURE OF CASE: Rehearing en banc, after remand from the Supreme Court, of an appeal of a conviction for racketeering.

FACT SUMMARY: At trial, the court refused to admit two witnesses' grand jury testimony denying knowledge of certain criminal activities under Rule 804(b)(1), since the government (P) had not had a "similar motive" to develop the testimony.

CONCISE RULE OF LAW: Similarity of motive for Rule 804(b)(1) is shown where the party resisting the offered testimony at a pending proceeding had, at a prior proceeding, an interest of substantially similar intensity to prove (or disprove) the same side of a substantially similar issue.

FACTS: While testifying before a grand jury, two witnesses, Bruno and DeMateis, principals in a company that was alleged to be a member of a racketeering scheme, denied knowledge of the scheme. They were confronted with inconsistent wiretapped conversations, but the two did not change their story. At the subsequent criminal trial, the two invoked the privilege against self-incrimination when called by DiNapoli's (D) attorney. DiNapoli (D) then sought to admit the grand jury testimony under Rule 804(b)(1). The district court ruled that "similar motive" was not satisfied and excluded the testimony. DiNapoli (D) was convicted. On appeal, his conviction was overruled for failure to admit the testimony. The Supreme Court then reversed the reversal and remanded. On remand, the appellate court ruled that the "similar motive" requirement was satisfied. The appellate court then granted the government's (P) motion for rehearing en banc.

ISSUE: Is similarity of motive for Rule 804(b)(1) shown where the party resisting the offered testimony at a pending proceeding had, at a prior proceeding, an interest of substantially similar intensity to prove (or disprove) the same side of a substantially similar issue?

HOLDING AND DECISION: (Newman, C.J.) Yes. Similarity of motive for Rule 804(b)(1) is shown where the party resisting the offered testimony at a pending proceeding had, at a prior proceeding, an interest of substantially similar intensity to prove (or disprove) the same side of a substantially similar issue. It is not enough that a questioner takes the same side of the same issue at two proceedings. The motives of a questioner can be very different if the two proceedings were of a different nature. In this case, the government's (P) interest at the grand jury proceeding was merely to uncover further information since the

defendants had already been indicted. There was no real need to show the witness testimony to be false. Given the low level of intensity with which the witnesses were challenged, it cannot be said that the government (P) would have developed information in the same manner at trial. The trial court's exclusion of the witnesses' grand jury testimony was entirely correct. The convictions are affirmed.

DISSENT: (Pratt, J.) The issue that the government (P) sought to prove in both proceedings was the same: whether the racketeering scheme existed. The majority has effectively rewritten the rule to require the "same motive," as opposed to a "similar motive."

DISSENT: (Miner, J.) The record is very clear in this case. The government (P) was clearly trying to prove the falsity of the witnesses' testimony at the grand jury proceeding through the use of impeaching questions. It is hard to see how the government (P) did not get a fair chance to develop the issue in front of the grand jury.

EDITOR'S ANALYSIS: The majority reads Rule 804(b)(1) as requiring a high degree of similarity between the levels of importance of an issue at two proceedings. Although the dissent complains of this, it seems more than just to protect a party from the admission of hearsay testimony unless that party had a prior chance to examine the testifier with a virtually identical mindset. Otherwise hearsay testimony from prior proceedings could be used as a weapon against a party that had not considered an issue to be as important at one proceeding as it is in another.

[For more information on former testimony, see Casenote Law Outline on Evidence, Chapter 10, § XII, The Former Testimony Exception.]

QUICKNOTES
MOTIVE - Reason or other impetus inciting one to action.

RACKETEERING – A conspiracy organized for the commission or attempted commission of extortion or coercion.

NOTES:

WILSON v. STATE
Murderer (D) v. State (P)
Nev. Sup. Ct., 86 Nev. 320, 468 P.2d 346 (1970).

NATURE OF CASE: Appeal from a murder conviction.

FACT SUMMARY: The court admitted a statement by the victim that Wilson (D) had shot him as a dying declaration without a showing that he believed in God.

CONCISE RULE OF LAW: All that is required to admit a dying declaration is that the declarant is dying and is aware of that fact. The weight given to the declaration is a question for the jury.

FACTS: After leaving a supper club with Wilson (D), Feltus returned bleeding and stated he was shot. In response to the question asking who had shot him, Feltus stated that Wilson (D) had done it. At trial, the court allowed Feltus' statements into evidence on a showing that at the time the statements were made, he was dying and that he was aware of his condition.

ISSUE: To admit a dying declaration, is it necessary to prove that the declarant believed in God?

HOLDING AND DECISION: (Batjer, J.) No. The only requirements for the admission of a dying declaration is that the statement was made when the declarant is aware of the fact that he is dying and is beyond a possible recovery. The fact that the declarant didn't believe in God or that the statement was not credible for some other reason does not affect its admissibility but rather should be weighed by the jury. Therefore, once the foundational requirements are met, it would be error to take the statement away from the jury. Once the statement is admitted, then the accused may impeach its credibility and in fact is given great latitude in so doing. However, credibility is a question not of admissibility, but one for the jury to weigh.

EDITOR'S ANALYSIS: The objection of Wilson's (D) attorney that a dying declaration not be admitted unless the declarant believed in God is based an the original theory behind the hearsay exception. It was believed that a man would not go to his maker with a lie on his lips; therefore, if a man knew he was dying, he would be truthful. It is interesting, however, that as this case indicates, the declarant must be aware he is dying, but he need not believe in God. The modern rationale seems to be that a dying man has no reason to lie. Many courts have recognized the fallacy in this logic and have begun instructing juries that the weight given to a dying declaration should not be as great as other types of evidence.

[For more information on dying declarations, see Casenote Law Outline on Evidence, Chapter 10, § XIII, Dying Declarations.]

BOWERS v. FIBREBOARD CORPORATION
Decedent's stepson (P) v. Asbestos manufacturer (D)
Wash. App. Ct., Div. 2, 66 Wash. App. 454, 832 P.2d 523 (1992).

NATURE OF CASE: Appeal of damage award for asbestos-induced injuries.

FACT SUMMARY: Bowers (P) offered into evidence an ancient Naval Dictionary listing the locations of naval ships at different times to prove that her deceased stepfather had been on ships at the same time as harmful asbestos products.

CONCISE RULE OF LAW: Ancient documents, if authenticated, are presumed reliable by their nature, and no further evidence of reliability is required for admission of the document into evidence.

FACTS: Bowers' (P) stepfather served in the Navy on different vessels and worked in a shipyard, where he was exposed to harmful asbestos manufactured by Fibreboard (D). To prove that he had been on the ships at the same time as the asbestos products, Bowers (P) offered into evidence a Naval Dictionary under the "ancient documents" exception to the hearsay rule. The dictionary listed the locations of various vessels at different times. Bowers (P) prevailed, and Fibreboard Corporation (D) appealed, assigning error to the admission of the dictionary. Fibreboard (D) contended that the dictionary was a learned treatise, and should have been proven reliable through testimonial foundation.

ISSUE: Must evidence of reliability be offered before an authenticated document of more than twenty years of age is admitted to evidence?

HOLDING AND DECISION: (Seinfeld, J.) No. Ancient documents, if authenticated, are presumed reliable by their nature, and no further evidence of reliability is required for admission of the document into evidence. While it is somewhat arbitrary to assume that twenty years is an important threshold in document reliability, there are good reasons for so presuming. First, it is exceptionally unlikely that a document would be falsified for trial more than twenty years before it was needed. Second, readers would have had more than twenty years to detect errors in the document. Here, the dictionary was self-authenticating since it was issued by a public authority. Beyond authentication, the ancient quality of the document was sufficient indicia of reliability under Washington Evidence Rule 803(a)(16). Affirmed.

EDITOR'S ANALYSIS: The ancient documents exception to the hearsay rule is quite firm. Virtually any document meeting the descriptive requirements of the rule may be admitted, whether the contents of the document are fact, speculation, or opinion. In one case, an unpublished document that questioned industry toxin exposure limits was admitted as an ancient document over the objections of the defendant that the conclusions in the report were untested. See George v. Celotex Corp., 914 F.2d 26 (2d Cir. 1990).

[For more information on ancient documents, see Casenote Law Outline on Evidence, Chapter 10, § IX, Miscellaneous Hearsay Exceptions.]

QUICKNOTES
ANCIENT DOCUMENTS – A document that is admissible into evidence without authentification if, on its face, it shows evidence of being twenty years old or more and it in the proper location.

FOUNDATION - The validity of proffered evidence that must be established prior to as admission at trial, usually by demonstrating its authenticity or that it is what it purports to be.

AUTHENTICATION (OF DOCUMENTARY EVIDENCE) - The validity of documentary evidence that must be established prior to its admission into evidence, usually by showing that a document is that it purports to be.

NOTES:

GRAHAM v. WYETH LABORATORIES

Injured vaccine user (P) v. Vaccine manufacturer (D)

906 F.2d 1399 (10th Cir. 1990), cert. den., 498 U.S. 981 (1990).

NATURE OF CASE: Appeal of a jury verdict awarding damages in a products liability suit.

FACT SUMMARY: An American Medical Association Report on vaccination injuries was admitted into evidence as a learned treatise, redacted to exclude the fact that the report was intended to discuss legislative compensation, and given to the jurors.

CONCISE RULE OF LAW: Since the purpose of the creation of a document pertains directly to its reliability as a learned treatise, it is not proper, under Rule 803(18), to admit a document into evidence as a learned treatise while redacting the purpose of its creation.

FACTS: Wyeth Labs (D) was sued by Graham (P) for injuries caused by a a defective DTP vaccine manufactured by Wyeth (D). At trial, an American Medical Association Ad Hoc Panel Report was admitted into evidence over Wyeth's (D) objections. The stated purpose of the report was to explore a legislative compensation scheme for mandatory vaccine programs. However, the court redacted the statement of purpose sua sponte before the document was read to the jury. The jury awarded $15,000,000 to Graham (P). Wyeth (D) appealed.

ISSUE: Is it proper, under Rule 803(18), to admit into evidence a document purporting to be a learned treatise while redacting the stated purpose of the creation of the document?

HOLDING AND DECISION: (Garth, J.) No. Since the purpose of the creation of a document pertains directly to its reliability as a learned treatise, it is not proper, under Rule 803(18), to admit a document into evidence as a learned treatise while redacting the purpose of its creation. Learned treatises present a risk that a jury will attribute too great an accuracy to claims within. To prevent such a danger, all information pertaining to accuracy of the treatise must be available for admission to evidence. In this case, the court acted improperly when it redacted the purpose of the report. The jury might have considered it very relevant that the report was generated to discuss legislative compensation, not to scientifically address DTP dangers. By redacting, the learned treatise lacked sufficient indicia of reliability to present hearsay information unchallenged. Because this error was compounded by other errors, the judgment in Graham's (P) favor must be reversed and remanded.

EDITOR'S ANALYSIS: Learned treatises, unlike ancient documents, require evidence of reliability. Of particular difficulty is when experts differ on the reliability of a treatise. At a certain point, the trier of fact is forced to evaluate the usefulness of a treatise by comparing the apparent merit of differing witnesses' opinions on the treatise; at such a point, opinion is resting on opinion.

[For more information on learned treatises, see Casenote Law Outline on Evidence, Chapter 10, § IX, Miscellaneous Hearsay Exceptions.]

QUICKNOTES

SUA SPONTE - An action taken by the court by its own motion and without the suggestion of one of the parties.

NOTES:

ROBINSON v. SHAPIRO
Wrongful death action (P) v. Owner of building (D)
646 F.2d 734 (2d Cir. 1981).

NATURE OF CASE: Appeal from judgment in a wrongful death case.

FACT SUMMARY: A coworker of Mrs. Robinson's (P) deceased husband was permitted to testify as to certain statements the deceased had told him had been made by the superintendent of the building where the deceased was doing work when he received the injuries from which he died.

CONCISE RULE OF LAW: To be admissible under the residual hearsay exception provided for in the Federal Rules of Evidence, evidence offered must fulfill five requirements relating to its trustworthiness, its materiality, its probative importance, whether its admission will best serve the interests of justice, and whether the opponent received adequate notice of its use.

FACTS: Mrs. Robinson (P) brought a wrongful death action after her husband died from injuries received while he was part of a crew cleaning debris from a garage roof. After the owners of the building did not respond to interrogatories attempting to obtain the address of the party who had been superintendent at the time, the trial judge allowed one of Mr. Robinson's coworkers to testify as to certain relevant statements Robinson had told him the superintendent had made to Robinson. Admissibility was based on the residual hearsay exception to the Federal Rules of Evidence. The superintendent let the crew use his apartment window to reach the roof because he did not want his rugs soiled. The superintendent was not available to testify at trial. On appeal, Shapiro (D) and the others whom Mrs. Robinson (P) sued for damages argued that this testimony was not admissible under the residual hearsay exception in the Federal Rules of Evidence.

ISSUE: Is there a residual hearsay exception in the Federal Rules of Evidence?

HOLDING AND DECISION: (Meskill, J.) Yes. The residual hearsay exception within the Federal Rules of Evidence renders admissible a statement not specifically covered by the enumerated exceptions but having "equivalent circumstantial guarantees of trustworthiness" if the court determines that (A) it is offered as evidence of a material fact; (B) it is more probative on the point for which it is offered than any other evidence which the proponent can procure through reasonable efforts; and (C) the general purposes of the rules and the interests of justice will best be served by its admission. It also provides that the statement may not be admitted unless its proponent gave sufficient notice to provide the adverse party with a fair opportunity to meet the statement (which requires notice of intention to offer it and notice of its particulars, including the name and address of the declarant). In this case, the trial court did not abuse its discretion in deciding these requirements were met and admitting the testimony.

EDITOR'S ANALYSIS: Rule 804 deals specifically with hearsay exceptions where the declarant is unavailable, with subsection (b)(5) thereof stating the residual hearsay exception relied on in this case. The same exception, worded exactly the same, appears again as subsection (24) of Rule 803, which covers hearsay exceptions that apply even if the declarant is available.

[For more information on the residual exceptions, see Casenote Law Outline on Evidence, Chapter 10, § X, The "Wildcard" Exceptions.]

QUICKNOTES
PROBATIVE - Tending to establish proof.

NOTES:

WHITE v. ILLINOIS
Convicted sexual offender (D) v. State (P)
112 S.Ct. 736 (1992).

NATURE OF CASE: Appeal from denial of motion for a mistrial.

FACT SUMMARY: In Illinois' (P) criminal action against White (D), the appellate court, affirming the trial court's ruling, denied White's (D) motion for a mistrial based on the admissibility of extrajudicial testimony, even though his accuser was present during trial.

CONCISE RULE OF LAW: The Sixth Amendment Confrontation Clause does not prohibit the admission of testimony under the "spontaneous declaration" and "medical examination" exceptions to the hearsay rule.

FACTS: After White (D) was convicted by a jury for aggravated criminal sexual assault, residential burglary, and unlawful restraint, the appellate court, affirming the trial court's ruling, denied his motion for a mistrial in lieu of the trial court's determination that S.G.'s, his alleged victim's, extrajudicial, accusatory statements were admissible under the spontaneous declaration and medical examination exceptions to the hearsay rule, despite her presence and failure to testify at trial.

ISSUE: Does the Sixth Amendment Confrontation Clause prohibit the admission of testimony under the "spontaneous declaration" and "medical examination" exceptions to the hearsay rule?

HOLDING AND DECISION: (Rehnquist, C.J.) No. The Sixth Amendment Confrontation Clause does not prohibit the admission of testimony under the "spontaneous declaration" and "medical examination" exceptions to the hearsay rule. The Confrontation Clause and the hearsay rule generally conform to the same purpose, which is the promotion of fact-finding integrity. In this end, certain "firmly-rooted" exceptions to the hearsay rule carry sufficient corroborative weight so as to satisfy the reliability requirement posed by the Confrontation Clause. In the instant case, since the trial court determined that the statements S.G. made triggered the application of the spontaneous declaration and medical examination exceptions to the hearsay rule, and since these exceptions are "firmly rooted" in this country's jurisprudence, White's (D) motion for a mistrial is denied. Affirmed.

CONCURRENCE: (Thomas, J.) The Confrontation Clause is implicated by extra-judicial statements only insofar as they are contained in formalized testimonial matters, such as affidavits, depositions, prior testimony, or confessions.

EDITOR'S ANALYSIS: Despite having no textual basis in the Sixth Amendment to reach its result, the majority above assumes that the Confrontation Clause limits admission of hearsay evidence insofar as it does not bear a particularized guarantee of trustworthiness. Notwithstanding this ostensibly even-handed rule, however, courts accordingly will have wide discretionary latitude in determining a statement's trustworthiness.

[For more information on excited utterances, see Casenote Law Outline on Evidence, Chapter 10, § III, Excited Utterances.]

NOTES:

IDAHO v. WRIGHT
State (P) v. Sexual molesters (D)
110 S. Ct. 3139 (1990).

NATURE OF CASE: Appeal of reversal of conviction for sexual molestation.

FACT SUMMARY: In a child sexual molestation prosecution, statements of the child-victim were admitted under the residual hearsay exception.

CONCISE RULE OF LAW: The admission of statements of a child-victim in a molestation prosecution under the residual hearsay exception may violate the Confrontation Clause.

FACTS: Wright (D) and Giles (D), a couple, were arrested for allegedly molesting Wright's (D) two daughters from a previous marriage, ages 5½ and 2½. The older daughter had informed her father's companion, who informed the police. Pursuant to official investigation, the younger daughter, Kathy, was examined by one Dr. Jambura. During the course of the exam, Kathy made certain statements indicating that she had been molested. At trial, the court allowed admission of the statements under Idaho's (P) residual hearsay objection, despite Kathy's incompetency to testify and the lack of detailed notes or recording of the exam. The trial court concluded that other evidence sufficiently corroborated the statements so as to bring them within the residual hearsay exception. Wright (D) and Giles (D) were convicted. The Idaho Supreme Court reversed, holding that admission of the statement violated the Confrontation Clause. The U.S. Supreme Court granted review.

ISSUE: May the admission of statements of a child-victim in a molestation prosecution under the residual hearsay exception violate the Confrontation Clause?

HOLDING AND DECISION: (O'Connor, J.) Yes. The admission of statements of a child-victim in a molestation prosecution under the residual hearsay exception may violate the Confrontation Clause. The Confrontation Clause has not been held to prohibit the admission of hearsay statements in a criminal prosecution. However, this Court has held that, for the clause to be satisfied, it must be shown that the declarant is unavailable and that the statement bears some indicia of reliability. As to what constitutes an indication of reliability, one such indication would be that the statement falls within a time-honored hearsay exception. The residual hearsay exception, almost by definition, is not such an exception. Consequently, a statement admitted thereunder, to satisfy the Confrontation Clause, must bear some other intrinsic indicia of reliability. What constitutes such indicia cannot be detailed in one opinion. Rather, it must be decided on a case-by-case basis. The broad, guiding principle should be that the statement must be sufficiently reliable so that it would be unlikely for cross-examination of the declarant to impeach the statement.

Here, the statement was obtained in an interview by a doctor in highly suggestive circumstances. This situation did not bear the necessary indicia of reliability to meet the standard for admissibility articulated above, and consequently, the statement should not have been admitted. Affirmed.

DISSENT: (Kennedy, J.) The Court's view that reliability must be intrinsic is erroneous. A trial court should be able to employ corroborating extrinsic evidence.

EDITOR'S ANALYSIS: The residual hearsay exception is recognized in most states. It is codified in Fed. R. Ev. 803(24). Its details vary from state to state, but the usual requirement is twofold. The statement must have some indication of reliability, and the declarant must be unavailable to testify.

[For more information on the medical diagnosis exception in child abuse cases, see Casenote Law Outline on Evidence, Chapter 10, § V, Statements for Medical Diagnosis.]

QUICKNOTES

EXTRINSIC EVIDENCE - Evidence that is not contained within the text of a document or contract but which is derived from the parties' statements or the circumstances under which the agreement was made.

CONFRONTATION CLAUSE - A provision in the Sixth Amendment to the United States Constitution that an accused in a criminal action has the right to confront the witnesses against him, including the right to attend the trial and to cross-examine witnesses called on behalf of the prosecution.

NOTES:

5

CHAPTER 5
CIRCUMSTANTIAL PROOF: FURTHER PROBLEMS

QUICK REFERENCE RULES OF LAW

1. **Evidence of Other Crimes.** Character is never an issue in a criminal prosecution unless the defendant chooses to make it one. (People v. Zackowitz)

   [For more information on the admission of character evidence, see Casenote Law Outline on Evidence, Chapter 6, § II, Character in Issue.]

2. **Evidence of Other Crimes.** Specific intent cannot be inferred from a person's general bad character. (United States v. Accardo)

   [For more information on using character to prove conduct, see Casenote Law Outline on Evidence, Chapter 6, § III, Character to Prove Conduct.]

3. **Evidence of Other Crimes.** Otherwise admissible evidence which is relevant to the present criminal charge is not made inadmissible merely because it may tend to show commission of a previous crime. (United States v. Montalvo)

   [For more information on evidence of prior criminal acts, see Casenote Law Outline on Evidence, Chapter 6, § IV, The "Other Crimes" Loophole.]

4. **Evidence of Other Crimes.** Evidence of other transactions by the defendant, if independently relevant, may be admissible even though they adversely reflect on the character of the accused. (People v. Steele)

   [For more information on evidence of past criminal activity, see Casenote Law Outline on Evidence, Chapter 6, § IV, The "Other Crimes" Loophole.]

5. **Evidence of Other Crimes.** Evidence of other criminal or immoral conduct may be admitted as part of the People's case on rebuttal if it has a tendency to disprove the defendant's claim that he was legally insane at the time of the crime. (People v. Santarelli)

   [For more information on using character to prove conduct, see Casenote Law Outline on Evidence, Chapter 6, § III, Character to Prove Conduct.]

6. **Evidence of Other Crimes.** Evidence of a defendant's similar crimes or acts must be relevant to some disputed issue in the trial to be admissible into evidence. (United States v. Figueroa)

   [For more information on evidence of similar crimes, see Casenote Law Outline on Evidence, Chapter 6, § IV, The "Other Crimes" Loophole.]

7. **Evidence of Other Crimes.** Proof of similar acts constituting separate and distinct crimes is admissible for the purpose of permitting the trier of facts to draw an inference from the evidence of a general scheme or plan that the defendant did commit the crime with which he is charged. (State v. Bock)

   [For more information on evidence of unchanged conduct, see Casenote Law Outline on Evidence, Chapter 6, § IV, The "Other Crimes" Loophole.]

8. **Evidence of Other Crimes.** The depraved sexual instinct exception to the general rule against admissability of prior bad acts should no longer be recognized. (Lannan v. State)

[For more information on uncharged misconduct, see Casenote Law Outline on Evidence, Chapter 6, § IV, The "Other Crimes" Loophole.]

9. **Evidence of Other Crimes.** A court need not make, prior to admitting post acts introduced to show motive or knowledge, a preliminary finding that the acts occurred. (Huddleston v. United States)

10. **Evidence of Other Crimes.** If evidence admissible against a defendant on other crimes with which he was charged in counts dismissed on appeal so affected the trial as to deny the defendant his right to have the jury fairly evaluate only the evidence admissible against him on the counts remaining, there must be a retrial as to those remaining counts. (People v. Castillo)

11. **Evidence of Criminal Defendant's Reputation and Opinion Evidence of His Character; Evidence of Victim's Character.** Where a defendant introduces evidence of his good character/reputation in the community, the prosecution may cross-examine these character witnesses about events or crimes, in defendant's past, which would tend to adversely affect defendant's reputation. (Michelson v. United States)

   [For more information on character testimony, see Casenote Law Outline on Evidence, Chapter 6, § II, Character in Issue.]

12. **Evidence of Criminal Defendant's Reputation and Opinion Evidence of His Character; Evidence of Victim's Character.** Evidence of specific past acts of violence and violent reputation of the victim is admissible to show that the defendant acted in self-defense only where such acts and reputation were known to the defendant. (Burgeon v. State)

   [For more information on the admissibility of character evidence, see Casenote Law Outline on Evidence, Chapter 6, § I, Definitions and Distinctions.]

13. **Evidence of Criminal Defendant's Reputation and Opinion Evidence of His Character; Evidence of Victim's Character.** The Rape Shield Law disallows evidence of a victim's past sexual conduct unless it is necessary and directly relevant to the defense. (White v. State)

   [For more information on rape shield laws, see Casenote Law Outline on Evidence, Chapter 6, § III, Character to Prove Conduct.]

14. **Evidence of Reputation and Opinion of Character in Civil Cases.** In a civil action, evidence of a victim's character is admissible where such character is an ultimate fact to be determined. (Crumpton v. Confederation Life Insurance Co.)

   [For more information on character in issue, see Casenote Law Outline on Evidence, Chapter 6, § II, Character in Issue.]

15. **Similar Occurrences.** Evidence of similar transactions or conduct on other occasions is not competent to prove the commission of a particular act charged unless the acts are connected in some special way, indicating a relevancy beyond mere similarity in certain particulars. (Dallas Railway & Terminal Co. v. Farnsworth)

   [For more information on evidence of routine practices, see Casenote Law Outline on Evidence, Chapter 6, § VI, Evidence of Habit or Routine Practice.]

16. **Habit and Custom.** At least where the issue involves proof of a deliberate and repetitive practice, a party should be able to introduce evidence of habit or regular usage to allow the inference of its persistence and hence negligence on a particular occasion. (Halloran v. Virginia Chemicals, Inc.)

[For more information on evidence of habit, see Casenote Law Outline on Evidence, Chapter 6, § VI, Evidence of Habit or Routine Practice.]

17. **Repairs, Liability Insurance.** Evidence of subsequent remedial measures may be admitted to impeach a defendant's testimony only when there has been self-serving, false, or misleading statements. (Phar-Mor, Inc. v. Goff)

[For more information on subsequent remedial measures, see Casenote Law Outline on Evidence, Chapter 7, § II, Subsequent Remedial Measures.]

18. **Compromises.** Settlement offers are excluded from evidence only when they are made after a controversy has arisen. (Hiram Ricker & Sons v. Students International Meditation Society)

[For more information on the exclusion of settlement offers, see Casenote Law Outline on Evidence, Chapter 7, § III, Compromise and Settlement Negotiations.]

19. **Compromises.** Under Federal Rule of Evidence 408, agreements in compromise of a claim are generally inadmissible on the issue of liability on such claim but not when offered for another purpose, such as proving bias or prejudice of a witness. (John McShain, Inc. v. Cessna Aircraft Co.)

[For more information on evidence of compromise agreements, see Casenote Law Outline on Evidence, Chapter 7, § III, Compromise and Settlement Negotiations.]

20. **Forensic Argument.** In argument to the jury, an attorney may state any reasonable inferences that may be drawn from the evidence as long as it relates to matters at issue in the trial. (Harvey v. Aubrey)

[For more information on inferences drawn from evidence, see Casenote Law Outline on Evidence, Chapter 2, § III, Is the "Evidence" Relevant?]

21. **Forensic Argument.** Flagrantly abusive statements, from one counsel to another, unsupported by the evidence and introducing matters clearly irrelevant to the jury's deliberation of the jury's issues justify a new trial. (Robinson v. Pennsylvania Railroad Co.)

PEOPLE v. ZACKOWITZ
State (P) v. Murderer (D)
N.Y. Ct. App., 254 N.Y. 192, 172 N.E. 466 (1930).

NATURE OF CASE: Prosecution for first-degree murder.

FACT SUMMARY: The decedent insulted Zackowitz's (D) wife, and Zackowitz (D) later, while in a rage and under the influence of alcohol, shot and killed him.

CONCISE RULE OF LAW: Character is never an issue in a criminal prosecution unless the defendant chooses to make it one.

FACTS: Coppola, the decedent, was one of four men who insulted Zackowitz's (D) wife. Zackowitz (D) threatened to kill them if they did not leave within five minutes. Zackowitz (D) walked his wife home, where she told him that the men had propositioned her. Zackowitz (D) had been drinking and went into a rage. He either armed himself with a pistol or had previously been carrying one (he offered two different stories, the latter one at trial) and went back to see if the men were still there. There were words and a fight, during which Zackowitz (D) shot Coppola. Zackowitz (D) left the scene and was subsequently arrested about two months later. The question at trial was Zackowitz's (D) state of mind. Was the murder premeditated or was it done in the heat of a liquor-induced rage (second-degree murder)? The prosecution was allowed to introduce, over Zackowitz's (D) objection, testimony showing that Zackowitz (D) owned three other pistols and a tear gas gun. These weapons had been obtained prior to the shooting, and there was no claim made that they were carried by Zackowitz (D) when he shot Coppola. The evidence was introduced to show that Zackowitz (D) was "a desperate type of criminal," a "person criminally inclined." Zackowitz (D) was convicted of first-degree murder.

ISSUE: Should a defendant's guilt of a specific crime be inferable from his general character?

HOLDING AND DECISION: (Cardozo, J.) No. It is a fundamental rule that character is never an issue in a criminal prosecution unless the defendant chooses to make it one. In a very real sense, a defendant starts his life anew. His guilt must be established with regard to the particular crime with which he is charged. The law has made a policy decision to exclude evidence of this nature in order to protect the innocent. "The natural and inevitable tendency of the tribunal — whether judge or jury — is to give excessive weight to the vicious record of crime thus exhibited, and either to allow it to bear too strongly on the present charge, or to take the proof of it as justifying a condemnation irrespective of guilt of the present charge." The evidence of the hidden guns would be admissible if they had been purchased subsequent to Zackowitz's (D) wife being insulted in order to show motive or design or if Zackowitz (D) had been carrying all of them (act of preparation). However, the fact that Zackowitz (D) had the guns at home does not tend to prove, even inferentially, his murder of Coppola was premeditated. Ownership of weapons was not relevant to the charge.

DISSENT: (Pound, J.) The possession of these weapons was a separate crime. The people may prove other crimes against the defendant in a criminal prosecution if such proof tends to establish (1) motive; (2) intent; (3) absence of mistake or accident; (4) common scheme or plan embracing two or more crimes so related to one another that proof of one tends to establish the other; (5) the identity of the person charged with the crime. The weapons have a bearing on the crime in general. If Zackowitz (D) had been carrying them at the time of the murder, such evidence would have been admissible. The fact that they were a short distance away in his apartment should not make a difference. Zackowitz (D) was presented to the jury as a man having dangerous weapons in his possession, making a selection from them, and then going out to kill those whom he previously had threatened. The prosecution did not seek to introduce the evidence as to general character but to show that Zackowitz (D), having the means and opportunity to carry out his threat, proceeded to do so.

EDITOR'S ANALYSIS: Aside from the prejudicial nature of character evidence in criminal prosecutions is the question of its probative value. If its introduction will not prove one of the elements of the crime charged, is it really relevant? Does the fact that Zackowitz (D) had weapons available prove, either directly or inferentially, that the killing was premeditated? If it does, why can't the same reasoning apply to anyone owning a single handgun, switchblade, etc.? The question here is whether Zackowitz (D) had a rational intent to murder Coppola prior to the commission of the killing. Does the fact that he had a weapon or weapons at home bear any relevance to intent? The law has made it a general policy that what a party was or had previously done (with the exception of the five points listed by the Dissent) is not relevant to the current charges against him. If the defendant introduces testimony as to his good character, the prosecution may rebut by introducing evidence as to his past crimes, misconduct, or reputation. So, while a defendant in a criminal prosecution may always introduce testimony as to his good character, he does so at the risk of allowing the prosecution to introduce contrary evidence of a like nature. The rationale is that the prosecution always has the right to rebut direct testimony and the fact that this would prejudice defendant is irrelevant.

[For more information on the admission of character evidence, see Casenote Law Outline on Evidence, Chapter 6, § II, Character in Issue.]

QUICKNOTES

CHARACTER EVIDENCE - Evidence of someone's moral standing in a community based on reputation.

UNITED STATES v. ACCARDO
Federal Government (P) v. Tax Fraud Suspect (D)
298 F.2d 133 (7th Cir. 1962).

NATURE OF CASE: Prosecution for false statements and fraudulent deductions in income tax returns.

FACT SUMMARY: The jury which convicted Accardo (D) of false statements and fraudulent deduction in his income tax returns had been exposed to newspaper articles which were highly damaging to Accardo's (D) character and reputation.

CONCISE RULE OF LAW: Specific intent cannot be inferred from a person's general bad character.

FACTS: Accardo (D), though unemployed, claimed to be an agent of Premium Beer Sales, Inc. on three tax returns and deducted automobile expenses. During the jury selection, newspapers and television labeled him a crook and spoke of his previous criminal record. During the trial, which was highly publicized, the media continued to present accounts prejudicial to Accardo (D). The jury was not sequestered during the trial and was undoubtedly exposed to this publicity. The trial judge admonished the jury not to be influenced by these accounts. The element of the crime charged was that the false statements and deductions were made in Accardo's (D) tax return in bad faith. Testimony was admitted that Accardo (D) was not employed. One statement made by the trial judge was that Accardo (D) was a gambler and that professional gambling was a malignancy which permeated all levels of society. Accardo (D) was convicted.

ISSUE: Can bad faith be inferred from proof of an ulterior motive or general bad character?

HOLDING AND DECISION: (Kiley, J.) No. Specific intent cannot be inferred from a person's general bad character. To convict Accardo (D) of the charges against him, bad faith in the preparation of his return was required. The willful, or bad faith, element is the deliberate making of false statements, not the making of an honest mistake of judgment. The motive for the willfulness is not at issue. The creating of a facade to report gambling income is not relevant to the charge. The testimony that Accardo (D) was not employed by Premium and, therefore, could not lawfully claim a deduction would allow the jury to infer that the claim was willful and made in bad faith. The problem in this case was that the jury's access to prejudicial publicity, the inadequate instructions by the judge about disregarding them, ineffective safeguards against the effect of the publicity during voir dire, and the introduction of testimony concerning Accardo's (D) motive does not allow a reviewing court to determine on what grounds the jury found Accardo (D) guilty. Most of the evidence introduced at trial was concerning Accardo's (D) violation of Illinois' antigambling laws, an offense Accardo (D) was not charged with. This is prejudicial character evidence which is inadmissible in a criminal prosecution. Since its admission was not relevant to the charges against Accardo (D) and was highly prejudicial, the conviction must be reversed and the case remanded for a new trial.

EDITOR'S ANALYSIS: The jury will not be permitted to infer bad faith from a defendant's motives where the motives are not relevant to the crime charged. In the case of Accardo (D), he was not charged with gambling violations or past misdeeds. Evidence of other crimes may be admitted where it tends to establish a motive for the crime charged but, as is shown in Accardo, only where motive is at issue. In civil litigation, character evidence is generally not admissible to reflect on the commission or noncommission of an act or on the quality of a party's conduct on a particular occasion. However, where character is at issue (e.g., defamation, chastity, fraud, or deceit, etc.) evidence (with certain exceptions) may be admitted. Since defendant's bad character was not at issue, it was improper for the jury to be allowed to infer guilt from past misconduct.

[For more information on using character to prove conduct, see Casenote Law Outline on Evidence, Chapter 6, § III, Character to Prove Conduct.]

NOTES:

UNITED STATES v. MONTALVO
Federal government (P) v. Heroin dealer (D)
271 F.2d 922 (2d Cir. 1959).

NATURE OF CASE: Appeal from criminal conviction.

FACT SUMMARY: Rovira (D) was suspected of trafficking in heroin. When he was observed in the vicinity of a recently seized stash of heroin, he was arrested and searched. The search produced a penknife with traces of heroin on it.

CONCISE RULE OF LAW: Otherwise admissible evidence which is relevant to the present criminal charge is not made inadmissible merely because it may tend to show commission of a previous crime.

FACTS: Rovira (D) and Montalvo (D) were seen handling a brown paper bag. What appeared to be the same bag was seized in a search of Montalvo's (D) apartment. When Rovira (D) appeared at the apartment by driving by it slowly twice, he was arrested and searched. The search revealed a penknife that had traces of heroin on its blade. The knife was introduced as evidence of Rovira's (D) involvement with heroin. He was convicted and appealed, contending that the penknife was inadmissible, among other grounds.

ISSUE: Will evidence be rendered inadmissible merely because it tends to show involvement in a prior criminal act where the evidence is relevant to the present criminal charge?

HOLDING AND DECISION: (Friendly, J.) No. The penknife was not introduced to show that because Rovira (D) had committed a previous narcotics offense he was capable of involvement in the presently charged act. It was introduced to show a continuing pattern of conduct, including the necessary tools, that was leading to the rejoining of Montalvo (D) to conclude their illegal plan. The fact that the evidence may have tended to show involvement in a previous criminal act did not render it inadmissible to prove the present charge. The relevance was a discretionary decision by the judge, and we find he did not violate his discretion.

EDITOR'S ANALYSIS: Introduction of evidence showing prior acts of misconduct are never admissible where the sole purpose is to discredit the character of the defendant. But where the evidence can be shown to have independent relevance to the case, it will be admitted, despite the adverse inferences thereby raised.

[For more information on evidence of prior criminal acts, see Casenote Law Outline on Evidence, Chapter 6, § IV, The "Other Crimes" Loophole.]

QUICKNOTES

CHARACTER EVIDENCE - Evidence of someone's moral standing in a community based on reputation.

NOTES:

PEOPLE v. STEELE
State (P) v. Drug dealer (D)
Ill. Sup. Ct., 22 Ill.2d 142, 174 N.E.2d 848 (1961).

NATURE OF CASE: Indictment for offering to sell a narcotic drug and then selling a quantity of a purported narcotic drug.

FACT SUMMARY: Steele (D), although offering to sell narcotics, intentionally sold a nonnarcotic drug.

CONCISE RULE OF LAW: Evidence of other transactions by the defendant, if independently relevant, may be admissible even though they adversely reflect on the character of the accused.

FACTS: An informant had been told by Steele (D) that he sold narcotics. The informant telephoned Steele (D), who offered to sell him narcotics. Several narcotics agents listened to the conversation. A meeting was set up. A narcotics agent went with the informant and paid Steele (D) $400 for the purported narcotics. When the agent tested the drug, he found that it was a nonnarcotic. When arrested, Steele (D) denied dealing in narcotics and said it was only a confidence game for "suckers." Steele (D) was tried under an Illinois statute making it illegal to offer to sell narcotics and then to sell a nonnarcotic drug. The trial court admitted testimony concerning Steele's (D) previous drug dealings. Steele (D) was convicted.

ISSUE: Can evidence of a defendant's past criminal activity be admitted to show that the present charge involved an ongoing activity or a course of conduct?

HOLDING AND DECISION: (Schaeffer, J.) Yes. Evidence of earlier dealings in narcotics supports an inference that those early sales laid the groundwork for Steele's (D) current confidence game. They also tend to show that Steele (D) represented the substance to be a narcotic when he knew that it was not. The evidence of other transactions was thus independently relevant apart from its tendency to show the bad character of the accused, and so its admission was not improper. The element of deceit is a principal ingredient in the charge. Evidence introduced that Steele (D) knew the substance offered was not a narcotic (fraudulent intent) and that he had misrepresented it (false statement) are admissible as tending to prove the elements of the crime. It is irrelevant that it tends to expose Steele's (D) bad character if its probative value outweighs its prejudicial quality. This is discretionary with the trial judge who will only be reversed if he has abused this power.

EDITOR'S ANALYSIS: Prior criminal activity is admissible to show a common scheme, ongoing activity, scienter, intent, lack of mistake, or identity. The proffered evidence of criminal activity must be of a similar nature to the crime charged, relevantly bear on an element of the crime, and not be too remote in time.

Admission of evidence of past misdeeds is generally circumstantial evidence. It allows the jury to infer one or more of the elements of the crime charged. It should never be allowed unless it would logically lead to such an inference. Admission for an improper purpose would most likely lead to an automatic reversal.

[For more information on evidence of past criminal activity, see Casenote Law Outline on Evidence, Chapter 6, § IV, The "Other Crimes" Loophole.]

QUICKNOTES
CHARACTER EVIDENCE - Evidence of someone's moral standing in a community based on reputation.

RELEVANCE - The admissibility of evidence based on whether it has any tendency to prove or disprove a matter at issue to the case.

NOTES:

PEOPLE v. SANTARELLI
State (P) v. Murderer (D)
425 N.Y.S.2d 77, 401 N.E.2d 199 (1980).

NATURE OF CASE: Appeal from conviction of murder in the second degree.

FACT SUMMARY: To rebut Santarelli's (D) defense of "temporary insanity," the Government (P) introduced into evidence testimony of witnesses who had seen him commit a number of other violent acts and claimed that this showed he had an "explosive personality" — a character trait not rising to the level of legal insanity.

CONCISE RULE OF LAW: Evidence of other criminal or immoral conduct may be admitted as part of the People's case on rebuttal if it has a tendency to disprove the defendant's claim that he was legally insane at the time of the crime.

FACTS: Santarelli (D) admitted that he had fired five blasts from a sawed-off shotgun into his brother-in-law, two of them proving fatal. However, he claimed that he had been "temporarily insane" at the time, that his acts had been the product of a "paranoid delusion." In cross-examining the psychiatrists that Santarelli (D) had put on in support of this claim, the Government (P) attempted to establish that Santarelli's (D) conduct also could be explained as a symptom of a "personality disorder" commonly called an "explosive personality." Moreover, the Government (P) elicited from the witnesses that one suffering from an explosive personality would not be classified as legally insane. Thereafter, the Government (P), over defense objections, was permitted to introduce into evidence the testimony of witnesses as to various violent acts or other crimes committed by Santarelli (D). For example, Vincent Christina, a close friend of Santarelli's (D) testified that it had been Santarelli (D) and he who went to a particular shop steward's place of business and beat him up. The shop steward had previously testified that he had been attacked and badly beaten by two men but that he was unable to identify his assailants. Santarelli's (D) probation officer was permitted to testify that Santarelli (D) had previously been convicted of possession of a sawed-off shotgun. He also testified concerning several incidents in which Santarelli (D) had resorted to violence in the face of relatively mild provocation. Grover testified that he had observed Santarelli (D) participate in a barroom scuffle, although he did not know how it had started or what provocation there had been. Police officer Monroney testified that he saw Santarelli (D) standing behind a bar throwing bottles and glasses around the room, but he likewise did not know how the incident began. Finally, testimony was presented regarding Santarelli's (D) relationship to organized crime. The Government (P) used this particular testimony in attempting to show that Santarelli (D) was under considerable emotional stress at the time he shot his brother-in-law, that it was related to the fact that his friend

Christina had been the subject of an attempted murder, and that this caused Santarelli (D) to be fearful for his own safety to the point that he considered asking for FBI protection. The implication was that Santarelli's (D) fears were based on his knowledge of local organized crime activities, that the shooting had been precipitated by the considerable emotional pressure under which Santarelli (D) had been laboring, but that it resulted from this "explosive personality" rather than any condition rising to the level of "temporary insanity." The admission of all of this evidence was again challenged in appealing the resulting conviction of murder in the second degree. Noting that the challenged evidence "carried little potential for prejudice in this case," the appellate division had upheld the trial court's ruling on the basis of what it perceived to be a "general rule" that once a defendant asserts the insanity defense, "any and all prior conduct of the accused having some bearing on the subject is admissible, even though it might also tend to show him guilty of other crimes."

ISSUE: If the defendant claims that he was legally insane at the time of the crime, can the government be permitted to introduce evidence of uncharged criminal or immoral conduct that has a tendency to disprove the defendant's claim?

HOLDING AND DECISION: (Gabrielli, J.) Yes. Once a defendant places his mental state before the trier of fact by alleging that he was insane at the time of the crime, he cannot complain when the Government (P) seeks to bring forth additional evidence bearing upon that issue. That is why evidence of uncharged criminal or immoral conduct may be admitted as part of the Government's (P) case on rebuttal if it has a tendency to disprove the defendant's claim that he was legally insane at the time of the crime. However, a defendant who asserts an insanity defense "opens the door" to the Government's (P) "character evidence" only to the extent that such evidence has a natural tendency to disprove his specific claim. In this case, therefore, to the extent that evidence of Santarelli's (D) prior violent acts and his relationship with organized crime had a direct bearing upon the validity of the Government's (P) "explosive personality" theory, it was clearly admissible. The problem arises in this case, however, because the trial judge failed to evaluate with sufficient particularity whether each piece of evidence offered by the Government (P) was actually relevant and material to their "explosive personality" theory. In deciding whether to admit evidence of prior criminal or immoral conduct in rebuttal to an insanity claim, the trial court must take special care to ensure not

Continued on next page.

only that the evidence bears some articulable relation to the issue but that its probative value in fact warrants its admission despite its potential for prejudice. The danger in cases involving the insanity defense is that every fact in the accused's life may in some sense be said to have a bearing upon the issue of his mental state. The danger is particularly great that the jury will become confused by the mass of evidence presented and will decide to convict the defendant not because they find he was legally sane at the time of the act, but rather because they are convinced that he is a person of general criminal intent. In looking at the individual pieces of evidence offered in this case, it is clear that some of the testimony related to acts of violence others saw Santarelli (D) commit. However, in at least two instances, those testifying had no notion of what provoked those acts. Thus, such testimony had no bearing on the "explosive personality" theory and should not have been admitted. Nor should the trial court have admitted testimony regarding Santarelli's (D) alleged participation in the cold-blooded act of helping another track down and beat up a shop steward. Such evidence would have no logical purpose other than demonstrating Santarelli's (D) general propensity toward criminality. It certainly would have no bearing on the "explosive personality" theory. One last piece of testimony that should not have been admitted was that of the probation officer to the effect that Santarelli (D) had been convicted of possession of a sawed-off shotgun. This bears no relationship to whether or not Santarelli (D) had an "explosive personality." At any rate, whatever arguable probative value it may have had was greatly outweighed by its potential for prejudicing the jury. That testimony regarding Santarelli's (D) participation in acts of violence upon little provocation was, however, directly relevant to the question of Santarelli's (D) reaction patterns and was thus properly admitted despite the danger of prejudice. Similarly, the testimony elicited by the prosecutor regarding Santarelli's (D) relationship to organized crime had a tendency to support the Government's (P) trial theory and was therefore properly admitted into evidence. Reversed and remitted for further proceedings on the indictment.

DISSENT: (Jasen, J.) The restrictive rule adopted by the majority unfairly limits the Government's (P) use of evidence of prior crimes and antisocial conduct offered solely for the purpose of proving a defendant's mental condition. It overemphasizes the possibility of prejudice to the defendant. It also ties the prosecutor to one particular "theory" of sanity, even though his burden is not to set forth a single unitary theory of sanity but to prove a defendant's sanity beyond a reasonable doubt. Most of the evidence which the majority contends should have been excluded offered an inference of Santarelli's (D) "predisposition toward violence." Such an inference is altogether different from the inference of "criminal predisposition" which the authorities cited by the majority seek to prevent.

EDITOR'S ANALYSIS: Just as a claim of insanity may let in evidence of other crimes, so may a claim of self-defense. In one particular case, a wife claimed she had killed her husband in self-defense. The court hearing her appeal held that the trial court had not erred in admitting evidence that a number of weeks after the fatal confrontation with her husband, the wife had shot a male acquaintance when he said he could not repay a debt. Halliburton v. State, Tex. Crim. App., 528 S.W.2d 216 (1975).

[For more information on using character to prove conduct, see Casenote Law Outline on Evidence, Chapter 6, § III, Character to Prove Conduct.]

QUICKNOTES

CHARACTER EVIDENCE - Evidence of someone's moral standing in a community based on reputation.

INSANITY (DEFENSE) - An affirmative defense to a criminal prosecution that the defendant suffered from a mental illness, thereby relieving him of liability for his conduct.

NOTES:

UNITED STATES v. FIGUEROA
Federal government (P) v. Heroin dealer (D)
618 F.2d 934 (2d Cir. 1980).

NATURE OF CASE: Appeal from conviction of drug-related offenses.

FACT SUMMARY: Acosta (D), on trial with Figueroa (D) and another for heroin-related offenses, challenged the admission into evidence of his 1968 conviction for selling heroin, insisting that it was not relevant to any disputed issue in the trial.

CONCISE RULE OF LAW: Evidence of a defendant's similar crimes or acts must be relevant to some disputed issue in the trial to be admissible into evidence.

FACTS: Three persons, including Acosta (D) and Figueroa (D), were jointly tried and found guilty of conspiracy to possess and distribute heroin and possession of heroin with intent to distribute. At trial, Acosta's (D) attorney had made it clear that his client was not bringing the issue of intent into dispute but rather was adopting a defense that the alleged incidents in which it was claimed he had participated had not in fact occurred at all but had been fabricated by the undercover Drug Enforcement Agent involved in the investigation. Nonetheless, the trial judge admitted evidence of Acosta's (D) 1968 conviction for selling heroin. It was admitted at the conclusion of the prosecution's case-in-chief, before it had been ascertained that the defendants were indeed going to rest without presenting evidence. Acosta (D) claimed its introduction was improper because it was not relevant to any disputed issue.

ISSUE: In order to be admissible, must evidence of a defendant's similar crimes or acts be relevant to some disputed issue in the trial?

HOLDING AND DECISION: (Newman, J.) Yes. To be admissible, evidence of a defendant's similar crimes or acts must be relevant to some disputed issue in the trial (e.g., to prove the defendant's knowledge or intent, to prove identity or common scheme, etc.). Of course, even then, its probative value must not be substantially outweighed by the risk of unfair prejudice. Applying these principles to this particular case, it becomes clear that the evidence of Acosta's (D) prior conviction should not have been admitted. His counsel clearly stated that he was not disputing the issues suggested by the trial court as providing the basis for admissibility, primarily intent. Reversed and remanded.

EDITOR'S ANALYSIS: It is, of course, the job of defense counsel to make it sufficiently clear to the court that the issues as to which a prior conviction might legitimately relate are not being disputed. He must communicate this well enough that the court would be justified (a) in sustaining objection to any subsequent cross-examination or jury argument that seeks to raise the issue and (b) in charging the jury that if they find all other elements established beyond a reasonable doubt, they can resolve the issue against the defendant because it is not disputed. See United States v. Mohel, 604 F.2d 748 (2d Cir. 1979).

[For more information on evidence of similar crimes, see Casenote Law Outline on Evidence, Chapter 6, § IV, The "Other Crimes" Loophole.]

QUICKNOTES

CHARACTER EVIDENCE - Evidence of someone's moral standing in a community based on reputation.

FRE 403 - Provides that a court may dismiss otherwise relevant evidence where its prejudicial effect on the proceeding outweighs any probative value it has.

HABIT - A practice or custom of repeated behavior in response to a specific set of circumstances.

RELEVANCE - The admissibility of evidence based on whether it has any tendency to prove or disprove a matter at issue to the case.

NOTES:

STATE v. BOCK
State (P) v. Check forger (D)
Minn. Sup. Ct., 229 Minn. 449, 39 N.W.2d 887 (1949).

NATURE OF CASE: Prosecution for second-degree forgery.

FACT SUMMARY: Bock (D) was accused of passing a bad check stolen from the General Roofing Co. Evidence was admitted at the trial to show that Bock (D) had also subsequently passed three other bad checks.

CONCISE RULE OF LAW: Proof of similar acts constituting separate and distinct crimes is admissible for the purpose of permitting the trier of facts to draw an inference from the evidence of a general scheme or plan that the defendant did commit the crime with which he is charged.

FACTS: Twenty-seven blank checks were stolen from the General Roofing Company. The next day, a man attempted to cash one of them. When a cashier became suspicious, the man fled. Bock (D) was later picked up by the police and was charged with attempting to pass a bad check. At the trial, the prosecution introduced testimony that Bock (D) had been identified as the party attempting to pass forged checks on nonexistent accounts on three subsequent occasions (Exhibits B, D, and F). Bock (D) countered with an alibi for the time the General Roofing checks were stolen and for the times when Exhibits B, D, and F were alleged to have been passed by him. Bock (D) also unsuccessfully attempted to introduce evidence of two other checks which had been passed with the same signatures as Exhibits B, D, and F. He offered to show that witnesses said he was not the party passing them. After Bock's (D) conviction, Miller was arrested by the police, and he confessed to the passing of Exhibits B, D, and F. Bock (D) appealed from the trial judge's ruling denying a new trial.

ISSUE: Is it error to admit evidence of collateral crimes of which the defendant is neither charged nor convicted?

HOLDING AND DECISION: (Knutsch, J.) No. This can be sustained under either of two exceptions to the general rule that evidence of past or subsequent criminal acts are not admissible. While inadmissible to prove guilt, it is clearly admissible to prove identity if the crimes are similar and closely connected in time and place. It is also admissible in order to show an ongoing scheme or plan. The fact that these activities extended over a month does not make them remote as to time. This is largely a matter of discretion with the trial judge, and the court will not overrule his decision unless there is a clear showing of abuse. Bock (D) also contended error regarding the trial court's failure to allow the introduction of his proof that similar checks had been passed by a third party. Objection to the admission was based on the contention that this evidence did not show that Bock (D) hadn't passed Exhibits B, D, and F. The trial judge's error was that Bock

(D) ought to be able to refute the inferences raised by Exhibits B, D, and F as to identity and common scheme or plan. By introducing evidence that another party was guilty of passing the checks, he can attempt to negate the inference that he alone was guilty of all these acts. This rebuttal would cast doubt on his being guilty of passing Exhibits B, D, and F, and might destroy the validity of all the identifications. Bock's (D) third contention of error was that Miller's affidavit alone should be grounds for a new trial. The trial judge contended that the affidavit was only of an impeaching nature and was cumulative of the other denials that Bock (D) had not passed the checks. While the granting of a new trial is discretionary with the trial judge and it will normally not be granted because of newly discovered evidence of a cumulative or corroborative nature, it is also true that cumulative evidence of an erroneous nature is as apt to lead to unjust results as cumulative evidence that leads to a correct one. Since it is impossible to determine the weight of the evidence concerning Exhibits B, D, and F on the jury due to its prejudicial nature, the defendant should be granted a new trial.

EDITOR'S ANALYSIS: Generally, the admission of evidence tending to show the defendant was involved in other acts of misconduct for which he has not been convicted is prohibited. This type of evidence is character evidence, and the prosecution cannot attempt to prove guilt by evidence of bad character. Several exceptions to this rule are generally recognized, however. Where the defendant puts on evidence of his own good character, the prosecution is allowed to rebut this testimony by showing prior acts of misconduct. The second major area of exceptions is recognized where the prosecution can show the other acts of misconduct have relevance independent of their use as evidence of bad character. The instant case is an example of showing a plan or scheme engaged in by the defendant of which the charged offense is only one instance. This type of exception is also allowed where the evidence will show a unique "modus operandi" or where it will support an inference of intentional conduct or provide a motive for the charged crime.

[For more information on evidence of unchanged conduct, see Casenote Law Outline on Evidence, Chapter 6, § IV, The "Other Crimes" Loophole.]

QUICKNOTES

ABUSE OF DISCRETION - A determination by an appellate court that a lower court's decision was based on an error of law.

CHARACTER EVIDENCE - Evidence of someone's moral standing in a community based on reputation.

MOTIVE - Reason or other impetus inciting one to action.

LANNAN v. STATE

Child molester (D) v. State (P)

Ind. Sup. Ct., 600 N.E.2d 1334 (1992).

NATURE OF CASE: Appeal from conviction for child molestation.

FACT SUMMARY: Lannan (D) was convicted of child molestation after testimony regarding prior, uncharged acts of molestation was introduced at trial.

CONCISE RULE OF LAW: The depraved sexual instinct exception to the general rule against admissability of prior bad acts should no longer be recognized.

FACTS: Lannan (D) was charged with molesting a child. At trial, the alleged victim also testifed with regard to an act that was not charged. Additionally, another girl testified that Lannan (D) had also molested her in the past. This testimony was admitted pursuant to the depraved sexual instinct exception to the usual rules regarding uncharged misconduct. Lannan (D) was convicted and appealed.

ISSUE: Should the depraved sexual instinct exception to the general rule against admissability of prior bad acts continue to be recognized?

HOLDING AND DECISION: (Shepard, C.J.) No. The depraved sexual instinct exception to the general rule against admissability of prior bad acts should no longer be recognized. The exception originated at a time when accusations of child molesting appeared impropable. The exception was thought to be needed in order to bolster the testimony of children. Also, it was thought that sexual predators had a higher recidivism rate than other criminals. Sadly, the first rationale is no longer required and there is no clear and valid evidence supporting the latter justification. However, the general rule prohibiting the introduction of character evidence that shows the defendant was a bad person remains fundamental. The justification for maintaining the exception is outweighed by its very broad nature. The rule does not require any similarity between the prior bad acts and the crime charged. In order for prior bad acts to come into evidence, courts must insist that such evidence be used only to prove an element of the crime. Thus, prior sexual misconduct can be admitted if it proves motive, opportunity, intent, plan, knowledge, or identity. In the present case, the testimony regarding Lannan's (D) misconduct with another girl at a different location has no connection to the charged conduct. Therefore, it should not have been admitted into evidence. However, this was harmless error, and Lannan's (D) conviction is affirmed.

CONCURRENCE: (Givan, J.) The reasons for the depraved sexual instinct exception remain today and the rule should be maintained.

EDITOR'S ANALYSIS: Other states have also rejected the depraved sexual instinct exception. Delaware and Tennessee have determined that there are no valid reasons for maintaining different rules for sexual misconduct. Rule 404 governs character evidence and prior bad acts.

[For more information on uncharged misconduct, see Casenote Law Outline on Evidence, Chapter 6, § IV, The "Other Crimes" Loophole.]

NOTES:

HUDDLESTON v. UNITED STATES

Seller of stolen goods (D) v. Federal government (P)

485 U.S. 681 (1988).

NATURE OF CASE: Review of conviction based on buying and selling stolen goods.

FACT SUMMARY: In a prosecution based on dealing in stolen goods, the trial court did not make a preliminary finding as to the accuracy of evidence of similar acts introduced to show motive and knowledge, prior to admission of the evidence.

CONCISE RULE OF LAW: A court need not make, prior to admitting post acts introduced to show motive or knowledge, a preliminary finding that the acts occurred.

FACTS: Huddleston (D) was indicted on charges of buying and selling stolen goods. At trial, the prosecution sought to introduce evidence of prior similar transactions by Huddleston (D). The court, without making any preliminary findings that the alleged prior acts had occurred, admitted the evidence based on Fed. R. Evid. 404(b), which permits the introduction of evidence of prior acts to show motive or knowledge. Huddleston (D) was convicted, and the court of appeals affirmed. The Supreme Court accepted review.

ISSUE: Must a court make, prior to admitting past acts introduced to show motive or knowledge, a preliminary finding that the acts occurred?

HOLDING AND DECISION: (Rehnquist, C.J.) No. A court need not make, prior to admitting past acts introduced to show motive or knowledge, a preliminary finding that the acts occurred. Fed. R. Evid. 404(b) prohibits the use of evidence of prior acts to prove conduct in conformity therewith, but permits the introduction of such evidence to prove knowledge, motive, opportunity or the like. Huddleston (D) argues that the court must preliminarily find that the prior acts did in fact occur. However, this runs contrary to the structure of the Rules of Evidence. Relevant evidence is to be admitted. Evidence of prior conduct, if relevant to show a legitimate item such as motive or knowledge, is equally admissible. It is for the jury to decide whether the prior act occurred. The only determination the court need make is that the evidence is relevant, which is to say, that a jury could find that the prior acts do in fact show motive or knowledge. Here, the court appears to have done just that. Affirmed.

EDITOR'S ANALYSIS: Fed. R. Evid. 404(b) is essentially an exclusionary section. It prohibits otherwise relevant evidence of prior acts to be introduced to prove conduct in conformity therewith. The rationale behind this is that the possibility of prejudice inherently outweighs whatever probative value exists. However, prior acts introduced to prove other than acts in conformity therewith are admissible.

QUICKNOTES

MOTIVE - Reason or other impetus inciting one to action.

NOTES:

PEOPLE v. CASTILLO

State (P) v. Attempted burglar (D)

N.Y. Ct. App., 47 N.Y.2d 270, 391 N.E.2d 997 (1979).

NATURE OF CASE: Appeal following a criminal conviction.

FACT SUMMARY: Castillo (D) sought a new trial on the one remaining count, claiming that the evidence admitted at his trial on the counts thereafter dismissed on appeal had tainted the original trial.

CONCISE RULE OF LAW: If evidence admissible against a defendant on other crimes with which he was charged in counts dismissed on appeal so affected the trial as to deny the defendant his right to have the jury fairly evaluate only the evidence admissible against him on the counts remaining, there must be a retrial as to those remaining counts.

FACTS: At his trial, Castillo (D) was convicted on charges stemming from two separate incidents — the first being the assault of an adult daughter in her bedroom of the family's apartment by an intruder and the second being the victim's father and brother awakening two days later to find a man outside the window ledge attempting to open the bathroom window. The appellate division dismissed all counts except for an attempted burglary count arising in connection with the second incident. Instead of ordering a new trial on that count, it simply remanded for sentencing thereon. Castillo (D) claimed that the evidence admitted in connection with the dismissed counts had so tainted his trial as to require a new trial on the one count that had not been dismissed.

ISSUE: If some counts for other crimes are dismissed, does a defendant have the right to have the jury fairly evaluate only the evidence admissible against him on the counts that remain?

HOLDING AND DECISION: (Fuchsberg, J.) Yes. A defendant has the right to have the jury fairly evaluate only the evidence admissible against him on the counts he faces. When some of the counts against a defendant are dismissed (on appeal or otherwise), he is thus entitled to have the jury render a verdict on the remaining counts in line with the aforementioned right. That means that a new trial on the remaining counts is required if the evidence admitted in connection with the dismissed counts at the original trial so tainted that trial as to deny the defendant that right. The circumstances of this case are such that a new trial on the remaining count should have been ordered because of the taint of the evidence introduced on the counts dismissed. Reversed and remanded.

EDITOR'S ANALYSIS: Drew v. United States, 331 F.2d 85 (D.C. Cir. 1964), in recognizing the liberal rule of joinder of offenses that prevails, states: "(E)ven where the evidence would not have been admissible in separate trials, if, from the nature of the crimes charged, it appears that the prosecutor might be able to present the evidence in such a manner that the accused is not confounded in his defense and the jury will be able to treat the evidence relevant to each charge separately and distinctly, the trial judge need not order a severance or election at the commencement of the trial."

NOTES:

MICHELSON v. UNITED STATES

Bribery suspect (D) v. Federal government (P)

335 U.S. 469 (1948).

NATURE OF CASE: Appeal from a conviction of bribery.

FACT SUMMARY: While admitting he was guilty of giving money to the federal officer, Michelson (D) claimed that it was done in response to the agent's threats, demands, and solicitation.

CONCISE RULE OF LAW: Where a defendant introduces evidence of his good character/reputation in the community, the prosecution may cross-examine these character witnesses about events or crimes, in defendant's past, which would tend to adversely affect defendant's reputation.

FACTS: At trial, Michelson (D) claimed entrapment. He stated that the federal officer had threatened, demanded, and solicited the bribe Michelson (D) had given him. Michelson (D) called five witnesses to testify as to his good character/reputation in the community. All were asked by the prosecution if they had heard that Michelson (D) had been arrested for receiving stolen goods 27 years ago. On direct, Michelson (D) had mentioned that he had once been arrested about 20 years before. The judge scrupulously instructed the jury to disregard the actual event and view the comment as merely testing the witness's standard of opinion as to Michelson's (D) reputation. The judge, before the prosecution was allowed to even ask this question, met with both sides and ascertained that this was an actual event which would probably result in some comment among acquaintances, if not injury, to Michelson's (D) reputation. Michelson (D) was convicted and appealed from the trial judge's allowance of this cross-examination.

ISSUE: May the prosecution question character witnesses concerning past events or crimes which would tend to damage defendant's reputation?

HOLDING AND DECISION: (Jackson, J.) Yes. The law in this area is purely decisional. It is archaic and illogical yet so widespread that we must weigh the value of an almost imperceptible logical advancement in the law against the confusion and error it would engender. The policy of the law is to exclude testimony concerning a person's past reputation or crimes. This is not because the evidence has no probative value, but because of the prejudice it does to the defendant. The likelihood of the jury giving too great a weight to this testimony outweighs the inferences provided by the evidence. However, no such restrictions are placed on the defendant in a criminal prosecution. He may, as Michelson (D) did, call various witnesses to testify as to his general character. General character is synonymous with reputation. The witness must establish that he knows the defendant and is a member of the community in which the defendant resides. Testimony as to specific acts or conduct is not permitted. The witness may only testify as to hearsay concerning the community's perception of defendant's reputation. This tends to help establish defendant as a person incapable of committing the crime charged and may even be sufficient, in certain circumstances, to be so favorable as to raise a reasonable doubt of guilt. Edgington v. United States, 164 U.S. 361 (1896). A jury, in federal court, may be so instructed if the case warrants it. However, once defendant opens the door, his witnesses may be cross-examined as to acts which, if they were aware of them, might tend to damage defendant's character in the community. Further, they may shed light on factors the witnesses have used to form their opinion and on how well they really know the defendant. "The witness must qualify to give an opinion by showing such acquaintance with the defendant, the community in which he has lived, and the circle in which he has moved, as to speak with authority of the terms in which he is regarded." While, generally speaking, the assumption is that if no ill is reported, defendant's reputation must be good, it is only viable if the witness has had access to said information. Michelson (D) was arrested 27 years before the current conviction. Several of his witnesses testified that they had known him for 30 years. While rehabilitation may have occurred, the question at issue is how Michelson's (D) community receives him. An arrest without conviction may be as damaging to a reputation as a conviction. The fact that the crimes are not similar is irrelevant as the issue is general character. The trial judge should be given great latitude in allowing or excluding this type of cross-examination. Being there, observing the witnesses, makes him a far more competent party to determine this matter. While this is an illogical paradoxical situation (admitting evidence that would not be normally admissible), the judge's jury instructions and warnings are alleged to be adequate protection. This is admittedly a rather fallacious assumption, but the substitution of a new rule prohibiting this type of cross-examination (followed by only one state) would lead to far greater difficulties. Judgment affirmed.

EDITOR'S ANALYSIS: The general rule that a witness may only testify as to a defendant's reputation in the community has been somewhat changed by the holding in United States v. Parker, 447 F.2d 826 (7th Cir. 1971). There, the court held that a character witness could testify concerning defendant's reputation among his coworkers. Generally speaking, character evidence is introduced to bolster defendants' protestations of innocence. The testimony is supposed to establish that defendant lacks the criminal propensities necessary to having committed the crime. A good reputation tends to show that defendant has not been in trouble, either legally or morally. Therefore, specific acts, conduct, or the witness's own opinion are irrelevant. It is the way that the community views the defendant which is to be established. Rationally, most character witnesses will be testifying as to how they view the defendant.

[For more information on character testimony, see Casenote Law Outline on Evidence, Chapter 6, § II, Character in Issue.]

BURGEON v. STATE

Murder suspect (D) v. State (P)

Nev. Sup. Ct., 714 P.2d 576 (1986).

NATURE OF CASE: Appeal from conviction for second-degree murder.

FACT SUMMARY: Burgeon (D) contended that the trial court erred in excluding evidence of the deceased's violent reputation and past acts of violence.

CONCISE RULE OF LAW: Evidence of specific past acts of violence and violent reputation of the victim is admissible to show that the defendant acted in self-defense only where such acts and reputation were known to the defendant.

FACTS: Burgeon (D) was arrested for second-degree murder of Badillo. Salas, an eyewitness, testified that Badillo did not point a gun at Burgeon (D), yet Burgeon (D), pleading self-defense, claimed he did. The defense unsuccessfully attempted to introduce evidence of Badillo's past acts of violence and his reputation as a violent person to establish the act of self-defense. The court excluded the evidence because Burgeon (D) had no knowledge of the victim's acts or reputation at the time of the shooting. Burgeon (D) was convicted and appealed.

ISSUE: Is evidence of violent acts and reputation of a victim admissible to show the defendant acted in self-defense only if the defendant knew of such acts or reputation?

HOLDING AND DECISION: (Per curiam) Yes. Evidence of specific acts of violence and violent reputation of the victim is admissible to show that the defendant acted in self-defense only if the defendant knew of such violent propensities. Self-defense requires the defendant believe his actions are necessary to protect himself from harm. Actions by the victim may give rise to an inference of danger based upon a violent reputation. If the defendant is unaware of such reputation, the actions must be objectively dangerous. In this case, the absence of knowledge of the reputation rendered the evidence of such irrelevant. Thus, it was properly excluded. Affirmed.

EDITOR'S ANALYSIS: The defense also contended it would introduce evidence of the victim's general character. While the defendant need not be aware of the victim's character as a prerequisite to admissibility, an offer of proof concerning the poor character is necessary. Such character can be established through the opinion of persons knowing the victim, but it cannot be established through specific acts.

[For more information on the admissibility of character evidence, see Casenote Law Outline on Evidence, Chapter 6, § I, Definitions and Distinctions.]

CRUMPTON v. CONFEDERATION LIFE INS. CO.

Estate of decedent (P) v. Insurer (D)

672 F.2d 1248 (5th Cir. 1982).

NATURE OF CASE: Appeal from recovery of insurance benefits.

FACT SUMMARY: Confederation (D) contended that evidence of its insured's character was inadmissible because his character was not in issue and it could not be used to prove he acted in conformance with his character.

CONCISE RULE OF LAW: In a civil action, evidence of a victim's character is admissible where such character is an ultimate fact to be determined.

FACTS: Crumpton was shot by a neighbor who accused him of raping her five days before. The neighbor thought he was going to attack her again, and she shot him. His beneficiary sued Confederation (D), contending she was entitled to the insurance proceeds payable upon accidental death. Confederation (D) refused payment, contending Crumpton committed the rape and should have known he would be killed in retaliation. It claimed, as a matter of law, that the death was not accidental. The jury found for the beneficiary, Crumpton (P), and Confederation (D) appealed. It contended that evidence of the insured Crumpton's character was inadmissible as such was not in issue, and it could not be used to show that he acted in conformity with such character. The district court denied Confederation's (D) motions for new trial and judgment n.o.v. Confederation (D) appealed.

ISSUE: In a civil action, is evidence of character admissible where such is an ultimate fact to be ascertained in the case?

HOLDING AND DECISION: (Brown, J.) Yes. In a civil action, evidence of a victim's character is admissible where such character is an ultimate fact to be determined. Whether the neighbor was mistaken about Crumpton's intention to attack her is related to his character. As such, character was in issue, and evidence thereof was admissible. The verdict thus was properly entered. Affirmed.

EDITOR'S ANALYSIS: This case was decided based upon Federal Rule of Evidence 404. While this rule usually applies only to criminal cases, in this case, the rape was a central issue, and the court thus felt this an appropriate case for its application.

[For more information on character in issue, see Casenote Law Outline on Evidence, Chapter 6, § II, Character in Issue.]

QUICKNOTES

ULTIMATE FACT - A fact upon which a judicial determination is made and which is inferred from the evidence presented at trial.

WHITE v. STATE
Rapist (D) v. State (P)
Md. Ct. App., 598 A.2d 187 (1991).

NATURE OF CASE: Appeal from rape conviction.

FACT SUMMARY: White (D) sought to introduce evidence of the victim's past sexual conduct to defend against rape charges.

CONCISE RULE OF LAW: The Rape Shield Law disallows evidence of a victim's past sexual conduct unless it is necessary and directly relevant to the defense.

FACTS: White (D) was charged with raping and kidnapping a woman. At trial, White (D) sought to introduce evidence that the victim had previously offered or exchanged sex for drugs. White's (D) defense was that there was no sexual conduct between them after White (D) declined a sex-for-drugs proposition by the victim. He was offering the evidence about the victim's prior sex-for-drug conduct to show her ulterior motive in accusing him of rape. The trial court rejected this evidence under the Rape Shield Law which prohibits evidence of the victim's sexual past.

ISSUE: Does the Rape Shield Law disallow evidence of a victim's past sexual conduct unless it is necessary and directly relevant to the defense?

HOLDING AND DECISION: (Chasanow, J.) Yes. The Rape Shield Law disallows evidence of a victim's past sexual conduct unless it is necessary and directly relevant to the defense. Maryland's Rape Shield statute provides that evidence relating to a victim's chastity is not admissible in a rape trial. Evidence of specific instances of prior sexual conduct may be admitted if it is material and relevant. It may be used to show ulterior motive for the accusations or to impeach testimony. One purpose of the law is to protect rape victims from defense attorneys who try to shift the focus of the case toward the victim. It also encourages rape victims to report crimes. Federal Rule of Evidence 412 was enacted for the same reasons. In the present case, White (D) has not demonstrated how evidence that the victim had previously offered sex for drugs is relevant to charges that White (D) raped the victim. Nothing in this testimony is at odds with the victim's version of the facts. On the other hand, the testimony would paint a picture of the victim as immoral. Thus, the inflammatory nature of this evidence combined with its negligible probative value shows that it should not have been admitted. Affirmed.

EDITOR'S ANALYSIS: The opinion is certainly wrong that White's (D) offered testimony is consistent with the victim's version of events. Since White (D) maintained that the victim had offered sex for drugs on the night in question while the victim maintained that she had been grabbed against her will, the evidence was certainly inconsistent with the victim's account of

the evening. Thus, this case is better viewed as finding that the probative value of this evidence was outweighed by its extremely prejudicial nature.

[For more information on rape shield laws, see Casenote Law Outline on Evidence, Chapter 6, § III, Character to Prove Conduct.]

QUICKNOTES
CHARACTER EVIDENCE - Evidence of someone's moral standing in a community based on reputation.

CHARACTER EVIDENCE OF VICTIM - Evidence of the character of a victim that is admissible at trial, under certain circumstances.

NOTES:

DALLAS RAILWAY AND TERMINAL CO. v. FARNSWORTH

Bus company (D) v. Injured bus passenger (P)

Tex. Sup. Ct., 148 Texas 584, 227 S.W.2d 1017 (1950).

NATURE OF CASE: Tort action for negligent operation of a streetcar.

FACT SUMMARY: Farnsworth (P) claimed that she was injured by Dallas' (D) bus after she alighted from it.

CONCISE RULE OF LAW: Evidence of similar transactions or conduct on other occasions is not competent to prove the commission of a particular act charged unless the acts are connected in some special way, indicating a relevancy beyond mere similarity in certain particulars.

FACTS: Farnsworth (P) was struck by the overhang of Dallas' (D) streetcar after alighting from it. She testified that the streetcar started to speed off the second she had gotten off, and she had no time to get out of the way of the overhang. Farnsworth (P) had two other witnesses who testified that the movement of the car was abrupt and that the car was moving rapidly for the intersection. Farnsworth (P) then was permitted to testify, over objections, that twice before, on this same trip, the driver had sped off in a similar manner, barely missing other alighting passengers. Dallas Railway (D) objected on the grounds that past conduct was not admissible to prove the commission of a given act. The jury found for Farnsworth (P).

ISSUE: Is evidence of similar transactions of conduct on other occasions admissible to prove the commission of a particular act?

HOLDING AND DECISION: (Smedley, J.) No. When the question is whether or not a person has been negligent in doing, or in failing to do, a particular act, evidence is not admissible to show that he has been guilty of a similar act of negligence or even habitually negligent on a prior occasion. This would raise collateral issues which would not be relevant to prove that defendant had committed the particular act in issue. An exception occurs when the prior occurrences are connected in some special way, indicating a relevancy beyond mere similarities in certain particulars. An example of this is where an inspector has repeatedly failed to inspect the wheels of a train and the issue is whether or not he had inspected them on the day of an accident. Evidence was allowed on the theory that it tended to show the inspector's mental condition or quality, that is, that he was inattentive and thoughtless and this had a direct bearing on whether he had probably inspected the wheels on the day of the accident. Farnsworth's (P) testimony concerned the same trip and tended to establish that the driver was in a hurry (state of mind or nerves) and had independent probative value. The driver's actions were so close in time that they could be considered part of the conduct of the operator that caused Farnsworth's (P) injury. Therefore, the evidence was properly admitted.

EDITOR'S ANALYSIS: The court's rationale is that past or repeated actions of a similar nature are not relevant to support a jury inference that the defendant was guilty of the current act. Similar occurrences are generally admissible in cases where proof is required that a specific product has caused the harm complained of. Also, in accident cases it may be admitted to show that defendant knew of a dangerous condition and failed to take remedial action. It may be applied to the doctrine of respondeat superior with regard to punitive damages, i.e., previous acts of negligence or misconduct by an agent which the employer should have been aware of. Only past occurrences are admissible; negligence or accidents subsequent to the one complained of are not. Finally, other sales or property values in similar areas may be used to establish the price which should be paid in a condemnation action. In all of the above, the evidence has some independent relevance from which the jury may make a permissible inference of fact. The prior occurrences must have been of a similar nature so that no independent variable could have affected the result, i.e., the fact that prior accidents had happened on a bridge does not automatically mean that it is unsafe (speed, driving conditions, and causes must all be similar). There must be a reasonable connection between the similar occurrences and the action complained of, so that the jury may infer that defendant had knowledge or caused the injury. Examples of this might be introducing testimony that thirty people who had tried a certain ointment received skin rashes.

[For more information on evidence of routine practices, see Casenote Law Outline on Evidence, Chapter 6, § VI, Evidence of Habit or Routine Practice.]

QUICKNOTES

NEGLIGENCE - Conduct falling below the standard of care that a reasonable person would demonstrate under similar conditions.

RELEVANCE - The admissibility of evidence based on whether it has any tendency to prove or disprove a matter at issue to the case.

NOTES:

HALLORAN v. VIRGINIA CHEMICALS, INC.
Auto mechanic (P) v. Chemical company (D)
N.Y. Ct. App., 42 N.Y.2d 386, 393 N.Y.S. 2d 341, 361 N.E.2d 991 (1977).

NATURE OF CASE: Personal injury products liability action.

FACT SUMMARY: The trial judge refused to allow Virginia Chemicals (D) to introduce evidence that Halloran (P) had previously used an immersion heating coil to heat cans of refrigerant to show that he was acting in such a negligent fashion when one of the cans blew up and injured him.

CONCISE RULE OF LAW: At least where the issue involves proof of a deliberate and repetitive practice, a party should be able to introduce evidence of habit or regular usage to allow the inference of its persistence and hence negligence on a particular occasion.

FACTS: Halloran (P), an automobile mechanic, sued Virginia Chemicals (D) for the injuries he sustained when a can of refrigerant they produced exploded while he was using it to service the air-conditioning system in a car. The trial judge refused to permit Virginia Chemicals (D) to introduce evidence that Halloran (P) had, on previous occasions, ignored the label warnings on the can by using an immersion coil to heat the can so the refrigerant would flow easier. The appellate division agreed that evidence of habit or usage was never admissible to establish that one persisted in such habit and hence acted negligently on a particular occasion.

ISSUE: Can evidence of habit or particular usage ever be introduced to prove negligence on a particular occasion?

HOLDING AND DECISION: (Breitel, J.) Yes. The statement that evidence of habit or regular usage is never admissible to establish negligence is too broad. At least in this kind of case, where the issue involves proof of a deliberate and repetitive practice, a party should be able, by introducing evidence of such habit or regular usage, to allow the inference of its persistence and hence negligence on a particular occasion. Of course, conduct which involves other persons or independently controlled instrumentalities cannot produce a regular usage because of the likely variation of the circumstances in which such conduct will be indulged. However, proof of a deliberate repetitive practice by one in complete control of the circumstances, as in this case, is quite another matter and should be admissible because it is so highly probative. Of course, Virginia Chemicals (D) must be able to show on voir dire a sufficient number of instances of the conduct in question to justify introduction of habit or regular usage. Remitted for a new trial on the issue of liability.

EDITOR'S ANALYSIS: Since the days of the common law reports, habit evidence has generally been admissible to prove conformity on specified occasions. However, where negligence is at issue, many courts have resisted allowing evidence of specific acts of carelessness or carefulness to create an inference that such conduct was repeated when like circumstances were again presented.

_____

[For more information on evidence of habit, see Casenote Law Outline on Evidence, Chapter 6, § VI, Evidence of Habit or Routine Practice.]

QUICKNOTES
HABIT - A practice or custom of repeated behavior in response to a specific set of circumstances.

NOTES:

PHAR-MOR, INC. v. GOFF
Store (D) v. Injured customer (P)
Ala. Sup. Ct., 594 So.2d 1213 (1992).

NATURE OF CASE: Appeal from award of damages in action for negligence.

FACT SUMMARY: Goff (P) introduced evidence that Phar-Mor (D) had undertaken subsequent remedial measures, maintaining that such evidence was necessary to impeach a Phar-Mor (D) witness.

CONCISE RULE OF LAW: Evidence of subsequent remedial measures may be admitted to impeach a defendant's testimony only when there has been self-serving, false, or misleading statements.

FACTS: Goff (P) allegedly fell at a Mobile Phar-Mor (D) store. She claimed that her foot was caught under a display basket that was negligently maintained in the store aisles. At trial, Phar-Mor's (D) store manager testifed that the basket had been erected in accordance with the manufacturer's instructions. The trial court allowed introduction of pictures that showed that Phar-Mor (D) baskets were stored differently at the time of the trial. Goff (P) argued that this proved that Phar-Mor (D) had previously negligently maintained the basket display. Goff (P) was awarded damages, and Phar-Mor (D) appealed.

ISSUE: May evidence of subsequent remedial measures always be admitted to impeach a defendant's testimony?

HOLDING AND DECISION: (Ingram, J.) No. Evidence of subsequent remedial measures may be admitted to impeach a defendant's testimony only when there has been self-serving, false, or misleading statements. The general rule excluding evidence of subsequent remedial measures is based on two rationales. First, evidence showing subsequent repairs is irrelevant to show antecedent negligence. Second, public policy favors the removal of disincentives to safety innovations. Evidence of this type may be admitted only when the defendant testifies and gains an unfair advantage through self-serving, false, or misleading statements that would go unchallenged under the exclusionary rule. In the present case, Goff (P) used the photos of the subsequent changes to argue that Phar-Mor (D) appreciated the danger posed when the baskets were maintained as they were when Goff (P) was injured. Therefore, it clearly falls within the exclusion and should have been rejected by the trial court. Reversed and remanded.

EDITOR'S ANALYSIS: Federal Rule of Evidence 407 governs the subsequent remedial measures rule in federal courts. Another reason for the rule not mentioned in this decision is that the jury could be distracted by evidence that is only slightly relevant. The rule generally applies to strict liability cases as well as to negligence actions.

[For more information on subsequent remedial measures, see Casenote Law Outline on Evidence, Chapter 7, § II, Subsequent Remedial Measures.]

QUICKNOTES

NEGLIGENCE - Conduct falling below the standard of care that a reasonable person would demonstrate under similar conditions.

NOTES:

HIRAM RICKER & SONS v. STUDENTS INT'L MEDITATION SOCIETY
Resort owners (P) v. Resort guests (D)
501 F.2d 550 (1st Cir. 1974).

NATURE OF CASE: Appeal from award of damages for breach of contract.

FACT SUMMARY: Ricker (P) introduced evidence that Students International Meditation Society (SIMS) (D) had offered to pay a certain amount to discharge its contractual obligations to Ricker (P).

CONCISE RULE OF LAW: Settlement offers are excluded from evidence only when they are made after a controversy has arisen.

FACTS: Ricker (P) owned a resort in Maine that hosted an event by SIMS (D). SIMS (D) was to pay an amount based on the number of participants at the event. Ricker (P) complained that SIMS (D) had not given an accurate count. On the last day of the event, Ricker's (P) president, Feldman, testified that an executive for SIMS (D) wrote a note offering to pay a certain amount in return for a release from all future bills. SIMS (D) sought to strike this testimony on the grounds that this was an inadmissible offer of settlement. Ricker (P) was awarded damages, and SIMS (D) appealed.

ISSUE: Are settlement offers always excluded from evidence?

HOLDING AND DECISION: (McEntee, J.) No. Settlement offers are excluded from evidence only when they are made after a controversy has arisen. Evidence of settlement offers is generally inadmissible. However, there is a well-recognized exception for admissions of fact as distinct from hypothetical concessions conditioned on settlement. In the present case, the note passed to Feldman on the final day of the event was an assertion of what SIMS (D) thought it actually owed to Ricker (P). It was not conditional or hypothetical. It was not made in order to forestall litigation costs. In fact, until Ricker (P) received this offer, Ricker (P) did not know whether an actual controversy would arise. Settlement negotiations would not be encouraged by excluding offers made before a controversy has even arisen. Accordingly, Ricker's (P) evidence was properly admitted. Reversed and remanded for other reasons.

EDITOR'S ANALYSIS: Fed. R. Evid. 408, covering settlement offers, was enacted by Congress in 1975. Irrelevance is given as one reason for the rule, but the primary policy behind it is probably promotion of compromise and settlement of disputes. It is unclear how probable the existence of a dispute needs to be in order to invoke the rule.

[For more information on the exclusion of settlement offers, see Casenote Law Outline on Evidence, Chapter 7, § III, Compromise and Settlement Negotiations.]

QUICKNOTES
SETTLEMENT OFFER - An offer made by one party to a lawsuit to the other agreeing upon the determination of rights and issues between them, thus disposing of the need for judicial determination.

NOTES:

JOHN McSHAIN, INC. v. CESSNA AIRCRAFT CO.
Pilot (P) v. Aircraft company (D)
563 F.2d 632 (3d Cir. 1977).

NATURE OF CASE: Action for damages resulting from an alleged design defect.

FACT SUMMARY: McShain (P), which brought suit after having two landing-gear accidents in a Cessna-built (D) plane, objected to the introduction into evidence of a pretrial release he had signed with another party.

CONCISE RULE OF LAW: Under Federal Rule of Evidence 408, agreements in compromise of a claim are generally inadmissible on the issue of liability on such claim but not when offered for another purpose, such as proving bias or prejudice of a witness.

FACTS: Cessna (D) manufactured the plane McShain (P) had purchased used from another party. After McShain (P) had flown the plane for 147 hours, the main landing gear collapsed as the plane landed on the runway. McShain (P) had Butler do some $11,739 in repairs, during the course of which Cessna (D) representatives paid a visit. After just five hours of further flight, the landing gear once again gave way on touchdown and necessitated another $24,681 in repairs. After filing a state action to rescind the original sales contract and recover the purchase price, McShain (P) sued Cessna (D) in district court, alleging defective design in the landing gear and failure to correct that design despite knowledge of the defects. At trial, McShain (P) objected to the introduction of evidence concerning a pretrial release by which he released Butler from any liability for the accident in exchange for $10 and the right to engage an employee of Butler's sister corporation as a consultant to testify at trial in support of the design-defect contention.

ISSUE: Are agreements in compromise of a claim admissible to prove a witness' bias or prejudice?

HOLDING AND DECISION: (Per Curiam) Yes. Federal Rule of Evidence 408 specifically provides that agreements in compromise of a claim are generally inadmissible on the issue of liability. However, it also specifically provides that it does not require such evidence to be excluded when offered for another purpose, such as proving bias or prejudice of a witness, although it can still be excluded if the prejudice which may eventuate from its admission outweighs its probative value. In this instance, the court did not fully set forth its underlying rationale, but admission of the release was not an abuse of discretion so "inconsistent with substantial justice" as to require a new trial. Affirmed.

EDITOR'S ANALYSIS: Rule 408 somewhat expands on the common law rule by covering not only the agreement itself but "conduct or statements made in compromise negotiations." It also lists two other examples of purposes for which evidence regarding compromise agreements may be admitted: to negative a contention of undue delay or prove an effort to obstruct a criminal investigation or prosecution.

_____

[For more information on evidence of compromise agreements, see Casenote Law Outline on Evidence, Chapter 7, § III, Compromise and Settlement Negotiations.]

QUICKNOTES
ADMISSION – A voluntary acknowledgment by a party as to the existence of specific facts.

BIAS - Predisposition; preconception; refers to the tendency of the judge to favor or disfavor a particular party.

SETTLEMENT OFFER - An offer made by one party to a lawsuit to the other agreeing upon the determination of rights and issues between them, thus disposing of the need for judicial determination.

NOTES:

HARVEY v. AUBREY
Tenant (D) v. Landlord (P)

Ariz. Sup. Ct., 53 Ariz. 210, 87 P.2d 482 (1939).

NATURE OF CASE: Suit for unlawful detainer of a leased premises.

FACT SUMMARY: Aubrey (P) brought suit against Harvey (D) to evict him from premises leased to Harvey (D) at the end of the lease. Harvey (D) sought to argue that a clause in the old lease implied the existence of a new lease.

CONCISE RULE OF LAW: In argument to the jury, an attorney may state any reasonable inferences that may be drawn from the evidence as long as it relates to matters at issue in the trial.

FACTS: Aubrey (P) sought to evict Harvey (D) from premises leased to Harvey (D) after the lease expired. He brought an unlawful detainer action against Harvey (D). The old lease contained a clause that the parties could, if agreeable to both, enter into a new lease at the expiration of the old lease. Harvey's (D) lawyer sought to argue to the jury that existence of that clause could infer the existence of a new lease. Upon objection, this argument was excluded by the judge. From a judgment in favor of Aubrey (P), Harvey (D) appealed.

ISSUE: May an attorney argue that certain inferences may be drawn from evidence when such inference is not reasonable or is unsupported?

HOLDING AND DECISION: (Lockwood, J.) No. While attorneys must be given wide latitude in jury argument, their argument must be confined to direct evidence or reasonable inference arising therefrom. They may not argue a matter not at issue unless it is relevant to an issue in the case. It is not reasonable to argue that a clause in a lease which permits the parties to enter into a new lease at the expiration of the old implies that such new lease actually exists. No such inference could reasonably arise, and the trial court properly excluded the argument.

EDITOR'S ANALYSIS: While expressed in somewhat different terms (not wholly unreasonable, made in good faith, and reasonable), the case illustrates a virtually universal rule. Some courts have stated, however, that the question of reasonableness is one for the jury. Where the judge is allowed to comment on the evidence, as in federal courts, the degree of latitude is greater in arguing inferences. It is usually held, however, that argument for a particular inference does not require the judge to point out alternatives.

[For more information on inferences drawn from evidence, see Casenote Law Outline on Evidence, Chapter 2, § III, Is the "Evidence" Relevant?".]

NOTES:

ROBINSON v. PENNSYLVANIA RAILROAD
Injured employee (P) v. Employer (D)
214 F.2d 798 (3d Cir. 1954).

NATURE OF CASE: Personal injury action under the Federal Employer's Liability Act.

FACT SUMMARY: During the trial, both counsel made numerous personal references which tended to cloud the issues of the case.

CONCISE RULE OF LAW: Flagrantly abusive statements, from one counsel to another, unsupported by the evidence and introducing matters clearly irrelevant to the jury's deliberation of the jury's issues justify a new trial.

FACTS: Robinson (P) was injured while working for the Pennsylvania Railroad (D). Robinson (P) brought an action under the Federal Employer's Liability Act for compensation. During the trial, both counsel made numerous inflammatory and highly prejudicial remarks toward one another. They brought in situations and tactics relating to other trials and raised numerous inferences wholly unsupported by the evidence. The trial judge never admonished either counsel or the jury concerning these diversionary tactics. Neither counsel objected to most of the statements made. Judgment was for Robinson (P).

ISSUE: Can frequent abuses of trial etiquette which tend to cloud the issues and which are not objected to by opposing counsel be considered proper grounds for the granting of a new trial?

HOLDING AND DECISION: (Staley, J.) Yes. Where the conduct of counsel is sufficient to obscure the issues and prevent the jury from fairly deciding the issues based on the facts and the law, an appellate court may order a new trial. In cases such as this one, it is entirely possible that the jury was utterly confused by these diversionary tactics, so that in the end, their verdict might well represent their judgment of which lawyer was in the right as to the false unsupported or irrelevant issues, leaving the real issue undecided. This conclusion is strengthened by the fact that none of the improper remarks evoked a reprimand by the trial judge or even a direction to the jury that they should be disregarded. The trial judge even stated in his charge to the jury that the lawyers had argued the case thoroughly and well. In short, "We are firmly convinced that the conduct of both counsel was of such a nature as to vitiate the entire trial." Case is remanded for a new trial.

EDITOR'S ANALYSIS: Where the attorneys make the issue personal, there is too great a chance that the jury will decide the matter on factors totally irrelevant to the facts at bar. Canon 15 of the Canons of Professional Ethics states that it is improper for an attorney to assert in argument his personal belief in his client's innocence or the justice of his cause. However, it is not a violation of ethics for a prosecutor to express his personal belief, based on the evidence, of defendant's guilt. Further, it is highly improper for an attorney to make himself an unsworn witness as to facts not admitted in evidence.

NOTES:

CHAPTER 6
EXPERT EVIDENCE

QUICK REFERENCE RULES OF LAW

1. **The Nature and Function of Expert Evidence.** Where a criminal defendant's identity is in issue, lay opinion testimony based on a perception that another, unavailable person was the one depicted in photographs admitted into evidence is admissible. (United States v. Robinson)

    [For more information on lay opinion evidence, see Casenote Law Outline on Evidence, Chapter 12, § II, Lay Witness Opinions.]

2. **The Nature and Function of Expert Evidence.** The rule excluding opinion evidence is to be applied sparingly, if at all, so that the jury may have all evidence that may aid them in their determination of the facts. (Een v. Consolidated Freightways)

    [For more information on expert opinion testimony, see Casenote Law Outline on Evidence, Chapter 12, § III, Expert Opinions.]

3. **The Nature and Function of Expert Evidence.** An expert opinion does not need to be generally accepted in the scientific community to be admissible. (Daubert v. Merrell Dow Pharmaceuticals, Inc.)

    [For more information on expert witnesses, see Casenote Law Outline on Evidence, Chapter 12, § III, Expert Opinions.]

4. **The Nature and Function of Expert Evidence.** DNA testing is admissible under Fed. R. Evid. 702 regarding expert testimony. (United States v. Chischilly)

    [For more information on the validity of scientific evidence, see Casenote Law Outline on Evidence, Chapter 12, § III, Expert Opinions.]

5. **The Nature and Function of Expert Evidence.** A plaintiff who seeks to hold a hospital or a physician liable for breach of duty as to medical care must produce some expert testimony supporting an inference of negligence from the fact of the accident itself, before a res ipsa loquitur instruction will be given. An exception to the general rule requiring the plaintiff to submit expert testimony exists when the subject matter of the case is such that lay people could infer as a matter of common knowledge that the injury would not have occurred unless the defendant were negligent. (Meier v. Ross General Hospital)

6. **The Nature and Function of Expert Evidence.** The trial judge should limit a psychiatrist's use of medical labels, and psychiatrists should be prohibited from testifying whether the alleged offense was the "product" of mental illness, since that is an issue to be decided by the jury. (Washington v. United States)

    [For more information on expert opinion testimony, see Casenote Law Outline on Evidence, Chapter 12, § III, Expert Opinions.]

7. **The Nature and Function of Expert Evidence.** Experts may not offer opinions embodying legal conclusions. (United States v. Scop)

    [For more information on the "ultimate issue" opinion, see Casenote Law Outline on Evidence, Chapter 12, § II, Lay Witness Opinions.]

8. **The Nature and Function of Expert Evidence.** Experts may not testify as to ultimate questions of law. (Specht v. Jensen)

> *[For more information on the "ultimate issue" opinion, see Casenote Law Outline on Evidence, Chapter 12, § II, Lay Witness Opinions.]*

9. **The Nature and Function of Expert Evidence.** A psychiatrist's testimony may not be excluded on the basis of the psychiatrist's inadmissible opinion on the ultimate issue. (United States v. West)

> *[For more information on the ultimate issue and the insanity defense, see Casenote Law Outline on Evidence, Chapter 12, § II, Lay Witness Opinions.]*

10. **The Basis of Expert Testimony.** The requirement that a hypothetical question must be used to secure an expert opinion is abandoned; the complete foundation for the opinion need not be put by hypothesis or otherwise prior to eliciting the opinion. (Rabata v. Dohner)

> *[For more information on the use of hypothetical questions in expert testimony, see Casenote Law Outline on Evidence, Chapter 12, § III, Expert Opinions.]*

11. **The Basis of Expert Testimony.** Expert witnesses may not offer opinions based on their personal assessment of the credibility of another witness's testimony. (United States v. Scop)

> *[For more information on basis for expert opinions, see Casenote Law Outline on Evidence, Chapter 12, § III, Expert Opinions.]*

12. **The Basis of Expert Testimony.** Expert testimony is not appropriate when an untrained lay person could determine the issue without expert assistance. (Pelster v. Ray)

> *[For more information on expert testimony defined, see Casenote Law Outline on Evidence, Chapter 12, § III, Expert Opinions.]*

13. **The Basis of Expert Testimony.** Courts may reject admission of expert opinions founded on plainly unreliable facts. (Christophersen v. Allied-Signal Corp.)

> *[For more information on discriminatory exclusion of evidence, see Casenote Law Outline on Evidence, Chapter 5, § IV, Limited Admissibility.]*

14. **The Basis of Expert Testimony.** Experts may disclose the underlying facts on which they base their opinions even if those facts are inadmissible. (People v. Anderson)

> *[For more information on the basis for expert opinions, see Casenote Law Outline on Evidence, Chapter 12, § III, Expert Opinions.]*

15. **Court-Appointed Experts, Discovering Expert Opinion, Compelling Expert Testimony.** It is within the discretion of the trial court to appoint an expert. (Scott v. Spanjer Bros., Inc.)

> *[For more information on court-appointed experts, see Casenote Law Outline on Evidence, Chapter 12, § III, Expert Opinions.]*

16. **Court-Appointed Experts, Discovering Expert Opinion, Compelling Expert Testimony.** A district court may appoint a neutral expert to assist it in fact-finding. (Students of California School for the Blind v. Honig)

[For more information on court-appointed experts, see Casenote Law Outline on Evidence, Chapter 12, § III, Expert Opinions.]

17. **Court-Appointed Experts, Discovering Expert Opinion, Compelling Expert Testimony.** The fact that an expert's opinion was obtained at the expense of a party and for its information and use only does not mean that the expert may not testify at the request of an opposing party without the former party's consent. (Rancourt v. Waterville Urban Renewal Authority)

   [For more information on expert opinion testimony, see Casenote Law Outline on Evidence, Chapter 12, § III, Expert Opinions.]

18. **Court-Appointed Experts, Discovering Experts Opinion, Compelling Expert Testimony.** A trial court may quash a subpoena when the equities of a case make it appropriate. (Buchanan, Plaintiff American Motors Corp., Defendant-Appellant In re Snyder, Non-Party Appellee)

UNITED STATES v. ROBINSON
Federal government (P) v. Convicted robber (D)
544 F.2d 110 (2d Cir. 1976); cert. denied, 434 U.S. 1050 (1978).

NATURE OF CASE: Appeal from conviction for bank robbery.

FACT SUMMARY: The court in Robinson's (D) robbery trial excluded the testimony of a prison official who believed that the surveillance photograph of the actual robber resembled one Turner, not Robinson (D), and a police officer was barred from testifying that Turner was suspected of other armed robberies and was at large.

CONCISE RULE OF LAW: Where a criminal defendant's identity is in issue, lay opinion testimony based on a perception that another, unavailable person was the one depicted in photographs admitted into evidence is admissible.

FACTS: Robinson (D) was arrested for bank robbery after FBI seized his coat after a search of his home permitted by his wife. Surveillance photographs of the bank robbery incident depicted three men, the identity of two of whom was undisputed. The third man was alleged by the Government (P) to be Robinson (D). Robinson (D) denied this, and sought to introduce the testimony of a prison official prepared to state that the bank photographs depicted a man resembling one Eli Turner. The official and his staff made this identification after a search of prison files. Turner was suspected of two other local armed robberies, and was still at large, according to the local police captain. Robinson's (D) first trial ended in mistrial. At his second trial, the judge excluded the testimony of the prison official and of the police captain. The court desired to avoid repetitive testimony as to whether the figure in the photograph resembled Robinson (D) or not, and concluded that the jury could view the evidence and decide for itself. Robinson (D) appealed.

ISSUE: Where a criminal defendant's identity is in issue, is lay opinion testimony based on perception that another, unavailable person was the one depicted in photographs admitted into evidence admissible?

HOLDING AND DECISION: (Meskill, J.) Yes. The concern for limiting testimony as to whether Robinson (D) was the man in the photographs was a legitimate one. But the testimony proffered here had another purpose: that of establishing that Turner was the man in the photograph. While the jury could compare Robinson (D) with the photograph, they could not compare Turner, who was at large and unavailable, to the photograph or to Robinson (D). The testimony would thus be "helpful" in determining identity, and was based on the rational perception of the proffered witness. Where a criminal defendant's identity is in issue, lay opinion testimony based on perception that another, unavailable person

was the one depicted in photographs admitted into evidence is admissible. The issue here was identity, and it was entirely proper for Robinson (D) to disprove the government's contention by proving that the third man in the photograph was someone else. Reversed and remanded.

EDITOR'S ANALYSIS: Rule 701 of the Federal Rules of Evidence (F.R.E.) grants the trial judge considerable leeway in determining which lay opinion evidence is "helpful to a clear understanding" of the fact in issue. The judge's determination may of course give rise to appellate review in cases such as this one, where helpful, relevant evidence is excluded as a time-saving or convenience device.

[For more information on lay opinion evidence, see Casenote Law Outline on Evidence, Chapter 12, § II, Lay Witness Opinions.]

QUICKNOTES
LAY WITNESS – A witness that is not an expert with respect to the testimony he is giving.

NOTES:

EEN v. CONSOLIDATED FREIGHTWAYS
Driver of car (P) v. Truck company (D)
120 F. Supp. 289 (D.N.D. 1954), aff'd 220 F.2d 82 (8th Cir. 1955).

NATURE OF CASE: Action to recover damages for personal injuries.

FACT SUMMARY: This action arose out of a collision between Een's (P) car and a Consolidated Freight (D) truck. Holcomb, a law enforcement officer with 17 years' experience in investigating accidents, was allowed to testify that he believed the accident occurred on Consolidated's (D) side of the highway.

CONCISE RULE OF LAW: The rule excluding opinion evidence is to be applied sparingly, if at all, so that the jury may have all evidence that may aid them in their determination of the facts.

FACTS: There was a collision between a car driven by Een (P), now an incompetent, and a truck owned by Consolidated (D). At trial, Holcomb testified that, from his observations, he believed that the collision took place on Consolidated's (D) side of the highway. Holcomb was a law enforcement officer with 17 years' experience in investigating accidents. He arrived at the accident scene an hour and twenty minutes after its occurrence, but before the damaged vehicles had been moved and the highway opened to traffic. The jury returned a verdict for Consolidated (D), and Een (P) moved for a new trial.

ISSUE: Is the location of a collision the proper subject of expert testimony by a witness who personally observed the scene of the collision shortly after its occurrence and who had many years' experience in investigating such collisions?

HOLDING AND DECISION: (Vogel, J.) Yes. Whether an expert is sufficiently qualified to give an opinion is within the discretion of the trial court. Hence, the question before this court in this case is whether the matter testified to by Holcomb was a proper subject for opinion testimony. Modern legal thinking indicates that the rule excluding opinion evidence is to be applied sparingly, if at all, so that the jury may have all evidence that may aid them in determining the facts. Wigmore states that the true test is whether the opinion testimony on the subject will appreciably assist the jury. In this case, contrary inferences as to which side of the road the accident occurred on were argued by opposing counsel. It was not a case where the conclusion as to where the accident occurred is so obvious that any reasonable person, trained or not, could easily draw an inference. Rather, in such a case, it would seem that experts in the field would be of considerable assistance to the jury. Holcomb's opinion was properly admitted.

EDITOR'S ANALYSIS: As stated in this case, the true function of expert testimony is to aid the understanding of the jury. To warrant use of expert testimony, two elements are required. The subject of inference must be so distinctively related to some science, profession, business, or occupation as to be beyond the knowledge of the jury. Secondly, the witness must have sufficient skill, knowledge, or experience in that field that it appears that his opinion will aid the jury in its determination of the facts. The practice as to experts' qualifications is recognized as a matter for the trial judge's discretion.

[For more information on expert opinion testimony, see Casenote Law Outline on Evidence, Chapter 12, § III, Expert Opinions.]

QUICKNOTES

EXPERT TESTIMONY - Testimonial evidence about a complex area of subject matter relevant to trial, presented by a person competent to inform the trier of fact due to specialized knowledge or training.

OPNINON EVIDENCE – Evidence as to the witness' opinion rather than facts and which are not admissible at trial.

NOTES:

DAUBERT v. MERRELL DOW PHARMACEUTICALS, INC.
Birth defect claimant (P) v. Drug manufacturer (D)
113 S. Ct. 2786 (1993).

NATURE OF CASE: Review of summary judgment dismissing product liability action.

FACT SUMMARY: Daubert's (P) proffered expert witnesses were excluded because the opinions they intended to introduce were not based on methods generally accepted in the scientific community.

CONCISE RULE OF LAW: An expert opinion does not need to be generally accepted in the scientific community to be admissible.

FACTS: Daubert (P) and Schuller (D) filed a lawsuit against Merrell Dow Pharmaceuticals, Inc. (D), alleging that they suffered in utero injuries due to maternal ingestion of the drug Bendectin. Merrell (D) moved for summary judgment, introducing expert opinions to the effect that there was no causal link between Bendectin and birth defects. Daubert (P) and Schuller (P) countered with a series of declarations from eight medical experts, contending that such a link existed. The district court held that the plaintiff's experts had used methodologies not generally accepted in the scientific community. Specifically, they had based their opinions on in vitro and animal studies, as well as chemical structure analysis. Merrell's (D) motion for summary judgment was granted, dismissing the action. The Ninth Circuit affirmed, and the Supreme Court granted review.

ISSUE: Does an expert opinion need to be generally accepted in the scientific community to be admissible?

HOLDING AND DECISION: (Blackmun, J.) No. An expert opinion does not need to be generally accepted in the scientific community to be admissible. The admissibility of expert opinions is governed by Fed.R.Evid. 702. The Rule provides that "If scientific . . . or other specialized knowledge will assist the trier of fact to understand the evidence or to determine a fact in issue," an expert may testify thereto. Nothing in this Rule provides that general scientific acceptance is a condition to admissibility. This being so, the broad relevance requirement of Fed.R.Evid. 401 takes over, which also provides no such requirement. Consequently, no such requirement should be inferred. However, this does not mean that there are no limits on admissibility of expert testimony. The Rule requires "knowledge," so guesses or speculation are inadmissible. A necessary corollary to this is that the expert must base his opinion on sound principles and valid deductions. In this analysis, such factors as peer review, publication, and even general acceptance may be relevant. No one issue will be determinative, however. Here, the courts below held general acceptance to be determinative, and this was erroneous. Reversed.

CONCURRENCE AND DISSENT: (Rehnquist, C.J.) Everything in the present opinion going beyond the main holding that general acceptance is not required is dicta and should not have been included.

EDITOR'S ANALYSIS: The "general acceptance" rule was first enunciated in Frye v. U.S., 293 F. 1013 (1923). For seventy years after Frye, the general acceptance requirement was adopted by most courts, although the rule was a matter of great controversy. The present opinion appears to have settled this issue.

[For more information on expert witnesses, see Casenote Law Outline on Evidence, Chapter 12, § III, Expert Opinions.]

QUICKNOTES

EXPERT TESTIMONY - Testimonial evidence about a complex area of subject matter relevant to trial, presented by a person competent to inform the trier of fact due to specialized knowledge or training.

NOTES:

UNITED STATES v. CHISCHILLY
Federal government (P) v. Sexual assault suspect (D)
30 F.3d 1144 (9th Cir. 1994), cert. den., 115 S. Ct. 946 (1995).

NATURE OF CASE: Appeal from aggravated sexual assault conviction.

FACT SUMMARY: Chischilly (D) maintained that DNA testing evidence was not reliable enough to be admitted.

CONCISE RULE OF LAW: DNA testing is admissible under Fed. R. Evid. 702 regarding expert testimony.

FACTS: Chischilly (D), a Native American, was charged with aggravated sexual assault and murder. FBI tests revealed that there was a match between Chischilly's (D) blood sample and the semen found on the victim's clothing. At trial, the government (P) presented evidence that there was a 1 in 2,563 chance of a similar match with a randomly selected Native American. Chischilly (D) opposed this evidence on many grounds. Chischilly (D) maintained that there could have been contaminants in the testing process that affected the reliability of the DNA evidence. Chischilly (D) also claimed that the statistical methods used to produce probabilities of a random match were inaccurate largely because the sample size of Native Americans was too small. Following his conviction, Chischilly (D) appealed.

ISSUE: Is DNA testing is admissible under Fed. R. Evid. 702?

HOLDING AND DECISION: (Choy, J.) Yes. DNA testing is admissible under Fed. R. Evid. 702. Rule 702 allows expert testimony that will assist the trier of fact to determine relevant facts. Objections to the reliability of DNA testing goes to the weight of the evidence rather than to its admissability. Scientific evidence is admissible as long as it is generally accepted in the relevant community. DNA testing for matches between suspects and found evidence is clearly acceptable in the forensic community. Chischilly's (D) objections to the statistical techniques are strong. He has presented substantial evidence that the testing of individuals from ethnic groups that are homogenous might cause the probability of random match to be overstated. Although there is healthy debate in the scientific community over this statistical sampling, the support for the government's (P) position is not so minimal as to raise concerns over admissability. Still, trial courts must be careful that DNA testing is not misused at trial. They must take care to make sure that the jury is not distracted or places inordinate weight on the DNA evidence. The jury might misunderstand the statistical evidence and equate a "match" with guilt. In the present case, the trial court provided the proper oversight. The government (P) presented its evidence carefully. Chischilly (D) adequately contested its validity. Accordingly, it was not an abuse of discretion to admit the DNA evidence under Rule 702. Affirmed.

EDITOR'S ANALYSIS: The case of Daubert v. Merrell Dow Pharmaceuticals, Inc., 509 U.S. 579 (1993), is the key case governing the admissability of scientific evidence under Rule 702. In Chischilly, the court seemed to base part of its decision on the fact that Chischilly (D) had vigorously disputed the validity of the testing at trial. Thus, the jury had a good opportunity to weigh any disputes before they made their decision. If Chischilly had not had the resources to effectively challenge the evidence, the result may have been different.

[For more information on the validity of scientific evidence, see Casenote Law Outline on Evidence, Chapter 12, § III, Expert Opinions.]

QUICKNOTES
EXPERT TESTIMONY - Testimonial evidence about a complex area of subject matter relevant to trial, presented by a person competent to inform the trier of fact due to specialized knowledge or training.

NOTES:

MEIER v. ROSS GENERAL HOSPITAL
Wrongful death plaintiff (P) v. Hospital (D)
Cal. Sup. Ct., 69 Cal. 2d 420, 445 P.2d 519 (1968).

NATURE OF CASE: Action to recover damages for wrongful death.

FACT SUMMARY: Meier's (P) deceased committed suicide while under psychiatric care at Ross General Hospital (D). Meier (P) presented no expert testimony at trial. Her request for a res ipsa loquitur instruction to the jury was denied.

CONCISE RULE OF LAW: A plaintiff who seeks to hold a hospital or a physician liable for breach of duty as to medical care must produce some expert testimony supporting an inference of negligence from the fact of the accident itself, before a res ipsa loquitur instruction will be given. An exception to the general rule requiring the plaintiff to submit expert testimony exists when the subject matter of the case is such that lay people could infer as a matter of common knowledge that the injury would not have occurred unless the defendant were negligent.

FACTS: After Meier, Meier's (P) deceased, attempted to commit suicide, Meier (P) brought him to Ross (D) for psychiatric care. The hospital had adopted the open door policy for its psychiatric patients. This method de-emphasizes physical restraint. No mechanical security devices are used, and the doors are not locked, nor are the windows barred. Meier committed suicide while under the care of Ross (D) by jumping through an operable window in his room. The window through which Meier jumped was operable by a crank. The crank could have been removed and the window secured. Meier (P) produced evidence showing that other hospitals used secured windows, and that secured windows would not have been incompatible with Ross' (D) open-door methods. Ross (D) produced experts who testified that Ross' (D) psychiatric facilities, including the operable window, comported with accepted medical standards. Meier (P) produced no expert witnesses. Ross (D) offered evidence of the difficulty, bordering on impossibility, of preventing an attempted suicide by any sort of physical restraint. The court refused to give the res ipsa loquitur instruction requested by Meier (P).

ISSUE: Must a plaintiff who seeks to hold a hospital or a physician liable for a breach of duty as to medical care produce some expert testimony supporting an inference of negligence from the fact of the accident itself, before a res ipsa loquitur instruction will be given?

HOLDING AND DECISION: (Tobriner, J.) No. Ordinarily, where a plaintiff seeks to hold a hospital or a physician liable for a breach of duty as to medical care, the courts refuse to give a res ipsa loquitur instruction unless the plaintiff produces some expert testimony supporting an inference of negligence. However, the courts have established an exception to this requirement for the testimony of experts if the subject matter of the case is such that lay people could infer as a matter of common knowledge that the injury would not have occurred unless the defendant were negligent. An obvious case in which expert testimony is not required exists where the facts support a finding of ordinary negligence unrelated to medical questions. In this case, there was testimony that the operable windows did not constitute an essential, or even relevant, element of the open-door policy of Ross (D). The jury could, therefore, find negligence in this case without regard to the propriety or impropriety of an asserted medical justification. The judgment for Ross (D) is reversed, and a new trial is ordered.

EDITOR'S ANALYSIS: Other cases where expert testimony was not required were a clamp left in the incision following surgery, failure to examine a hip despite complaints of pain in that area, rectal abscess following routine presurgical enema, patient unconsciousness for a month following operation for a fractured jaw, hospital nurses failing to look at a child although the mother had told them of symptoms, and patient falling during x-rays and the nurse failing to tell the radiologist of the patient's history of dizziness.

[For more information on the admission of expert testimony, see Casenote Law Outline on Evidence, Chapter 12, § III, Expert Opinions.]

QUICKNOTES

EXPERT TESTIMONY - Testimonial evidence about a complex area of subject matter relevant to trial, presented by a person competent to inform the trier of fact due to specialized knowledge or training.

NEGLIGENCE - Conduct falling below the standard of care that a reasonable person would demonstrate under similar conditions.

RES IPSA LOQUITUR - A rule of law giving rise to an inference of negligence where the instrument inflicting the injury is in the exclusive control of the defendant and where such harm could not ordinarily result in the absence of negligence.

NOTES:

WASHINGTON v. UNITED STATES
Convicted rapist (D) v. State (P)
129 U.S. App. D.C. 29, 390 F.2d 444 (D.C. Cir. 1967).

NATURE OF CASE: Appeal from conviction of rape.

FACT SUMMARY: Washington (D) contended that the trial court should have entered judgment of acquittal because of insanity.

CONCISE RULE OF LAW: The trial judge should limit a psychiatrist's use of medical labels, and psychiatrists should be prohibited from testifying whether the alleged offense was the "product" of mental illness, since that is an issue to be decided by the jury.

FACTS: Washington (D) sought reversal of a conviction for rape on the ground that the trial court should have entered judgment of acquittal because of insanity.

ISSUE: Can a psychiatrist testify whether an alleged offense was the "product" of mental illness?

HOLDING AND DECISION: No. In Durham v. U.S., 214 F.2d 862 (1954), a new test for insanity was announced: an accused is not criminally responsible if his unlawful act was the product of a mental disease or defect. It was hoped that the new test would clarify the roles of the expert and the jury by reducing the emphasis on conclusory labels. The legal and moral question of culpability is distinctly separate from the medical-clinical concept of illness. Likewise, the roles of the psychiatrist and the jury are separate. The former is to state medical-clinical facts and opinions and the latter is to pass legal and moral judgment. Testimony in terms of "mental disease or defect" seems to leave the psychiatrist too free to testify according to his judgment about the criminal responsibility of the defendant. Hence, this court holds that psychiatrists should be prohibited from testifying whether the alleged offense was the "product" of mental illness, since this is part of the ultimate issue to be decided by the jury. Psychiatrists should limit their testimony to an explanation of how the defendant's disease or defect relates to the alleged offense. Also, the trial judge should limit the psychiatrist's use of medical labels, such as schizophrenia, paranoia, neurosis, etc. Unexplained labels are not enough, since description and explanation of the origin, development, and manifestations of the alleged disease are the chief functions of the expert witness. To insure that expert witnesses, counsel, and the jury are advised of the restrictions expressed in this opinion, the trial judge should give the explanatory instruction in open court to the first psychiatric witness immediately after he is qualified as a witness. A copy of the explanatory instruction which should be given is set out in the appendix to this opinion. In this case, it appears that conclusory labels may have served more to confuse the jury than to guide it. However, the lower court did not err in refusing to enter judgment of acquittal.

EDITOR'S ANALYSIS: The problem considered by the court in Washington is seen by many courts to involve the "ultimate issue" doctrine. This doctrine prohibits expert witnesses from invading the province of the trier of fact by testifying to their opinions on ultimate issues. This often necessitates a difficult and rather unconvincing verbal process of splitting up the ultimate issues or otherwise seeking to get at least one inferential step away from them. When the question involves application of a mixed legal-scientific concept, application of the ultimate fact doctrine may be justified according to Korn, Law, Fact, and Science in the Courts, 66 Colum. L.Rev. The expert's opinion may be unwanted because the court feels it would unduly influence the jury or because legal and scientific issues cannot be separated. However, he feels, the doctrine should have no place in cases in which the requisite inferences call for purely scientific knowledge.

[For more information on expert opinion testimony, see Casenote Law Outline on Evidence, Chapter 12, § III, Expert Opinions.]

QUICKNOTES
EXPERT WITNESS - A witness providing testimony at trial who is specially qualified regarding the particular subject matter involved.

NOTES:

UNITED STATES v. SCOP

Federal government (P) v. Fraudulent company officer (D)

846 F.2d 135 (2d Cir. 1988).

NATURE OF CASE: Appeal from mail and securities fraud conviction.

FACT SUMMARY: Whitten, an SEC investigator, testified as an expert for the prosecution and repeatedly stated legal conclusions.

CONCISE RULE OF LAW: Experts may not offer opinions embodying legal conclusions.

FACTS: Scop (D) and others were involved in the initial offering and trading of stock in an auto dealership. As a participant in the public offering, Scop (D) was prohibited from purchasing any stock during the offering period. However, Scop (D) attempted to circumvent this rule by using the names and accounts of friends. Another participant then engaged in a scheme to artificially inflate the price of the stock. Scop (D) and other co-conspirators were charged with fraud and illegal securities practices. At trial, the government (P) called Whitten, an SEC investigator, as an expert witness. Whitten was allowed, over defense objections, to testify as to whether there was a scheme to defraud investors. He continuously used the language of the statute and accompanying regulations concerning manipulation and fraud. Scop (D) was convicted and appealed.

ISSUE: May experts offer opinions embodying legal conclusions?

HOLDING AND DECISION: (Winter, J.) No. Experts may not offer opinions embodying legal conclusions. Expert witnesses may provide testimony as to their opinions on the material issues of the trial. However, experts may not give legal conclusions. The admission of an expert's legal conclusions is highly prejudicial and gives the appearance that the court is shifting the responsibility to decide the case to the witness. Witnesses should not instruct the jury as to applicable principles of law. Whitten's testimony in Scop's (D) trial consistently involved terms such as "manipulation," "scheme to defraud," and "fraud," which are not self-defining terms, but legal terms drawn directly from the statutes at issue. Whitten made no attempt to couch his opinion testimony in even conclusory factual statements. Accordingly, his testimony was improper, and the conviction is reversed.

EDITOR'S ANALYSIS: Fed. R. Evid. 704 provides that expert opinion testimony is not objectionable because it embraces an ultimate issue to be decided by the trier of fact. This rule changed the traditional rule regarding ultimate issues. However, opinions that are phrased in strictly legal conclusions are still barred, as

demonstrated in the above case.

[For more information on the "ultimate issue" opinion, see Casenote Law Outline on Evidence, Chapter 12, § II, Lay Witness Opinions.]

NOTES:

SPECHT v. JENSEN
Victim of illegal search (P) v. Officer (D)
853 F.2d 805 (10th Cir. 1988), cert. den., 488 U.S. 1008 (1989).

NATURE OF CASE: Appeal of an award of damages for an illegal search.

FACT SUMMARY: Specht (P) called as his expert witness an attorney who stated his views as to what constituted an illegal search pursuant to the Fourth Amendment.

CONCISE RULE OF LAW: Experts may not testify as to ultimate questions of law.

FACTS: Specht (P) filed a § 1983 suit for damages as a result of an illegal search. A key issue at the trial is whether the defendant's conduct amounted to a "search" within the meaning of the Fourth Amendment. The issue of consent to the search was also critical. Specht (P) called an attorney as an expert witness. This attorney testified that based on a series of hypothetical questions tailored to reflect Specht's (P) view of the evidence, there had been no consent given, and an illegal search had occurred. Jensen (D) objected to this testimony, arguing that it was beyond the scope of Rule 702. Specht (P) was awarded damages, and Jensen (D) appealed.

ISSUE: May experts testify as to ultimate questions of law?

HOLDING AND DECISION: (Moore, J.) No. Experts may not testify as to ultimate questions of law. The trial judge has the sole responsibility to state the law to the jury. It would be misleading and redundant if the attorneys and witnesses were allowed to state the law to the jury. Fed. R. Evid. 704 allows expert witnesses to give their opinions on ultimate facts. However, while testimony on ultimate facts is authorized, testimony on ultimate questions of law is not favored. Several of the federal circuit courts have barred expert testimony on ultimate questions of law. These courts have drawn a clear line between testimony on factual issues and testimony that articulates the ultimate principles of law. The latter tends toward directing a jury to a particular verdict. In the present case, Specht's (P) expert crossed this line. The jury heard an array of legal conclusions that touched on nearly every element of Specht's (P) burden of proof. Thus, the judge allowed the expert to supplant the judge's duty to set forth the law. The jury may have drawn the conclusion that the expert was more knowledgeable than the judge in that area of the law. Accordingly, the award of damages must be reversed and the case remanded.

DISSENT: (Seymour, J.) The trial judge followed the dictates of Rule 702, which allow expert testimony, because he clearly instructed the jury that it was to follow his instructions of law and to determine the weight of the expert testimony. Jensen (D) has not shown any prejudicial effect arising from the expert testimony at issue.

EDITOR'S ANALYSIS: The majority decision did acknowledge that it is a very narrow line between permissible expert testimony on ultimate issues of fact and impermissible questions of law. The dissent certainly makes a good point that the jury confusion rationale behind the rule is virtually eliminated by an instruction that only the court determines the applicable law. This issue remains a difficult one for courts to enforce.

[For more information on the "ultimate issue" opinion, see Casenote Law Outline on Evidence, Chapter 12, § II, Lay Witness Opinions.]

QUICKNOTES

ULTIMATE FACT - A fact upon which a judicial determination is made and which is inferred from the evidence presented at trial.

NOTES:

UNITED STATES v. WEST
Federal government (P) v. Robber (D)
962 F.2d 1243 (7th Cir. 1992).

NATURE OF CASE: Appeal from robbery conviction.

FACT SUMMARY: West (D) wanted to introduce a psychiatrist's opinion of his mental condition even though the psychiatrist had the ultimate opinion that he was not legally insane.

CONCISE RULE OF LAW: A psychiatrist's testimony may not be excluded on the basis of the psychiatrist's inadmissible opinion on the ultimate issue.

FACTS: West (D) was charged with bank robbery. His sole defense was that he was legally insane at the time of the holdup. Dr. Jeckel, a court-appointed psychiatrist, examined West (D). Jeckel concluded that West (D) was suffering from a severe mental disorder called schizoaffective disorder at the time of the robbery. However, Jeckel also determined that West (D) understood the wrongfulness of his actions at the time of the crime. Therefore he was not insane under the legal federal definition. West (D) sought to have Jeckel testify at trial regarding his mental state. The government (P) moved to have Jeckel's testimony excluded. The trial court excluded the testimony based on Jeckel's ultimate conclusion on the insanity issue and also refused to charge the jury on the insanity defense. West (D) was convicted and appealed.

ISSUE: May a psychiatrist's testimony be excluded on the basis of the psychiatrist's inadmissible opinion on the ultimate issue?

HOLDING AND DECISION: (Will, J.) No. A psychiatrist's testimony may not be excluded on the basis of the psychiatrist's inadmissible opinion on the ultimate issue. Rule 704(b) forbids experts in criminal cases from testifying with respect to ultimate issues of a defendant's mental state or condition. In an insanity defense case, the ultimate issue is whether the defendant appreciated the wrongfulness of his acts. This question is for the jury alone to decide. Therefore, Jeckel's opinion as to what West (D) understood during the crime was inadmissible and legally insignificant. However, Jeckel's opinion on the ultimate issue should have played no role in determining whether Jeckel could testify as to West's (D) mental state. Rule 704(b) permits the jury to find a defendant insane even if no expert would draw that conclusion. Conversely, a defendant may be found sane although every expert finds him insane. Since the trial court's ruling deprived West (D) of the only defense he had, the conviction must be reversed.

CONCURRENCE: (Manion, J.) Although Jeckel's testimony should not have been excluded, he can still be asked whether West's (D) mental disorder would prevent West (D) from understanding the nature and wrongfulness of his acts.

EDITOR'S ANALYSIS: The court also noted that Jeckel's testimony should not have been excluded under Rule 403 as too confusing for the jury. The decision stated that all psychiatric testimony involves unfamiliar terminology. The court felt that the trial judge was too concerned with the jury reaching the "right" conclusion.

[For more information on the ultimate issue and the insanity defense, see Casenote Law Outline on Evidence, Chapter 12, § II, Lay Witness Opinions.]

QUICKNOTES

FRE 403 - Provides that a court may dismiss otherwise relevant evidence where its prejudicial effect on the proceeding outweighs any probative value it has.

ULTIMATE FACT - A fact upon which a judicial determination is made and which is inferred from the evidence presented at trial.

NOTES:

RABATA v. DOHNER
Injured Plaintiff (P) v. Defendant (D)
Wis. Sup. Ct., 45 Wis. 2d 111, 172 N.W.2d 409 (1969).

NATURE OF CASE: Action to recover damages for personal injuries.

FACT SUMMARY: Rabata's (P) counsel refused to use a hypothetical question in eliciting an opinion from an expert.

CONCISE RULE OF LAW: The requirement that a hypothetical question must be used to secure an expert opinion is abandoned; the complete foundation for the opinion need not be put by hypothesis or otherwise prior to eliciting the opinion.

FACTS: This case arose out of an automobile accident. At trial, Rabata's (P) attorney called Vik, who testified that he had examined the scene of the accident, the vehicles, and the police photographs showing road conditions at the time of the accident. Rabata's (P) attorney then asked if Vik had an opinion as to how the accident occurred. Dohner's (D) attorney objected that the question was not in hypothetical form.

ISSUE: Must a hypothetical question be used to elicit an opinion from an expert?

HOLDING AND DECISION: (Heffernan, J.) No. The requirement that a hypothetical question must be used to secure an opinion of an expert is abandoned. The complete foundation for the opinion need not be put to the witness by hypothesis or otherwise prior to eliciting the opinion. "The use of hypothetical questions frequently has a stultifying effect on the jury and presents to them at one time so great a quantity of assumed facts that it is not reasonable to expect them to have any clear idea of the basis on which the opinion is formed." Such questions are a dangerous device which can lead to slanted questions, jury fatigue, and obfuscation of the facts. The trial judge may, in his discretion, insist that a hypothesis be used if he thinks it will aid the jury. He may also insist that some foundation be put in the record. Generally, however, it will be the duty of opposing counsel to draw out the data on which the expert arrived at his opinion. The lower court was correct in not requiring Rabata's (P) attorney to propound a hypothetical question. Judgment for Rabata (P) is affirmed.

EDITOR'S ANALYSIS: McCormick states that this is a landmark decision, which should be followed in other jurisdictions. He also states that while the hypothetical question is an ingenious and logical device for enabling the jury to apply the expert's knowledge to the facts, in practice it is a failure and an obstruction to the administration of justice. If counsel is required to recite all relevant facts in the question, it becomes intolerably wordy (Donner's attorney's hypothetical was four pages long in this case), but if counsel is allowed to select only the material facts it may result in one-sided questions. McCormick feels that the remedy announced in this case is the most satisfactory.

[For more information on the use of hypothetical questions in expert testimony, see Casenote Law Outline on Evidence, Chapter 12, § III, Expert Opinions.]

NOTES:

UNITED STATES v. SCOP

Federal government (P) v. Fraudulent company officer (D)

846 F.2d 135 (2d Cir. 1988).

NATURE OF CASE: Appeal from mail and securitites fraud conviction.

FACT SUMMARY: The expert witness for the government (P) based his testimony on his opinion that another government (P) witness was telling the truth.

CONCISE RULE OF LAW: Expert witnesses may not offer opinions based on their personal assessment of the credibility of another witness's testimony.

FACTS: Scop (D) and others were involved in the initial offering and trading of stock in an auto dealership. As a participant in the public offering, Scop (D) was prohibited from purchasing any stock during the offering period. However, Scop (D) attempted to circumvent this rule by using the names and accounts of friends. Another participant then engaged in a scheme to artificially inflate the price of the stock. Scop (D) and other co-conspirators were charged with fraud and illegal securities practices. At trial, the government (P) called Whitten, an SEC investigator, as an expert witness. On cross-examination, Scop's (D) attorney elicited from Whitten that his opinions were based on his positive assessment of the trustworthiness and accuracy of the government's (P) other witnesses. Scop (D) was convicted and appealed.

ISSUE: May expert witnesses offer opinions based on their personal assessment of another witness's credibility?

HOLDING AND DECISION: (Winter, J.) No. Expert witnesses may not offer opinions based on their personal assessment of another witness's credibility. The credibility of witnesses is exclusively for the determination by the jury. Witnesses may not opine as to the credibility of other witnesses. Even experts possessed of medical knowledge and skills that directly relate to credibility may not state an opinion as to whether another witness is credible. Rule 705 allows an expert to state an opinion without disclosing the basis for it. Thus, Scop (D) need not have elicited the basis for Whitten's opinions. Still, such testimony is prejudicial and also renders secondary opinion based upon it inadmissible. Whitten's testimony clearly was based on his assessment of the credibility of one government (P) witness in particular. Scop's (D) conviction must be reversed.

CONCURRENCE: (Pierce, J.) The result is correct, but the majority is incorrect on this issue. An expert's reliance on the testimony of a witness whose credibility is in question may be brought out on cross-examination and does not affect the foundation for admission of the opinion itself.

EDITOR'S ANALYSIS: The dissent is more persuasive on this issue. After all, every opinion is based on some assessment of the credibility of the underlying information. The majority opinion simply forces all expert opinion to be couched in terms of hypotheticals.

_____

[For more information on basis for expert opinions, see Casenote Law Outline on Evidence, Chapter 12, § III, Expert Opinions.]

NOTES:

PELSTER v. RAY
Plaintiff (P) v. Defendant (D)
987 F.2d 514 (8th Cir. 1993).

NATURE OF CASE: Appeal from award of damages for fraud.

FACT SUMMARY: Pelster's (P) expert testifed as to the information on easily understandable title documents.

CONCISE RULE OF LAW: Expert testimony is not appropriate when an untrained lay person could determine the issue without expert assistance.

FACTS: Pelster (P) brought an action against Morton (D) [Ray is unidentified] for fraud in putting up for auction a used car which Morton knew had had its odometer rolled back. At the trial, Pelster's (P) expert, Ley, testified about investigative techniques and odometer fraud. Ley testified regarding various documents that had accompanied the subject car through its sales and transfers. Ley testified that based on these documents, he believed that the odometer on the car had been rolled back. Morton (D) objected to this testimony on the basis that the odometer readings on the documents were hearsay and did not require expert opinion to be understandable. When Pelster (P) prevailed at trial, Morton (D) appealed.

ISSUE: Is expert testimony appropriate when an untrained lay person could determine the issue without expert assistance?

HOLDING AND DECISION: (Wollman, J.) No. Expert testimony is not appropriate when an untrained lay person could determine the issue without expert assistance. Under Fed. R. Evid. 702, the test for determining the appropriateness of expert testimony is whether the untrained layman would be qualified to determine intelligently the particular issue without enlightenment from those having specialized understanding of the subject. In the present case, any lay person has the ability to compare odometer readings on documents. Ley's testimony only provided Pelster (P) with a shortcut based on evidence that may have been inadmissible on its own. Pelster (P) may not bring inadmissible hearsay under the guise of expert testimony to prove facts that the jury is entitled to decide on its own. Therefore, the judgment must be reversed and the case remanded.

EDITOR'S ANALYSIS: The court also noted that Ley's status as a criminal investigator may have posed an additional danger by giving it extra weight. The court did find, however, that Ley could properly testify as an expert as to other matters. It held that the jury might need assistance on issues such as how titles are altered, and how used car sales are completed.

[For more information on expert testimony defined, see Casenote Law Outline on Evidence, Chapter 12, § III, Expert Opinions.]

NOTES:

CHRISTOPHERSEN v. ALLIED-SIGNAL CORP.
Toxic tort claimant (P) v. Company (D)
939 F.2d 1106 (5th Cir. 1991), cert. den., 503 U.S. 912 (1992).

NATURE OF CASE: Appeal from summary judgment for the defense in toxic tort action.

FACT SUMMARY: Miller, an expert, testified that Christophersen's (P) exposure to fumes from heavy metals caused his cancer, although Miller had not been given accurate dosage and exposure information.

CONCISE RULE OF LAW: Courts may reject admission of expert opinions founded on plainly unreliable facts.

FACTS: Christophersen (P) died in 1986 as a result of a rare form of cancer. Christophersen (P) had worked for Marathon (D) [Allied-Signal not identified] for fourteen years at a plant that produced nickel/cadmium batteries. Christophersen (P) was allegedly exposed to the fumes resulting from the manufacturing process and the exposure caused the cancer. Marathon (D) moved for summary judgment on Christophersen's (P) marketing defect claim. The trial court ruled that Christophersen's (P) expert affidavit, from Dr. Miller, should be excluded from consideration. Miller's opinion was premised on factual data about Christophersen's (P) exposure to fumes that came from the affidavit of another Marathon (D) employee. The court ruled that Miller's opinion was based on inaccurate facts contained in the underlying affidavit. Christophersen (P) responded that any defects in the underlying facts went only to the weight of the opinion rather than its admissability. The court granted summary judgment to Marathon (D), and Christophersen (P) appealed.

ISSUE: May courts reject admission of expert opinions founded on plainly unreliable facts?

HOLDING AND DECISION: (Per curiam) Yes. Courts may reject admission of expert opinions founded on plainly unreliable facts. Rule 703 allows expert opinion evidence when it is based on facts and data of a type reasonably relied upon by experts in the particular field. The inquiry into the types of facts and data underlying an expert's testimony is not limited to whether the underlying facts would be admissible. District courts must have the discretion to reject and disallow opinions that are founded on critical facts that are plainly untrustworthy. These opinions cannot be helpful to the jury. Nothing in Rule 703 suggests that a court is required to admit an opinion based on facts that are indisputably wrong and contradict the record. Even if Rule 703 did not bar such evidence, the general rule and principles requiring relevance would eliminate such opinions from consideration. In the present case, Dr. Miller's opinion was based on facts that were clearly and plainly wrong. Additionally, Dr. Miller did not have essential facts regarding the physical facilities of the Marathon (D) plant. Therefore, the district court did not abuse its discretion in rejecting the Miller affidavit. Affirmed.

CONCURRENCE: (Clark, C.J.) Trustworthiness of facts or data not tested for admissability is gained through the assurance that the expert's scientific community reasonably relies upon them for the same purpose. This has nothing to do with whether the expert's particular facts and data provide sufficient support for a particular opinion. Thus, the only proper basis for exclusion of Miller's opinion is Rule 403.

DISSENT: (Reavley, J.) Judge Clark's concurrence would have a new and drastic effect. Judges would be able to weigh contradictory evidence and exclude any evidence considered unreliable.

EDITOR'S ANALYSIS: This issue is a very contentious one. An especially difficult dilemma occurs when summary judgment is based on expert testimony that itself is based on inadmissible hearsay. In that situation, the losing party has no opportunity to challenge the basis for the opinion. On the other hand, summary judgment could always be defeated if expert testimony were allowed based on any underlying facts, reliable or not.

[For more information on discriminatory exclusion of evidence, see Casenote Law Outline on Evidence, Chapter 5, § IV, Limited Admissibility.]

QUICKNOTES

FRE 403 - Provides that a court may dismiss otherwise relevant evidence where its prejudicial effect on the proceeding outweighs any probative value it has.

NOTES:

PEOPLE v. ANDERSON
State (P) v. Convicted murderer (D)
Ill. Sup. Ct., 495 N.E.2d 485 (1986), cert. den., 479 U.S. 1012.

NATURE OF CASE: Appeal from murder conviction.

FACT SUMMARY: Anderson's (D) expert was not allowed to disclose the contents of the psychiatric reports on which he based his diagnosis of insanity.

CONCISE RULE OF LAW: Experts may disclose the underlying facts on which they base their opinions even if those facts are inadmissible.

FACTS: Anderson (D) shot and killed the manager and the engineer of the apartment building where he was employed as a janitor. His defense at trial was insanity. A psychiatrist hired by the defense interviewed Anderson (D) and reviewed various psychiatric and criminal records as well as other documents. The psychiatrist testified at trial that Anderson (D) could not appreciate the criminality of his acts and could not conform his conduct to the law. The trial court did not allow the psychiatrist to disclose to the jury that one basis for his diagnosis was the contents of medical reports from the Army and California prison that he had read. The doctor was only allowed to state that he had utilized these reports. Anderson (D) was convicted and appealed.

ISSUE: May experts disclose the underlying facts on which they base their opinions even if those facts are inadmissible?

HOLDING AND DECISION: (Simon, J.) Yes. Experts may disclose the underlying facts on which they base their opinions even if those facts are inadmissible. Rule 703, previously adopted by this state through case law, was designed to broaden the basis for expert opinions and to bring judicial practice in line with the practice of the experts themselves. The range of information available to the trier of fact was thereby expanded. Since opinions based on underlying facts are allowed, it would be illogical to deprive the jury of the reasons supporting the opinion. To prevent the expert from referring to the contents of materials upon which he relied in reaching his conclusion places an unreal stricture on the expert and causes the jury to think that the opinion is based upon reasons that are flimsy and inconclusive. Hearsay documents and materials are allowed before the jury through expert testimony because they are not offered for their truth but for the limited purpose of explaining the basis for the expert opinion. A limiting instruction should forestall any misuse of this hearsay by the jury. In the present case, Anderson's (D) psychiatrist should have been allowed to testify as to the basis for his insanity diagnosis. Therefore, the conviction must be reversed and the case is remanded.

EDITOR'S ANALYSIS: The rule allowing experts to use hearsay testimony goes back many years. In Finnegan v. Fall River Gas Works Co., 34 N.E. 523 (Mass. 1893), the court found that experts, competent in their fields, must be allowed to testify as to a fact that they could not personally verify because their expertise gave it the requisite authority. Ordinarily, courts defer to the experts themselves on the issue of what type of materials are relied upon and used by experts in that field.

[For more information on the basis for expert opinions, see Casenote Law Outline on Evidence, Chapter 12, § III, Expert Opinions.]

QUICKNOTES
EXPERT WITNESS - A witness providing testimony at trial who is specially qualified regarding the particular subject matter involved.

INSANITY (DEFENSE) - An affirmative defense to a criminal prosecution that the defendant suffered from a mental illness, thereby relieving him of liability for his conduct.

NOTES:

SCOTT v. SPANJER BROS., INC.
Infant plaintiff (P) v. Defendant (D)
298 F.2d 928 (2d Cir. 1962).

NATURE OF CASE: Action to recover damages for personal injuries.

FACT SUMMARY: The court appointed a physician to examine Scott (P), an infant, shortly before the trial.

CONCISE RULE OF LAW: It is within the discretion of the trial court to appoint an expert.

FACTS: This action was brought by infant and parents, Scott (P). Shortly before the trial, the judge appointed a physician to examine Wayne Scott (P), an infant. Spanjer (D) was not informed of the appointment until the day before the trial. Scott (P) was awarded a verdict and Spanjer (D) appealed on the basis of the appointment and the lack of earlier notice of it.

ISSUE: Is it within the discretion of the trial court to appoint a medical expert to examine one of the parties without notifying the opposing party of the appointment until shortly before the trial?

HOLDING AND DECISION: (Hincks, J.) Yes. The appointment of an impartial medical expert by the court is an equitable and forward-looking technique for promoting the fair trial of a lawsuit. Such an appointment is within the discretion of the trial court, and is proper even when, as in this case, the appointment occurs shortly before trial. In this case, the court stated that the reason for its appointment of a physician to examine Wayne Scott (P) was that because Wayne Scott (P) is an infant, the court has the important duty to protect an infant's rights. The appointment was proper, and judgment for Scott (P) is affirmed.

DISSENT: Such an appointment is proper only when reasonable notice of the names of the appointed experts is given to the parties. Such notice was not given in this case. Further, in considering the desirability of court-appointed experts, it should not be overlooked that in many fields experts are divided into opposing schools of thought. Under conventional trial techniques, the parties will call experts favoring their position. But a judge making an appointment, often unaware of the existence of opposing schools in the field, may appoint an expert who is precommitted to a particular school.

EDITOR'S ANALYSIS: In favor of court-appointed experts, it has been suggested that such experts will more effectively educate the triers of fact on the disputed issues and will produce findings more nearly approximating the truth, that settlements will be encouraged, and that experts of high competence who are unwilling to testify for a party may be willing to serve as court-appointed experts. Against the use of such experts, it has been urged that they carry too much weight with the jury, that lawyers will be afraid to cross-examine them vigorously for fear of jury disapproval, and that the experts selected, although nominally impartial, will unavoidably be biased one way or the other.

[For more information on court-appointed experts, see Casenote Law Outline on Evidence, Chapter 12, § III, Expert Opinions.]

NOTES:

STUDENTS OF CALIFORNIA SCHOOL FOR THE BLIND v. HONIG

Blind students (P) v. Department of Education (D)

736 F.2d 538 (9th Cir. 1984); vacated, 471 U.S. 148 (1985).

NATURE OF CASE: Appeal of order granting preliminary injunction.

FACT SUMMARY: In construction of a school, a district court appointed a neutral expert to help it decide.

CONCISE RULE OF LAW: A district court may appoint a neutral expert to assist it in fact-finding.

FACTS: The Students of California School for the Blind (P) objected, based on seismological considerations, to a proposed location for a school for the blind. The students (P) sought an injunction preventing construction. After hearing evidence, the district court sua sponte reopened the cases to obtain an opinion from a neutral expert. The court eventually granted a preliminary injunction, and the Department of Education (D) appealed.

ISSUE: May a district court appoint a neutral expert to assist it in fact-finding?

HOLDING AND DECISION: (Pregerson, J.) Yes. A district court may appoint a neutral expert to assist it in fact-finding. Federal Rule of Evidence 706 permits courts to appoint such experts on their own motion where doing so will prevent injustice and the parties are allowed to cross-examine, which they did here. The standard of review is abuse of discretion, and in this particular instance, considering the complex, technical nature of the issues involved, the use of such an expert was well within the district court's discretion. Affirmed.

EDITOR'S ANALYSIS: The Dept. of Education (D) challenged the expert's credentials. Rule 706 does not specifically state what qualifications are necessary for appointment under the Rule. The court noted that the court's decisions regarding qualifications are to be held to an abuse of discretion standard, and ruled without comment that no such abuse existed.

[For more information on court-appointed experts, see Casenote Law Outline on Evidence, Chapter 12, § III, Expert Opinions.]

BUCHANAN v. AMERICAN MOTORS CORP. IN RE SNYDER

Wrongful death plaintiff (P) v. Automobile manufacturer (D)

697 F.2d 151 (6th Cir. 1983).

NATURE OF CASE: Appeal of order quashing subpoena.

FACT SUMMARY: American Motors (D) sought to depose Snyder, whose only relation to the action was authorship of a paper adverse to AMC's (D) position.

CONCISE RULE OF LAW: A trial court may quash a subpoena when the equities of a case make it appropriate.

FACTS: Buchanan (P) sued American Motors (D) for wrongful death following a jeep accident. Buchanan's (P) expert relied on a research paper written by Snyder, who had no other connection with the litigation. The paper was not prepared pursuant to the litigation. AMC (D) served a deposition subpoena upon Snyder, to examine him about his conclusions. Snyder obtained an order quashing the subpoena, and AMC (D) appealed.

ISSUE: May a trial court quash a subpoena when the equities of a case make it appropriate?

HOLDING AND DECISION: (Merritt, J.) Yes. A trial court may quash a subpoena when the equities of a case make it appropriate. The applicable Federal Rules of Civil Procedure give the trial court the discretion to make such orders as are necessary to effectuate justice. These orders will be disturbed only upon a showing of abuse. Here, Snyder, who was a total stranger to the present litigation, was faced with the prospect of a lengthy deposition which would have involved substantial preparation time. It was no abuse of discretion for a court to decide that a stranger to the litigation should not be subject to such an inquisition. Affirmed.

EDITOR'S ANALYSIS: Discovery of expert opinions by an opposing party has always been somewhat problematic, as it pushes into the realm of work product and the attorney-client privilege. In the last couple of decades, statutory procedures for expert witness disclosure, usually near trial, have been created. Examples include F.R.C.P. 26(b)(4) and California Code of Civil Procedure § 2034. These sections would have been inapplicable here, however, as Snyder had not been retained by either party.

QUICKNOTES

ATTORNEY-CLIENT PRIVILEGE - A doctrine precluding the admission into evidence of confidential communications between an attorney and his client made in the course of obtaining professional assistance.

SUBPOENA - A mandate issued by court to compel a witness to appear at trial.

WORK PRODUCT - Work performed by an attorney in preparation of litigation that is not subject to discovery.

RANCOURT v. WATERVILLE URBAN RENEWAL AUTHORITY
Property owner (P) v. Government entity (D)
Me. Sup. Ct., 223 A.2d 303 (1966).

NATURE OF CASE: Action for damages for taking of property by eminent domain.

FACT SUMMARY: An appraiser who had been employed by Waterville (D) to appraise Rancourt's (P) property was called as a witness by Rancourt (D).

CONCISE RULE OF LAW: The fact that an expert's opinion was obtained at the expense of a party and for its use only does not mean that the expert may not testify at the request of an opposing party without the former party's consent.

FACTS: St. Pierre was called by Rancourt (P) in rebuttal. He testified that in 1963 he had made an appraisal of Rancourt's (P) property for Waterville (D), and that, in his opinion, the value of the property was $27,500. Rancourt (P) called St. Pierre for the purpose of impeaching the testimony of Waterville's (D) expert witness. Waterville (D) contended that Rule 26(b) M.R.C.P. creates a privilege against a party's use as a witness of an expert who was employed by the opposing party. Rule 26(b) provides, "nor shall the deponent be required to produce or submit for inspection any part of a writing which reflects an attorney's mental impressions, conclusions, opinions, or legal theories, or . . . the conclusions of an expert."

ISSUE: Can an expert whose opinion was obtained at a party's expense and for its use only testify at the request of an opposing party without the former party's consent?

HOLDING AND DECISION: (Williamson, J.) Yes. There is no privilege on the part of the employer of an expert which will prohibit that expert's testimony at the request of an opposing party. Rule 26(b) was designed to regulate the discovery and deposition process before trial and to protect a party against being compelled to disclose the "work product." The rule is neither limited by, nor does it limit, the admissibility of evidence at trial. The fact that an expert's opinion was obtained at a party's expense and for its use only does not force the conclusion that the expert may not testify at the request of an opposing party without the former party's consent. There was no error in the admission of St. Pierre's testimony, even though he was employed by Waterville (D) and called as a witness by Rancourt (P).

EDITOR'S ANALYSIS: In State ex rel. State Highway Commission v. Steinkraus, 417 P.2d 431 (1966), which is in accord with Rancourt, the court makes the point that it is not unfair that the expert has been paid for his or her opinion out of state funds. In Town of Thomaston v. Ives, 239 A.2d 515 (1968), an expert employed by the condemnor was compelled to testify for the condemnee as to the value of the condemnee's land over the objections of both condemnor and the expert. In Atlantic Coast R.R. v. Dixon, 207 F.2d 899 (5th Cir. 1953), it was held permissible for the plaintiff's attorney to ask the defendant's medical expert on cross-examination what he thought of the qualifications of plaintiff's medical expert.

[For more information on expert opinion testimony, see Casenote Law Outline on Evidence, Chapter 12, § III, Expert Opinions.]

QUICKNOTES
EXPERT TESTIMONY - Testimonial evidence about a complex area of subject matter relevant to trial, presented by a person competent to inform the trier of fact due to specialized knowledge or training.

NOTES:

CHAPTER 7
PROCEDURAL CONSIDERATIONS

QUICK REFERENCE RULES OF LAW

1. **Allocating Burdens.** The Due Process Clause does not require that a state assume the burden of disproving beyond a reasonable doubt the nonexistence of all affirmative defenses to the crime charged. (Patterson v. New York)

   [For more information on allocation of the burden of proof, see Casenote Law Outline on Evidence, Chapter 4, § III, Presumptions in Criminal Cases.]

2. **Allocating Burdens.** A state may require a criminal defendant to meet the burden of proving an affirmative defense to the crime charged. (Martin v. Ohio)

   [For more information on allocations of the burden of proof, see Casenote Law Outline on Evidence, Chapter 4, § III, Presumptions in Criminal Cases.]

3. **Weight of Burden of Producing Evidence.** The standard of evidence necessary for a judge to send a criminal case to the jury is whether, giving full play to the right of the jury to determine credibility, weigh the evidence, and draw justifiable inferences of fact, a reasonable mind might fairly conclude guilt beyond a reasonable doubt. (United States v. Taylor)

4. **Weight of Burden of Persuasion.** When a juvenile is charged in an adjudicatory hearing with acts which would constitute a crime if committed by an adult, his guilt must be proved beyond a reasonable doubt. (In re Winship)

   [For more information on the Due Process Clause standard, see Casenote Law Outline on Evidence, Chapter 4, § III, Presumptions in Criminal Cases.]

5. **Weight of Burden of Persuasion.** While individual states may apply a stricter rule, it does not offend constitutional standards in criminal cases to determine the reasonableness of a confession, challenged as involuntary, by a preponderance of the evidence. (Lego v. Twomey)

6. **Weight of Burden of Persuasion.** When the fact of membership in organized crime will result in a much longer and harsher sentence, it must be established by "clear, unequivocal and convincing evidence." (United States v. Fatico)

   [For more information on the weight of the burden of proof, see Casenote Law Outline on Evidence, Chapter 4, § I, Burdens of Proof.]

7. **Weight of Burden of Persuasion.** The party upon whom rests the burden of proof does not lift that burden by merely producing a preponderance of evidence. (Anderson v. Chicago Brass Co.)

   [For more information on the weight of the burden of proof, see Casenote Law Outline on Evidence, Chapter 4, § I, Burdens of Proof.]

8. **Presumptions and Related Subjects.** A rebuttable presumption, once established, persists until contrary evidence persuades the fact finder that it is as probable that the presumed fact does not exist as that it does exist. (Hinds v. John Hancock Mutual Life Insurance Co.)

   [For more information on rebuttable presumptions, see Casenote Law Outline on Evidence, Chapter 4, § II, Presumptions in Civil Cases.]

9. **Presumptions and Related Subjects.** Congress may require a criminal defendant to rebut presumptions concerning bail if such represents a reasonable response to a subject of legitimate legislative concern and if the presumption does not increase the risk of an erroneous deprivation of liberty. (United States v. Jessup)

[For more information on rebuttable presumptions, see Casenote Law Outline on Evidence, Chapter 4, § II, Presumptions in Civil Cases.]

10. **Presumptions and Related Subjects.** Where a presumption rests upon the fact that the circumstances involved in the issue are peculiarly within the knowledge of one party, the presumption will not be rebutted by the production of substantial countervailing evidence but will only be rebutted when the party against whom it has been revoked has proven certain countervailing facts. (O'Dea v. Amodeo)

[For more information on rebuttable presumptions, see Casenote Law Outline on Evidence, Chapter 4, § II, Presumptions in Civil Cases.]

11. **Presumptions and Related Subjects.** Once a prima facie case of employment discrimination has been established, the burden shifts to the employer-defendant to articulate some legitimate, nondiscriminatory reason for the employee's rejection — and that is all that is required at that point. (Texas Department of Community Affairs v. Burdine)

[For more information on presumptions affecting burden of proof, see Casenote Law Outline on Evidence, Chapter 4, § II, Presumptions in Civil Cases.]

12. **Presumptions and Related Subjects.** A permissive presumption is constitutional if there is a "rational connection" between the proved fact and the ultimate fact presumed and the latter is more likely than not to flow from the former. (County Court of Ulster County v. Allen)

[For more information on presumptions in criminal cases, see Casenote Law Outline on Evidence, Chapter 4, § III, Presumptions in Criminal Cases.]

13. **Presumptions and Related Subjects.** A mandatory rebuttable presumption in favor of the prosecution on any fact necessary to prove the crime charged is unconstitutional. (Francis v. Franklin)

[For more information on the burden of proof in criminal cases, see Casenote Law Outline on Evidence, Chapter 4, § III, Presumptions in Criminal Cases.]

14. **Presumptions and Related Subjects.** Jury instructions which erroneously shift the burden of proof on an element of the crime are not necessarily reversible error. (Rose v. Clark)

[For more information on allocation of the burden of proof, see Casenote Law Outline on Evidence, Chapter 4, § I, Burdens of Proof.]

PATTERSON v. NEW YORK
Murder suspect (D) v. State (P)
432 U.S. 197 (1977).

NATURE OF CASE: Appeal from conviction for second-degree murder.

FACT SUMMARY: When he was tried for murder, Patterson (D) faced the burden, under New York law, of proving the affirmative defense of extreme emotional disturbance.

CONCISE RULE OF LAW: The Due Process Clause does not require that a state assume the burden of disproving beyond a reasonable doubt the nonexistence of all affirmative defenses to the crime charged.

FACTS: New York's law recognized as an affirmative defense to a murder charge the fact that the defendant "acted under the influence of extreme emotional disturbance for which there was a reasonable explanation or excuse." It also provided that one who intentionally killed another under circumstances that did not constitute murder because he acted under the extreme influence of emotional disturbance would be guilty of the separate crime of manslaughter. Patterson (D) appealed his conviction for second-degree murder on the grounds that New York violated the Due Process Clause by assigning to the defendant the burden of proving his affirmative defense of extreme emotional disturbance. The court of appeals held that the due process had not been violated. It pointed out that there had been no shifting of the burden to the defendant to disprove any fact essential to the offense charged since the New York affirmative defense of extreme emotional disturbance bore no direct relationship to any element of murder.

ISSUE: Does the Due Process Clause require that a state assume the burden of disproving beyond a reasonable doubt the nonexistence of all affirmative defenses to the crime charged?

HOLDING AND DECISION: (White, J.) No. The teaching of previous cases has been that the Due Process Clause requires the prosecution to prove beyond a reasonable doubt all of the elements included in the definition of the offense with which the defendant is charged. Proof of the nonexistence of all affirmative defenses has never been constitutionally required. Thus, New York's practice does not violate the Due Process Clause.

DISSENT: (Powell, J.) The Due Process Clause requires that the prosecutor bear the burden of persuasion beyond a reasonable doubt if the factor at issue makes a substantial difference in punishment and stigma, which it does in this case.

EDITOR'S ANALYSIS: A majority of states had already assumed the burden of disproving affirmative defenses when this case was decided. The real import of the decision was its "apparent dilution of the force of Mullaney.

MARTIN v. OHIO
Murder suspect (D) v. State (P)
480 U.S. 288, 107 S. Ct. 1098 (1987).

NATURE OF CASE: Appeal from conviction for murder.

FACT SUMMARY: Martin (D) contended that an Ohio statute placing the burden of proof on the criminal defendant to prove self-defense violated her due process rights.

CONCISE RULE OF LAW: A state may require a criminal defendant to meet the burden of proving an affirmative defense to the crime charged.

FACTS: Martin (D) was charged with the murder of her husband, and she defended, contending that she acted in self-defense. The trial court instructed the jury, based on Ohio law, that the defendant had the burden of proving self-defense by a preponderance of the evidence. Martin (D) was convicted and appealed, contending her due process rights were denied by forcing her to bear the burden of proof on this issue. The court of appeals and the Ohio Supreme Court affirmed. The U.S. Supreme Court granted certiorari.

ISSUE: May a state constitutionally require a criminal defendant to meet the burden of proving an affirmative defense to the crime charged?

HOLDING AND DECISION: (White, J.) Yes. A state may require a criminal defendant to meet the burden of proving an affirmative defense to the crime charged. Proving self-defense does not require the defendant to disprove the existence of any element of the crime charged. Thus, the burden of proving each element of the offense beyond a reasonable doubt rests with the prosecution. Because proof of self-defense does not shift the burden to an element of the crime, the burden is not unconstitutionally placed on the defendant. Affirmed.

DISSENT: (Powell, J.) The opinion allows a criminal defendant to be convicted of a crime if he does not prove self-defense. Thus, the jury may convict even though a reasonable doubt exists whether the accused acted in self-defense. This is an improper allocation of the burden of proof.

EDITOR'S ANALYSIS: Burdens of proof differ according to the nature of the action and the issue within the action. As a general proposition, the prosecution in a criminal case has the most difficult burden. It must prove each element of the crime beyond a reasonable doubt. The civil plaintiff must only prove his case by a preponderance of the evidence. If the issue relates to an affirmative defense, the civil defendant must present a preponderance of evidence to prevail. A failure to meet these burdens requires an adverse finding as to that party.

UNITED STATES v. TAYLOR
Federal government (P) v. Counterfeitor (D)
464 F.2d 240 (2d Cir. 1972).

NATURE OF CASE: Appeal from a criminal conviction.

FACT SUMMARY: Taylor (D) claimed that the evidence had not been sufficient to warrant submission to the jury of the question whether he had committed the crime with which he was charged.

CONCISE RULE OF LAW: The standard of evidence necessary for a judge to send a criminal case to the jury is whether, giving full play to the right of the jury to determine credibility, weigh the evidence, and draw justifiable inferences of fact, a reasonable mind might fairly conclude guilt beyond a reasonable doubt.

FACTS: Taylor (D) and his companion were stopped for routine questioning when they attempted to cross into New York from Canada by car. They had no proof of ownership of the car and were asked into the customs office for further investigation. Meanwhile, an inspection of the vehicle began and produced a number of counterfeit bills stuck in a magazine and four road maps. In appealing his resulting criminal conviction, Taylor (D) insisted the evidence had not been sufficient to warrant submission to the jury of the question whether he "with intent to defraud" kept in his possession and concealed the counterfeit bills found in the car. For years, the Second Circuit had followed a "single test" standard of evidence, i.e., the standard of evidence necessary to send a case to the jury was considered to be the same in both civil and criminal cases.

ISSUE: Is the test for determining whether a criminal case should be sent to the jury whether a reasonable mind might fairly conclude guilt beyond a reasonable doubt?

HOLDING AND DECISION: (Friendly, J.) Yes. Despite our reverence for Judge Hand, and perhaps in part because of our desire to remove one of his rare ill-advised opinions from public debate, it is now time to overrule the "single test" standard. The true rule to be applied in criminal cases is whether upon the evidence, giving full play to the right of the jury to determine credibility, weigh the evidence, and draw justifiable inferences of fact, a reasonable mind might fairly conclude guilt beyond a reasonable doubt. If the judge concludes that upon the evidence it might, he must send the case to the jury. If he concludes that there is no evidence upon which a reasonable mind might fairly conclude guilt beyond a reasonable doubt, he cannot send the case to the jury and must grant the motion of acquittal. In this case, the proper standard of evidence would have been met, so Taylor's (D) victory on the legal point is, for him, an empty one. Affirmed.

EDITOR'S ANALYSIS: Judge Learned Hand, who enunciated the "single test" standard, supported his position in pointing out that few cases would be differently resolved upon application of the type of test set forth in this case, rather than the "single test" standard. Still, standards for resolving issues in criminal law are commonly different from the standards used in civil matters to resolve substantially similar issues. Though the difference may appear minimal, it would not seem so to the criminal defendant who is acquitted by virtue of it.

QUICKNOTES

AFFIRMATIVE DEFENSE - A manner of defending oneself against a claim not by denying the truth of the charge but by the introduction of some evidence challenging the plaintiff's right to bring the claim.

NOTES:

IN RE WINSHIP
State (P) v. Juvenile thief (D)
397 U.S. 358 (1970).

NATURE OF CASE: Appeal from New York Family Court juvenile hearing.

FACT SUMMARY: Winship (D), a juvenile, was charged with an act which would have constituted larceny had he been over 16 years old.

CONCISE RULE OF LAW: When a juvenile is charged in an adjudicatory hearing with acts which would constitute a crime if committed by an adult, his guilt must be proved beyond a reasonable doubt.

FACTS: Winship (D), when 12 years old, entered a locker and stole $112 from a woman's purse. He thus came within the New York Family Court Act definition of a juvenile delinquent as "a person over 7 or less than 16 years of age who does any act which, if done by an adult, would constitute a crime." The Family Court judge determined that Winship (D) was guilty of the offense charged, relying upon a provision of the Family Court Act which permitted such a determinant "on a preponderance of the evidence." Winship (D) appealed, contending that the Fourteenth Amendment required the application of the "reasonable doubt" standard before a determination of guilt could be reached.

ISSUE: Is proof beyond a reasonable doubt, as opposed to some lesser standard, constitutionally required during the adjudicatory stage of a juvenile hearing where the defendant is charged with acts which would constitute a crime if committed by an adult?

HOLDING AND DECISION: (Brennan, J.) Yes. Justice Brennan announced the explicit holding of the court that "the Due Process Clause protects the accused against conviction except upon proof beyond a reasonable doubt of every fact necessary to constitute the crime with which he is charged." In other words, the court accepted the notion that juveniles were entitled to the same protection as adults, at least with respect to the standard of proof in cases of a criminal nature. Brennan relied heavily upon history, authority, and logic to buttress his opinion. He noted that the "reasonable doubt" standard had long been a fixture of American jurisprudence "dat[ing] from our early years as a Nation." He cited numerous opinions of the Supreme Court which showed that "it has long been assumed that proof of a criminal charge beyond a reasonable doubt is constitutionally required." Such an assumption is a "safeguard" which "plays a vital role in the American scheme of criminal procedure." Such a standard is necessary, Brennan concludes, in order that "the moral force of the criminal law not be diluted by a standard of proof that leaves people in doubt whether innocent men are being condemned." Application of a high standard of proof, such as the reasonable doubt test, helps to insure that innocent defendants will not be convicted in adult criminal trials. Application of such a standard is also logical in juvenile adjudications where, as here, a youth is charged with a serious offense. Harlan, in a concurring opinion, essentially agreed with the majority, noting the higher standard of proof in criminal cases was justified by the greater disutility of convicting an innocent man than acquitting a guilty man.

EDITOR'S ANALYSIS: In Re Winship stands for the proposition that proof beyond a reasonable doubt is among the essentials of due process and fair treatment required during the adjudicatory stage when a juvenile is charged with an act which would constitute a crime if committed by an adult. Winship appears to fit into a recent trend by Supreme Court to ensure due process for juveniles. See, for example, In Re Gault, 387 U.S. 1 (1967). Juvenile adjudications, like civil and criminal lawsuits, essentially rest upon probability. When the trier of fact is confronted with allegations and defenses, there is a margin of error which must be anticipated. In a civil trial, a mistaken judgment for the plaintiff is no worse than an erroneous decision for the defendant. Various factors such as judicial economy outweigh the need for absolute certainty in a civil trial. In a criminal case, however, society deems a mistaken judgment convicting an innocent man much worse than an erroneous decision freeing a guilty man. This is the fundamental rationale of the reasonable doubt standard. The court in Winship and other juvenile cases merely extends this logic to cases in which youths are changed with serious offenses.

[For more information on the Due Process Clause standard, see Casenote Law Outline on Evidence, Chapter 4, § III, Presumptions in Criminal Cases.]

QUICKNOTES
BURDEN OF PROOF - The duty of a party to introduce evidence to support a fact that is in dispute in an action.

PRESUMPTION - A rule of law requiring the court to presume certain facts to be true based on the existence of other facts, thereby shifting the burden of proof to the party against whom the presumption is asserted to rebut.

NOTES:

LEGO v. TWOMEY

Confessor (P) v. State (D)

404 U.S. 477 (1972).

NATURE OF CASE: Appeal from a conviction for armed robbery on grounds challenging the voluntariness of a confession.

FACT SUMMARY: Lego (P) sought a writ of habeas corpus on the ground that the voluntariness of his confession, which he alleges was obtained by a police beating, to the crime of armed robbery should have been determined by a "reasonable doubt" standard rather than by a "preponderance of the evidence" standard.

CONCISE RULE OF LAW: While individual states may apply a stricter rule, it does not offend constitutional standards in criminal cases to determine the reasonableness of a confession, challenged as involuntary, by a preponderance of the evidence.

FACTS: Lego (P) was convicted of the crime of armed robbery and sentenced to prison for 25 to 50 years. Introduced at trial was a confession made by Lego (P). He did not deny making the confession but did deny making it voluntarily. He alleged he confessed because the police had beaten him about the head with a pistol butt. The police testified at a preliminary hearing that Lego (P) was not beaten. Lego (P) introduced a photograph of himself showing his swollen face and traces of blood which he claimed did not result from an admitted scuffle with the robbery victim. The judge, by a preponderance of the evidence, determined the confession was voluntary. Lego (P) sought a writ of habeas corpus, claiming that the standard applied by the judge was error in that where a confession found voluntary by a preponderance of the evidence is introduced, it is impossible to find the defendant guilty beyond a reasonable doubt.

ISSUE: In criminal trials, shall the voluntariness of a confession be determined by a preponderance of the evidence?

HOLDING AND DECISION: (White, J.) Yes. Voluntariness of a confession may be determined by a preponderance of the evidence, although each state is free to apply a stricter standard. In Jackson v. Denno, 378 U.S. 368 (1964), the Supreme Court stated that no conviction could stand if an involuntary confession had been introduced, even if without it there is sufficient evidence to support the conviction. Voluntariness of a confession is not determined at trial; it is determined at a pretrial hearing. Such hearing is not intended to serve the purpose of strengthening the reliability of jury verdicts. Therefore, judging voluntariness of a confession by a preponderance of the evidence does not undermine the fundamental right that protects "the accused against conviction except upon proof beyond a reasonable doubt." Lego (P) does not challenge that standard. As he does

not maintain that either his confession or its voluntariness is an element of the crime with which he was charged, the standard "beyond a reasonable doubt" actually has no application to the issue of voluntariness at all. Neither do the values served by exclusionary rules show that the Constitution requires voluntariness to be proved beyond a reasonable doubt. From experience, there is no substantial evidence that federal rights have suffered by application of the preponderance of the evidence standard as applied here.

DISSENT: (Brennan, J.) The Jackson decision does not provide sufficient protection against the danger of an involuntary confession being used in a criminal trial where the preponderance of the evidence standard is applied. When two self-serving accounts of an event are given, the standard of persuasion will, in many instances, be of controlling significance in the fact finder's determination of the question.

EDITOR'S ANALYSIS: The voluntariness hearing being a matter outside the province of the jury and, therefore, unrelated to the reliability of jury verdicts does not use the right to proof beyond a reasonable doubt. The majority stated it has not been established that the values upon which the exclusionary rules are based had or would suffer by application of the preponderance of the evidence standard. Application of this standard, the court believes, would be consistent with the traditional allocation of functions between judge and jury. While this decision may appear to have settled the question, it was decided on a 4-3 vote, two newly appointed justices not participating, and remains vulnerable.

QUICKNOTES

BURDEN OF PROOF - The duty of a party to introduce evidence to support a fact that is in dispute in an action.

NOTES:

UNITED STATES v. FATICO
Federal government (P) v. Mob member (D)
458 F.Supp. 388 (E.D. N.Y. 1978); aff'd, 603 F.2d 1053 (2d Cir.1979); cert.
denied, 444 U.S. 1073 (1980).

NATURE OF CASE: Sentencing proceeding following criminal conviction.

FACT SUMMARY: The Government (P) sought to prove that Fatico (D) was a "made" member of an organized crime family, in which case the sentence to be imposed on him could be substantially increased.

CONCISE RULE OF LAW: When the fact of membership in organized crime will result in a much longer and harsher sentence, it must be established by "clear, unequivocal and convincing evidence."

FACTS: Fatico (D) faced the possibility that the sentence imposed for the crimes to which he had pleaded guilty would be substantially enhanced if the Government (P) could establish a critical fact not proved at his criminal trial, i.e., that he was a "made" member of an organized crime family. The question was what burden of proof the Government (P) had to meet in establishing that critical fact.

ISSUE: Must the fact of a defendant's membership in organized crime be established by "clear, unequivocal and convincing evidence" if that fact will result in a much longer and harsher sentence?

HOLDING AND DECISION: (Weinstein, J.) Yes. Fatico (D) faces the possibility of a higher sentence based on proof of a fact not established at his criminal trial. When the fact of membership in organized crime will result in a much longer and harsher sentence, it must be established by "clear, unequivocal and convincing evidence." Since this is a federal conviction, not a habeas corpus proceeding, this Court need not determine whether this holding rests on due process or upon the judicial responsibility to properly administer litigation. Furthermore, it should be noted that this court does not hold that this standard of proof is fixed for all possible disputed facts at sentencing. Where the sentencing judge will give a matter only slight weight, a preponderance standard might be suitable. At the other end of the spectrum, where there is a dispute about a recent serious felony conviction, ease of proof suggests that the court should require proof beyond a reasonable doubt if its existence will enhance the sentence. Turning to the facts of this particular case, it is plain that the testimony the Government (P) originally proffered would not have proved by a preponderance, and certainly not by "clear, unequivocal and convincing evidence," that Fatico (D) was a "made" member of the Gambino organized crime family. However, when viewed with the other evidence introduced at the sentencing hearing, a much more compelling

case is made out. In fact, the combined evidence meets the rigorous burden of establishing Fatico's (D) membership in an organized crime family by "clear, unequivocal and convincing evidence."

EDITOR'S ANALYSIS: The "clear, unequivocal and convincing evidence" standard had been established for deportation hearings on the notion that a person should not be "banished from this country upon no higher degree of proof than applies in a negligence case." It has also been applied to expatriation and denaturalization cases, while a simple "clear and convincing" standard has been imposed for civil commitment proceedings.

[For more information on the weight of the burden of proof, see Casenote Law Outline on Evidence, Chapter 4, § I, Burdens of Proof.]

QUICKNOTES
BURDEN OF PROOF - The duty of a party to introduce evidence to support a fact that is in dispute in an action.

NOTES:

ANDERSON v. CHICAGO BRASS CO.
Injured plaintiff (P) v. Defendant (D)
Wis. Sup. Ct., 127 Wis. 273, 106 N.W. 1077 (1906).

NATURE OF CASE: Action to recover damages for personal injuries.

FACT SUMMARY: In his instruction to the jury, the trial judge defined burden of proof as meaning that the party affirmatively asserting an allegation must establish it by a fair preponderance of the evidence.

CONCISE RULE OF LAW: The party upon whom rests the burden of proof does not lift that burden by merely producing a preponderance of evidence.

FACTS: The court charged the jury on the subject of burden of proof and preponderance of evidence as follows: "By burden of proof I mean that it is incumbent on the party affirmatively asserting an allegation to establish it by a fair preponderance of the credible evidence, facts, and circumstances proven at trial, and by `preponderance of evidence' it is meant the greater convincing power of evidence."

ISSUE: Does the party upon whom the burden of proof rests lift that burden by merely producing a preponderance of evidence?

HOLDING AND DECISION: (Winslow, J.) No. To lift the burden of proof, a party must do more than produce a preponderance of evidence. In this case, the definition of preponderance of evidence was correct, but the definition of burden of proof was not. This is because while a party may produce a preponderance, that is, evidence of slightly greater convincing power than the evidence produced by the adverse party, the evidence may still be weak and leave the mind in doubt. In order to be entitled to a finding in its favor, a party's evidence must not only be of greater convincing power, but it must be such as to satisfy the minds of the jury of the truth of the party's contention. This idea, in some definite form, must be given to the jury. Its omission is fatal. Since it was omitted here, the judgment is reversed.

EDITOR'S ANALYSIS: In most civil cases, the plaintiff must prove its case by a "preponderance of the evidence." In criminal cases, a fact must be proved "beyond a reasonable doubt" and in certain civil cases "by clear, strong and convincing evidence." There is some conflict as to the definition of "preponderance of evidence." One group of cases rejects the idea that a jury need only find the facts to be more probable than not. They hold, "a preponderance of the evidence is that evidence which convinces us as to its truth." Another line of cases emphasizes probabilities and defines preponderance of evidence as meaning that the greater probability lies in favor of the party producing it.

[For more information on the weight of the burden of proof, see Casenote Law Outline on Evidence, Chapter 4, § I, Burdens of Proof.]

UNITED STATES v. JESSUP
Federal government (P) v. Narcotics law violator (D)
757 F.2d 378 (1st Cir. 1985).

NATURE OF CASE: Appeal from denial of bail.

FACT SUMMARY: Jessup (D) contended a federal statute requiring judicial officers to apply a rebuttable presumption in bail decisions that one charged with a serious drug offense will likely flee before trial deprived him of his constitutional rights to due process.

CONCISE RULE OF LAW: Congress may require a criminal defendant to rebut presumptions concerning bail if such represents a reasonable response to a subject of legitimate legislative concern and if the presumption does not increase the risk of an erroneous deprivation of liberty.

FACTS: Jessup (D) was arrested for violation of federal narcotics laws. At his bail hearing, the defendant failed to present evidence to rebut the statutory presumption that persons accused of serious drug offenses will flee, and bail was denied. Jessup (D) appealed, contending the presumption denied him due process of law.

ISSUE: May Congress require a criminal defendant to rebut presumptions concerning bail if such represents a reasonable response to a problem of legitimate legislative concern and does not increase the risk of erroneous deprivations of liberty?

HOLDING AND DECISION: (Breyer, J.) Yes. Congress may require a criminal defendant to rebut presumptions concerning bail if such represents a reasonable response to a problem of legitimate legislative concern and if the presumption does not increase the risk of an erroneous deprivation of liberty. Exhaustive legislative hearings were held prior to the enactment of the Bail Reform Act. Such hearings provided statistical evidence of the evil of drug use and drug dealing, leading Congress to enact the rebuttable presumption. The desire to curtail drug violations is clearly a legitimate concern of Congress. The use of the presumption allows judicial officers to legitimately deny bail where the release of the defendant poses an actual threat of continued criminal conduct. As a result, no great risk of erroneous deprivations of liberty exists. Therefore, the presumption was valid. Affirmed.

EDITOR'S ANALYSIS: The Court also concluded the presumption involved in this case places the burden of production of rebutting evidence on the defendant. It does not shift the burden of persuading the judicial officer that he will not flee. The actual burden then is merely to produce some evidence to rebut the presumption and is a lower standard.

[For more information on rebuttable presumptions, see Casenote Law Outline on Evidence, Chapter 4, § II, Presumptions in Civil Cases.]

HINDS v. JOHN HANCOCK MUTUAL LIFE INSURANCE CO.
Decedent's estate (P) v. Insurer (D)
Me. Sup. Jud. Ct., 155 Me. 349, 155 A.2d 721, 95 A.L.R.2d 703 (1959).

NATURE OF CASE: Suit to recover proceeds of life insurance policy.

FACT SUMMARY: Donald Hinds died from a gunshot wound to his head. His son (P) brought suit to recover the double indemnity portion of a life insurance policy, which John Hancock Life (D) refused to pay on the grounds the death was not accidental.

CONCISE RULE OF LAW: A rebuttable presumption, once established, persists until contrary evidence persuades the fact finder that it is as probable that the presumed fact does not exist as that it does exist.

FACTS: Donald Hinds was insured by John Hancock Mutual Life (D) by a $9,000 life insurance policy. The policy provided, however, that an additional $9,000 was payable if the insured died through violent, external, and accidental means causing bodily injury. Donald Hinds was found dead from a gunshot wound to his right temple, and he was extremely intoxicated at time of death. All of the physical evidence pointed toward suicide. His wife, who was present in the house at time of death, refused to testify, asserting her privilege against self-incrimination. A police officer, who was prepared to testify that the wife told him the deceased committed suicide, was not permitted to do so. The policy obligation to pay the additional $9,000 would not arise if Donald Hinds committed suicide. The jury rendered a verdict for the additional $9,000 in favor of Hinds' son (P), the beneficiary, and John Hancock (D) appealed.

ISSUE: Will a rebuttable presumption against suicide cease to operate if the party against whom it is asserted produces any evidence to contradict the presumed fact?

HOLDING AND DECISION: (Webber, J.) No. The court is faced with the task of determining when a rebuttable presumption ceases to operate. At the outset, the son (P) was aided by a presumption against suicide in the case of death under disputed circumstances. A rebuttable presumption shifts the burden of going forward with the evidence to the other party. The party against whom the presumption operates must then produce some measure of evidence in rebuttal to cause the presumption to disappear. The question before this court is to resolve what measure of evidence is required. There are four prevalent theories on this point. (1) The presumed fact will exist until the adverse party has produced evidence sufficient for a finding the presumed fact does not exist. Under this view, any relevant evidence, actually believed or not, will cause the presumption to disappear. (2) The presumed fact will exist until the adverse party produces substantial evidence of its nonexistence. Under this view, the existence of the presumed fact is a question for the jury.

The problem with this view is the difficulty in defining the term substantial. (3) The presumed fact will exist until the evidence of its nonexistence convinces the jury that its nonexistence is at least as probable as its existence. (4) The presumed fact will exist until the jury finds that the nonexistence of the presumed fact is more probable than its existence. Under this view, once the presumption is created, the burden of proof shifts to the adverse party to prove its nonexistence. The Uniform Rules of Evidence proposed a split approach to presumptions by applying Number (1) above where the basic facts have no tendency to establish the presumed fact but the presumption exists as a matter of expediency and applying Number (4) where the basic facts tend to prove the existence of the presumed fact. This view has found little judicial following. In examining the various alternatives available, this court finds that the view which gives rebuttable presumptions the maximum force without shifting the burden of proof is the view that requires the presumed fact to be controlling until the fact finder is convinced that the existence of the presumed fact is as likely as not. This requires that the rebuttal evidence, in fact, be believed by the trier of fact and avoids the difficulty of defining substantial evidence. Using this rule, the judge, in most instances, will be able to refrain from referring specifically to the presumption in charging the jury. In the instant case, Hinds' son (P) was able to establish that his father's death was caused by violent and external means, and the presumption against suicide aided his case in establishing it was accidental. However, the physical evidence was sufficient to establish that suicide was as likely as not, and the presumption ceased to operate. The wife's refusal to testify and the prevention of the officer's testimony certainly raised a clear inference that the wife was responsible for the death. This inference was not dispelled by the jury instructions. Proof of criminal acts in a civil trial must be clear and convincing evidence, not inference. In the face of a preponderance of physical evidence, uncontradicted, that the death was suicide, the jury's verdict was clearly erroneous. Unless the son (P) remits the additional $9,000, a new trial is ordered.

EDITOR'S ANALYSIS: The majority rule remains that the presumption will operate until the adverse party produces any relevant evidence that the presumed fact does not exist. However, in recent years there has been a shift toward requiring the adverse party to produce more than just minimal evidence in rebuttal. In a civil case, at the outset, the plaintiff has the burden of going forward with the evidence. Once he has presented a prima facie case, the burden of going forward shifts to the defendant. However, in the absence of presumptions, the burden of proof remains with the plaintiff. Where the defendant is required to establish that a presumed fact is more likely not to exist, the burden of proof, as well as the burden of going forward, has shifted.

[For more information on rebuttable presumptions, see Casenote Law Outline on Evidence, Chapter 4, § II, Presumptions in Civil Cases.]

O'DEA v. AMODEO
Injured passenger (P) v. Driver/owner of car (D)
Conn. Sup. Ct. Err., 118 Conn. 58, 170 A. 2d 486 (1934).

NATURE OF CASE: Action to recover damages for personal injury.

FACT SUMMARY: O'Dea (P) was in an accident with a car driven by J. Amodeo (D). O'Dea (P) alleged that the car was owned by C. Amodeo (D), father of J. Amodeo (D). A statute provides that proof that a car was being driven by a member of the car owner's family raises a presumption that the vehicle was a family vehicle, and the defendant has the burden of rebutting this presumption.

CONCISE RULE OF LAW: Where a presumption rests upon the fact that the circumstances involved in the issue are peculiarly within the knowledge of one party, the presumption will not be rebutted by the production of substantial countervailing evidence but will only be rebutted when the party against whom it has been revoked has proven certain countervailing facts.

FACTS: O'Dea (P) was injured by a car driven by J. Amodeo (D) and alleged by O'Dea (P) to be owned by C. Amodeo (D), J. Amodeo's (D) father. A statute provides that proof that a car was being driven by a member of the car owner's family raises a presumption that the car was being operated as a family car with the owner's consent, and the defendant has the burden of rebutting this presumption. The jury returned a verdict against both C. Amodeo (D) and J. Amodeo (D). The trial court set aside the verdict against C. Amodeo (D) on the ground that there was no evidence that the car was a family car. C. Amodeo (D) agreed with the trial judge and contended that once substantial evidence was offered that the car was not a family car, the statute ceased to have any effect, and a plaintiff has the burden of proving that the car was a family car. Both Amodeos (D) testified that the car was not a family car.

ISSUE: Are presumptions which rest upon the fact that the circumstances involved in the issue are peculiarly within the knowledge of one party only rebuttable by that party's proof of countervailing circumstances?

HOLDING AND DECISION: (Maltbie, J.) Yes. Certain kinds of presumptions lose their effect as soon as substantial countervailing evidence is produced. Examples are presumptions which have their basis in convenience and serve to bring out the real issues in dispute or those which rest upon common experience and knowledge. However, there is a different rule as to presumptions which rest upon the fact that the circumstances involved in the issue are peculiarly within the knowledge of one of the parties. In those cases, the presumption is rebutted only when the party against whom it has been invoked has proven

countervailing facts. The presumption created by the statute involved in this case is of the latter class. Hence, if O'Dea (P) offered no evidence on the issue of whether the car was a family car and the trier of fact disbelieved the evidence offered by Amodeo (D) to prove that it was not a family car, O'Dea (P) would be entitled to recover. Here, O'Dea (P) did not offer any evidence other than that the car was operated by the son of the owner. Amodeo (D) and Amodeo (D) testified that the car was not a family car. The trial court stated that even if their testimony was disbelieved, O'Dea (P) would not be entitled to recover. This constituted error. The case is remanded.

EDITOR'S ANALYSIS: In this case, the court held that the presumption operated to fix the burden of persuasion upon the adversary. In terms of instructions to the jury, this means that regardless of whether the word "presumption" is ever mentioned to the jury, it is told that the opponent must prove the nonexistence of the presumed fact by a preponderance of the evidence. McCormick states that in such cases the court holds that the policies giving rise to the presumptions are stronger than the policies that fixed the burden of persuasion prior to the introduction of evidence. He feels that the decision is almost always a sound one.

[For more information on rebuttable presumptions, see Casenote Law Outline on Evidence, Chapter 4, § II, Presumptions in Civil Cases.]

QUICKNOTES

PRESUMPTION - A rule of law requiring the court to presume certain facts to be true based on the existence of other facts, thereby shifting the burden of proof to the party against whom the presumption is asserted to rebut.

REBUTTABLE PRESUMPTION - A rule of law, inferred from the existence of a particular set of facts, that is conclusive in the absence of contrary evidence.

NOTES:

TEXAS DEPARTMENT OF COMMUNITY AFFAIRS v. BURDINE

Employer (D) v. Employee (P)

450 U.S. 248 (1981).

NATURE OF CASE: Employment discrimination suit.

FACT SUMMARY: Once Burdine (P) established a prima facie case of gender-based discrimination, the question became the nature of the burden that thereby shifted to her employer, the Department (D).

CONCISE RULE OF LAW: Once a prima facie case of employment discrimination has been established, the burden shifts to the employer-defendant to articulate some legitimate, nondiscriminatory reason for the employee's rejection — and that is all that is required at that point.

FACTS: Burdine (P) brought an employment discrimination suit against the Department (D) under Title VII of the Civil Rights Act, alleging gender-based discrimination. The trial court held that none of the decisions made by the Department (D) had been based on gender discrimination. The court of appeals reversed the trial court's finding that the Department (D) had rebutted Burdine's (P) prima facie case of gender discrimination. It reiterated its view that the defendant in a Title VII case must rebut a prima facie case of discrimination by proving by a preponderance of the evidence the existence of legitimate nondiscriminatory reasons for the employment action and that those hired or promoted were better qualified than the plaintiff employee.

ISSUE: Is the only burden an employer must meet to rebut a prima facie case of employment discrimination that of articulating some legitimate, nondiscriminatory reason for its action?

HOLDING AND DECISION: (Powell, J.) Yes. When the plaintiff in a Title VII case alleging discriminatory treatment establishes a prima facie case of discrimination by a preponderance of the evidence, this effectively creates a presumption that the employer unlawfully discriminated. The burden then shifts to the employer-defendant to rebut the presumption of discrimination by articulating some legitimate, nondiscriminatory reason for the employment action it took. The employer is not required to assume the greater burden that the court of appeals would place on him. Once the employer-defendant articulates a legitimate, nondiscriminatory reason for its action, the plaintiff-employee then has the opportunity to prove by a preponderance of the evidence that the legitimate reasons offered by the employer-defendant were not its true reasons but were a pretext for discrimination. Since the court of appeals erred in its pronouncement of the burden faced by the Department (D), its judgment must be vacated and the case remanded.

EDITOR'S ANALYSIS: The Court's use of the word "presumption" is unique. In cases involving sex or race discrimination claims, the courts usually couch their decisions in terms of shifting "burdens" without employing that term. In fact, none of the statutes that underlie such cases use the term either.

[For more information on presumptions affecting burden of proof, see Casenote Law Outline on Evidence, Chapter 4, § II, Presumptions in Civil Cases.]

QUICKNOTES

BURDEN OF PROOF - The duty of a party to introduce evidence to support a fact that is in dispute in an action.

PRESUMPTION - A rule of law requiring the court to presume certain facts to be true based on the existence of other facts, thereby shifting the burden of proof to the party against whom the presumption is asserted to rebut.

NOTES:

COUNTY COURT OF ULSTER COUNTY v. ALLEN
State (P) v. Weapons possessor (D)
442 U.S. 140 (1979).

NATURE OF CASE: Appeal from a grant of a writ of habeas corpus.

FACT SUMMARY: Allen (P) claimed that one of the statutory presumptions that played a part in the trial in which he was convicted for weapons possession was unconstitutional.

CONCISE RULE OF LAW: A permissive presumption is constitutional if there is a "rational connection" between the proved fact and the ultimate fact presumed and the latter is more likely than not to flow from the former.

FACTS: Allen (P) was one of the passengers in a car stopped for speeding. In looking through the window, an officer spotted a handgun protruding from a purse near a female minor in the car. Two more weapons were found during a search. Allen (P) and the others were convicted for felonious possession of the weapons. A New York statute made the presence of a firearm in a car presumptive evidence that it was in the possession of all persons in the car. It was a constitutional challenge to this presumption that convinced the district court to grant Allen's (P) petition for a writ of habeas corpus. The court of appeals affirmed, holding there is no rational basis for the inference that possession of a gun by all occupants in a car is more likely than not to flow from the gun's presence in the vehicle.

ISSUE: Does the constitutionality of a permissive presumption depend on there being a rational connection between the proved fact and the ultimate fact presumed as well as the latter being more likely than not to flow from the former?

HOLDING AND DECISION: (Stevens, J.) Yes. The test of a permissive presumption's constitutionality is whether there is a rational connection between the proved fact and the fact presumed and if the latter is more likely than not to flow from the former. As applied to the facts of this case, the presumption of possession is entirely rational and meets the aforementioned standards of constitutionality. Here, it was highly improbable that the female minor was the sole custodian of the firearms in question. Her purse was open because the guns were too large to fit within it. The guns were in open view and within easy access of the driver and other passengers. Reversed.

EDITOR'S ANALYSIS: A presumption that was the sole and sufficient basis for a finding of guilt would have to satisfy a more stringent test than one upon which the prosecution can rely as one not-necessarily-sufficient part of its proof. Instead of the "rational connection" test, the Constitution would require that the evidence necessary to invoke the inference be sufficient for a rational jury to find the inferred fact beyond a reasonable doubt.

[For more information on presumptions in criminal cases, see Casenote Law Outline on Evidence, Chapter 4, § III, Presumptions in Criminal Cases.]

NOTES:

FRANCIS v. FRANKLIN
State (P) v. Prison escapee (D)
471 U.S. 307 (1965)

NATURE OF CASE: Appeal from conviction for murder.

FACT SUMMARY: Francis (P) contended that a jury instruction that indicated a presumption of intent was a permissive rebuttable presumption and thus did not shift the burden of proof or intent to Franklin (D).

CONCISE RULE OF LAW: A mandatory rebuttable presumption in favor of the prosecution on any fact necessary to prove the crime charged is unconstitutional.

FACTS: Franklin (D) shot an individual during the course of his prison escape. Franklin (D) was tried, and he contested only the element of intent. The trial judge instructed the jury that a rebuttable presumption applied, indicating that the acts of a person of sound mind are presumed to be intended by that person. Franklin (D) was convicted and appealed, contending this instruction shifted the burden of proof on that issue to him and thus violated his constitutional rights. Francis (P) contended that the instruction gave rise to a permissive presumption, allowing rather than requiring the jury to presume intent. The prosecution then still bore the burden of persuading the jury to make that presumption. The court of appeals reversed, and the Supreme Court granted a hearing.

ISSUE: Is a mandatory rebuttable presumption in favor of the prosecution on any fact necessary to prove the crime charged unconstitutional?

HOLDING AND DECISION: (Brennan, J.) Yes. A mandatory rebuttable presumption in favor of the prosecution on any fact necessary to prove the crime charged is unconstitutional. This instruction specifically states the acts of a person of sound mind are presumed international. This language points to a mandatory presumption. Such a mandatory presumption requires the jury to find a particular fact, unless the defense meets a burden of rebutting it. This shifts the burden of proof to the defense. Because the defense has the burden of disproving a necessary element of the crime, in this case intent, the constitutional requirement that the prosecution bear this burden is breached. Thus, the instruction was reversible error. Revered.

DISSENT: (Powell, J.) Standing alone, this instruction appears to require the jury to find a particular fact. However, when read in context with further explanatory language, it does not lead an ordinary juror to believe the instruction is a mandatory presumption. It leaves the burden of persuasion with the prosecution and thus is not unconstitutional.

DISSENT: (Rehnquist, J.) The holding in this case needlessly extends the holding in Sandstrom v. Montana, 442 U.S. 510 (1979). One or two sentences out of several pages of jury instructions should not be the sole basis of a reversal where the jury found guilt beyond a reasonable doubt.

EDITOR'S ANALYSIS: This case is based on Sandstrom v. Montana, 442 U.S. 510 (1979). In that case, the Court held that such an instruction, without an indication the presumption was rebuttable, was unconstitutional. This case expands upon this holding. Some commentators suggested that the holding in Francis should be limited as applying only where the burden is shifted on the only contested issue in this case.

[For more information on the burden of proof in criminal cases, see Casenote Law Outline on Evidence, Chapter 4, § III, Presumptions in Criminal Cases.]

QUICKNOTES

REBUTTABLE PRESUMPTION - A rule of law, inferred from the existence of a particular set of facts, that is conclusive in the absence of contrary evidence.

NOTES:

ROSE v. CLARK
State (P) v. Murder suspect (D)
478 U.S. 570 (1986).

NATURE OF CASE: Appeal from conviction for murder.

FACT SUMMARY: Clark (D) contended that the trial court's erroneous jury instruction, that malice is implied or presumed in all homicides, was reversible error.

CONCISE RULE OF LAW: Jury instructions which erroneously shift the burden of proof on an element of the crime are not necessarily reversible error.

FACTS: Clark (D) was arrested for murdering two people. The trial court instructed the jury that in order to convict Clark (D) of second-degree murder, malice must be shown. The court further instructed that malice is presumed in all homicides requiring Clark (D) to rebut such presumption. Clark (D) was convicted and appealed, contending the instruction was erroneous and as such was reversible error. The state court of appeals affirmed, holding the instruction did not shift the burden of proof to Clark (D). Clark (D) petitioned the federal court for habeas corpus relief, and such was granted. The court held the instruction violated Clark's (D) right to have the crime proved beyond a reasonable doubt. The court of appeals affirmed, holding the error was not harmless. The U.S. Supreme Court granted certiorari.

ISSUE: Are jury instructions which erroneously shift the burden of proof on an element of the crime necessarily reversible error?

HOLDING AND DECISION: (Powell, J.) No. Jury instructions which erroneously shift the burden of proof on an element of the crime are not necessarily reversible error. The prosecution must prove each element of the crime charged. Shifting the burden on any element to the defendant is unconstitutional. In this case, Clark (D) had a full opportunity to prove his innocence. The jury was instructed that guilt must be proved by the prosecution. Thus whether the error was harmless must be reanalyzed by the court of appeals. The case is thus remanded for this purpose.

CONCURRENCE: (Burger, C.J.) This was harmless error.

CONCURRENCE: (Stevens, J.) Harmless error applies to this case.

DISSENT: (Blackmun, J.) Clark (D) was deprived of his right to jury by this instruction. Thus, the error was reversible.

EDITOR'S ANALYSIS: This case was decided under the authority of Chapman v. California, 368 U.S. 18 (1967). That case held that errors of constitutional dimension do not necessarily result in reversible error. The reviewing court must find the error reversible beyond a reasonable doubt. If this standard is not met, the error is harmless and does not require reversal.

[For more information on allocation of the burden of proof, see Casenote Law Outline on Evidence, Chapter 4, § I, Burdens of Proof.]

NOTES:

CHAPTER 8
JUDICIAL NOTICE

QUICK REFERENCE RULES OF LAW

1. **Adjudicative Facts.** Because only those matters that are of common knowledge or capable of certain verification are subject to being judicially noticed, a judge is not authorized to make his personal knowledge of a fact not generally or professionally known the basis of his action. (In re Marriage of Tresnak)

   [For more information on judicial notice of adjudicative facts, see Casenote Law Outline on Evidence, Chapter 3, § II, Judicial Notice of Adjudicative Facts.]

2. **Adjudicative Facts.** The general rule permits judicial notice of a court's prior cases to support a motion for summary judgment, but the judge must inform the parties as to what was noticed. (Soley v. Star & Herald Co.)

   [For more information on judicial notice of adjudicative facts, see Casenote Law Outline on Evidence, Chapter 3, § II, Judicial Notice of Adjudicative Facts.]

3. **Adjudicative Facts.** Sufficient indication of the general reliability of VASCAR, a radar device used to calculate the speed of cars, is now available to warrant the court's taking judicial notice thereof so as to dispense with the necessity to use expert testimony in each case to establish same. (State v. Finkle)

   [For more information on requirements for judicial notice, see Casenote Law Outline on Evidence, Chapter 3, § II, Judicial Notice of Adjudicative Facts.]

4. **Legislative Facts.** Under the Federal Rules of Evidence, a court is not precluded from instructing the jury that it must accept as conclusive a "legislative" fact of which the court has taken judicial notice, *i.e.*, a fact, truth, or pronouncement that does not change from case to case but applies universally. (United States v. Gould)

   [For more information on judicial notice of legislative facts, see Casenote Law Outline on Evidence, Chapter 3, § I, Definitions and Distinctions.]

5. **Legislative Facts.** The Equal Protection Clause does not preclude a state from seeking to prevent illegitimate teenage pregnancies by prohibiting males from having sexual intercourse with minor females. (Michael M. v. Superior Court of Sonoma County)

   [For more information on judicial notice of legislative facts, see Casenote Law Outline on Evidence, Chapter 3, § I, Definitions and Distinctions.]

6. **Authority Determination by Nonjudicial Agency.** Whether a foreign government should be recognized is a political question that neither the United States Supreme Court nor any other American court may review. (Ren-Guey v. Lake Placid 1980 Olympic Games, Inc.)

7. **Effect of Judicial Notice.** Failure to plead a fact in a criminal proceeding may not be cured by judicial notice. (United States v. Jones)

   [For more information on requirements for judicial notice, see Casenote Law Outline on Evidence, Chapter 3, § IV, Procedure for Taking Judicial Notice.]

IN RE MARRIAGE OF TRESNAK
Father seeking custody (P) v. Mother seeking custody (D)
Iowa Sup. Ct., 297 N.W.2d 109 (1980).

NATURE OF CASE: Appeal from award of child custody.

FACT SUMMARY: In awarding custody to her husband, the trial court assumed that Linda Tresnak's plan to attend law school would necessitate her being away from her children a lot.

CONCISE RULE OF LAW: Because only those matters that are of common knowledge or capable of certain verification are subject to being judicially noticed, a judge is not authorized to make his personal knowledge of a fact not generally or professionally known the basis of his action.

FACTS: The court which dissolved the marriage of Linda and Jim Tresnak gave custody of their children to him. In its decision, the trial court stated that Linda's proposed plan to attend law school would necessitate much study and time away from her children. It also stated that Jim would be able to engage in "various activities with the boys, such as athletic events, fishing, hunting, mechanical training, and other activities that boys are interested in." In asking on appeal that the custody decision be reversed, Linda maintained that no evidentiary support existed for the court's assumptions about law school and the children's activities. She also contended that the assumed facts were not a proper subject of judicial notice.

ISSUE: Is it within the judge's authority to make his personal knowledge of a fact not generally or professionally known the basis of his action?

HOLDING AND DECISION: (McCormick, J.) No. To be capable of being judicially noticed, a matter must be of common knowledge or capable of certain verification. That means that judicial notice is limited to what a judge may properly know in his judicial capacity, and he is not authorized to make his personal knowledge of a fact not generally or professionally known the basis of his action. It is common knowledge in the legal profession that law school studies are demanding and time-consuming, but the requirements of a specific law school curriculum are not generally or professionally known. Nor is how a particular person will arrange his family responsibilities to accommodate his schooling. There is simply no legitimate basis for the assumption that Linda cannot continue to be a good mother while attending law school or why she could not participate in her children's activities as well as Jim could. In fact, she should be given custody. Reversed and remanded.

EDITOR'S ANALYSIS: The traditional approach to judicial notice, taken by Professor Morgan, is that it is limited to "indisputables," i.e., propositions of fact having a 100% degree of probability and which reasonable men would not dispute. This has not, however, stopped many courts from making "creative use" of judicial notice. Furthermore, there is a whole school which sees "convenience" as the primary goal and would limit judicial notice only in the face of valid objections made on fairness grounds.

[For more information on judicial notice of adjudicative facts, see Casenote Law Outline on Evidence, Chapter 3, § II, Judicial Notice of Adjudicative Facts.]

QUICKNOTES
JUDICIAL NOTICE - The discretion of a court to recognize certain well-known facts as being true, without the necessity of a party introducing evidence to establish the truth of the fact.

NOTES:

SOLEY v. STAR & HERALD CO.
Injured plaintiff (P) v. Newspaper (D)
390 F.2d 364 (5th Cir. 1968).

NATURE OF CASE: Appeal from dismissal of libel action.

FACT SUMMARY: Star & Herald Co.'s (D) motion to strike Soley's (P) libel complaint did not rebut any specific contentions or offer any affirmative defenses. The trial judge evidently came upon some evidence which he felt justified dismissal. However, he did not inform the parties as to what he noticed.

CONCISE RULE OF LAW: The general rule permits judicial notice of a court's prior cases to support a motion for summary judgment, but the judge must inform the parties as to what was noticed.

FACTS: In 1960 Soley (P) brought a negligence action against a bus company. Star & Herald (D) published an account of the trial which stated that the action was dismissed on the basis of proof that Soley (P) had been treated prior to his accident with the bus for a condition that he claimed was caused by the accident. Soley (P) brought a libel action against Star (D) in the same court. In it, he alleged that Star's (D) account was false and malicious, Star (D) knew it to be, and that he and his family had suffered damages as a result. Star's (D) motion to strike the complaint did not rebut any specific contentions or offer an affirmative defense. The motion was granted. The trial court made a reference to the prior suit but did not inform the parties of any facts of which he had taken judicial notice.

ISSUE: May a court take judicial notice of its prior cases?

HOLDING AND DECISION: (Goldberg, J.) Yes. The general rule permits judicial notice of a court's prior cases to support a motion for summary judgment. However, the court must inform the parties as to what it has noticed. In this case, Star's (D) motion to strike failed to rebut any specific contentions or to offer an affirmative defense. Since Soley's (P) pleadings did contain the allegations necessary to a libel action — publication, untruth, damages, and even malice — the trial judge evidently came upon some evidence outside the pleadings which he felt justified dismissal. It is probable that he found the article to be true. This assumption is based on his reference to Soley's (P) prior action, which indicates that evidence of Soley's (P) prior treatment for his condition had been introduced at that trial. A trial court may, in its consideration of a motion to dismiss, treat it as a motion for summary judgment and consider evidence outside of the pleadings. As stated above, the judge may take judicial notice of a court's prior cases. However, here, the judge did not inform the parties as to what he noticed. He says he referred to Soley's (P) prior case, but it is not clear whether that means he physically had it before him or that he recalled it. The case is reversed and remanded.

EDITOR'S ANALYSIS: Wigmore says that whether a court will notice a fact contained in the record of another case depends more or less on the practical notoriety and certainty of the fact under the circumstances of each case. Courts are more likely to notice the records of prior cases if the cases are related. Among the criteria used to determine "relatedness" are: (1) the second case involved the same factual pattern as the prior case; and (2) the evidence or finding of fact as to one who is a party in both cases is relevant to prove an issue in the second case.

[For more information on judicial notice of adjudicative facts, see Casenote Law Outline on Evidence, Chapter 3, § II, Judicial Notice of Adjudicative Facts.]

QUICKNOTES

JUDICIAL NOTICE - The discretion of a court to recognize certain well-known facts as being true, without the necessity of a party introducing evidence to establish the truth of the fact.

LIBEL - A false or malicious publication subjecting a person to scorn, hatred or ridicule, or injuring him or her in relation to his or her occupation or business.

SUMMARY JUDGMENT - Judgment rendered by a court in response to a motion by one of the parties, claiming that the lack of a question of material fact in respect to an issue warrants disposition of the issue without consideration by the jury.

NOTES:

STATE v. FINKLE
State (P) v. Speeder (D)

N.J. Super. Ct., 128 N.J. Super. 199, 319 A.2d 733 (1974); aff'd, 66 N.J. 139, 329 A.2d 65; cert. denied,423 U.S. 836 (1974).

NATURE OF CASE: Appeal from conviction for a traffic offense.

FACT SUMMARY: In prosecuting Finkle (D) for speeding, the State (P) took the position that the scientific reliability of its radar device was a proper subject to judicial notice.

CONCISE RULE OF LAW: Sufficient indication of the general reliability of VASCAR, a radar device used to calculate the speed of cars, is now available to warrant the court's taking judicial notice thereof so as to dispense with the necessity to use expert testimony in each case to establish same.

FACTS: In appealing his conviction for driving 75.3 miles per hour in a 55 m.p.h. zone, Finkle (D) claimed that the court had erred in not requiring expert testimony to establish the reliability of the radar device that had been used by the state trooper to measure his speed of travel. The State (P) maintained that the scientific reliability of the VASCAR device was a proper subject of judicial notice. Finkle (D) also objected to the court's having resorted to authoritative literature in the field to arrive at a decision on whether judicial notice of the device's reliability should be taken. He insisted that he should have had the right to confront and cross-examine the authors of the reports relied on by the court in making its decision.

ISSUE: Is there sufficient indication of the general reliability of VASCAR radar to warrant the court's taking judicial notice thereof?

HOLDING AND DECISION: (Conford, J.) Yes. At this point in time, sufficient indication of the general reliability of VASCAR radar is available to warrant the court's taking judicial notice thereof. In addition to facts that are so generally known or of such common notoriety that they cannot be reasonably disputed, judicial notice may be taken of "specific facts and propositions of generalized knowledge which are capable of immediate determination by resort to sources of reasonably indisputable accuracy." The very process of determination of whether grounds exist for the taking of judicial notice implies discretionary resort by the court to relevant authoritative literature in the particular field without any need for putting it through the adversarial trial process. The court below properly followed these principles in arriving at its decision to make use of judicial notice in regard to the reliability of the VASCAR device. Affirmed.

EDITOR'S ANALYSIS: There is a general concurrence that judicial notice of the scientific validity of radar is proper. Nonetheless, the accuracy of the particular radar instrument used

in a particular case must still be established. Some states have saved the courts from the need to resort to taking judicial notice. They have obviated the need by enacting statutes which specify that certain types of tests are admissible, e.g., blood tests, drunkometer or Breathalyzer tests, etc.

[For more information on requirements for judicial notice, see Casenote Law Outline on Evidence, Chapter 3, § II, Judicial Notice of Adjudicative Facts.]

QUICKNOTES

EXPERT TESTIMONY - Testimonial evidence about a complex area of subject matter relevant to trial, presented by a person competent to inform the trier of fact due to specialized knowledge or training.

JUDICIAL NOTICE - The discretion of a court to recognize certain well-known facts as being true, without the necessity of a party introducing evidence to establish the truth of the fact.

NOTES:

UNITED STATES v. GOULD
Federal government (P) v. Cocaine user (D)
536 F.2d 216 (8th Cir. 1976).

NATURE OF CASE: Appeal from conviction for a drug offense.

FACT SUMMARY: Gould (D) challenged the trial court's action in taking judicial notice of the fact that cocaine hydrochloride was a Schedule II controlled substance and instructing the jury hearing his drug case that it had to accept this fact as conclusive.

CONCISE RULE OF LAW: Under the Federal Rules of Evidence, a court is not precluded from instructing the jury that it must accept as conclusive a "legislative" fact of which the court has taken judicial notice, *i.e.*, a fact, truth, or pronouncement that does not change from case to case but applies universally.

FACTS: On appeal from a cocaine-related drug conviction, Gould (D) argued that the trial court had acted improperly in taking judicial notice of the fact that cocaine hydrochloride was a Schedule II controlled substance and in instructing the jury that it had to accept this fact as conclusive. At trial, there was no direct evidence to indicate that it was a derivative of coca leaves (and thus a Schedule II substance).

ISSUE: Is a federal court precluded by the Federal Rules of Evidence from instructing the jury that it must accept as conclusive a "legislative" fact of which it has taken judicial notice?

HOLDING AND DECISION: (Gibson, J.) No. There is nothing in the Federal Rules of Evidence to preclude a court from instructing the jury that it must accept as conclusive a "legislative" fact of which it has properly taken judicial notice. "Legislative" facts are those which involve universal facts, truths, or pronouncements that do not change from case to case, while "adjudicative" facts are those developed in a particular case. The fact that cocaine hydrochloride is derived from coca leaves is, if not common knowledge, at least a matter which is capable of certain, easily accessible, and indisputably accurate verification. It is thus a proper subject of judicial notice. Furthermore, it falls within the category of "legislative" facts as opposed to "adjudicative" facts (which are the facts that relate to the parties, their activities, their properties, their businesses — and that normally go to the jury in a jury case). As such, it is not subject to Rule 201 (g), which covers only adjudicative facts in calling for a jury instruction in civil cases that a judicially noticed fact is conclusive but providing that in criminal cases the jury shall be instructed that it may, but is not required to accept as conclusive, a judicially noticed fact. Thus, nothing prevents a court from instructing a jury that it must accept as conclusive the universal fact that cocaine hydrochloride is a derivative of coca. Affirmed.

EDITOR'S ANALYSIS: Not all agree with the attempted distinction between legislative and adjudicative facts. For example, Montana adopted a rule identical to Federal Rules of Evidence 201, except that instead of covering only "adjudicative facts" in terms of judicial notice, it covers "all facts" subject to judicial notice. It reasoned that the attempted distinction was confusing and could not be readily made in many situations.

[For more information on judicial notice of legislative facts, see Casenote Law Outline on Evidence, Chapter 3, § I, Definitions and Distinctions.]

QUICKNOTES

JUDICIAL NOTICE - The discretion of a court to recognize certain well-known facts as being true, without the necessity of a party introducing evidence to establish the truth of the fact.

NOTES:

MICHAEL M. v. SUPERIOR COURT OF SONOMA COUNTY
Statutory rapist (D) v. State (P)
450 U.S. 464 (1981).

NATURE OF CASE: Action to set aside an information.

FACT SUMMARY: Michael M. (P), who was charged with violating California's statutory rape law, asserted that the law was unconstitutional in that it made men alone criminally liable.

CONCISE RULE OF LAW: The Equal Protection Clause does not preclude a state from seeking to prevent illegitimate teenage pregnancies by prohibiting males from having sexual intercourse with minor females.

FACTS: Michael M. (P), a 17½-year-old male, was charged with having unlawful sexual intercourse with a female under the age of 18 (the girl was 16½). He sought to have the information dismissed on the grounds that the statutory rape law under which he was charged was not gender-neutral and thus violated the Equal Protection Clause. Eventually, after several intervening adverse decisions, Michael M. (P) brought his case to the Supreme Court.

ISSUE: Can a state, in seeking to prevent illegitimate pregnancies, pass a gender-based law which prohibits males from having sexual intercourse with minor females?

HOLDING AND DECISION: (Rehnquist, J.) Yes. The Equal Protection Clause does not prevent the passage of statutes involving a gender classification which realistically reflects the fact that the sexes are not similarly situated in certain circumstances. Teenage girls get pregnant; boys do not. Virtually all of the harmful effects of illegitimate teenage pregnancies fall on the girl involved. The legislature sought to prevent such pregnancies by enacting a law recognizing this fact. The Equal Protection Clause does not stand as an obstacle to that effort. Affirmed.

DISSENT: (Brennan, J.) A gender-neutral statutory rape law would be no more difficult to enforce and would be just as effective a deterrent.

DISSENT: (Stevens, J.) The evidence the plurality cites itself demonstrates that local custom and belief govern teenage sexual activity and not laws. However, I would have no doubt about the validity of a state law prohibiting all unmarried teenagers from engaging in sexual intercourse. Such a gender-neutral law would be constitutionally permissible, even if it would not solve the problem of illegitimate teenage pregnancies.

EDITOR'S ANALYSIS: In cases involving constitutional challenges to statutes, the courts must often take judicial notice of studies or other such information as a means of advancing a legitimate state interest. In many instances, judicial notice is involved in arriving at a decision as to precisely what the "purpose" of the statute is — what specific state interest it serves.

[For more information on judicial notice of legislative facts, see Casenote Law Outline on Evidence, Chapter 3, § I, Definitions and Distinctions.]

NOTES:

REN-GUEY v. LAKE PLACID 1980 OLYMPIC GAMES, INC.

Athlete (P) v. Olympic games (D)

N.Y. App. Div., 72 A.D.2d 439, 424 N.Y.S.2d 535, aff'd 49 N.Y.2d 771, 403 N.E.2d 178 (1980).

NATURE OF CASE: Action seeking a permanent injunction.

FACT SUMMARY: Ren-Guey (P), an athlete from Taiwan, sought to stay the 1980 Olympic Games unless he was allowed to use the flag, emblem, name, and anthem of the Republic of China despite the fact that the International Olympic Committee had said that only the People's Republic of China could use them.

CONCISE RULE OF LAW: Whether a foreign government should be recognized is a political question that neither the United States Supreme Court nor any other American court may review.

FACTS: The International Olympic Committee (IOC), after receiving notification that the United States had withdrawn diplomatic recognition of Taiwan, adopted a resolution allowing the National Olympic Committee from the People's Republic of China to use the nation's flag, anthem, and emblem. It also changed the name of the Taiwanese National Olympic Committee and required it to submit alternatives for the flag, anthem, and emblem to be used by the Taiwanese at the 1980 Olympic Games. Ren-Guey (P), an athlete selected by the Taiwanese to participate in the Games, sought a permanent injunction staying the Games unless Lake Placid, Inc. (D), the surrogate of the IOC that was established to operate the Winter Games, allowed him to use the flag, emblem, name, and anthem of the Republic of China. The U.S. State Department had a policy of deferring to the IOC on matters concerning national representation at the Olympics.

ISSUE: Will the courts review "political" questions?

HOLDING AND DECISION: (Per curiam) No. Whether a foreign government should be recognized is a political question that neither the U.S. Supreme Court nor any other American court may review. In essence, the plaintiff in this case is asking the courts to compel Lake Placid, Inc. (D), as a surrogate of the IOC, to recognize a symbol of national sovereignty. However, the IOC has already made a different determination. Furthermore, the fact is the Department of State, acting on the President's behalf, has elected to defer to the IOC on matters concerning national representation at the Olympics. Therefore, this case presents a political question, bound up as it is with questions of foreign policy, and is, for that reason, beyond the powers of this Court to review.

EDITOR'S ANALYSIS: The ability of the courts to take judicial notice of authoritative determinations made by nonjudicial agencies, such as the State Department, is not questioned. It provides one way for the courts to avoid becoming embroiled in matters that are properly the province of one of the other branches of the government under the Constitution.

NOTES:

UNITED STATES v. JONES
Federal government (P) v. Telephone tapper (D)
580 F.2d 219 (6th Cir. 1978).

NATURE OF CASE: Appeal from acquittal of illegal interception of telephone calls.

FACT SUMMARY: Jones (D) was acquitted of intercepting telephone calls illegally because the Government (P) failed to allege that the maker of the telephone, South Central Bell, was a common carrier providing facilities for interstate communication.

CONCISE RULE OF LAW: Failure to plead a fact in a criminal proceeding may not be cured by judicial notice.

FACTS: Jones (D) was charged with illegally intercepting telephone conversations by tapping the telephone of his estranged wife. The telephone was made by South Central Bell, part of an international corporation providing communications services throughout the world. The statute under which Jones (D) was charged required that the interception be from equipment of a common carrier providing facilities for the transmission of interstate communications. The Government (P) failed to allege South Central Bell's status as such a carrier, and Jones (D) was accordingly acquitted, despite a guilty verdict. The Government (P) appealed, seeking to cure the pleading defect by requesting judicial notice of Bell's status.

ISSUE: May a failure to plead a fact in a criminal proceeding be cured by judicial notice?

HOLDING AND DECISION: (Engel, J.) No. While the Federal Rule of Evidence 201(f) permits the request of judicial notice at any state of a proceeding, even on appeal, the value of judicial notice is different in a criminal proceeding such as this one than in a civil action. In a civil action, the jury must regard judicially noticed facts as conclusively established. However, in a criminal proceeding, the jury must pass on facts that are judicially noticed, despite the notice. Thus, even if judicial notice is taken in this case of South Central Bell's status as an interstate carrier, the jury would not be required to accept the fact. Thus, failure to plead a fact in a criminal proceeding may not be cured by judicial notice. The jury's right to reject the judicially noticed fact cannot be taken away by granting notice after the jury is discharged.

EDITOR'S ANALYSIS: The neglect of the Government's (P) attorney is on the one hand exactly the kind of mistake that Fed. R. Evid. 201(f) is intended to cure by allowing judicial notice on appeal. However, the right of the defendant to have the jury render its verdict with the ability to reject the judicial notice outweighs the policy for correction on appeal. The peculiar result in this case has been criticized.

[For more information on requirements for judicial notice, see Casenote Law Outline on Evidence, Chapter 3, § IV, Procedure for Taking Judicial Notice.]

QUICKNOTES

JUDICIAL NOTICE - The discretion of a court to recognize certain well-known facts as being true, without the necessity of a party introducing evidence to establish the truth of the fact.

NOTES:

CHAPTER 9
PRIVILEGES

QUICK REFERENCE RULES OF LAW

1. **Subpoenaed Documents.** The Fifth Amendment right against self-incrimination does not bar the government from summoning documents of an individual in the hands of his attorney pursuant to the attorney-client relationship. (Fisher v. United States)

   [For more information on the attorney-client privilege, see Casenote Law Outline on Evidence, Chapter 8, § II, The Attorney-Client Privilege.]

2. **Collective Entities.** Corporate and other collective entities, along with their officers, are not protected by the Fifth Amendment prohibition against self-incrimination. (Braswell v. United States)

   [For more information on privileges, see Casenote Law Outline on Evidence, Chapter 8, § I Privileges in General.]

3. **Required Records.** Persons who care for children pursuant to a custody order and who may be subject to a request for access to the child are not protected by the Fifth Amendment privilege against self-incrimination when asked by the state to produce the child. (Baltimore City Department of Social Services v. Bouknight)

   [For more information on privileges, see Casenote Law Outline on Evidence, Chapter 8, § I Privileges in General.]

4. **Immunity.** Immunity from use and derivative use of testimony is sufficient to compel testimony over the claim of the privilege against self-incrimination. (Kastigar v. United States)

5. **Exercise of the Privilege: Comment and Inference.** The Fifth Amendment is violated when a judge refuses a criminal defendant's request that the jury be instructed that his refusal to testify cannot be used as an inference of guilt and should not prejudice him in any way because he is not compelled to testify. (Carter v. Kentucky)

   [For more information on adverse inference from a claim of privilege, see Casenote Law Outline on Evidence, Chapter 8, § X, Privilege Procedure.]

6. **Prosecutorial Discovery.** Reciprocal discovery does not violate the privilege against self-incrimination. (Izazaga v. Superior Court)

7. **Basic Elements.** The attorney-client privilege applies to all confidential communications between attorneys and their clients relating to legal issues and advice. (In re Sealed Case)

   [For more information on the attorney-client privilege, see Casenote Law Outline on Evidence, Chapter 8, § II, The Attorney-Client Privilege.]

8. **The Identity of the Client, Fee Information, and Related Matters.** A fee payer's identity may not be compelled if it is intertwined with privileged confidential communications. (Ralls v. United States)

   [For more information on the attorney-client privilege, see Casenote Law Outline on Evidence, Chapter 8, § II, The Attorney-Client Privilege.]

9. **Required Reports under 26 U.S.C. Section 6050I and the Bank Secrecy Act.** Attorneys are not exempt

from laws requiring information regarding individuals who pay cash for services. (United States of America v. Goldberger & Dubin)

[For more information on the elements of the attorney-client privilege, see Casenote Law Outline on Evidence, Chapter 8, § II, The Attorney-Client Privilege.]

10. **Physical Evidence.** The attorney-client privilege usually provides protection for all observations resulting from privileged communication from a client leading defense counsel to physical evidence, but the original location and condition of that evidence loses the protection of the privilege if defense counsel chooses to remove the evidence to examine or test it. (People v. Meredith)

[For more information on the scope of the attorney-client privilege, see Casenote Law Outline on Evidence, Chapter 8, § II, The Attorney-Client Privilege.]

11. **Physical Evidence.** A criminal defendant cannot be compelled to produce evidence against him which is testimonial in nature and tends to incriminate him. (Commonwealth v. Hughes)

12. **The Corporation as the Client, Work Product and Related Matters.** In the case of a corporation claiming the attorney-client privilege, whether the privilege protects any particular communication must be determined on a case-by-case basis; the "control group" test does not govern. (Upjohn v. United States)

[For more information on the holder of the attorney-client privilege, see Casenote Law Outline on Evidence, Chapter 8, § II, The Attorney-Client Privilege.]

13. **The Attorney's Agents and Joint Defense Matters.** Communications made by a defendant to a psychiatrist retained by or at the request of his counsel to aid him in representing the defendant are protected by the attorney-client privilege. (People v. Lines)

[For more information on the scope of the attorney-client privilege, see Casenote Law Outline on Evidence, Chapter 8, § II, The Attorney-Client Privilege.]

14. **The Attorney's Agents and Joint Defense Matters.** Disclosures made by a defendant in confidence to a codefendant's attorney (or the attorney's client) for a common purpose related to both of their defenses are protected by the attorney-client privilege even if the co-defendant's defenses are not in all respects compatible. (United States v. McPartlin)

[For more information on the attorney-client privilege and joint clients, see Casenote Law Outline on Evidence, Chapter 8, § II, The Attorney-Client Privilege.]

15. **The Crime-Fraud Exception.** A district court, at the behest of the party opposing a claim of attorney-client privilege, may conduct an in-camera review of the materials in question. (United States v. Zolin)

[For more information on attorney-client privilege, see Casenote Law Outline on Evidence, Chapter 8, § II, The Attorney-Client Privilege.]

16. **The Privilege Against Adverse Spousal Testimony.** A criminal defendant cannot prevent his spouse from voluntarily giving testimony against him because the privilege against adverse spousal testimony belongs to the testifying spouse. (Trammel v. United States)

[For more information on adverse spousal testimony, see Casenote Law Outline on Evidence, Chapter 8, § V, Spousal Privileges.]

17. The Privilege Against Adverse Spousal Testimony. A government promise not to use privileged information in its prosecution allows a witness to be compelled to testify to the privileged matter. (In the Matter of Grand Jury Subpoena of Ford v. United States)

> *[For more information on governmental privilege, see Casenote Law Outline on Evidence, Chapter 8, § VII, Government Privileges.]*

18. The Husband-Wife Confidential Communication Privilege. The marital communications privilege does not apply to statements made in furtherance of joint criminal activity. (United States v. Marashi)

> *[For more information on exceptions to spousal privileges, see Casenote Law Outline on Evidence, Chapter 8, § V, Spousal Privileges.]*

19. The Physician-Patient, Psychotherapist-Patient, and Similar Counselor-Client Privileges. A psychotherapist-patient privilege should be recognized in federal courts. (Jaffee v. Redmond)

> *[For more information on federal recognition of the psychotherapist-patient privilege, see Casenote Law Outline on Evidence, Chapter 8, § IV, The Psychotherapist-Patient Privilege.]*

20. The Physician-Patient, Psychotherapist-Patient, and Similar Counselor-Client Privileges. The dangerous-patient exception to the psychotherapist-patient privilege applies if there is a reasonable belief in the dangerousness of the patient. (Menendez v. Superior Court of Los Angeles County)

> *[For more information on exceptions to the psychotherapist-patient privilege, see Casenote Law Outline on Evidence, Chapter 8, § IV, The Psychotherapist-Patient Privilege.]*

21. Peer Review Privilege and Critical Self-Analysis Privilege. There is no privilege for confidential peer review materials. (University of Pennsylvania v. EEOC)

> *[For more information on claims of privilege, see Casenote Law Outline on Evidence, Chapter 8, § X, Privilege Procedure.]*

22. Conflicts. Federal Rule of Evidence 501 provides that privileges "shall be governed by the principles of the common law as they may be interpreted by the courts of the United States in the light of reason and experience" except that "in civil actions and proceedings, with respect to an element of a claim or defense as to which State law supplies the rule of decision" privileges are to "be determined in accordance with State laws." (Ghana Supply Commission v. New England Power Co.)

> *[For more information on federal privilege law, see Casenote Law Outline on Evidence, Chapter 8, § I Privileges in General.]*

FISHER v. UNITED STATES
Taxpayer (D) v. Federal government (P)
425 U.S. 391 (1976).

NATURE OF CASE: Review of order of summons to produce documents.

FACT SUMMARY: The Government (P) sought production of documents by an attorney who received them from his taxpayer-client in connection with the attorney-client relationship.

CONCISE RULE OF LAW: The Fifth Amendment right against self-incrimination does not bar the government from summoning documents of an individual in the hands of his attorney pursuant to the attorney-client relationship.

FACTS: A taxpayer delivered certain documents to his attorney in connection with the attorney-client relationship. The Government (P) sought an order compelling the attorney to produce those documents. The taxpayer challenged the summons on the ground that his Fifth Amendment right against self-incrimination would be violated by the attorney's production of the papers.

ISSUE: Does the Fifth Amendment right against self-incrimination bar the government from summoning documents of an individual in the hands of his attorney pursuant to the attorney-client relationship?

HOLDING AND DECISION: (White, J.) No. While the elements of compulsion are clearly present, the act of producing the documents in question here would not involve testimonial self-incrimination. The testimonial aspects of the documents were reduced to writing by a wholly voluntary process. And while the act of producing the documents has some communicative value of its own, in this case the existence of the documents and their location was a foregone conclusion and not something the taxpayer was revealing by virtue of his attorney's production. The Fifth Amendment right against self-incrimination does not bar the government from summoning documents of an individual in the hands of his attorney pursuant to the attorney-client relationship. We do not address the question whether the right would shield the taxpayer from producing his own tax records.

CONCURRENCE: (Brennan, J.) I agree that the compulsion in this case of ordered production of nonpersonal business records does not violate the Fifth Amendment. However, the Court's treatment of the self-incrimination privilege is inadequate. The fact that the papers contain no declarations does not mean that they are not "testimonial." While business records of entities generally fall outside the scope of protection, not all economic records are unprotected. The act of producing the records, furthermore, implicitly admits the existence of the records and implicitly authenticates them. The fact that the government could otherwise know of the records is irrelevant because the protection does not depend on the strength of the government's case against a defendant.

EDITOR'S ANALYSIS: An individual cannot create immunity by transferring possession of papers to an attorney, at least not on Fifth Amendment grounds. But where the Fifth Amendment protects documents in the hands of an individual, his transfer of them to an attorney (within the attorney-client relationship) does not defeat the privilege. Thus, the self-incrimination analysis turns on the status of the person who claims he will be incriminated, not that of his agent.

[For more information on the attorney-client privilege, see Casenote Law Outline on Evidence, Chapter 8, § II, The Attorney-Client Privilege.]

QUICKNOTES

ATTORNEY-CLIENT PRIVILEGE - A doctrine precluding the admission into evidence of confidential communications between an attorney and his client made in the course of obtaining professional assistance.

SUBPOENA - A mandate issued by court to compel a witness to appear at trial.

NOTES:

BRASWELL v. UNITED STATES

Business owner (D) v. Federal government (P)

487 U.S. 99 (1988).

NATURE OF CASE: Appeal from denial of a motion to quash a federal grand jury subpoena to produce corporate business records held by the records custodian.

FACT SUMMARY: After Braswell (D), sole shareholder of two corporations, received a federal grand jury subpoena to produce the books and records of both corporations, he moved to quash the subpoena on the ground that producing the records would violate his Fifth Amendment privilege.

CONCISE RULE OF LAW: Corporate and other collective entities, along with their officers, are not protected by the Fifth Amendment prohibition against self-incrimination.

FACTS: Braswell (D) owned a business that he initially operated as a sole proprietorship, then later incorporated. A year later, he formed a second corporation. Braswell (D) was the sole shareholder of the second corporation, which was funded by the 100% interest he held in the first corporation. When Braswell (D) received a federal grand jury subpoena requiring him to produce the books and records of the two corporations, he moved to quash the subpoena, arguing that the act of producing the records would incriminate him and thus violate his Fifth Amendment privilege against self-incrimination. The district court denied the motion based on the collective entity doctrine. The court of appeals affirmed. Braswell (D) appealed.

ISSUE: Are corporate and other collective entities, along with their officers, protected by the Fifth Amendment prohibition against self-incrimination?

HOLDING AND DECISION: (Rehnquist, C.J.) No. Corporate and other collective entities, along with their officers, are not protected by the Fifth Amendment prohibition against self-incrimination. This doctrine — known as the collective entity rule — has a lengthy and distinguished pedigree. The Court has consistently recognized that the custodian of corporate or entity records holds those documents in a representative rather than a personal capacity. A custodian's assumption of his representative capacity leads to certain obligations, including the duty to produce corporate records on proper demand by the federal government (P). The custodian's act of production is not deemed a personal act, but rather an act of the corporation. Any claim of Fifth Amendment privilege asserted by the agent would be tantamount to a claim of privilege by the corporation, which of course possesses no such privilege. Affirmed.

DISSENT: (Kennedy, J.) The necessary effect of this decision is to avoid and manipulate basic Fifth Amendment principles. The collective entity rule provides no support for the majority's holding.

The privilege against self-incrimination does apply in the context of this case. Once the government (P) concedes there are testimonial consequences implicit in the act of production, it cannot escape the conclusion that compliance with the subpoena is indisputably Braswell's (D) own act.

EDITOR'S ANALYSIS: The majority's concern was that recognizing a Fifth Amendment privilege on behalf of the records custodians of collective entities would have a detrimental impact on the government's efforts to prosecute "white-collar crime," one of the most serious problems confronting law enforcement authorities. The greater portion of evidence of wrongdoing by an organization or its representatives is usually found in the official records and documents of that organization. Were the cloak of the privilege to be thrown around these impersonal records and documents, effective enforcement of many federal and state laws would be impossible.

[For more information on privileges, see Casenot Law Outline on Evidence, Chapter 8, § I Privilege in General.]

QUICKNOTES

SUBPOENA - A mandate issued by court to compel a witness to appear at trial

NOTES:

BALTIMORE CITY DEPARTMENT OF SOCIAL SERVICES v. BOUKNIGHT

Municipal agency (P) v. Parent (D)
493 U.S. 549 (1990).

NATURE OF CASE: Appeal from reversal of a judgment upholding a contempt order for failure of a parent custodian to produce a child as ordered.

FACT SUMMARY: Bouknight (D), who had custody of her son pursuant to a custody order, was found in contempt of court after she refused to produce him in response to a court order, claiming that producing the child would violate her Fifth Amendment right against self-incrimination.

CONCISE RULE OF LAW: Persons who care for children pursuant to a custody order and who may be subject to a request for access to the child are not protected by the Fifth Amendment privilege against self-incrimination when asked by the state to produce the child.

FACTS: Maurice M. (P), an abused child, was removed from his mother's control and placed in shelter care. Several months later, he was returned to his mother, Bouknight (D). At a hearing, the juvenile court asserted jurisdiction over Maurice (P), placing him under Baltimore City Department of Social Services' (BCDSS) (P) continuing oversight. Because Bouknight (D) later failed to cooperate with BCDSS (P) caseworkers, BCDSS (D) petitioned to place Maurice (P) in foster care. When Bouknight (D) refused to produce Maurice (P), the juvenile court imprisoned her, finding her in contempt. The court rejected Bouknight's (D) claim that the contempt order violated her Fifth Amendment right against self-incrimination. The court of appeals reversed. BCDSS (P) appealed.

ISSUE: Are persons who care for children pursuant to a custody order and may be subject to a request for access to the child protected by the Fifth Amendment privilege against self-incrimination when asked by the state to produce the child?

HOLDING AND DECISION: (O'Connor, J.) No. Persons who care for children pursuant to a custody order and may be subject to a request for access to the child are not protected by the Fifth Amendment privilege against self-incrimination when asked by the state to produce the child. Assuming control over items that are the legitimate object of the government's (P) noncriminal regulatory powers reduces the ability to invoke the privilege. Once Maurice (P) was adjudicated a child in need of assistance, his care and safety became the particular object of the state's regulatory interests. By accepting care of Maurice (P) subject to the custodial order's conditions, Bouknight (D) submitted to the routine operation of the regulatory system. She was properly found in contempt. The court of appeals is thus reversed.

EDITOR'S ANALYSIS: Orders to produce children cannot be characterized as efforts to gain some testimonial component of the act of production. The government demands production of the public charge entrusted to a custodian for compelling reasons unrelated to criminal law enforcement. But even when criminal conduct may exist, the court may properly request production and return of the child and enforce that request through exercise of the contempt power, especially where the child's safety is a concern.

[For more information on privileges, see Casenote Law Outline on Evidence, Chapter 8, § I Privileges in General.]

NOTES:

KASTIGAR v. UNITED STATES
Criminal defendant (P) v. Federal government (D)
406 U.S. 441 (1972).

NATURE OF CASE: Appeal from a contempt order.

FACT SUMMARY: Prior to testifying as to possibly incriminating matters, Kastigar (P) was granted immunity from having his testimony used against him.

CONCISE RULE OF LAW: Immunity from use and derivative use of testimony is sufficient to compel testimony over the claim of the privilege against self-incrimination.

FACTS: Kastigar (P) was subpoenaed to appear before a federal grand jury. The government believed that he might assert the privilege against self-incrimination. Therefore, prior to the testimony, Kastigar (P) was granted immunity from having his testimony used against him or any other evidence derived from the testimony. However, he still refused to answer and was held in contempt.

ISSUE: May testimony be compelled by granting immunity from the use of the compelled testimony and evidence derived therefrom?

HOLDING AND DECISION: (Powell, J.) Yes. Immunity from use and derivative use of testimony is sufficient to compel testimony over the claim of the privilege against self-incrimination. In prior cases, it has been held that the immunity must cover the entire transaction in order to override the privilege against self-incrimination. However, the immunity in this case is enough as it does afford protection against being forced to give testimony leading to the infliction of penalties affixed to criminal acts. All that is required of the immunity is that it protect the witness from future prosecution based on knowledge and sources of information obtained from the compelled testimony. It is not necessary to have total transactional immunity to afford this protection. The immunity involved in this case is sufficient.

DISSENT: (Brennan, J.) To overcome the privilege against self-incrimination, there must be total transactional immunity. The situation must be such as the witness is in the same position he would have been in had he not been compelled to testify.

EDITOR'S ANALYSIS: As this case indicates, the purpose of the Fifth Amendment privilege has been construed to protect a witness from legal criminal liability based on his testimony. Therefore, if immunity is granted, then there is no need for the privilege. There is, however, an agreement that would make the privilege absolute. As Justice Douglas has argued, the purpose of the Fifth Amendment privilege was also to protect the witness against infamy, which "was historically considered to be punishment as effective as fine and imprisonment." Under this

view, immunity would not be effective, regardless of its scope. However, no court has adopted this view, and virtually all states have immunity statutes.

QUICKNOTES
IMMUNITY FROM PROSECUTION - Statutory protection afforded to a witness against prosecution as a result of his testimony.

NOTES:

CARTER v. KENTUCKY
Burglar (D) v. State (P)
450 U.S. 288 (1981).

NATURE OF CASE: Appeal from conviction for burglary.

FACT SUMMARY: At his trial on burglary charges, Carter (D) demanded but the judge refused to give a jury instruction that a defendant is not compelled to testify and the fact that he does not testify cannot be used as an inference of guilt.

CONCISE RULE OF LAW: The Fifth Amendment is violated when a judge refuses a criminal defendant's request that the jury be instructed that his refusal to testify cannot be used as an inference of guilt and should not prejudice him in any way because he is not compelled to testify.

FACTS: Carter (D) was convicted of third-degree burglary and of being a persistent felony offender at a trial in which he chose not to testify after he was informed that his prior felony convictions could then be brought before the jury to impeach his credibility. In appealing his conviction, Carter (D) insisted that the trial judge had violated his Fifth Amendment privilege against compulsory self-incrimination by refusing his request to give the jury the following instruction: "The defendant is not compelled to testify and the fact that he does not cannot be used as an inference of guilt and should not prejudice him in any way."

ISSUE: Does the Fifth Amendment require a judge to give an instruction to the jury upon defendant's request that his refusal to testify cannot be used as an inference of guilt?

HOLDING AND DECISION: (Stewart, J.) Yes. The Fifth Amendment bars adverse comment on a criminal defendant's failure to testify. It also requires that the trial judge accede to a criminal defendant's request that the jury be instructed that a defendant is not compelled to testify and that his refusal to testify cannot be used as an inference of guilt and should not prejudice him in any way. A defendant must pay no court-imposed price for the exercise of his constitutional privilege not to testify. Even without adverse comment, the jury, unless instructed otherwise, may well draw adverse inferences from a defendant's silence. Thus, even if the defendant does not want such an instruction given, the trial judge can use the unique power of the jury instruction to prevent improper speculation by the jury as to why a defendant did not testify. He must always issue such an instruction when the defendant requests it. Reversed.

EDITOR'S ANALYSIS: A prosecutor cannot call the defendant as a witness to force him to claim his privilege in front of the jury. Once the defendant takes the stand, the prosecutor is, however, free to ask the defendant questions he knows will result in a string of repeated assertions of the privilege against self-incrimination. Furthermore, the trial judge does not commit error in permitting the prosecutor to proceed thusly. United States v. Hearst, 563 F.2d 1331 (9th Cir. 1977).

IZAZAGA v. SUPERIOR COURT
Suspected rapist-kidnapper (D) v. State (P)
Cal. Sup. Ct., 815 P.2d 304 (1991).

NATURE OF CASE: Appeal from denial of application for writ of mandate following discovery order in rape prosecution.

FACT SUMMARY: Izazaga (P) claimed that California's law requiring reciprocal discovery in criminal cases was barred by the Fifth Amendment's self-incrimination protection.

CONCISE RULE OF LAW: Reciprocal discovery does not violate the privilege against self-incrimination.

FACTS: California Prop. 115, titled the Crime Victims Justice Reform Act, included a provision authorizing reciprocal discovery in criminal cases. Izazaga (P) was charged with rape and kidnapping shortly after Proposition 115 passed. The prosecution served on Izazaga (P) a request for discovery which Izazaga (P) refused. Following a court order requiring the discovery, Izazaga (P) applied for a writ of mandate based on the unconstitutionality of the discovery provisions of Proposition 115. Izazaga (P) claimed that requiring advance disclosure of defense witnesses implicated the Self-Incrimination Clause of the U.S. and California Constitutions. The court of appeal denied the application, but the state supreme court issued an alternative writ.

ISSUE: Does reciprocal discovery violate the privilege against self-incrimination?

HOLDING AND DECISION: (Lucas, C.J.) No. Reciprocal discovery does not violate the privilege against self-incrimination. The Fifth Amendment states that no person can be compelled to testify against himself. Previously, the Supreme Court has ruled that states may require defendants intending to rely on an alibi defense to notify the prosecution in advance. The Supreme Court has found that four requirements trigger the privilege. The information must be (1) incriminating, (2) personal to defendant, (3) obtained by compulsion; and (4) testimonial or communicative in nature. Statutorily mandated discovery of evidence that meets these four requirements is prohibited. All other evidence is discoverable. In the present case, the names of defense witnesses merely force defendant to divulge at an earlier date information that the defendant is planning on revealing at trial. Such information is not personal to defendant and thus does not meet the requirements triggering the self-incrimination privilege. Timing of the disclosure does not affect any of the requirements. Accordingly, Izazaga (P) must comply with discovery order.

EDITOR'S ANALYSIS: This issue is important to defendants because otherwise they would be able to see the prosecution's case before choosing a defense. A defendant may alter his alibi if the prosecution goes in an unexpected direction. Therefore, in a certain sense, reciprocal discovery alters the basic presumption of innocence accorded to defendants.

IN RE SEALED CASE
Parties not named.
737 F.2d 94 (D.C. Cir 1984).

NATURE OF CASE: Appeal from order mandating testimony in grand jury investigation.

FACT SUMMARY: The attorney-client privilege was asserted by a company's (D) general counsel as to conversations he had with the company's (D) president.

CONCISE RULE OF LAW: The attorney-client privilege applies to all confidential communications between attorneys and their clients relating to legal issues and advice.

FACTS: An unnamed company (D) was investigated by a grand jury. The general counsel, and a vice president, of the company (D) was called before the grand jury to testify. He testified about his activities and observations during his time with the company (D). However, on instruction from counsel, he asserted the attorney-client privilege with respect to five matters. The first was an overheard conversation that he related to the president of the company (D). The second was the bases for a hunch he had regarding the company's (D) involvement in bid rigging. The third matter was a conversation with a company (D) senior executive. The fourth was conversations with the president in the course of periodic status reviews of the company's (D) legal affairs. The last was a conversation with the president on an airplane. The government (P) brought a motion to compel testimony on these five matters and the court ruled that the general counsel had not established entitlement to the privilege except as to the conversation with the senior executive. The company (D) appealed the remaining matters.

ISSUE: Does the attorney-client privilege apply to all confidential communications between attorneys and their clients relating to legal issues and advice?

HOLDING AND DECISION: (Ginsburg, J.) Yes. The attorney-client privilege applies to all confidential communications between attorneys and their clients relating to legal issues and advice. However, the attorney must be acting as a lawyer for purposes of the conversation. Additionally, strangers cannot be present. Furthermore, the conversation may not be for the purpose of committing a crime or tort. Communications from attorney to client are shielded when they rest on confidential information obtained from the client. When an attorney conveys facts obtained from other sources, the privilege is not in effect. The status of in-house attorney does not dilute the privilege. With regard to the matters at issue, the general counsel cannot claim the privilege with respect to an overheard conversation. This simply does not qualify as confidential information. The bases for hunches about bid rigging are also not protected by the privilege because they are based upon the general counsel's observations. No confidential communication was involved. The conversations with the president at the status review meetings qualify for the privilege because they were intertwined with the general counsel's legal advice. Also, the plane conversation is privileged even though there was no express request by the president to keep the matter confidential. There were no other parties to the conversation and it was carried out in a manner suggesting that it was intended to be confidential. Therefore, the order compelling testimony is affirmed in part and reversed in part.

EDITOR'S ANALYSIS: As noted in the decision, the privilege only attaches when the communication relates to legal matters. Thus, when corporate counsel also plays a management role, difficulties can sometimes arise. Of course, the client can waive the privilege at any time.

[For more information on the attorney-client privilege, see Casenote Law Outline on Evidence, Chapter 8, § II, The Attorney-Client Privilege.]

QUICKNOTES
ATTORNEY-CLIENT PRIVILEGE - A doctrine precluding the admission into evidence of confidential communications between an attorney and his client made in the course of obtaining professional assistance.

CONFIDENTIAL COMMUNICATIONS - A communication made between specified classes of persons which is privileged.

NOTES:

RALLS v. UNITED STATES
Criminal defense attorney (P) v. Federal government (D)
52 F.3d 223 (9th Cir. 1995).

NATURE OF CASE: Appeal from denial of motion to quash grand jury subpoena.

FACT SUMMARY: Ralls (P), a lawyer, refused to divulge the identity of a client, asserting the attorney-client privilege.

CONCISE RULE OF LAW: A fee payer's identity may not be compelled if it is intertwined with privileged confidential communications.

FACTS: Ralls (P), a criminal defense attorney, was paid by someone to represent Bonnette at an initial appearance and detention hearing for drug smuggling charges. The government (D) later issued a grand jury subpoena to Ralls (P), seeking to discover the name of the person who hired Ralls (P) and the amount of the fee. Ralls (P) moved to quash the subpoena. The district court ordered Ralls (P) to testify about the fee payer's identity and fee arrangements. Ralls (P) appealed.

ISSUE: May a fee payer's identity be compelled under the attorney-client privilege?

HOLDING AND DECISION: (Choy, J.) No. A fee payer's identity may not be compelled if it is intertwined with privileged confidential communications. The party asserting the attorney-client privilege has the burden of establishing the relationship and the privileged nature of the communication. Generally, the attorney-client privilege does not safeguard against disclosure of the identity of the fee payer and the fee arrangements. This is because the privilege only applies to confidential communications and the fee is usually an incidental matter. However, an attorney may invoke the privilege to protect the client's identity if disclosure would convey information that ordinarily would be part of the usual confidential communications. The application of the privilege is not triggered by the fact that identity and fee arrangements would incriminate the fee payer. It can be used only when the information would infringe on a privileged communication. Thus, if the disclosure of the client's identity would also reveal the confidential purpose, the identity is privileged. In the present case, Ralls (P) has revealed through sealed affidavit that the fee payer specifically discussed his own criminal liability in connection with the same crime involving Bonnette. Thus, the identity is so intertwined with privileged communications that disclosure of the identity would destroy the privilege. Accordingly, the district court's denial of Ralls' (P) motion to quash the subpoena is reversed.

EDITOR'S ANALYSIS: Generally, courts no longer inquire whether the identity of a client would be incriminating in order to determine applicability of the attorney-client privilege. Ralls (P) had argued that the last-link doctrine prevented disclosure. The last-link doctrine involves cases where the identity of a client would be the final step in the chain of evidence needed to prosecute a person. The court found that the last-link doctrine does not apply any differently from the test it used above.

[For more information on the attorney-client privilege, see Casenote Law Outline on Evidence, Chapter 8, § II, The Attorney-Client Privilege.]

QUICKNOTES
CONFIDENTIAL COMMUNICATIONS - A communication made between specified classes of persons which is privileged.

ATTORNEY-CLIENT PRIVILEGE - A doctrine precluding the admission into evidence of confidential communications between an attorney and his client made in the course of obtaining professional assistance.

NOTES:

UNITED STATES v. GOLDBERGER & DUBIN
Federal government (P) v. Attorneys (D)
935 F.2d 501 (2d Cir. 1991).

NATURE OF CASE: Appeal from order to provide information.

FACT SUMMARY: Goldberger (D) and other attorneys (D) maintained that they did not have to disclose the identity of clients who paid large fees in cash.

CONCISE RULE OF LAW: Attorneys are not exempt from laws requiring information regarding individuals who pay cash for services.

FACTS: Goldberger (D) and other attorneys (D) received fees from clients in cash in amounts exceeding $10,000. Internal Revenue Code § 6050I requires that any person engaged in a trade or business who receives more than $10,000 in cash is required to file a form including the payor's name and identifying information. Goldberger (D) and the other attorneys (D) filed the form but did not disclose the payor's identity. When they refused to disclose this information, the government (P) sought to enforce summons mandating disclosure. The district court ruled that Goldberger (D) and the other attorneys (D) must comply and provide the payor information. Goldberger (D) appealed, maintaining that this information was privileged under the attorney-client privilege.

ISSUE: Are attorneys exempt from laws requiring information regarding individuals who pay cash for services?

HOLDING AND DECISION: (Van Graafeiland, J.) No. Attorneys are not exempt from laws requiring information regarding individuals who pay cash for services. Financial reporting legislation plays an important role in the economic life of the country. The reporting provisions of the Internal Revenue Code are very useful in tax and criminal investigations. Absent special circumstances, there has been no evidence presented that identification of clients on the IRS forms is a disclosure of confidential information. There is absolutely no direct linkage between the identification and the incrimination of the client in § 6050I. Since the practice of law is a trade or business as contemplated by § 6050I, there is no reason to believe that attorneys were to be exempt from its application. To the extent that the attorney-client privilege slightly conflicts with § 6050I, Congress intended that the privilege give way to importance of proper tax recording. Therefore, the district court's order that Goldberger (D) and the other attorneys (D) disclose the client identity information is affirmed.

EDITOR'S ANALYSIS: The court also dismissed the attorney's argument that § 6050I conflicted with the Fourth and Fifth Amendments. The decision noted that these types of contentions had been rejected consistently with regard to similar reporting requirements of the Bank Secrecy Act. The court also dismissed the Sixth Amendment argument that disclosure deprived the anonymous clients of their right to counsel.

[For more information on the elements of the attorney-client privilege, see Casenote Law Outline on Evidence, Chapter 8, § II, The Attorney-Client Privilege.]

QUICKNOTES
ATTORNEY-CLIENT PRIVILEGE - A doctrine precluding the admission into evidence of confidential communications between an attorney and his client made in the course of obtaining professional assistance.

NOTES:

PEOPLE v. MEREDITH
State (P) v. Convicted felons (D)
Cal. Sup. Ct., 29 Cal.3d 682, 631 P.2d 46 (1981).

NATURE OF CASE: Appeal from conviction for murder and robbery.

FACT SUMMARY: Scott (D), whose communications with his attorney led a defense investigator to find the murder victim's wallet (which was removed but later turned in to the police), maintained that his privilege against self-incrimination barred the investigator from testifying to the location of the wallet.

CONCISE RULE OF LAW: The attorney-client privilege usually provides protection for all observations resulting from privileged communication from a client leading defense counsel to physical evidence, but the original location and condition of that evidence loses the protection of the privilege if defense counsel chooses to remove the evidence to examine or test it.

FACTS: Scott (D) and Meredith (D) were both convicted of the first-degree murder and first-degree robbery of David Wade. When Schenk, Scott's (D) first appointed attorney, visited him in jail, Scott (D) told him that the victim's wallet (which he had tried to burn) was in a plastic bag in a burn barrel behind his house. Schenk proceeded to retain an investigator, Frick, and sent Frick to find the wallet. Frick found the wallet and brought it back to Schenk, who turned it over to police after examining its contents and determining that it contained credit cards with Wade's name. Schenk only told the police that to the best of his knowledge the wallet had belonged to Wade. On appeal, Scott (D) conceded that the wallet itself was admissible but insisted that his privilege against self-incrimination was a bar to Frick's testimony as to where the wallet had been located.

ISSUE: If defense counsel removes evidence to which he has been led by a privileged communication from his client, does the original location and condition of the evidence lose the protection of the client's privilege against self-incrimination?

HOLDING AND DECISION: (Tobriner, J.) Yes. Normally, the attorney-client privilege is not strictly limited to communications but extends to protect all observations made as a consequence of protected communication. If, therefore, a privileged communication leads defense counsel to some physical evidence, his observations thereof are insulated from revelation as long as he leaves the evidence where he discovers it. If, however, he makes the tactical decision of removing the evidence to examine or test it, the original location and condition of that evidence loses the protection of the privilege. Thus, the location of the wallet was not protected information in this case. Affirmed.

EDITOR'S ANALYSIS: As a tactical maneuver designed to prevent the jury from connecting the defendant with the party who "discovered" the evidence (as the result of privileged communications), the defense will sometimes offer to enter into a stipulation simply informing the jury as to the location or condition of the evidence. The prosecutor cannot refuse simply in the hopes of providing the opportunity for the jury to make such a connection.

[For more information on the scope of the attorney-client privilege, see Casenote Law Outline on Evidence, Chapter 8, § II, The Attorney-Client Privilege.]

NOTES:

COMMONWEALTH v. HUGHES
State (P) v. Assaulter (D)
Mass. Sup. Jud. Ct., 380 Mass. 583, 404 N.E.2d 1239 (1980), cert. denied 449
U.S. 900 (1980).

NATURE OF CASE: Appeal from contempt citation.

FACT SUMMARY: Commonwealth (P) contended that Hughes (D) could be compelled to produce the suspected assault weapon.

CONCISE RULE OF LAW: A criminal defendant cannot be compelled to produce evidence against him which is testimonial in nature and tends to incriminate him.

FACTS: Hughes (D) was charged with assault. The Commonwealth (P) moved for an order requiring him to produce a gun registered to him and believed to have been used in the assault. Hughes (D) refused to produce the gun, contending such would violate his right not to incriminate himself. The court found him in contempt of its order, and Hughes (D) appealed.

ISSUE: Can a criminal defendant be compelled to produce evidence against him of a testimonial nature?

HOLDING AND DECISION: (Kaplan, J.) No. A criminal defendant cannot be compelled to produce evidence against him which is testimonial in nature and tends to incriminate him. Production of the gun will supply the prosecution with the serial number and other identifying information. This will allow the gun to be traced to Hughes (D) and imply his guilt. As a result, production is testimonial in nature and cannot be compelled. Reversed.

EDITOR'S ANALYSIS: Defendants can be required to submit to blood testing and to provide handwriting samples without violating the self-incrimination protection. These activities are not testimonial in nature and thus are not applicable to self-incrimination analysis.

NOTES:

UPJOHN CO. v. UNITED STATES
Company (D) v. Federal government (P)
449 U.S. 383 (1981).

NATURE OF CASE: Appeal from denial of privilege in tax investigation.

FACT SUMMARY: Upjohn (D) claimed the IRS was not entitled to production of its questionnaires to and interviews of Upjohn (D) employees concerning possibly illegal payments made by Upjohn (D), as they were privileged communications and an attorney's work product.

CONCISE RULE OF LAW: In the case of a corporation claiming the attorney-client privilege, whether the privilege protects any particular communication must be determined on a case-by-case basis; the "control group" test does not govern.

FACTS: In January 1976, independent accountants discovered that a foreign subsidiary of Upjohn (D) had made payments to or for the benefit of foreign government officials. Upjohn's (D) general counsel conducted an investigation of these "possibly illegal" payments, which included interviews of all foreign general and area managers and various other Upjohn (D) employees and questionnaires to the foreign managers. The IRS conducted its own investigation to determine the tax consequences of the payments. It demanded production of all Upjohn's (D) relevant files, including the questionnaires and memoranda of the interviews. Upjohn (D) claimed these were privileged and also protected as the work product of an attorney in anticipation of litigation. Upjohn (D) appealed the enforcement of the summons. The Sixth Circuit affirmed to the extent that officers and employees not responsible for directing Upjohn's (D) actions in response to legal advice were not "clients" whose communications could come within the attorney-client privilege. The case was remanded to district court for a determination as to who was not within the "control group." The district court was not to consider the work product doctrine, which the Sixth Circuit found inapplicable to administrative summonses. Upjohn (D) appealed.

ISSUE: In the case of a corporation claiming the attorney-client privilege, does the privilege for any communication turn on whether the employee making the communication was responsible for directing the corporation's actions?

HOLDING AND DECISION: (Rehnquist, J.) No. The "control group" test adopted by the Sixth Circuit, which grants the attorney-client privilege only to those communications made by employees responsible for directing the corporation's actions in response to legal advice, frustrates the very purpose of the privilege; this is so because it discourages communication of relevant information by employees of the client corporation to attorneys seeking to render their best legal advice to the

corporate control group. Further, it invites unpredictability of application, as those whose communications receive the privilege must play a "substantial role" in directing corporate actions in response to the advice. Thus, in the case of a corporation claiming the privilege, the control group test does not govern; whether any particular communication is privileged must be determined on a case-by-case basis. Here, the communications in question were made by Upjohn (D) employees to its counsel at the direction of its officers so that they might get advice from the counsel. Thus, these communications, the questionnaires, and notes reflecting responses to interviews are privileged. Regarding the notes which go beyond recording responses to interviews, Federal Rule 26 offers special protection to work product revealing an attorney's mental processes. While a sufficient showing of necessity can overcome protection as to tangible items and documents, a far stronger showing is required as to material revealing a lawyer's mental impressions. Here, the lesser standard was erroneously applied by the district court to the attorney's memoranda of interviews which went beyond the recording of responses. Reversed and remanded.

CONCURRENCE: (Burger, C.J.) The majority is right to reject the "control group" test, but it should articulate a standard: A communication should be privileged whenever an employee speaks at the direction of management regarding conduct within the scope of employment.

EDITOR'S ANALYSIS: Before the Upjohn case, the weight of authority favored the control group test. A broader test that some courts employed extended the privilege to embrace any communication by an employee involving his corporate duties and made at the direction of his corporate employer. This latter test was favored by Burger in Upjohn, although the majority declined to formulate a standard. While avoiding some of the problems of the control group test, the broader test seems to unduly extend the shield of privilege.

[For more information on the holder of the attorney-client privilege, see Casenote Law Outline on Evidence, Chapter 8, § II, The Attorney-Client Privilege.]

QUICKNOTES
ATTORNEY-CLIENT PRIVILEGE - A doctrine precluding the admission into evidence of confidential communications between an attorney and his client made in the course of obtaining professional assistance.

NOTES:

PEOPLE v. LINES
State (P) v. Murder suspect (D)
Cal. Sup. Ct., 13 Cal.3d 500, 531 P.2d 793 (1975).

NATURE OF CASE: Appeal from a conviction for second-degree murder.

FACT SUMMARY: Lines (D) contended that the communications he had made to the psychiatrists the court had appointed at his lawyer's request to provide him with the information needed to properly represent Lines (D) were protected by the attorney-client privilege.

CONCISE RULE OF LAW: Communications made by a defendant to a psychiatrist retained by or at the request of his counsel to aid him in representing the defendant are protected by the attorney-client privilege.

FACTS: Lines (D) appealed his second-degree murder conviction on the grounds the court had erred in letting in certain psychiatric testimony. His attorney had requested the court to appoint two doctors to examine Lines (D) to provide him with information he needed so that he could properly advise Lines (D) whether to enter a plea based on insanity or present a defense based on his mental condition. After two sessions with doctors Markman and Tweed, Lines (D) entered a plea of not guilty by reason of insanity. Thereupon, the court acted in accord with the law and appointed three doctors to examine Lines (D) and investigate his sanity so that they could testify on that issue at trial. Two of the doctors appointed were Markman and Tweed. At trial, Lines (D) objected to Markman's testimony insofar as it was based on the first two sessions he had with Lines (D), arguing that the communications he made therein were protected by the attorney-client privilege.

ISSUE: Are the communications a defendant makes to a psychiatrist appointed to aid his counsel in representing him protected by the attorney-client privilege?

HOLDING AND DECISION: (Sullivan, J.) Yes. The attorney-client privilege covers communications made to third persons "to whom disclosure is reasonably necessary for ... the accomplishment of the purpose for which the lawyer is consulted." Thus, when counsel retains or requests the appointment of a psychiatrist to aid him in representing his client-defendant, the communications by the defendant to the psychiatrist and the information obtained by the psychiatrist in connection therewith remains protected from disclosure — even if the client places his physical or mental condition in issue. While it thus appears that an error was committed in this case, it was harmless. Affirmed.

EDITOR'S ANALYSIS: Friendenthal disagrees with the notion that a doctor in this type of situation functions as a mere "interpreter" between client and attorney. He adds, says Friendenthal, "an important increment of knowledge of his own." "It seems," he writes, "that this knowledge should be treated just like the knowledge of any other witness and should be discoverable from the doctor himself." Discovery and Use of an Adverse Party's Expert Information, 14 Stan.L.Rev.455 (1962).

[For more information on the scope of the attorney-client privilege, see Casenote Law Outline on Evidence, Chapter 8, § II, The Attorney-Client Privilege.]

QUICKNOTES

ATTORNEY-CLIENT PRIVILEGE - A doctrine precluding the admission into evidence of confidential communications between an attorney and his client made in the course of obtaining professional assistance.

NOTES:

UNITED STATES v. McPARTLIN
Federal government (P) v. Co-conspirator (D)
595 F.2d 1321 (7th Cir. 1979); cert. denied, 444 U.S. 833.

NATURE OF CASE: Appeal from criminal conviction.

FACT SUMMARY: McPartlin (D) claimed that statements he made in confidence to an investigator working for his codefendant's attorney were protected by the attorney-client privilege because they had been made for a common purpose related to both of their defenses.

CONCISE RULE OF LAW: Disclosures made by a defendant in confidence to a codefendant's attorney (or the attorney's client) for a common purpose related to both of their defenses are protected by the attorney-client privilege even if the codefendant's defenses are not in all respects compatible.

FACTS: McPartlin (D) and one of his codefendants, Ingram (D), knew that the Government's (P) case against them hinged largely on Benton's testimony and that it was imperative that an effort be made to discredit his diaries, which corroborated much of his testimony. With his counsel's consent, McPartlin (D) thus gave two interviews to an investigator acting for Ingram's (D) counsel, the purpose being to determine if there was a basis for challenging the truth of some of the diary entries. In the second interview, McPartlin (D) made certain statements that Ingram (D) felt tended to support his defense. When Ingram's (D) counsel sought to offer evidence of these statements at trial, McPartlin's (D) counsel objected on the grounds that they were covered by the attorney-client privilege inasmuch as they were made in confidence to an attorney for a codefendant for a common purpose related to both of their defenses.

ISSUE: Does the attorney-client privilege protect statements made by a defendant in confidence to a codefendant's attorney for a common purpose related to both of their defenses?

HOLDING AND DECISION: (Tone, J.) Yes. Uninhibited communication among joint parties and their counsel about matters of common concern is often important to the protection of their interests. That is why the attorney-client privilege extends its protection to statements made by a defendant in confidence to a codefendant's attorney (or the attorney's agent) for a common purpose related to both of their defenses. It is not required that the codefendant's defenses must be in all respects compatible for this joint-defense privilege to be applicable. The privilege protects pooling of information for any defense purpose common to the participating defendants. Thus, McPartlin's (D) objections were well founded.

EDITOR'S ANALYSIS: A somewhat different result obtains in noncriminal cases where parties who consulted jointly have a falling out thereafter. If the parties then become involved in litigation between themselves, the privilege does not apply to the statements they made during such consultations insofar as that litigation is concerned.

[For more information on the attorney-client privilege and joint clients, see Casenote Law Outline on Evidence, Chapter 8, § II, The Attorney-Client Privilege.]

NOTES:

204

UNITED STATES v. ZOLIN
Federal government (P) v. Attorney (D)
491 U.S. 554 (1989).

NATURE OF CASE: Appeal from a judgment finding no crime-fraud exception to the attorney-client privilege in IRS investigation.

FACT SUMMARY: When the IRS (P) sought access to documents filed by the Church of Scientology (D) in connection with litigation, Zolin (D) asserted the attorney-client privilege as a bar, and the IRS (P) urged the court to conduct an in-camera review before making its privilege ruling.

CONCISE RULE OF LAW: A district court, at the behest of the party opposing a claim of attorney-client privilege, may conduct an in-camera review of the materials in question.

FACTS: In conjunction with an investigation of the tax returns of the founder of the Church of Scientology (D), the IRS (P) sought access to documents filed in litigation involving the Church (D). IRS (P) agents were permitted to inspect and copy some of the summoned materials, including two tapes. Zolin (D) asserted the attorney-client privilege as a bar to disclosure of the tapes. The IRS (P) argued, however, that the tapes fell within the crime-fraud exception to the attorney-client privilege and urged the district court to listen to the tapes in camera before making its privilege ruling. The district court ruled that the tapes contained confidential attorney-client communications and that the crime-fraud exception did not apply. Zolin (D) appealed, and the IRS (P) cross-appealed. The court of appeals affirmed the district court's ruling. The IRS (P) appealed.

ISSUE: May a district court, at the behest of the party opposing a claim of attorney-client privilege, conduct an in-camera review of the materials in question?

HOLDING AND DECISION: (Blackmun, J.) Yes. A district court, at the behest of the party opposing a claim of attorney-client privilege, may conduct an in-camera review of the materials in question. Before engaging in in-camera review, the court should require a showing of a factual basis adequate to support a good-faith belief by a reasonable person that in-camera review may reveal evidence to establish the claim that the exception applies. Once that showing has been made, the decision to engage in in-camera review rests with the discretion of the court. The party opposing the privilege may use any nonprivileged evidence in support of its request for in camera review, even if that evidence is not independent of the contested communications. Because the court of appeals considered only independent evidence, its judgment is vacated on this issue, and the case is remanded.

EDITOR'S ANALYSIS: The attorney-client privilege encourages full and frank communication between attorneys and their clients. However, the crime-fraud exception prevents the privilege from extending to communications concerning the commission of a future crime or fraud. The Court emphasized that Federal Rule 104(a) does not comport with the California rule, which bars disclosure of privileged information in order to rule on the claim of privilege.

[For more information on attorney-client privilege, see Casenote Law Outline on Evidence, Chapter 8, § II, The Attorney-Client Privilege.]

QUICKNOTES
ATTORNEY-CLIENT PRIVILEGE - A doctrine precluding the admission into evidence of confidential communications between an attorney and his client made in the course of obtaining professional assistance.

IN CAMERA - In private chambers.

NOTES:

TRAMMEL v. UNITED STATES

Heroin importer (D) v. Federal government (P)

445 U.S. 40 (1980).

NATURE OF CASE: Appeal from convictions for conspiracy to import and importing heroin.

FACT SUMMARY: Trammel's (D) wife agreed to testify against her husband in return for lenient treatment for herself, but Trammel (D) argued he had the right to prevent her from testifying against him.

CONCISE RULE OF LAW: A criminal defendant cannot prevent his spouse from voluntarily giving testimony against him because the privilege against adverse spousal testimony belongs to the testifying spouse.

FACTS: In return for lenient treatment for herself, Mrs. Trammel, an unindicted coconspirator, agreed to testify against her husband at his trial for conspiracy to import and importing heroin. The district court ruled she could testify to any act she observed during the marriage and to any communication made in the presence of a third person but not as to confidential communications between herself and her husband because they fell within the privilege attaching to confidential marital communications. On appeal, Trammel (D) contended that he was entitled to invoke the privilege against adverse spousal testimony so as to exclude the voluntary testimony of his wife. The court of appeals rejected this contention and affirmed the convictions.

ISSUE: Can a criminal defendant invoke the privilege against adverse spousal testimony so as to prevent his spouse from voluntarily offering adverse testimony against him?

HOLDING AND DECISION: (Burger, C.J.) No. Inasmuch as the privilege against adverse spousal testimony belongs solely to the testifying spouse, a criminal defendant cannot invoke the privilege to prevent his spouse from offering adverse testimony against him. The Hawkins case left the federal privilege for adverse spousal testimony where it found it at the time, thus continuing a rule which barred the testimony of one spouse against the other unless both consented. However, since that 1958 decision, support for that conception of the privilege has eroded further, and the trend in state law is toward divesting the accused of the privilege to bar adverse spousal testimony. The ancient foundations for so sweeping a privilege involved a conception of the wife as her husband's chattel to do with as he wished, and they have long since disappeared. Nor is the desire to protect the marriage a valid justification for affording an accused such a privilege. If his spouse desires to testify against him, simply preventing her from doing so is not likely to save the marriage. Affirmed.

EDITOR'S ANALYSIS: The Model Code of Evidence and the Uniform Rules of Evidence completely abolished the notion of a privilege against adverse spousal testimony and limited themselves to recognizing a privilege covering confidential marital communications. Several state legislatures have followed suit.

[For more information on adverse spousal testimony, see Casenote Law Outline on Evidence, Chapter 8, § V, Spousal Privileges.]

NOTES:

IN THE MATTER OF GRAND JURY SUBPOENA OF FORD v. UNITED STATES

Subpoened witness (D) v. Federal government (P)

756 F.2d 249 (2d Cir. 1985).

NATURE OF CASE: Appeal from contempt citation.

FACT SUMMARY: Ford (D) appealed his contempt citation on the basis he could not, due to the spousal privilege, be compelled to give grand jury testimony against his wife, even where the Government (P) agreed not to use such testimony against her.

CONCISE RULE OF LAW: A government promise not to use privileged information in its prosecution allows a witness to be compelled to testify to the privileged matter.

FACTS: Ford (D) was subpoenaed to testify before a grand jury investigating his wife. He moved to quash the subpoena on the basis his testimony was privileged by the spousal relationship. The Government (P) agreed not to use the testimony in its case against the wife. Ford (D) still refused and was cited for contempt. He appealed.

ISSUE: Does a government promise not to use privileged information in its prosecution allow a witness to testify to privileged information?

HOLDING AND DECISION: (Timbers, J.) Yes. A government promise not to use privileged information in its prosecution allows a witness to be compelled to testify to the privileged matter. If the testimony or its fruits cannot be used in the prosecution of the spouse, the dangers sought to be avoided by the privilege are avoided. No confidential information will destroy the marital relationship, and thus the privilege is sufficiently met. As a result, Ford (D) was properly ordered to testify. Affirmed.

EDITOR'S ANALYSIS: The Government (P) in this case assured against the use of the testimony by screening out the prosecutor from the testimony. A "Chinese wall" was placed around him so that no inadvertent use of the testimony was made. Ford (D) was eventually released after six months' confinement.

[For more information on governmental privilege, see Casenote Law Outline on Evidence, Chapter 8, § VII, Government Privileges.]

UNITED STATES v. MARASHI
Federal government (P) v. Tax evader (D)
913 F.2d 724 (9th Cir. 1990).

NATURE OF CASE: Appeal from tax evasion conviction.

FACT SUMMARY: Marashi (D) claimed that the marital communications privilege should apply to discussions he had with his wife about his tax evasion plans.

CONCISE RULE OF LAW: The marital communications privilege does not apply to statements made in furtherance of joint criminal activity.

FACTS: Sharon Marashi discovered that her husband Mohammad (D) was having an affair with his secretary. The secretary's husband met with Sharon to discuss ways in which to get revenge on their unfaithful spouses. Sharon mentioned that Marashi (D) had underreported his income for several years and the secretary's husband contacted the IRS, which started an investigation. Eventually, Sharon was persuaded to testify against Marashi (D) with regard to his alleged tax evasion scheme. Marashi (D) moved to suppress Sharon's testimony, and all of the evidence that resulted from it, on the basis of the marital communications privilege. The motion was denied and Marashi (D) was convicted. He appealed.

ISSUE: Does the marital communications privilege apply to statements made in furtherance of joint criminal activity?

HOLDING AND DECISION: (Hall, J.) No. The marital communications privilege does not apply to statements made in furtherance of joint criminal activity. In general, the marital communications privilege bars testimony concerning statement privately communicated between spouses. The nontestifying spouse may invoke the privilege even after dissolution of the marriage. However, the privilege extends only to words or acts intended as communication to the other spouse in a valid marriage. Furthermore, the communication must have been intended as confidential, although marital communications are presumptively confidential. However, the privilege will be construed narrowly because it obstructs the truth-seeking process. The government (P) conceded that certain communications between Sharon and Marashi (D) were privileged, but urged an exception to the general rule. Every jurisdiction considering the question has ruled that the privilege does not extend to communication regarding future crimes in which both spouses are participants. We believe that this exception is proper. The exception also applies even if both spouses are not charged with criminal activity. The government must be free to prosecute one spouse in order to secure the testimony of the other spouse. Therefore, Marashi's (D) statements to Sharon about his tax evasion scheme are admissible under the partnership-in-crime exception to the marital communications privilege. Affirmed.

EDITOR'S ANALYSIS: This exception virtually swallows the privilege. After all, the privilege is usually invoked as to criminal matters. If the communication in question did not relate to criminal activity, the party probably would not invoke the privilege.

[For more information on exceptions to spousal privileges, see Casenote Law Outline on Evidence, Chapter 8, § V, Spousal Privileges.]

QUICKNOTES
CONFIDENTIAL COMMUNICATIONS - A communication made between specified classes of persons which is privileged.

SPOUSAL PRIVILEGE - A common law doctrine precluding spouses from commencing actions against one another for their torts.

NOTES:

JAFFEE v. REDMOND
Decedent's estate (P) v. Police officer (D)
116 S. Ct. 1923 (1996).

NATURE OF CASE: Appeal from reversal and remand following award of damages in wrongful death action.

FACT SUMMARY: Redmond (D), a police officer, claimed that her counseling sessions following a shooting were privileged.

CONCISE RULE OF LAW: A psychotherapist-patient privilege should be recognized in federal courts.

FACTS: Redmond (D) worked as a police officer in Illinois and shot Allen while on patrol duty. Jaffee (P), Allen's estate administrator, filed suit for wrongful death. During pretrial discovery, Jaffee (P) learned that Redmond (D) had participated in about fifty counseling sessions with Beyer, a psychotherapist. Jaffee (P) sought the notes from these sessions. Redmond (D) opposed disclosure of the notes, invoking the psychotherapist-patient privilege. The district court rejected this contention and ordered disclosure. When Redmond (D) continued to refuse, the court instructed the jury at trial that it could presume that the notes would have been unfavorable to Redmond (D). Jaffee (P) prevailed at trial but the court of appeals reversed. Jaffee (P) appealed.

ISSUE: Should a psychotherapist-patient privilege be recognized in federal courts?

HOLDING AND DECISION: (Stevens, J.) Yes. A psychotherapist-patient privilege should be recognized in federal courts. Rule 501 of the Federal Rules of Evidence authorizes federal courts to define new privileges by interpreting common law principles in the light of reason and experience. Recognition of privileges based on confidential relationships should be based on a case-by-case basis under Rule 501. Thus, privileges could be added by federal courts over time. Privileges are exceptions to the general rule that the public has the right to every man's evidence. However, exceptions may be justified by a public good that overrides the general rule. As with the spousal and attorney-client privileges, the psychotherapist-patient privilege is rooted in the imperative need for confidence and trust. Effective psychotherapy depends on an atmosphere of confidence and trust in which the patient feels free to make complete disclosure of facts and emotions. The privilege serves the public interest by facilitating the provision of appropriate treatment for individuals suffering from the effects of mental problems. Without the privilege, patients would no longer have confidential conversations when circumstances indicate that litigation would be probable. On the other hand, the evidentiary benefit that would result from denial of the privilege would be modest at best. Therefore, the privilege should apply to all confidential communications between patients and psychiatrists, psychologists, and licensed social workers. Finally, if the purpose of the privilege is to be upheld, courts should not balance the privacy interest against the evidentiary need for the information. Accordingly, the award of damages to Jaffee (P) must be overturned and the court of appeals is affirmed.

DISSENT: (Scalia, J.) The majority does not address the fact that occasional injustice will result from application of this privilege. They ignore the traditional judicial preference for the truth. Additionally, the privilege is vast and ill-defined.

EDITOR'S ANALYSIS: The majority is not on solid ground with respect to its contention that persons may be deterred from seeking counseling if there is no privilege. It seems arguable that people will not treat themselves on the slim chance of later forced disclosure. Commentators have noted that people rarely go to doctors with thoughts of litigation.

[For more information on federal recognition of the psychotherapist-patient privilege, see Casenote Law Outline on Evidence, Chapter 8, § IV, The Psychotherapist-Patient Privilege.]

QUICKNOTES
CONFIDENTIAL COMMUNICATIONS - A communication made between specified classes of persons which is privileged.

NOTES:

MENENDEZ v. SUPERIOR COURT OF LOS ANGELES COUNTY

Murderer brothers (P) v. State (D)

Cal. Sup. Ct., 834 P.2d 786 (1992).

NATURE OF CASE: Motion to exclude evidence in murder trial.

FACT SUMMARY: Oziel (P), a psychologist, revealed confidential communications from his patients, the Menendez brothers (P), because he was afraid of them.

CONCISE RULE OF LAW: The dangerous-patient exception to the psychotherapist-patient privilege applies if there is a reasonable belief in the dangerousness of the patient.

FACTS: The parents of Erik and Lyle Menendez (P) were killed in their home. Several months later, Erik and Lyle (P) met with Dr. Oziel (P), a psychologist. The brothers (P) told Oziel (P) incriminating information at these sessions. Oziel (P) then told both his wife and his mistress about the brothers' confidential communications. Subsequently, Oziel's (P) mistress relayed the information to the police, who searched Oziel's (P) office for audiotape recordings and notes of the meetings with the Menendez brothers (P). Oziel (P) and the Menendez brothers (P) sought by motion to claim the psychotherapist-patient privilege and prevent disclosure of the audiotapes. The government responded that the dangerous-patient exception contained in California Evidence Code § 1024 applied to the privilege claim.

ISSUE: Does the dangerous-patient exception to the psychotherapist-patient privilege apply if there is a reasonable belief in the dangerousness of the patient?

HOLDING AND DECISION: (Mosk, J.) Yes. The dangerous-patient exception to the psychotherapist-patient applies if there is a reasonable belief in the dangerousness of the patient. The psychotherapist-patient privilege applies to confidential communications between patients and their psychotherapists. Certainly, this privilege applies to the information that Oziel (P) learned from the Mendendez brothers (P) at their counseling sessions. However, there is an exception to the general rule of privilege. If the psychotherapist has reasonable cause to believe that the patient is dangerous to the psychotherapist or other persons, the confidential communications can be disclosed. This reasonable belief must be determined in light of the standards of the psychotherapeutic community and is an objective test. The exception can apply even where the patient is not a threat to others in the community. In the present case, Oziel (P) had reasonable cause to believe that the brothers (P) were a threat to himself, his wife, and his mistress. Accordingly, disclosure of the communications was not barred by application of the privilege.

EDITOR'S ANALYSIS: The court did apply the privilege to two sessions where there was insufficient evidence that disclosure was necessary under the exception. At the trials of the Menendez brothers (P), the tapes discussed by the court were played and they revealed that the brothers (P) had admitted to killing their parents (although they did not indicate why they had done so). A psychotherapist's responsibility to warn people about dangerous patients was established by the California Supreme Court in Tarasoff v. Regents of University of California, 551 P.2d 334 (1976).

[For more information on exceptions to the psychotherapist-patient privilege, see Casenote Law Outline on Evidence, Chapter 8, § IV, The Psychotherapist-Patient Privilege.]

QUICKNOTES

CONFIDENTIAL COMMUNICATIONS - A communication made between specified classes of persons which is privileged.

NOTES:

UNIVERSITY OF PENNSYLVANIA v. EEOC
University (D) v. Government agency (P)
493 U.S. 182 (1990).

NATURE OF CASE: Appeal from enforcement of subpoena.

FACT SUMMARY: Pennsylvania U. (D) claimed that it could not be forced to disclose confidential peer review materials in a lawsuit by a professor denied tenure.

CONCISE RULE OF LAW: There is no privilege for confidential peer review materials.

FACTS: Tung was a professor at the Wharton School of Business at the University of Pennsylvania (Penn) (D). In 1985, she was denied tenure. Tung filed a charge of discrimination with the EEOC (P), claiming that the department chairman had sexually harassed her. Tung believed that he had then submitted a negative letter to the tenure committee. The EEOC (P) investigated the charges and sought information from Penn (D). However, Penn (D) refused to produce a number of tenure documents. It did not want to disclose confidential peer review materials. The EEOC (P) applied to the district court to enforce the subpoena and the court issued an order for Penn (D) to disclose the materials. The court of appeals affirmed, and Penn (D) appealed to the Supreme Court.

ISSUE: Is there a privilege for confidential peer review materials?

HOLDING AND DECISION: (Blackmun, J.) No. There is no privilege for confidential peer review materials. Fed. R. Evid. 501 allows federal courts to adopt privileges that accord with common law principles. A privilege should be created and applied only when it promotes sufficiently important interests to outweigh the need for probative evidence. And such privileges should be strictly construed. When Congress enacted Title VII and extended it to educational institutions and provided for extensive EEOC subpoena powers, it did not create a privilege for peer review materials. This is a strong indication that Congress did not intend for a privilege to apply to confidential peer review materials. Thus, tenure determinations are subject to the same standards as other employment decisions. Furthermore, Penn's (D) contention that the First Amendment protects these materials is also misplaced. The confidentiality of peer review materials does not implicate academic freedom in any respect. The subpoena power possessed by the EEOC (P) does not direct the content of university discourse toward or away from particular subjects or points of view. Finally, confidentiality is not even the norm in all peer review systems. Accordingly, the district court order enforcing the EEOC (P) subpena is affirmed.

EDITOR'S ANALYSIS: Prior to this decisions, some courts had acknowledged a limited privilege. In those decisions, the confidentiality claims were balanced against the plaintiff's need for disclosure. Courts have also generally rejected privileges in hospital peer review situations.

[For more information on claims of privilege, see Casenote Law Outline on Evidence, Chapter 8, § X, Privilege Procedure.]

QUICKNOTES

SUBPOENA - A mandate issued by court to compel a witness to appear at trial.

NOTES:

GHANA SUPPLY COMMISSION v. NEW ENGLAND POWER CO.

Foreign entity (P) v. Utility company (D)

83 F.R.D. 586 (D. Mass. 1979).

NATURE OF CASE: Motion to compel discovery in a civil case.

FACT SUMMARY: Ghana Supply (P), which sued New England Power (D) for unlawful conversion of fuel oil, claimed executive privilege with regard to certain information New England (D) sought to discover.

CONCISE RULE OF LAW: Federal Rule of Evidence 501 provides that privileges "shall be governed by the principles of the common law as they may be interpreted by the courts of the United States in the light of reason and experience" except that "in civil actions and proceedings, with respect to an element of a claim or defense as to which State law supplies the rule of decision" privileges are to "be determined in accordance with State laws."

FACTS: Ghana Supply (P) brought suit charging New England Power (D) with unlawful conversion of fuel oil. Three months later the appropriate governmental agency in Ghana created a Committee of Inquiry to investigate the underlying situation in an in camera proceeding. The Committee was given the power to compel attendance and testimony of witnesses. Testimony was completed and briefs filed, but no final report had issued when New England (D) sought to use the various methods of discovery to obtain much of the information from the aforementioned official inquiry. The Republic of Ghana produced most of the requested material but claimed an executive privilege as to those documents created solely for the Committee and all oral testimony before the Committee.

ISSUE: Are there instances where a state's rule of decision as to privileges applies in a federal case?

HOLDING AND DECISION: (Garrity, J.) Yes. According to Federal Rule of Evidence 501, privileges "shall be governed by the principles of common law as they may be interpreted by the courts of the United States in the light of reason and experience" except that "in civil actions and proceedings, with respect to an element of a claim or defense as to which State law supplies the rule of decision" privileges are to "be determined in accordance with State law." In this diversity case, the claim involves a common law tort (conversion), and there is no federal law or strong federal interest involved. Under such circumstances, Erie mandates that state law provide the rule of decision as to claims and defenses. Rule 501 thus requires that the court look to state law for resolution of the privilege question. Since the purpose of Rule 501 is to create the same effect for the law of privilege as now exists for substantive law in diversity cases, this court should follow the rule of Klaxon and look to the conflicts law of

Massachusetts, the forum state. Massachusetts applies its own law, characterizing questions of privilege as procedural. Thus, the controlling law on the subject of privilege in this case is that of Massachusetts, the forum state. After searching Massachusetts and federal authority to attempt and predict what the Massachusetts Supreme Judicial Court would hold when presented with this issue, it would appear to follow the majority position and hold that the Republic of Ghana, by instituting this civil action through Ghana Supply (P), has waived any privilege it might have otherwise had to prevent disclosure of information sought by New England Power (D) that is material to New England Power's (D) defense. In so holding, the court has given some consideration to the impact on the Republic of Ghana resulting from disclosure. It appears to us that the disclosure will not infringe seriously on any legally recognized privilege. Furthermore, an order to produce documents and testimony in the instant case merely puts the Ghanaian government as plaintiff to a choice. If it wants to continue the litigation, it must make an exception to its nondisclosure order, which it almost certainly has the power to do, or face sanctions for failure to comply with the discovery order. It also has the option to dismiss the lawsuit voluntarily at any time. No party to this case is placed in the position of risking violation of foreign law by complying with a discovery order of this court.

EDITOR'S ANALYSIS: The draft of the Federal Rules of Evidence originally proposed by the Advisory Committee was quite different from Rule 501 as enacted by Congress in that the subject of privileges was more thoroughly covered by a number of detailed provisions. One of the concerns voiced by those who objected to this approach was that state evidentiary privileges might not be honored in the federal courts. Rule 501, as it eventually was enacted, deals directly with this concern.

[For more information on federal privilege law, see Casenote Law Outline on Evidence, Chapter 8, § I Privileges in General.]

QUICKNOTES

PRIVILEGE - A benefit or right conferred upon a person or entity beyond those conferred upon the general public.

DISCOVERY - Pretrial procedure during which one party makes certain information available to the other.

DIVERSITY - The authority of a federal court to hear and determine cases involving $10,000 or more and in which the parties are citizens of different states, or in which one party is an alien.

ERIE DOCTRINE - Federal courts must apply state substantive law and federal procedural law.

GLOSSARY
COMMON LATIN WORDS AND PHRASES ENCOUNTERED IN THE LAW

A FORTIORI: Because one fact exists or has been proven, therefore a second fact that is related to the first fact must also exist.

A PRIORI: From the cause to the effect. A term of logic used to denote that when one generally accepted truth is shown to be a cause, another particular effect must necessarily follow.

AB INITIO: From the beginning; a condition which has existed throughout, as in a marriage which was void ab initio.

ACTUS REUS: The wrongful act; in criminal law, such action sufficient to trigger criminal liability.

AD VALOREM: According to value; an ad valorem tax is imposed upon an item located within the taxing jurisdiction calculated by the value of such item.

AMICUS CURIAE: Friend of the court. Its most common usage takes the form of an amicus curiae brief, filed by a person who is not a party to an action but is nonetheless allowed to offer an argument supporting his legal interests.

ARGUENDO: In arguing. A statement, possibly hypothetical, made for the purpose of argument, is one made arguendo.

BILL QUIA TIMET: A bill to quiet title (establish ownership) to real property.

BONA FIDE: True, honest, or genuine. May refer to a person's legal position based on good faith or lacking notice of fraud (such as a bona fide purchaser for value) or to the authenticity of a particular document (such as a bona fide last will and testament).

CAUSA MORTIS: With approaching death in mind. A gift causa mortis is a gift given by a party who feels certain that death is imminent.

CAVEAT EMPTOR: Let the buyer beware. This maxim is reflected in the rule of law that a buyer purchases at his own risk because it is his responsibility to examine, judge, test, and otherwise inspect what he is buying.

CERTIORARI: A writ of review. Petitions for review of a case by the United States Supreme Court are most often done by means of a writ of certiorari.

CONTRA: On the other hand. Opposite. Contrary to.

CORAM NOBIS: Before us; writs of error directed to the court that originally rendered the judgment.

CORAM VOBIS: Before you; writs of error directed by an appellate court to a lower court to correct a factual error.

CORPUS DELICTI: The body of the crime; the requisite elements of a crime amounting to objective proof that a crime has been committed.

CUM TESTAMENTO ANNEXO, ADMINISTRATOR (ADMINISTRATOR C.T.A.): With will annexed; an administrator c.t.a. settles an estate pursuant to a will in which he is not appointed.

DE BONIS NON, ADMINISTRATOR (ADMINISTRATOR D.B.N.): Of goods not administered; an administrator d.b.n. settles a partially settled estate.

DE FACTO: In fact; in reality; actually. Existing in fact but not officially approved or engendered.

DE JURE: By right; lawful. Describes a condition that is legitimate "as a matter of law," in contrast to the term "de facto," which connotes something existing in fact but not legally sanctioned or authorized. For example, de facto segregation refers to segregation brought about by housing patterns, etc., whereas de jure segregation refers to segregation created by law.

DE MINIMUS: Of minimal importance; insignificant; a trifle; not worth bothering about.

DE NOVO: Anew; a second time; afresh. A trial de novo is a new trial held at the appellate level as if the case originated there and the trial at a lower level had not taken place.

DICTA: Generally used as an abbreviated form of obiter dicta, a term describing those portions of a judicial opinion incidental or not necessary to resolution of the specific question before the court. Such nonessential statements and remarks are not considered to be binding precedent.

DUCES TECUM: Refers to a particular type of writ or subpoena requesting a party or organization to produce certain documents in their possession.

EN BANC: Full bench. Where a court sits with all justices present rather than the usual quorum.

EX PARTE: For one side or one party only. An ex parte proceeding is one undertaken for the benefit of only one party, without notice to, or an appearance by, an adverse party.

EX POST FACTO: After the fact. An ex post facto law is a law that retroactively changes the consequences of a prior act.

EX REL.: Abbreviated form of the term ex relatione, meaning, upon relation or information. When the state brings an action in which it has no interest against an individual at the instigation of one who has a private interest in the matter.

FORUM NON CONVENIENS: Inconvenient forum. Although a court may have jurisdiction over the case, the action should be tried in a more conveniently located court, one to which parties and witnesses may more easily travel, for example.

GUARDIAN AD LITEM: A guardian of an infant as to litigation, appointed to represent the infant and pursue his/her rights.

HABEAS CORPUS: You have the body. The modern writ of habeas corpus is a writ directing that a person (body) being detained (such as a prisoner) be brought before the court so that the legality of his detention can be judicially ascertained.

IN CAMERA: In private, in chambers. When a hearing is held before a judge in his chambers or when all spectators are excluded from the courtroom.

IN FORMA PAUPERIS: In the manner of a pauper. A party who proceeds in forma pauperis because of his poverty is one who is allowed to bring suit without liability for costs.

INFRA: Below, under. A word referring the reader to a later part of a book. (The opposite of supra.)

IN LOCO PARENTIS: In the place of a parent.

IN PARI DELICTO: Equally wrong; a court of equity will not grant requested relief to an applicant who is in pari delicto, or as much at fault in the transactions giving rise to the controversy as is the opponent of the applicant.

IN PARI MATERIA: On like subject matter or upon the same matter. Statutes relating to the same person or things are said to be in pari materia. It is a general rule of statutory construction that such statutes should be construed together, i.e., looked at as if they together constituted one law.

IN PERSONAM: Against the person. Jurisdiction over the person of an individual.

IN RE: In the matter of. Used to designate a proceeding involving an estate or other property.

IN REM: A term that signifies an action against the res, or thing. An action in rem is basically one that is taken directly against property, as distinguished from an action in personam, i.e., against the person.

INTER ALIA: Among other things. Used to show that the whole of a statement, pleading, list, statute, etc., has not been set forth in its entirety.

INTER PARTES: Between the parties. May refer to contracts, conveyances or other transactions having legal significance.

INTER VIVOS: Between the living. An inter vivos gift is a gift made by a living grantor, as distinguished from bequests contained in a will, which pass upon the death of the testator.

IPSO FACTO: By the mere fact itself.

JUS: Law or the entire body of law.

LEX LOCI: The law of the place; the notion that the rights of parties to a legal proceeding are governed by the law of the place where those rights arose.

MALUM IN SE: Evil or wrong in and of itself; inherently wrong. This term describes an act that is wrong by its very nature, as opposed to one which would not be wrong but for the fact that there is a specific legal prohibition against it (malum prohibitum).

MALUM PROHIBITUM: Wrong because prohibited, but not inherently evil. Used to describe something that is wrong because it is expressly forbidden by law but that is not in and of itself evil, e.g., speeding.

MANDAMUS: We command. A writ directing an official to take a certain action.

MENS REA: A guilty mind; a criminal intent. A term used to signify the mental state that accompanies a crime or other prohibited act. Some crimes require only a general mens rea (general intent to do the prohibited act), but others, like assault with intent to murder, require the existence of a specific mens rea.

MODUS OPERANDI: Method of operating; generally refers to the manner or style of a criminal in committing crimes, admissible in appropriate cases as evidence of the identity of a defendant.

NEXUS: A connection to.

NISI PRIUS: A court of first impression. A nisi prius court is one where issues of fact are tried before a judge or jury.

N.O.V. (NON OBSTANTE VEREDICTO): Notwithstanding the verdict. A judgment n.o.v. is a judgment given in favor of one party despite the fact that a verdict was returned in favor of the other party, the justification being that the verdict either had no reasonable support in fact or was contrary to law.

NUNC PRO TUNC: Now for then. This phrase refers to actions that may be taken and will then have full retroactive effect.

PENDENTE LITE: Pending the suit; pending litigation underway.

PER CAPITA: By head; beneficiaries of an estate, if they take in equal shares, take per capita.

PER CURIAM: By the court; signifies an opinion ostensibly written "by the whole court" and with no identified author.

PER SE: By itself, in itself; inherently.

PER STIRPES: By representation. Used primarily in the law of wills to describe the method of distribution where a person, generally because of death, is unable to take that which is left to him by the will of another, and therefore his heirs divide such property between them rather than take under the will individually.

PRIMA FACIE: On its face, at first sight. A prima facie case is one that is sufficient on its face, meaning that the evidence supporting it is adequate to establish the case until contradicted or overcome by other evidence.

PRO TANTO: For so much; as far as it goes. Often used in eminent domain cases when a property owner receives partial payment for his land without prejudice to his right to bring suit for the full amount he claims his land to be worth.

QUANTUM MERUIT: As much as he deserves. Refers to recovery based on the doctrine of unjust enrichment in those cases in which a party has rendered valuable services or furnished materials that were accepted and enjoyed by another under circumstances that would reasonably notify the recipient that the rendering party expected to be paid. In essence, the law implies a contract to pay the reasonable value of the services or materials furnished.

QUASI: Almost like; as if; nearly. This term is essentially used to signify that one subject or thing is almost analogous to another but that material differences between them do exist. For example, a quasi-criminal proceeding is one that is not strictly criminal but shares enough of the same characteristics to require some of the same safeguards (e.g., procedural due process must be followed in a parol hearing).

QUID PRO QUO: Something for something. In contract law, the consideration, something of value, passed between the parties to render the contract binding.

RES GESTAE: Things done; in evidence law, this principle justifies the admission of a statement that would otherwise be hearsay when it is made so closely to the event in question as to be said to be a part of it, or with such spontaneity as not to have the possibility of falsehood.

RES IPSA LOQUITUR: The thing speaks for itself. This doctrine gives rise to a rebuttable presumption of negligence when the instrumentality causing the injury was within the exclusive control of the defendant, and the injury was one that does not normally occur unless a person has been negligent.

RES JUDICATA: A matter adjudged. Doctrine which provides that once a court of competent jurisdiction has rendered a final judgment or decree on the merits, that judgment or decree is conclusive upon the parties to the case and prevents them from engaging in any other litigation on the points and issues determined therein.

RESPONDEAT SUPERIOR: Let the master reply. This doctrine holds the master liable for the wrongful acts of his servant (or the principal for his agent) in those cases in which the servant (or agent) was acting within the scope of his authority at the time of the injury.

STARE DECISIS: To stand by or adhere to that which has been decided. The common law doctrine of stare decisis attempts to give security and certainty to the law by following the policy that once a principle of law as applicable to a certain set of facts has been set forth in a decision, it forms a precedent which will subsequently be followed, even though a different decision might be made were it the first time the question had arisen. Of course, stare decisis is not an inviolable principle and is departed from in instances where there is good cause (e.g., considerations of public policy led the Supreme Court to disregard prior decisions sanctioning segregation).

SUPRA: Above. A word referring a reader to an earlier part of a book.

ULTRA VIRES: Beyond the power. This phrase is most commonly used to refer to actions taken by a corporation that are beyond the power or legal authority of the corporation.

ADDENDUM OF FRENCH DERIVATIVES

IN PAIS: Not pursuant to legal proceedings.

CHATTEL: Tangible personal property.

CY PRES: Doctrine permitting courts to apply trust funds to purposes not expressed in the trust but necessary to carry out the settlor's intent.

PER AUTRE VIE: For another's life; in property law, an estate may be granted that will terminate upon the death of someone other than the grantee.

PROFIT A PRENDRE: A license to remove minerals or other produce from land.

VOIR DIRE: Process of questioning jurors as to their predispositions about the case or parties to a proceeding in order to identify those jurors displaying bias or prejudice.

CASENOTE LEGAL BRIEFS